69|70 graphis annual

International Annual of Advertising Graphics

Internationales Jahrbuch der Werbegraphik

Art publicitaire graphique international

Edited by: / Herausgegeben von: / Réalisé par:

Walter Herdeg

Walter Herdeg, The Graphis Press, Zurich

Distributed in the United States by

Hastings House, Publishers, Inc.

10 EAST 40TH STREET, NEW YORK, N.Y. 10016

PUBLICATION N° 118

PAPER/PAPIER: BIBER-KUNSTDRUCK SK 3 ADMIRO HOCHWEISS, 120 GM² UND WERKDRUCKPAPIER SK 3 BIBER-OFFSET HOCHWEISS MASCHINENGLATT, 140 GM²
GEDRUCKT MIT FARBEN DER COLORA-GRAPHIKA AG, BERN / PRINTED WITH INKS OF COLORA-GRAPHIKA SA, BERNE
PRINTED IN SWITZERLAND

Contents

Inhalt

Sommaire

Abbreviations

Argentina .... ARG
Australia .... AUL
Austria .... AUS
Belgium .... BEL
Brazil .... BRA
Bulgaria .... BUL
Canada .... CAN
Cuba .... CUB
Czechoslovakia .... CSR
Denmark .... DEN
Finland .... FIN
France .... FRA
Great Britain .... GB
Greece .... GRE
Hungary .... HUN
India .... IND
Israel .... ISR
Italy .... ITA
Japan .... JAP
Luxembourg .... LUX
Mexico .... MEX
Netherlands .... NLD
Norway .... NOR
Poland .... POL
Spain .... SPA
Sweden .... SWE
Switzerland .... SWI
USA .... USA
West Germany .... GER

Abkürzungen

Argentinien .... ARG
Australien .... AUL
Belgien .... BEL
Brasilien .... BRA
Bulgarien .... BUL
Dänemark .... DEN
Finnland .... FIN
Frankreich .... FRA
Griechenland .... GRE
Grossbritannien .... GB
Indien .... IND
Israel .... ISR
Italien .... ITA
Japan .... JAP
Kanada .... CAN
Kuba .... CUB
Luxemburg .... LUX
Mexiko .... MEX
Niederlande .... NLD
Norwegen .... NOR
Österreich .... AUS
Polen .... POL
Schweden .... SWE
Schweiz .... SWI
Spanien .... SPA
Tschechoslowakei .... CSR
Ungarn .... HUN
USA .... USA
Westdeutschland .... GER

Abréviations

Allemagne d'Ouest .... GER
Argentine .... ARG
Australie .... AUL
Autriche .... AUS
Belgique .... BEL
Brésil .... BRA
Bulgarie .... BUL
Canada .... CAN
Cuba .... CUB
Danemark .... DEN
Espagne .... SPA
Etats-Unis .... USA
Finlande .... FIN
France .... FRA
Grande-Bretagne .... GB
Grèce .... GRE
Hongrie .... HUN
Inde .... IND
Israël .... ISR
Italie .... ITA
Japon .... JAP
Luxembourg .... LUX
Mexique .... MEX
Norvège .... NOR
Pays-Bas .... NLD
Pologne .... POL
Suède .... SWE
Suisse .... SWI
Tchécoslovaquie .... CSR

The introduction to this issue is by DR. MARKUS KUTTER, a Swiss author who has also made a name as a copywriter and in 1959 founded, with the artist and designer Karl Gerstner, one of the most successful Swiss advertising agencies. Born in 1925, Kutter studied history and modern languages in Basle, Geneva, Paris and Rome. In 1952 he joined J.R. Geigy as editor of their house organ and later headed their information department until the founding of the Gerstner, Gredinger + Kutter agency. He has published several books and writes for various Swiss newspapers and weeklies alongside his work for the agency.

Das Vorwort zu der vorliegenden Ausgabe wurde von DR. MARKUS KUTTER, einem bekannten Schweizer Publizisten und Copywriter, verfasst. Markus Kutter wurde im Jahre 1925 geboren, studierte Geschichte und moderne Sprachen an den Universitäten von Basel, Genf, Paris und Rom. Im Jahr 1952 trat er als Werkzeitungsredaktor der Firma J.R. Geigy AG bei und leitete später die Informationsabteilung dieser Firma. Im Jahr 1959 gründete er, zusammen mit dem Künstler und Designer Karl Gerstner, eine Werbeagentur, die sich durch den Beitritt von Paul Gredinger zur Agentur Gerstner, Gredinger + Kutter AG erweiterte und heute zu den führenden Schweizer Werbeagenturen gehört. Markus Kutter ist Autor verschiedener Werke und ist neben seiner beruflichen Tätigkeit als Mitinhaber der Agentur GGK publizistisch bei verschiedenen Schweizer Tages- und Wochenzeitungen tätig.

Ce numéro a été préfacé par le DR MARKUS KUTTER. Ce publiciste et rédacteur publicitaire suisse, né en 1925, est venu à la publicité par le biais des relations publiques. Il a étudié l'histoire et les langues vivantes aux universités de Bâle, de Genève, de Rome et de Paris avant d'être appelé en 1952 à diriger la revue d'entreprise, puis le département Publicité et Relations Publiques de la Société J.R. Geigy, l'un des grands des produits pharmaceutiques en Suisse. En 1959, il fondait avec l'artiste et designer Karl Gerstner l'agence publicitaire qui, avec le concours ultérieur de Paul Gredinger, devait s'imposer comme l'une des plus prestigieuses agences suisses sous le sigle de GGK. Markus Kutter a écrit plusieurs livres et collabore régulièrement à divers quotidiens et hebdomadaires suisses tout en s'occupant activement de son agence.

The items reproduced in this book were selected from 17000 entries from all parts of the world. It is gratifying to note that there has been a definite rise in the overall quality of work submitted in recent years. More entries are now coming in from Eastern Europe, and though a dirge for the poster is being sung in many quarters, the number of posters sent in is noticeably on the increase. The Editor extends his thanks to all contributors and regrets that space does not allow him to include more of their often excellent work.

Die Arbeiten, die in der vorliegenden Ausgabe gezeigt werden, wurden aus 17000 Einsendungen aus 45 Ländern ausgewählt. Wir stellen mit Freude fest, dass sich die Qualität im Vergleich mit vergangenen Jahren weiter verbessert hat. Erfreulich ist auch der Zuwachs an Einsendungen aus den östlichen Ländern. Obwohl oft der Untergang des Werbeplakats prophezeit wird, muss an dieser Stelle bemerkt werden, dass die Zahl der eingesandten Arbeiten ständig zunimmt. Wiederum dankt der Herausgeber allen Mitarbeitern und bedauert, dass es ihm aus Platzgründen nicht möglich ist, mehr der oft ausgezeichneten Arbeiten zu berücksichtigen.

Les travaux figurant dans le présent volume ont été sélectionnés parmi 17000 envois provenant de 45 pays. Nous constatons avec plaisir une hausse générale de qualité, ces dernières années. La contribution des pays de l'Europe de l'Est s'est accrue. Bien que des voix s'élèvent un peu partout pour prédire le déclin prochain de l'affiche, jamais les envois d'affiches n'ont été aussi nombreux. Une fois de plus, l'Editeur remercie tous ceux qui ont concouru au succès de l'entreprise, tout en regrettant de ne pas disposer de la place nécessaire pour reproduire un plus grand nombre de leurs travaux souvent d'excellente qualité.

The Hardships and Rewards of Being an Advertising Designer

Questions couched in general terms are not always the most astute, but are often the most difficult to answer.

And if one is asked what the role of the graphic designer is in commerce and society, in cultural and public affairs, one would do well to tread cautiously. It is perhaps wisest to circumnavigate the dangers as simply as possible by adopting an empirical approach. Thus one may legitimately ask: where are graphic designers most in evidence? And the answer (whether gratifying or not) is: in advertising.

Ninety per cent of all graphic design (or perhaps even more) is being done in advertising. Without advertising there would hardly be such a thing as graphic design at all (except perhaps for the design of traffic signs, certificates, medals and book covers). One might also turn the sentence round and say that without graphic design there would be no advertising, for even the simplest typographical advertisement needs somebody to indicate spacing and layout. And if the questioner still wants to know what the role of the graphic designer is in commerce and society, in cultural and public affairs, we can pick up a few useful cues by considering the answers to the same questions when applied to advertising.

It should be clear, however, that graphic design and advertising are not identical. Nor are the advertising man and the designer identical. The relationship of the two is one that it is not always easy to define. Is it polemic? Is it dialectical? Even when the designer is part of an advertising agency, his position still involves the same problems.

So we are left with two questions: What does advertising expect of the graphic designer? And what does the graphic designer expect of advertising?

Since I am an advertising man myself – from the copy side – and am accordingly perched on one end of this see-saw, I trust the reader will not mind if I restrict myself to the first of these questions, in the hope that a little light will also fall on the second.

The fanfares of the Bauhaus have died away

There are modest eras, and there are eras that are less modest. And in any of these eras there are modest and less modest opinions.

Advertising – believe it or not – has become more modest of late years. It can now prove (by scientific methods if necessary) how little effect it often has on the consumer's decision to buy, and it knows only too well how few the commodities and services are that it can really help to sell. (Just try to sell wheat, coal, cement or tram-rails by advertising.) Even fashions depend much less on advertising than people think. (When men decide not to wear hats, for instance, advertisers can only stand and wring their hands. And it is only now, when hippie fashions are beginning to fade, that advertising can gradually get its finger into that particular pie.)

In other words, changing the world, reforming society or shaping taste are no jobs for advertising. Its brief is smaller and more clearly defined: to provide information about a product or service, to offer the purchasing consumer a choice, at best to create a demand. And one major point should not be overlooked: there is no such thing as advertising in the absolute sense. Advertising is always tied to a definite product or group of products, to a firm or a service. It always has a specific assignment to fulfil.

Why should I linger over this? Because I should like to prove that graphic design, which generally speaking has ambitions in the way of educating the masses, influencing taste and improving the world around us, has no place in advertising unless it can reconcile these ambitions with the individual and clearly defined assignment.

Advertising is likewise, let us confess, a kind of nine-days'-wonder. Nothing else fades quite as quickly. Think back three years, five years: of the hundreds of advertising campaigns you then witnessed, how many have stuck in your memory? This does not mean for a moment that the graphic design used in a campaign is unimportant, and far less does it imply that bad, shallow and cheap design is in any way preferable to good, witty and talented work.

But what is good graphic design?

Let us, once more, start with advertising: what is good advertising?

Good advertising is clever. Not clever in the intellectual sense, and perhaps it would be better to say: shrewd. Why is this?

Barrows Mussey, an American living in Dusseldorf, knows better than most how advertising works and observes its shifts with a well-disposed but critical eye. He says: good advertising creates a suction effect. (It is accordingly the very opposite of what sales managers assert, for they think it should be used like a hammer.)

It does not talk people's heads off, but it puts a chair ready, so that if anybody feels like sitting down, he has something to sit on. Mussey adds: If you want to attract the birds, you shouldn't get your gun, but should try birdseed. And not a ton of seed – a handful will be quite enough. By far the best plan is to strew the seed yourself, so that the birds notice that somebody is standing them a meal – that always fetches them.

Good graphic design in advertising in perhaps just this gesture: the right way to strew birdseed. Or to put it in general terms: the approach that awakens interest, that attracts attention, that inspires curiosity. It has been said hundreds of times, but it cannot be said too often: people (and that's us) are not interested in advertising, but only in whatever they're interested in. Advertising therefore has to be interesting, and so does graphic design.

Good graphic design is not handsome design, then, but design that helps to make advertising interesting. If it fulfils this purpose, it may also be handsome, especially as handsomeness itself tends to be interesting.

The whole thing is as simple as that.

A question in passing: has graphic design anything to do with art?

Yes, definitely.

I also believe that art has something to do with the awakening of interest, with curiosity and discovery. An artist is one who perceives the world otherwise than we are accustomed to perceive it (and is capable of stating or demonstrating the fact). And since custom leads to established views, and established views are the opposite of perception as an active process, the result is that we perceive the world less and less, while the artist is continually perceiving it for the first time. That is why we need art. And why anybody who wishes to percieve the world around him must have recourse to art. He must take an active interest in it.

I can now say the opposite of what I said before: Even the simplest consumer has the desire to discover new ground, to undergo transsubstantiation and to change the world around him. If he sees advertising which satisfies this desire in the subject it deals with and in the way it deals with this subject, as a reader and viewer of this advertising he feels the suction effect of which I spoke above. Consequently it is a legitimate wish of graphic design to change the world, to reform society and to influence taste. Or at least to play a part in this process. Or even – no panic, please – to profane art.

For the artist who re-perceives the world first comes up against the resistance of established views. Then he finds the first people inclined to perceive the world as he perceives it. The perception gradually gains ground: a fashion develops, a trend. As a result more and more people move over into the new camp. Other spheres: fashion, architecture, interior decoration, graphic design and the poster assume the new style of perception. Art becomes profane.

Advertising art may (and perhaps should) take part in this process. It has repeatedly done so in the past – we need only think of the role played by *art nouveau* posters and advertisements, in which a fine art revival and advertising design advanced hand in hand. And it is therefore anything but surprising that good graphic designers should seek intellectual and even social contact with artists, avant-garde innovators, and poets; and should likewise be prepared to discard a successful style, a means of optical utterance that has found acceptance, and to try something new.

It would be dreadful if a recognized type of good graphic design were to establish itself in advertising once and for all. For one thing, it would be monotonous. And monotony is a deadly sin in advertising, as it is for that matter anywhere else.

Good design is obvious

Assuming a designer enters the advertising field: what is there expected of him? What does he have to achieve, provided that he has already mastered the technical side of graphic design?

The most difficult things that are required of him are two: to be good-humoured; and not to be noticed. On the subject of good humour, a statement by Robert Stalder (himself a copywriter who therefore writes about copywriters) deserves to be quoted: 'The copywriter should be a person who from time to time feels an irresistible urge to proclaim to his fellow-men that cars, soap, cigarettes, beer, bras and computers are not just things a decadent society has foisted on it merely in order to be able to complain about them afterwards, but things that all reasonably fulfil their purpose of making life pleasanter, and one of which fulfils it better than any other on the market. This latter is of course the one that he himself happens to be advertising. Self-confessed *joie de vivre* is the best rhetoric.'

Much the same applies to the graphic designer who works for advertising. The trouble is that being good-humoured is one of the most difficult of requirements to fulfil.

The other difficulty for the designer is the job of obliterating himself. Only the advertisement, poster or booklet should be visible. All the wishes, abilities, thoughts and feelings of the designer himself should disappear in the product, so that he is nowhere to be seen. The advertisement must say: I'm a good advertisement (or better still: I speak for a good product); it should never say: Look, what a good designer (or copywriter or photographer) made me!

In this sense good design is obvious design. Its point is that it helps to create an idea, a mood, a style to which it can later subscribe. If it succeeds in doing this, the short-lived entity known as an advertisement will be a living entity, however short-lived. The proof of its vitality lies in the fact that it is not forgotten as soon as the page is turned, that reader and viewer read and view it with pleasure. And that, led by curiosity or interest, they learn something without noticing it.

I would have liked to close with a list of practical qualifications for the prospective advertising designer. But I find that I cannot formulate these qualifications or even give any useful advice. Perhaps I have already been warped by practical work in an advertising agency. Certainly I have learned that, given the same technical abilities, it is only temperament, a creative vein and a knack of having ideas that decide whether a man is to become a good advertising designer or not. Some people (especially the doctrinaire types) never learn it at all.

Consequently it may be regrettable but is never really catastrophic if the schools that train graphic designers do not always teach the things that are needed in practice. Provided they do not teach the very opposite of what practical advertising calls for, one need not worry overmuch.

For one can safely assume that the designer who has a flair for advertising will finally find his way to it.

MARKUS KUTTER

Die entsagungsvolle, aber vielversprechende Kunst, Werbegraphiker zu sein

Allgemein formulierte Fragen sind immer die klügsten, aber oft die schwierigsten.

Und wenn man also gefragt wird, was die Rolle des Graphikers in der Wirtschaft, in der Gesellschaft, in der Kultur und in der Öffentlichkeit sei, so muss man sich davor hüten, aufs Glatteis zu geraten. Am besten ist es vielleicht, man zieht sich methodisch möglichst simpel aus der Klemme und geht sozusagen empirisch vor. Man fragt also: Wo gibt es denn am meisten Graphiker zu sehen? Und dann lautet die Antwort (ob sie gefällt oder nicht): in der Werbung.

Zu 90 (wenn nicht noch mehr) Prozent findet Graphik in der Werbung statt. Ohne Werbung gäbe es kaum eine Graphik (eine Verkehrstafelgraphik vielleicht, eine Militärabzeichen-, Urkunden-, Wegweiser- und Buchdeckelgraphik dazu) – man kann den Satz wohl auch umkehren: Ohne Graphik gäbe es auch keine Werbung – denn noch das schlichteste Schriftinserat braucht zu guter Letzt die Hand dessen, der die Satzangaben macht.

Und wenn man jetzt also wissen will, welches die Rolle des Graphikers in der Wirtschaft, in der Gesellschaft, in der Kultur und in der Öffentlichkeit ist, so wird man schon etwas klüger, wenn man darauf schaut, wie man diese Fragen für die Werbung zu beantworten hat.

Dabei ist es allerdings klar, dass Graphik und Werbung nicht identisch sind. Auch der Werbemann und der Graphiker sind nicht identisch. Werbung und Graphik stehen in einem Verhältnis, das zu formulieren nicht immer leicht fällt: ist es ein polemisches? ist es ein dialektisches? – Die Stellung des Graphikers selber in der Werbeagentur deutet auf dieselbe Problematik hin.

So bleiben zwei Fragen übrig: Was will die Werbung vom Graphiker? Und die andere: Was will der Graphiker von der Werbung?

Da ich als Werbemann, der vom Text herkommt, auf der einen Seite dieser Schaukel sitze, wird man mir erlauben, mich nur mit der ersten Frage auseinanderzusetzen – in der Hoffnung, dass dann aber auch ein wenig Licht auf die zweite Frage fällt.

Die Fanfaren des Bauhauses sind verklungen

Es gibt bescheidene Epochen und unbescheidene. Und es gibt in diesen Epochen wiederum bescheidene Meinungen und unbescheidene.

Die Werbung – ob man mir's glaubt oder nicht – ist eher bescheiden geworden. Sie kann (sogar wissenschaftlich) nachweisen, wie wenig entscheidend sie beim eigentlichen Kaufentschluss in vielen Fällen mitwirkt, und weiss nur zu gut, wie klein die Anzahl von Artikeln oder Dienstleistungen überhaupt ist, bei denen sie etwas auszurichten vermag. (Versuchen Sie einmal, Weizen, Flussfracht, Kohle, Zement oder Tramschienen mit Werbung zu verkaufen.) Auch das, was man Mode nennt, ist viel unabhängiger von Werbung, als sich die Leute so denken. (Ohnmächtig muss die Werbung zuschauen, wenn die Männer plötzlich keine Hüte mehr tragen wollen. Und erst jetzt, wo die Hippie-Mode langsam ihrem Ende entgegengeht, kann die Werbung sich langsam des Themas bemächtigen.)

Das heisst: kühn die Welt zu verändern, die Gesellschaft zu bekehren, den Geschmack grundlegend zu bilden, kann gar nicht Aufgabe der Werbung sein. Ihr Auftrag ist genau umrissen: über ein Produkt, eine Dienstleistung zu informieren, beim Kaufentscheid Wahlmöglichkeiten zu offerieren, bestenfalls Nachfrage zu schaffen. Und was vor allem wichtig ist: Es gibt keine Werbung an sich; Werbung wird immer für ein bestimmtes Produkt, eine Produktgruppe, eine Firma, eine Dienstleistung gemacht, sie hat immer einen spezifischen Auftrag, mit dem sie fertig werden muss.

Warum sage ich das? Weil ich nachweisen will, dass Graphik, die in einem allgemeinen Sinn ambitiös in Richtung auf Erziehung, Geschmacksbildung, Weltverbesserung ist, in der Werbung nur dann etwas zu suchen hat, wenn ihr Ehrgeiz sich mit dem einzeln definierten Auftrag verträgt.

Werbung, gestehen wir es, ist zudem eine Eintagsfliege: heute gemacht, morgen vergessen. Denken Sie nur drei oder fünf Jahre zurück: Von Tausenden von Werbekampagnen, deren Zeuge Sie waren – wieviel haben Sie im Gedächtnis behalten?

Das heisst nicht, dass es in der Werbung einerlei ist, was für Graphik auf dem Papier steht. Und noch weniger will ich damit sagen, dass schlechte Graphik der guten, anspruchslose der anspruchsvollen, dumme der einfallsreichen und billige der wertvollen vorgezogen werden soll.

Nur eben: Was heisst das – gute Graphik?

Fangen wir doch lieber bei der Werbung an – was heisst das: gute Werbung?

Gute Werbung ist klug. Nicht intellektuell klug – vielleicht muss ich eher sagen: ist listig. Wieso?

Barrows Mussey, der in Düsseldorf lebende Amerikaner, der wie wenig andere Leute begriffen hat, wie Werbung funktioniert und ihre Zuckungen mit so kritischen wie liebevollen Augen verfolgt, sagt: Gute Werbung schafft einen Sog. (Sie ist damit das Gegenteil von dem, was die Verkaufsdirektoren sagen – dass sie nämlich hämmern soll.) Sie schwatzt den Leuten nicht ein Loch in den Bauch, sondern stellt den Stuhl hin, auf den die Leute, wenn sie sich schon setzen wollen, dann gerne absitzen. Mussey sagt auch: Wenn Sie wollen, dass die Vögel kommen, dürfen Sie nicht die Schrotflinte, sondern müssen Körner nehmen; und zwar nicht eine Tonne Körner, eine Handvoll genügt. Noch besser ist es, Sie werfen diese Körner richtig vor sich hin, so dass die Vögel begreifen, dass hier einer Körner auswirft – dann kommen sie.

Vielleicht ist gute Graphik in der Werbung genau diese Geste: das richtige Werfen der Körner. Oder allgemeiner gesagt: der Auftritt, der lockt, der das Interesse holt, der die Neugierde weckt. Man hat es schon hundertmal gesagt, kann es aber nicht häufig genug wiederholen: die Leute (das sind wir alle) interessieren sich nicht für Werbung, sondern für das, was sie interessiert. Also müssen wir interessante Werbung machen und auch interessante Graphik.

Die gute Graphik ist also nicht die schöne Graphik, sondern die Graphik, die dazu hilft, dass die Werbung interessant wird. Leistet sie das, dann darf sie durchaus auch schön sein – weil das Schöne, auf seine Weise, eben auch interessant ist.

So einfach ist das.

Eine Zwischenfrage: Hat Graphik etwas mit der Kunst zu tun?

Gewiss.

Ich glaube auch, dass die Kunst etwas mit Sichinteressieren, mit Neugierde und Entdeckungen zu tun hat.

Künstler ist einer, der die Welt anders begreift (und das sagen, zeigen, demonstrieren kann), als wir die Welt zu begreifen gewohnt sind. Und da die Gewöhnung, etwas zu begreifen, feste Begriffe schafft, und da feste Begriffe das Gegenteil von Begreifen im Sinn eines aktiven Vorganges sind, läuft es darauf hinaus, dass wir die Welt immer weniger begreifen, der Künstler sie aber immer wieder zum ersten Mal begreift. Darum haben wir die Kunst so nötig. Und darum muss, wer die Welt begreifen will, zur Kunst gehen. Er muss sich für Kunst interessieren.

Jetzt kann ich also das Gegenteil von dem sagen, was ich vorher sagte: Es ist auch im einfachsten Konsumenten ein Verlangen da, Neues zu entdecken, sich zu ändern und die Welt zu ändern. Wenn er nun Werbung sieht, die ihm in der Sache, von der sie handelt, aber auch in der Art und Weise, wie sie von dieser Sache handelt, dieses Verlangen stillt, so gerät er als Leser und Betrachter dieser Werbung in den Sog, von dem ich vorher sprach. Und so darf auch die Graphik die Welt verändern wollen, die Gesellschaft bekehren, den Geschmack bilden. Oder sie darf an diesem Prozess teilhaben. Oder sie darf – erschrecken Sie nicht – die Kunst profanieren.

Denn der Künstler, der die Welt neu begreift, stösst zuerst auf den Widerstand der etablierten festen Begriffe. Dann findet er die ersten Leute, die die Welt auch so begreifen wollen, wie er sie begriffen hat. Nun breiten sich diese Begriffe langsam aus: Es entsteht eine Richtung, eine Mode, ein Trend. Resultat: Mehr und mehr Leute laufen ins neue Lager über. Andere «Branchen», die Mode, die Architektur, die Dekorateure, die Graphiker und Plakatmaler übernehmen die neue Art, die Welt zu begreifen. Die Kunst wird profan.

An diesem Prozess kann (oder soll?) die Werbegraphik teilhaben. Sie hat auch immer wieder daran teilgenommen – denken Sie nur an die Rolle der Jugendstilplakate und -anzeigen, wo künstlerische Erneuerung und Werbegraphik Hand in Hand gingen. Und darum ist es überhaupt nicht verwunderlich, dass sich gute Graphiker in der geistigen oder sogar gesellschaftlichen Nähe von Künstlern, Experimentatoren, Avantgardisten, Poeten und wie man sie immer heissen mag, niederlassen wollen. Und dass sie bereit sind, einen einmal erfolgreichen Stil, eine Art der optischen Aussage, die Anklang gefunden hat, wegzuschmeissen und etwas Neues zu probieren. Es wäre doch schrecklich, wenn es in der Werbung eine ein für alle Mal anerkannte und etablierte Art von guter Graphik gäbe. Es wäre nämlich langweilig. Und Langeweile ist eine Todsünde in der Werbung – wie überhaupt.

Das Gute ist das Selbstverständliche

Doch was soll der Graphiker, der in der Werbung geht, nun eigentlich können? Oder worin besteht seine Leistung – einmal abgesehen davon, dass er sein Handwerk technisch beherrscht?

Das Schwierigste, das von ihm verlangt wird, sind zwei Dinge: gute Laune zu haben und nicht bemerkt zu werden.

Zum Stichwort «gute Laune» ein Zitat von Robert Stalder (der selber Werbetexter ist und als solcher über Werbetexter schrieb):

«Der Werbetexter sollte einer sein, der von Zeit zu Zeit das unbändige Bedürfnis verspürt, seinen Mitmenschen zuzujauchzen, dass Autos, Seifen, Zigaretten, Bier und BH's und Computer durchaus nicht das sind, was eine dekadente Gesellschaft sich aus dem einzigen Grunde aufschwatzen lassen will, dass sie nachher Grund hat, über ihren Erwerb zu schimpfen, sondern, dass das Dinge sind, von denen je eines seinen Zweck, auf vernünftige Weise das Leben angenehmer zu machen, noch besser erfüllt als alle anderen, die auf dem Markt sind.

Nämlich jeweils das, für das er wirbt.

Demonstrierte Lebensfreude ist die beste Rhetorik.»

Das gilt sinngemäss auch für den Graphiker in der Werbung. Das Dumme ist nur, dass gute Laune zu haben einer der schwierigsten Vorsätze ist.

Die andere Schwierigkeit für den Graphiker besteht darin, sich unsichtbar zu machen. Sichtbar soll das Inserat, Plakat, die Broschüre sein. Alles Wollen, Können, Denken, Fühlen, Spüren des Graphikers muss in das nachher auf dem Tisch liegende Erzeugnis schlüpfen. Ihn selber soll man nicht mehr sehen. Das Inserat muss sagen: Ich bin ein gutes Inserat (oder noch besser: Hier spricht ein gutes Produkt), aber es darf nie sagen: Seht, was für ein guter Graphiker (oder Texter oder Photograph) hat mich gemacht!

In dem Sinn meine ich: Gute Graphik hat etwas Selbstverständliches. Ihr Witz liegt darin, dass sie hilft, eine Idee, eine Stimmung, einen einheitlichen Stilwillen zu schaffen, dem sie sich nachher unterordnen kann. Gelingt das, so erweist sich das kurzlebige Geschöpf, genannt Inserat, bei aller Kurzlebigkeit doch auch als ein lebendiges Geschöpf. Der Beweis seiner Lebendigkeit zeigt sich darin, dass man es nicht schon beim Umblättern vergessen hat, dass der Leser und Betrachter es gerne liest und gern betrachtet. Dass er, seiner Neugierde und seinen Wünschen folgend, etwas lernt, ohne es zu merken.

Ich hätte diesen Aufsatz gern mit einer Liste von praktischen Anforderungen an den zukünftigen Werbegraphiker abgeschlossen. Ich merke, dass ich diese Anforderungen nicht formulieren kann und auch um Ratschläge verlegen bin. Ich bin vielleicht durch die praktische Arbeit in einer Werbeagentur schon deformiert. Ich habe eben erlebt, dass bei gleichen technischen und handwerklichen Voraussetzungen nur Temperament, schöpferische Laune und Einfallskraft darüber entscheiden, ob einer ein guter Graphiker in der Werbung wird. Gewisse Leute (die doktrinären zuerst) lernen es nie.

Und darum ist es zwar manchmal bedauerlich, aber nicht katastrophal, wenn in den Schulen, die Graphiker ausbilden, nicht immer das gelehrt wird, was die Praxis eigentlich verlangt. Solange nicht gerade das Gegenteil von dem gelehrt wird, was die Werbung nachher in der Praxis braucht, wird man zufrieden sein. Man darf dabei darauf vertrauen, dass der für die Werbung begabte Graphiker selber den Weg zur Werbung findet.

Markus Kutter

De l'art difficile, plein d'abnégation, mais riche de promesses, d'être un artiste publicitaire

Les questions posées sous une forme générale ne sont pas toujours les plus judicieuses, mais souvent les plus difficiles à résoudre.

Si donc on se voit poser la question du rôle de l'artiste graphique dans la vie économique, sociale, culturelle et publique, on prendra garde de ne pas s'engager sur un terrain glissant. Peut-être la meilleure façon de répondre consiste-t-elle à adopter la méthode simpliste de l'empirisme et à se demander dans quel domaine on rencontre le plus de graphistes. La réponse est évidente (qu'elle vous plaise ou non): dans la publicité.

Les 90% (sinon davantage) de l'art graphique ont à faire avec la publicité. Sans publicité, il n'y aurait guère d'art graphique (peut-être tout au plus un art graphique des panneaux de signalisation, des insignes militaires, des documents et diplômes, des poteaux indicateurs et des couvertures de livres). On peut aussi inverser la phrase et dire que sans art graphique il n'y aurait pas non plus de publicité, puisque l'annonce rédactionnelle la plus simple de présentation ne peut se dispenser du concours du maquettiste. Si donc on tient à préciser le rôle de l'artiste graphique dans la vie économique, sociale, culturelle et publique, on verra plus clair en cherchant la solution de ces questions pour la publicité.

Il ne faut évidemment pas perdre de vue que l'art graphique et la publicité sont loin d'être identiques, pas plus que ne le sont le publicitaire et le graphiste. Quant à déterminer avec précision la relation entre la publicité et l'art graphique, bien malin qui saurait toujours décider s'il s'agit de rapports polémiques ou dialectiques. Il n'est que de considérer la position de l'artiste graphique au sein de l'agence publicitaire pour s'apercevoir de la complexité du problème.

Il reste donc deux questions: que demande la publicité à l'artiste graphique? et d'autre part: que demande l'artiste graphique à la publicité?

En tant que publicitaire ayant fait ses premières armes dans la rédaction de textes, je me trouve assis d'un côté déterminé de la balançoire, et l'on m'excusera donc de ne m'attaquer qu'à la première de ces deux questions, dont la solution ne manquera pas d'apporter quelque clarté à la seconde.

Les fanfares du Bauhaus se sont tues

Il est des époques emplies de modestie et d'autres qui en sont absolument dénuées. Il est d'autre part, au sein de ces époques, des opinions modestes et d'autres qui le sont très peu.

La publicité – qu'on veuille bien le croire ou non – s'est gantée de modestie. Elle est même en mesure de démontrer (par des moyens scientifiques, si besoin est) de quel poids minime elle pèse dans la décision d'achat en de nombreux cas. Elle sait de plus pertinemment qu'il n'est qu'un nombre très restreint d'articles et de services où elle ait quelque pouvoir. (Essayez donc de vendre avec du tam-tam publicitaire du blé, du fret fluvial, du charbon, du ciment ou des rails de tramway.) Même ce que l'on est convenu d'appeler la mode dépend dans une bien plus faible mesure de la publicité qu'on ne le pense communément. (La publicité en est réduite à croiser les bras quand les hommes n'ont d'un coup plus envie de porter un chapeau. Et ce n'est que maintenant où la mode hippie est sur le déclin que la publicité peut lentement songer à s'en emparer.)

Ce qui revient à dire que le rôle de la publicité n'est certainement pas de transformer le monde, de prêcher la société, de former le goût public de façon décisive. Le rôle qui lui est imparti est bien défini: renseigner sur un produit, un service, offrir une ou des options au moment de la décision d'achat, tout au plus aider à créer la demande. L'essentiel étant que la publicité en soi n'existe pas: la publicité se fait toujours pour un produit, un ensemble de produits, une société, un service déterminés, elle a toujours une mission bien définie, qu'elle doit remplir au mieux.

On se demandera pourquoi j'expose ceci. C'est pour démontrer que l'art graphique, qui a ses ambitions propres en ce qui concerne l'orientation générale de l'éducation, du goût et l'amélioration du monde, n'a de place dans la publicité que dans la mesure où ses ambitions s'accommodent d'une mission particulière bien définie au préalable.

Avouons que, de surcroît, la publicité n'est qu'un éphémère, lancé aujourd'hui, oublié demain. Reportez-vous en pensée il y a trois ou cinq ans: combien de campagnes publicitaires avez-vous encore présentes à la mémoire, sur les milliers que vous avez vues?

Ce qui ne veut pas dire que la qualité graphique de la création publicitaire n'a pas grande importance. Et je ne voudrais pas tendre la perche à ceux qui préfèrent dans le domaine graphique le médiocre au réussi, le banal au soigné, le plat à l'ingénieux et le bon marché à la valeur sûre.

Oui mais: qu'est-ce, au juste, l'art graphique de qualité?

Allons tout d'abord voir du côté de la publicité. Qu'est-ce, au juste, la publicité de qualité?

La publicité de qualité est intelligente ou, pour mieux dire, puisqu'il ne s'agit pas vraiment d'intellect: elle est astucieuse. Comment cela?

Barrows Mussey, l'Américain de Dusseldorf (Allemagne Fédérale), qui est l'un des rares professionnels à avoir compris le mécanisme de la publicité et qui en ausculte les palpitations et mouvements convulsifs avec autant de sens critique que d'affection, déclare que la publicité de qualité crée comme un appel d'air. (Elle représente par-là même le contraire de ce que prétendent les directeurs des ventes, à savoir qu'elle doit asséner des coups de marteau.) Elle ne harcèle pas les gens à la façon d'un moulin à paroles, mais avance la chaise qui sera utilisée avec plaisir lorsque l'on aura envie de s'asseoir. Mussey dit encore que pour attirer les oiseaux, il est préférable de se munir de graines plutôt que d'un fusil de chasse. Pas une tonne entière de graines, une poignée suffit amplement. Il vaut encore mieux, dit-il, jeter ces graines devant soi de la manière appropriée pour faire comprendre aux oiseaux qu'il y a là quelqu'un qui leur offre des graines – et vous les verrez arriver.

Peut-être l'art graphique de qualité au service de la publicité équivaut-il exactement à ce geste: jeter des graines devant soi de façon appropriée. En termes plus clairs: la démarche qui attire, qui en appelle à l'attention, qui éveille la curiosité. Des centaines de fois déjà, on a constaté (et il faut le redire et le redire) que les gens (c'est-à-dire nous tous) ne s'intéressent pas à la publicité, mais à ce qui les intéresse. D'où la nécessité de faire de la publicité intéressante et, partant, de la création graphique intéressante.

L'art graphique de qualité n'est donc pas la belle création graphique, mais celle qui aide à rendre intéressante la publicité. Dans la mesure où elle y réussit, elle a parfaitement le droit d'être belle, parce que la beauté, en son genre, contribue aussi à l'intérêt.

Ce n'est pas plus difficile que cela.

Parenthèse: est-ce que l'art graphique a quelque chose à voir avec l'art tout court?

Certainement.

Je crois aussi que l'art a quelque chose à voir avec l'intérêt qu'on prend aux choses, la curiosité, les découvertes.

Un artiste, c'est un homme qui voit le monde autrement (et sait l'exprimer, le montrer, le démontrer) que nous ne le faisons d'habitude. Et comme l'habitude transforme une vision, une conception données en normes rigides et que les normes rigides sont à l'antipode de l'effort d'appréhension en tant que phénomène actif, notre conception du monde s'écarte toujours davantage de la réalité, que nous voyons et comprenons de moins en moins, alors que l'artiste a de cette réalité une vision toujours neuve, parce que toujours renouvelée. C'est pourquoi nous avons tant besoin de l'art. Et c'est pourquoi celui qui veut voir le monde tel qu'il est et le comprendre doit s'enquérir de la vision des artistes, doit s'intéresser à l'art.

Je puis maintenant dire le contraire de ce que j'avançais tout à l'heure: tout consommateur, et jusqu'au plus fruste, désire au tréfonds de son être découvrir quelque chose de nouveau, changer, se transformer et transformer le monde. Lorsqu'il en vient à contempler une création publicitaire qui satisfait son attente par le thème qu'elle traite, mais aussi par la manière dont elle le traite, le consommateur même moyen est entraîné par l'appel d'air dont il était question tout à l'heure. C'est ainsi que l'art graphique se voit connaître le droit de transformer le monde, de prêcher la société, de former le goût public, ou du moins de participer à un processus de ce genre. Ce faisant, l'art graphique acquiert même un droit que j'aimerais écrire en toutes lettres, au risque de vous effrayer, celui de profaner l'art.

C'est que l'artiste qui a du monde une conception nouvelle se heurte d'emblée à la résistance des notions et conceptions consacrées. Par la suite, il rencontre quelques individus qui se rangent à sa conception, et leurs idées font tache d'huile jusqu'à constituer une tendance, une mode, un mouvement. Le résultat en est qu'un nombre croissant d'individus vient se ranger sous la bannière des novateurs. D'autres «branches», la mode, l'architecture, la décoration intérieure, l'art graphique, l'affiche s'emparent de l'interprétation nouvelle: l'art se profane.

L'art publicitaire peut (ou doit?) participer à ce processus. Il y a du reste participé à maintes reprises – que l'on se rappelle le rôle des affiches et annonces inspirées de l'Art Nouveau et qui alliaient la relance artistique à l'intérêt publicitaire. Et c'est bien la raison pour laquelle on ne saurait s'étonner de voir des artistes graphiques de valeur s'installer aux confins philosophiques ou même sociaux du domaine de l'Aventure que prospectent les artistes, les expérimentateurs, les créateurs d'avant-garde, les poètes et autres chercheurs d'Absolu. On ne saurait pas non plus s'étonner de voir ces mêmes artistes graphiques de valeur renoncer abruptement à un style qui pourtant avait consacré leur réussite, à une technique éprouvée d'expression visuelle qui avait rallié les suffrages, pour partir pour de nouvelles conquêtes.

Admettons que ce serait affreux qu'il y eût en publicité une seule manière, consacrée une fois pour toutes, de réaliser des créations graphiques de qualité. Il en résulterait un ennui indicible. Sans compter que l'ennui est, du point de vue publicitaire (et de bien d'autres), un péché capital.

La Qualité vient du naturel

Que doit-on en somme demander à l'artiste graphique qui s'engage dans la publicité? Evidemment, la connaissance parfaite de son métier. Mais ceci posé, où réside son apport personnel et irremplaçable?

Les deux choses les plus difficiles qu'on lui demande dans son travail publicitaire sont la bonne humeur, d'une part, la discrétion, de l'autre, soit l'aptitude à passer inaperçu.

Pour ce qui est de la bonne humeur, nous citerons un rédacteur de textes publicitaires qui a étudié sa propre profession, Robert Stalder:

«Un rédacteur, ce devrait être un homme qui éprouve de temps à autre le désir irrésistible de crier à la face des gens que les autos, les savons, les cigarettes, la bière, les soutiens-gorge et les ordinateurs ne sont pas du tout ce qu'une société décadente est prête à acheter à force de persuasion pour le seul plaisir de se plaindre après coup du baratin publicitaire et des achats inutiles, mais qu'il s'agit d'objets bénéfiques dont un certain remplit bien mieux sa mission d'apporter un confort raisonné à la vie que tous les autres objets du même genre qui se trouvent sur le marché. Il s'agit évidemment de l'objet auquel il voue ses soins de publicitaire.

La meilleure rhétorique consiste à démontrer aux gens ce que c'est que la vraie joie de vivre.»

On pourrait en dire autant de l'artiste publicitaire. L'ennui, c'est que la bonne humeur constante est une des choses les plus difficiles à garantir.

Nous disions que l'autre difficulté majeure que rencontre le graphiste est de passer inaperçu. Ce qui doit être visible, c'est l'annonce, l'affiche, la brochure. Le vouloir, le savoir, la pensée, les sentiments et le flair de l'artiste graphique doivent entrer tout entiers dans le produit publicitaire tel qu'il se présentera sous forme imprimée. Quant à lui-même, qu'il soit invisible! L'annonce doit exprimer ceci: Je suis une bonne annonce (ou mieux encore: c'est un bon produit qui vous parle), mais jamais, au grand jamais elle n'insinuera: Voyez donc quel artiste (ou rédacteur, ou photographe) de qualité m'a faite!

C'est en ce sens que j'entends que la qualité d'un travail graphique vient de son naturel. L'apport de l'artiste graphique consiste à aider à créer une idée, un état d'esprit, une volonté unique de style et de s'y soumettre ensuite. Dans la mesure où il réussit à cette tâche, la créature éphémère appelée annonce prouvera toute sa vitalité, bien que menacée de disparition à brève échéance. Cette vitalité se manifestera à la lecture, quand le lecteur reviendra sur ses pas pour la regarder de près, la contempler, au lieu de la faire sombrer dans l'oubli, sitôt entrevue au cours des pages. Sans s'en apercevoir, il aura ainsi appris quelque chose de nouveau en obéissant à sa curiosité, en obtempérant à ses désirs.

J'aurais aimé conclure cet exposé par une liste des exigences pratiques de la profession d'artiste publicitaire. Je m'aperçois néanmoins que je n'arrive pas à donner forme à ces exigences ni à des conseils utiles. C'est que je suis peut-être déjà victime de la déformation professionnelle qui atteint tout membre d'une agence publicitaire. C'est peut-être aussi que j'ai vu trop souvent le tempérament, la disposition créatrice du moment et la puissance imaginative décider de la réussite d'un artiste graphique que n'auraient pas avantagé vis-à-vis de ses collègues sa formation technique, son métier. On comprend que certains n'apprennent jamais à devenir de vrais créateurs, les doctrinaires encore moins que d'autres.

C'est pourquoi il est parfois regrettable, mais guère fatal que les écoles professionnelles qui forment des artistes graphiques n'enseignent pas toujours les côtés pratiques, réels du travail publicitaire, pour autant qu'elles n'enseignent rien de vraiment contraire aux exigences du métier. Faisons confiance à l'artiste graphique doué pour le travail publicitaire; il saura bien trouver le chemin de la publicité par lui-même.

Markus Kutter

Index to Designers and Artists
Verzeichnis der Entwerfer und Künstler
Index des maquettistes et artistes

Index to Art Directors
Verzeichnis der künstlerischen Leiter
Index des directeurs artistiques

Index to Agencies and Studios
Verzeichnis der Agenturen und Studios
Index des agences et studios

Index to Advertisers
Verzeichnis der Auftraggeber
Index des clients

NOTE: Where more than one name occurs in the crediting of an illustration, the name before the oblique is that of the artist, the designer's name follows. Two artists or designers, jointly responsible for one piece, are separated by a comma.

ANMERKUNG: Wenn in den Künstlerlisten für eine Illustration mehr als ein Name angegeben ist, bedeutet derjenige vor dem Schrägstrich den Künstler, derjenige nach dem Schrägstrich den Entwerfer. Sind zwei oder mehrere Künstler gleicherweise an einer Arbeit beteiligt, so sind die Namen durch Komma getrennt.

REMARQUE: Lorsque deux artistes sont responsables, l'un de la réalisation, l'autre de la maquette, leurs noms, dans la liste accompagnant les illustrations, sont séparés par un trait oblique: réalisation / maquette. Dans le cas où deux ou plusieurs artistes sont collectivement responsables de la réalisation, une virgule sépare leurs noms.

1

Posters

Plakate

Affiches

1

Artist / Künstler / Artiste:

1) J. DESGRIPPES
2) EDWARD MARSON
3) HEIKKI KASTEMAA
4) 7) GEORGES LEMOINE
5) GEORGE TSCHERNY
6) DONALD BRUN
8) ROBERT INDIANA

Art Director / Directeur artistique:

1) P. BAUDARD
3) HEIKKI KASTEMAA
4) 7) JACQUES LAVAUX
5) LEONARD H. SIENNICK
6) DONALD BRUN
8) RON IREBAUGH

Agency / Agentur / Agence – Studio:

1) DE PLAS, PARIS
2) GEORGE NELSON & CO., INC., NEW YORK
3) HEIKKI KASTEMAA, HELSINKI
5) GEORGE TSCHERNY, NEW YORK

2

3

5

6

Posters / Plakate / Affiches

4

7

8

1) Bus-side poster for an aperitif. (FRA)
2) Poster for *Rosenthal*, porcelain manufacturers, who have opened a new studio in New York. (USA)
3) Poster for a stereo studio and record shop in Helsinki. Red ground, blue 'ripples', green bird. (FIN)
4) Poster for school equipment from a store. (FRA)
5) Poster for General Dynamics about the resources of the Arctic. Artwork in blue-grey shades. (USA)
6) Poster for a brand of cigars. Polychrome. (SWI)
7) For an exhibition in a department store. (FRA)
8) Christmas poster for the *Neiman Marcus* stores. (USA)

1) Busplakat für den Aperitif *Dubonnet*. (FRA)
2) Plakat zur Eröffnung des *Rosenthal*-Studio-Hauses in New York. Schwarzweiss. (USA)
3) Plakat für ein Stereo- und Plattengeschäft in Helsinki. Roter Grund, Ringe blau, Vogel grün. (FIN)
4) Plakat für Schulausrüstungen aus einem Warenhaus. (FRA)
5) Plakat über die Forschungsarbeiten zur wirtschaftlichen Ausnützung der Arktis. (USA)
6) Plakat für *Meccarillos*-Zigarren. Mehrfarbig. (SWI)
7) Plakat für eine Ausstellung in einem Warenhaus. (FRA)
8) Weihnachtsplakat eines Warenhauses. (USA)

1) Affiche pour l'apéritif *Dubonnet*, à placarder sur les autobus. (FRA)
2) Affiche en noir pour un magasin de porcelaine. (USA)
3) Affiche pour un magasin de disques et d'appareils stéréophoniques. Fond rouge, cercles bleus, oiseau vert. (FIN)
4) Affiche pour les magasins *Prisunic*, Paris. (FRA)
5) Affiche de la General Dynamics, évoquant les ressources de l'Arctique. (USA)
6) Affiche pour les cigares *Meccarillos*. Polychrome. (SWI)
7) Pour une exposition dans un magasin *Prisunic*. (FRA)
8) Affiche de Noël d'un grand magasin de Dallas. (USA)

WO
FREUNDE
SIND, IST AUCH
MARTINI
MARTINI
9

Pepita
10

12

Halsfeger
KLEIN'S
HALS
FEGER
Fr. 1.-
13

11

14

Posters / Plakate / Affiches

9) 'Where there are friends, there's *Martini*.' Poster for an aperitif. (SWI)
10) Poster for a grapefruit-flavoured mineral water. (SWI)
11) Poster project for a book. (JAP)
12) Poster for the soft drink *Canada Dry*, also used as a prize in a company campaign. Polychrome. (SWI)
13) Poster for herbal coughdrops. (SWI)
14) Poster for toys sold by a co-operative society. (SWI)

9) Plakat für einen Aperitif. (SWI)
10) Plakat für das Mineralwasser *Pepita*. Mehrfarbig. (SWI)
11) Plakatentwurf für ein Buch mit dem Titel *Paraphrenie*. Mehrfarbig. (JAP)
12) Plakat als Preis innerhalb der Sammelaktion der Mineralwasserfirma Canada Dry Suisse S. A., Le Landeron. (SWI)
13) Plakat für *Klein's Halsfeger*. A. Klein AG, Neuewelt. (SWI)
14) Plakat für die Spielwarenabteilung der Firma *Co-op*. (SWI)

9) «Quand les amis se retrouvent, on trouve Martini». Affiche pour un apéritif. (SWI)
10) Affiche pour une boisson minérale aux pamplemousses. Polychrome. (SWI)
11) Maquette d'affiche pour un livre. Polychrome. (JAP)
12) Affiche pour les boissons minérales de la Canada Dry Suisse S. A., Le Landeron, utilisée comme prix dans le cadre d'une campagne de la société. (SWI)
13) Affiche pour des bonbons contre la toux. (SWI)
14) Affiche pour les jouets en vente dans les coopératives *Co-op*. (SWI)

Artist / Künstler / Artiste:

9) ATELIER GEORGES WICKY
10) HERBERT LEUPIN
11) TAKEYUKI SAKAGUCHI
12) HANS ULRICH
13) DONALD BRUN
14) WALTER GRIEDER

Art Director / Directeur artistique:

9) GEORGES WICKY
10) HERBERT LEUPIN
11) TAKEYUKI SAKAGUCHI
12) KREATIV-TEAM ULRICH+FEHLMANN
13) DONALD BRUN
14) KARL-HEINZ WITT

Agency / Agentur / Agence – Studio:

9) TRIO ADVERTISING S. A., LAUSANNE
12) JACQUES SENAUD, LAUSANNE

Posters / Plakate / Affiches

15) 16) Posters from a series for various stores in a shopping centre. Bright colours. (USA)
17) Poster for a fashion store. Blue and red. (SWI)
18) 19) Polychrome posters for a Greenwich Village newspaper. (USA)
20) Poster to advertise pecan nuts. Two colours. (ISR)
21) Polychrome poster for a bank offering customers advice on investment problems. (SWI)
22) For a coffee without caffeine. Polychrome. (SWI)
23) Poster for oven-ready chickens from a department store. (FRA)
24) Poster for fruit and vegetables. Four colours. (POL)
25) Polychrome poster for the New York State lottery. (USA)
26) Bus-side poster for a telephone directory with a classified section. Polychrome. (USA)

15) 16) Plakate für verschiedene Läden in einem Einkaufszentrum. Mehrfarbig. (USA)
17) Plakat für das Modehaus *Weilemann* in Bern. Blau und rot. (SWI)
18) 19) Plakate für die Zeitung THE VILLAGE VOICE des New Yorker Künstlerviertels Greenwich Village. Mehrfarbig. (USA)
20) Plakat für Pecannüsse. Zweifarbig. (ISR)
21) Plakat für die Abteilung Anlageberatung der Schweizerischen Kreditanstalt. Mehrfarbig. (SWI)
22) Plakat für den koffeinfreien Kaffee *Idol*. Mehrfarbig. (SWI)
23) Plakat für ofenfertige Hühnchen aus einem Warenhaus. (FRA)
24) Plakat für Gemüse und Obst. Mehrfarbig. (POL)
25) Plakat für die Lotterie des Staates New York. (USA)
26) Plakat einer Telephongesellschaft, das auf ein Telephonbuch mit Branchenverzeichnis aufmerksam macht. (USA)

15) 16) Affiches pour les magasins d'un centre d'achat. Polychrome. (USA)
17) Affiche pour une maison de confection. Bleu et rouge. (SWI)
18) 19) Affiches en couleur pour THE VILLAGE VOICE, revue du quartier des artistes de New York, Greenwich Village. Polychrome. (USA)
20) Affiche en faveur des noix de pécan. Deux couleurs. (ISR)
21) Affiche en couleur pour les services d'une banque en matière d'investissements. (SWI)
22) Affiche pour le café décaféiné *Idol*. Polychrome. (SWI)
23) Affiche pour les poulets en vente dans les magasins *Prisunic*. (FRA)
24) Affiche en faveur des fruits et des légumes polonais. (POL)
25) Affiche en couleur pour la loterie de l'Etat de New York. (USA)
26) Affiche pour un annuaire de téléphone, donnant la listes des abonnés par professions. Polychrome. (USA)

15

16

18

19

21

22

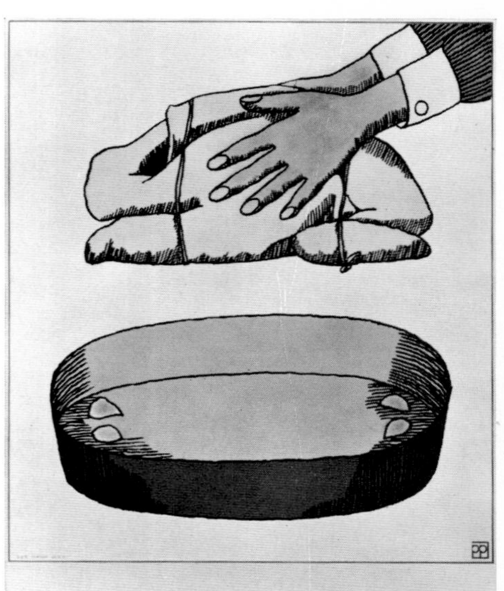

23

17

25

20

26

24

Artist / Künstler / Artiste:

15) 16) JAMES ODGERS
17) HANS-ULRICH OSTERWALDER
18) 19) 25) TOMI UNGERER
20) DAN ARNON
21) GÉRARD MIEDINGER
22) ROMANO CHICHERIO/CESARE BIANCHI
23) GEORGES LEMOINE
24) KAROL SLIWKA
26) ED RENFRO

Art Director / Directeur artistique:

15) 16) HERB ROSENTHAL
18) 19) TOMI UNGERER
21) GÉRARD MIEDINGER
22) ROMANO CHICHERIO
23) GEORGES LEMOINE
25) GEORGE CINFO
26) RAY ALBAN/AL SCHEER

Agency / Agentur / Agence – Studio:

17) HABLÜTZEL+DR. JACQUET, BERN
20) STUDIO HBM, TEL AVIV
22) ROMANO CHICHERIO, LUGANO
23) PRISUNIC, BUREAU D'ÉTUDES, PARIS
24) W.H.Z., WARSCHAU
25) FULLER, SMITH & ROSS, INC., LOS ANGELES
26) REACH MC CLINTON CO., INC., NEWARK, N.J.

27) Showcard for a make of socks. Silver, blue, red and black. (SPA)
28) Poster for the Post Office Savings Bank, reproduced by permission of Her Britannic Majesty's Postmaster General. (GB)
29) Poster for a fashion magazine. Two colours. (GB)
30) For the Finnish Post Office. 'Someone is expecting your letter.' (FIN)
31) Poster for anti-asthmatic drugs for use in autumn. (ITA)
32) Poster for an 'independent' newspaper. (SWI)
33) Poster for a brand of French-flavour cigarettes. (SWI)
34) Poster for a book and record club. (SWI)

27) Aufstellplakat für eine Sockenmarke. (SPA)
28) Plakat für die englische Postsparkasse. (GB)
29) Plakat für eine Modezeitschrift. Zweifarbig. (GB)
30) Plakat für die finnische Post. «Jemand erwartet Ihren Brief.» (FIN)
31) Plakat für Pillen gegen Asthmabeschwerden im Herbst. (ITA)
32) Plakat zur Werbung für die NATIONALZEITUNG, Basel. (SWI)
33) Plakat für die Zigarette *Gauloise.* (SWI)
34) Plakat für Bücher und Schallplatten von *Ex Libris Verlag AG*, Zürich. (SWI)

Artist / Künstler / Artiste:

27) PLA NARBONA
28) DONALD SMITH
29) ALAN CRACKNELL/TOM WOLSEY
30) LASSE HIETALA
31) GIORGIO TONTI
32) ROLF RAPPAZ
33) CELESTINO PIATTI
34) MICHEL FRITSCHER

Art Director / Directeur artistique:

27) PLA NARBONA
28) WENDY MONCK
29) TOM WOLSEY
30) LASSE HIETALA
31) GIORGIO TONTI
32) ROLF RAPPAZ
33) ANDRÉ BERGONZOLI
34) OSWALD DUBACHER

Agency / Agentur / Agence – Studio:

27) DORIA-PUBLICIDAD Y EDICIONES, BARCELONA
29) LENNON, NEWELL & WOLSEY, LONDON
31) STUDIO ZERO, MILAN

27

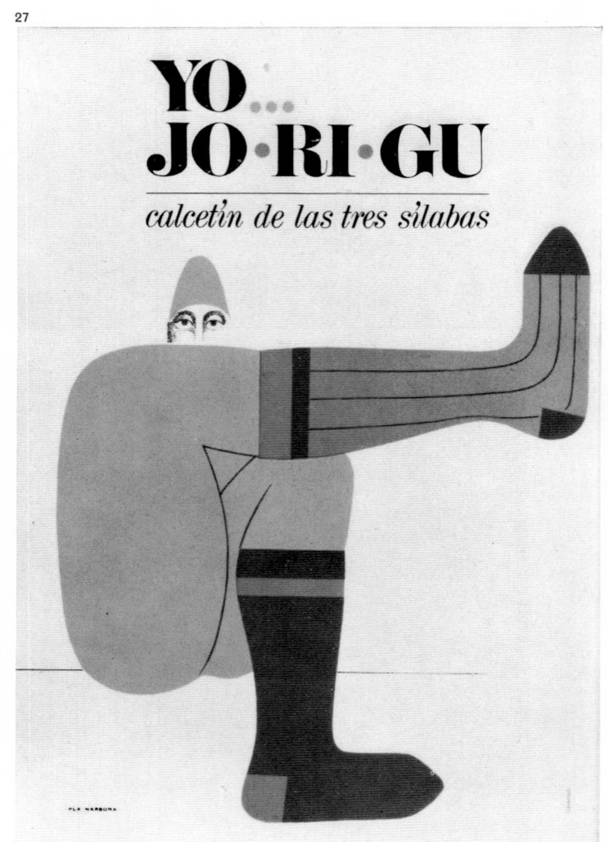

28

30

31

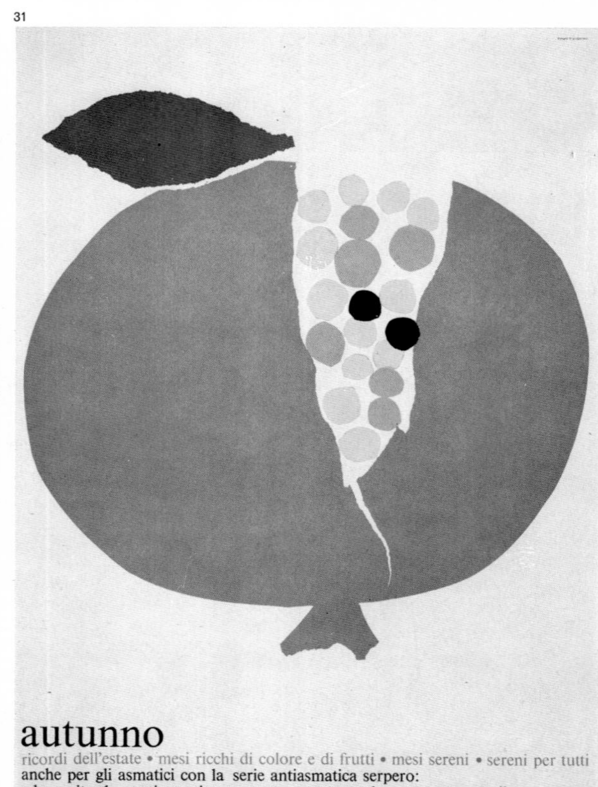

27) Affiche d'étalage pour les chaussettes José Rieva Gubau. (SPA)
28) Affiche pour la Caisse d'épargne des Postes britanniques. (GB)
29) Affiche pour une revue de mode. Deux couleurs. (GB)
30) Affiche pour les Postes finlandaises. (FIN)
31) Affiche pour des dragées contre l'asthme de Serpero S.p.A. (ITA)
32) Affiche pour un quotidien «indépendant». (SWI)
33) Affiche pour les cigarettes *Gauloises*, de Rinsoz & Ormond SA. (SWI)
34) Affiche pour un club du livre et du disque. (SWI)

29

33

32

34

35

35) 36) Complete poster and detail, for car loans from the Chemical Bank New York Trust Company. (USA)

37) Poster for an exhibition of advertising from the Great Ideas of Western Man campaign of the Container Corporation of America. (USA)

38) Industrial poster to encourage engineers and personnel to use microfilm records. Polychrome. (USA)

39) Polychrome recruitment poster addressed to college graduates by the American Telephone & Telegraph Co. (USA)

40) Poster for *Olivetti* typewriters. (ITA)

35) 36) Vollständiges Plakat und Illustration für Bankdarlehen beim Kauf von Autos. (USA)

37) Plakat für eine Ausstellung über die Werbekampagne «Grosse Gedanken des Abendlandes», veranstaltet von der Container Corporation of America. (USA)

38) Industrieplakat, das Ingenieure und Personal dazu anregt, Mikrofilme zu verwenden. (USA)

39) Plakat einer Telephongesellschaft zur Anwerbung von College-Absolventen. (USA)

40) Plakat für *Olivetti*-Schreibmaschinen. Mehrfarbig. (ITA)

36

35) 36) Affiche et son illustration, pour le financement des voitures par une banque de New York. (USA)
37) Affiche pour une exposition d'annonces de la série «Grande idées de l'homme occidental», organisée par la Container Corporation of America. (USA)
38) Affiche encourageant les ingénieurs et le personnel d'une usine à utiliser le classement sur microfilms. (USA)
39) Affiche en couleur destinée à recruter des universitaires pour une compagnie de téléphone. (USA)
40) Affiche pour les machines à écrire *Olivetti*. Polychrome. (ITA)

37

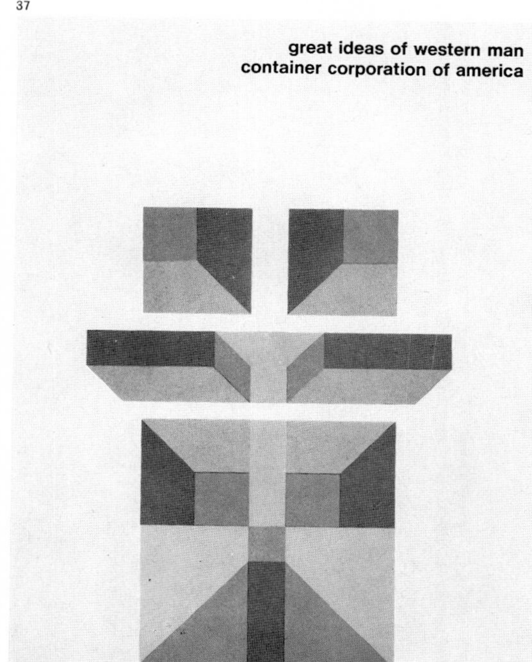

39

38

40

Artist / Künstler / Artiste:

35) 36) PAUL DAVIS/ZOLTAN MEDVECKY
37) JOHN MASSEY
38) EUGENE HOFFMAN
39) ABE GURVIN
40) JEAN MICHEL FOLON

Art Director / Directeur artistique:

35) 36) ZOLTAN MEDVECKY
37) JOHN MASSEY
38) EUGENE HOFFMAN
39) AL CATALANO
40) GIORGIO SOAVI

Agency / Agentur / Agence – Studio:

35) 36) BENTON & BOWLES, INC., NEW YORK

41

42

43

46

47

48

Artist | Künstler | Artiste:

41) JOHANNES REGN
42) 43) CHARLES SAXON
44) ROBERT LANTERIO/MARCO BERGAMASCHI
45) HESELER & HESELER
46) WOLFGANG BÄUMER
47) BERNARD VILLEMOT
48) CHARLES H. AFFOLTER
49) FRED BAUER-BENOIS
50) RUEDI KÜLLING
51) LOUIS SILVERSTEIN

41)–43) From a series of posters designed by well-known illustrators on different grades of paper made by the International Paper Co. (USA)
44) Poster for the Italian branch of IBM. (ITA)
45) Poster for a lecture on modern educational methods. Yellow, red and black. (GER)
46) 'Why lose your head? Play Lotto.' Poster for a weekly national lottery. (GER)
47) Poster for natural fruit juices. Polychrome. (FRA)
48) Poster for a French-Swiss lottery. Full colour. (SWI)
49) Poster for a national lottery. Blue and red. (SWI)
50) Poster for *Bic* ball-point pens. Four colours. (SWI)
51) Poster for THE NEW YORK TIMES to encourage holiday reading. Sepia shades, red lettering. (USA)

Art Director/Directeur artistique:

41)–43) IRVING D. MILLER
44) MARCO BERGAMASCHI
45) HESELER & HESELER
50) RUEDI KÜLLING
51) LOUIS SILVERSTEIN

Agency/Agentur/Agence – Studio:

41)–43) IRVING D. MILLER, INC., NEW YORK
45) HESELER & HESELER, WUPPERTHAL
47) DE PLAS, PARIS
49) ROBERT BLOCH, ZÜRICH
50) ADVICO AG, ZÜRICH

44

45

49

50

51

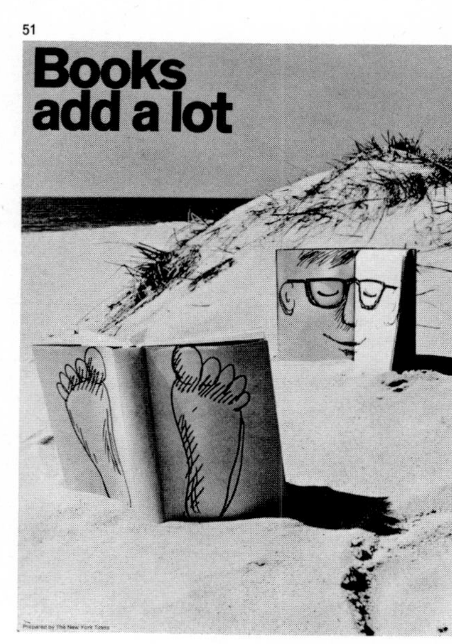

41)–43) Aus einer Serie von Plakaten für eine Papierfabrik, die jeweils von bekannten Illustratoren entworfen und auf verschiedenen Papierqualitäten gedruckt wurden. (USA)
44) Plakat für IBM in Italien. (ITA)
45) Plakat für eine Vorlesung über moderne Erziehungsmethoden anlässlich der Eröffnung des Frühjahrsemesters 1968 der Volkshochschule Wuppertal. Gelb, rot, schwarz. (GER)
46) Plakat für die Nordwestlotto in Nordrhein-Westfalen. (GER)
47) Plakat für natürliche Fruchtsäfte. Mehrfarbig. (FRA)
48) Plakat für eine Westschweizer Landeslotterie. (SWI)
49) Plakat für eine interkantonale Landeslotterie. (SWI)
50) Plakat für den Kugelschreiber *Bic*. Mehrfarbig. (SWI)
51) Plakat der NEW YORK TIMES, das zur Ferienlektüre ermuntern will. Sepiatöne, rote Schrift. (USA)

41)–43) D'une série d'affiches réalisées par des illustrateurs célèbres sur les différentes qualités de papier d'un fabricant américain. (USA)
44) Affiche pour IBM, Milan. (ITA)
45) Affiche pour une conférence sur les méthodes modernes d'éducation. Jaune, rouge et noir. (GER)
46) «Pourquoi perdre la tête? Tentez votre chance.» Affiche pour une loterie hebdomadaire. (GER)
47) Affiche pour les jus de fruits C.P.C., Paris. (FRA)
48) Affiche pour la Loterie romande, Lausanne. (SWI)
49) Affiche pour la Loterie intercantonale. (SWI)
50) Affiche pour les stylos à bille *Bic*, Lugano. (SWI)
51) Affiche du NEW YORK TIMES, encourageant à la lecture en vacances. Plusieurs tons de sépia, texte en rouge. (USA)

早川良雄作品展『顔たち』
一九六八年一月五日－二十日　大阪・今橋画廊
"THE FACE" From The Works of yoshio HAYAKAWA
JAN 5–20 1968 IMABASHI Gallery

52

P.B.GRANDPRIX
START

53

JEAN GENET
ジャン・ジュネ全集

55

タコタよさらば

56

54

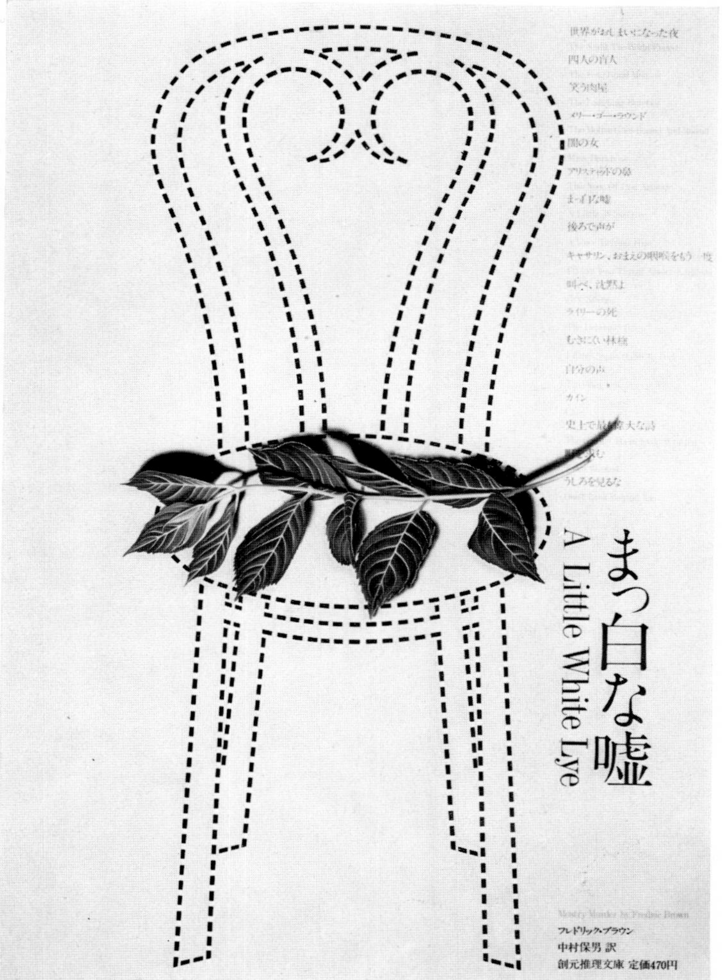

57

Posters / Plakate / Affiches

52) Poster for 'The Face', an exhibition of work by Yoshio Hayakawa. (JAP)
53) Poster for a men's weekly. (JAP)
54) Polychrome poster for a book. (JAP)
55) Poster project for the collected works of the playwright Jean Genet. (JAP)
56) Poster for an American best-seller published by Kodansha Ltd. (JAP)
57) Poster project for a book. (JAP)

52) Plakat für «Das Gesicht», eine Ausstellung der Arbeiten von Yoshio Hayakawa. (JAP)
53) Plakat für die japanische Ausgabe des PLAYBOY. (JAP)
54) Plakat für ein Buch. Mehrfarbig. (JAP)
55) Plakatentwurf für die gesammelten Werke des Schriftstellers Jean Genet. (JAP)
56) Plakat für einen Roman, herausgegeben von Kodansha Ltd., Tokyo. (JAP)
57) Plakatentwurf für ein Buch mit dem Titel «Eine kleine Notlüge». (JAP)

52) Affiche pour une exposition des œuvres de Yoshio Hayakawa, intitulée «Le visage». (JAP)
53) Affiche pour l'édition japonaise de PLAYBOY. (JAP)
54) Affiche en couleur pour un livre. (JAP)
55) Maquette d'affiche pour les œuvres complètes de Jean Genet. (JAP)
56) Affiche pour l'édition japonaise d'un roman américain à succès. (JAP)
57) Maquette d'affiche pour un livre intitulé «Un petit mensonge innocent». (JAP)

Artist / Künstler / Artiste:

52) YOSHIO HAYAKAWA
53) KEIICHI TANAAMI
54) TADANORI YOKOO
55) TOSHIKI OHASHI/KEISUKE KONISHI
56) YASUO SHIGEHARA
57) KEIKO TAKEMURA

Art Director / Directeur artistique:

53) KEIICHI TANAAMI
54) TADANORI YOKOO
57) KEIKO TAKEMURA

Agency / Agentur / Agence – Studio:

56) MADISON ADV. OFFICE, TOKYO
57) LIGHT PUBLICITY LTD., TOKYO

58) Poster for an international campaign in favour of museums. Red shades, black. (BEL)
59) Poster for a book of poems by Alan Ginsberg. (JAP)
60) Poster for an exhibition of work by Kazumasa Nagai. Red shades, blue, black. (JAP)
61) Poster project for an exhibition of modern arts and crafts. (JAP)
62) Poster for a radio symphony concert. Red, white and blue sectors on black. (GER)
63) Poster for a concert as part of a Czech week on the Hessian radio. (GER)
64) Poster for a week of experimental theatre in Frankfort. (GER)

58

Belgique
1968
2e campagne
internationale
des musées

59

Artist / Künstler / Artiste:

58) ANDRÉ PASTURE
59) SHIRO TATSUMI/TOSHIKI OHASHI
60) KAZUMASA NAGAI
61) TAKAKO MISHIMA
62) HANS FÖRTSCH/SIGRID VON BAUMGARTEN
63) 64) HANS MICHEL

Art Director / Directeur artistique:

62) HANS FÖRTSCH/SIGRID VON BAUMGARTEN

Agency / Agentur / Agence – Studio:

60) NIPPON DESIGN CENTER, TOKYO
62) HANS FÖRTSCH/SIGRID VON BAUMGARTEN, BERLIN

62

58) Plakat für die 2. Internationale Museumskampagne. Rottöne und Schwarz. (BEL)
59) Plakat für einen Gedichtband von Alan Ginsberg. (JAP)
60) Plakat für eine Ausstellung der Arbeiten von Kazumasa Nagai. (JAP)
61) Plakatentwurf für eine Ausstellung moderner kunstgewerblicher Arbeiten. (JAP)
62) Plakat für ein Konzert des Strassburger Radio-Symphonie-Orchesters. (GER)
63) Plakat für eine tschechoslowakische Woche des Hessischen Rundfunks. (GER)
64) Plakat für eine Woche experimentellen Theaters in Frankfurt/M. (GER)

58) Affiche pour une campagne internationale en faveur des musées. (BEL)
59) Affiche pour un recueil de poèmes d'Alan Ginsberg. (JAP)
60) Affiche pour une exposition des œuvres de Kazumasa Nagai. Rouge, bleu, noir. (JAP)
61) Maquette d'affiche pour une exposition d'art décoratif moderne. (JAP)
62) Affiche pour l'orchestre symphonique de la radio de Strasbourg. (GER)
63) Affiche pour une programme radiodiffusé de musique populaire tchèque. (GER)
64) Affiche pour une semaine de théâtre expérimental à Francfort. (GER)

60

61

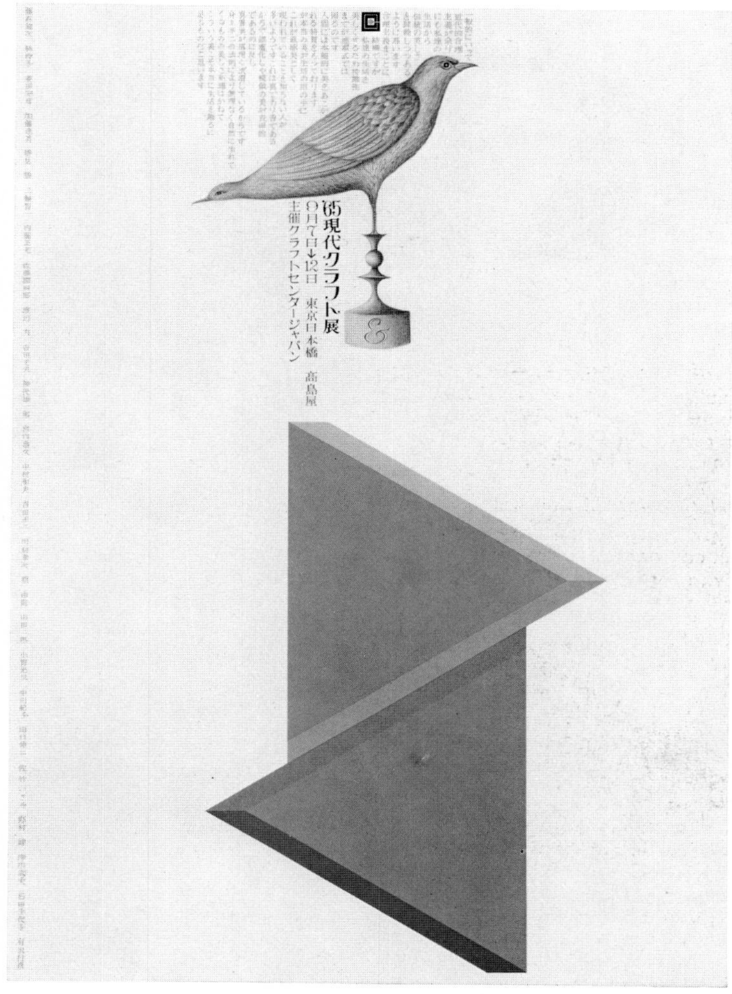

63

64

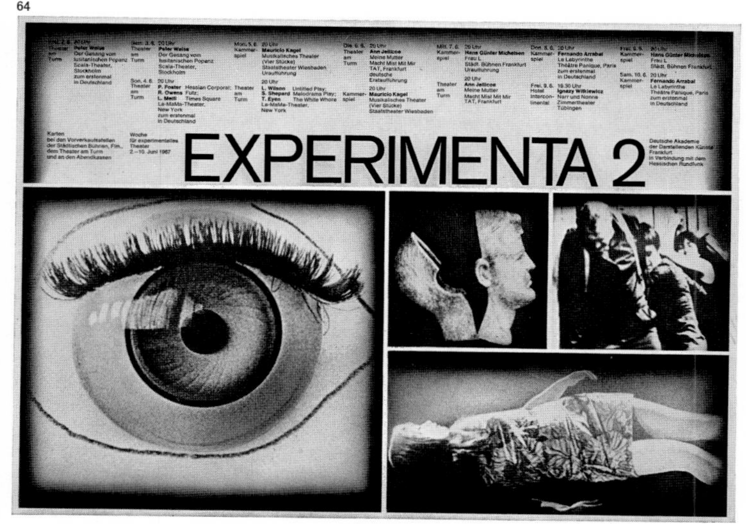

Posters / Plakate / Affiches

Artist / Künstler / Artiste:

65) GIUSEPPE LUCCI
66) SHIGEO FUKUDA
67) JEAN MICHEL FOLON
68) GIULIO CITTATO
69) SUSUMU EGUCHI
70) JOSEF FLEJŠAR

Art Director / Directeur artistique:

65) GIUSEPPE LUCCI
66) SHIGEO FUKUDA
68) GIULIO CITTATO
69) SUSUMU EGUCHI

Agency / Agentur / Agence – Studio:

65) GARDNER ADVERTISING, NEW YORK
68) CONTAINER CORPORATION OF AMERICA, CHICAGO
69) TOKYO ADV., TOKYO

65) Poster announcing the 12th Annual Report Exhibition of the Mead Library of Ideas. Black and white. (USA)
66) Poster for EXPO '70 in Osaka. (JAP)
67) Poster for an exhibition of the artist's work. (FRA)
68) Poster for Chicago art galleries, from a series on aspects of the city's cultural life. Grey, black and white. (USA)
69) Poster for a children's science exhibition in the *Tobu* department store. (JAP)
70) Poster for a tapestry exhibition in a Prague art gallery. Black and white. (CSR)

65) Plakat für die 12. Ausstellung von amerikanischen Jahresberichten, veranstaltet von der Mead Library of Ideas in New York. (USA)
66) Plakat für die EXPO '70 in Osaka. (JAP)
67) Plakat für eine Ausstellung der Arbeiten von Folon. (FRA)
68) Aus einer Serie von Plakaten für die Stadt Chicago, hier für die Kunstmuseen. Grau, schwarz und weiss. (USA)
69) Plakat für eine wissenschaftliche Ausstellung für Kinder im Warenhaus *Tobu*. (JAP)
70) Plakat für eine Ausstellung von Tapisserien in einem Prager Museum. Schwarzweiss. (CSR)

65) Affiche pour une exposition de rapports annuels, organisée par la «Bibliothèque aux idées» d'une fabrique de papier. Noir et blanc. (USA)
66) Affiche pour l'EXPO '70, à Osaka. (JAP)
67) Affiche pour une exposition des œuvres de Folon. (FRA)
68) Affiche tirée d'une série pour la ville de Chicago, ici en faveur des musées d'art. Gris, noir, blanc. (USA)
69) Affiche annonçant une exposition scientifique pour les enfants dans un grand magasin de Tokyo. (JAP)
70) Affiche pour une exposition de tapisseries dans un musée de Prague. Noir et blanc. (CSR)

65

68

EXPO'70 日本万国博
人類の進歩と調和
昭和45年3月開会・大阪
財団法人日本万国博覧会協会 大阪市東区本町4丁目27−1

66

FOLON
GALERIE DE FRANCE

67

ちびっこ
あつまれ〜ェ
夏休みは東武の6階!
主催—財団法人日本児童文化研究所 後援—東京都
史上最大 子供の科学展
8月17日〈水〉→28日〈日〉●6階催物場
整理料—おとな・こども 50円
月曜定休
池袋駅西口
東武

69

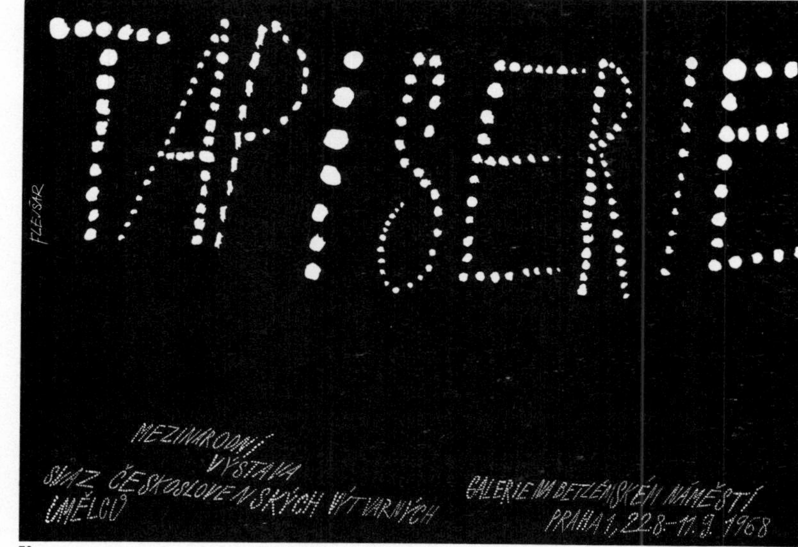
TAPISERIE
FLEIŠAR
MEZINÁRODNÍ VÝSTAVA
SVAZ ČESKOSLOVENSKÝCH VÝTVARNÝCH UMĚLCŮ
GALERIE NA BETLÉMSKÉM NÁMĚSTÍ
PRAHA 1, 22.8-11.9.1968

70

71) Poster for the presentation of a cultural prize. (GER)
72) Poster for a soirée of the National Society of Interior Designers. (USA)
73) For an issue of GRAPHIC DESIGN with a designer/copywriter dialogue. (JAP)
74) For an exhibition of modern European painting. Blue, red, black. (FRA)
75) Poster for the French pavilion at the Milan Triennale. (FRA)
76) Poster for an exhibition of toys in Bremen. (GER)
77) Poster for a theatrical performance. (JAP)

71) Plakat für die Verleihung eines Kulturpreises, in den Landesfarben gehalten. (GER)
72) Einladungsplakat zum Jahresfest einer Vereinigung von Innenarchitekten. (USA)
73) Plakat für eine Nummer der Zeitschrift GRAPHIC DESIGN. (JAP)
74) Plakat für eine Ausstellung zeitgenössischer europäischer Malerei. (FRA)
75) Plakat für den französischen Pavillon an der Mailänder Triennale. (ITA)
76) Plakat für eine Verkaufsaustellung von Spielzeugen in Bremen. (GER)
77) Plakat für eine Theateraufführung. (JAP)

71

72

74

75

71) Affiche pour la remise d'une récompense culturelle. (GER)
72) Affiche pour la soirée annuelle d'une association d'ensembliers. (USA)
73) Affiche pour une revue d'art graphique. (JAP)
74) Affiche pour une exposition au Musée des Arts décoratifs de Paris. (FRA)
75) Affiche pour le pavillon français à la Triennale de Milan. (ITA)
76) Affiche pour une exposition de jouets à Brême. (GER)
77) Affiche pour une représentation théâtrale. (JAP)

73

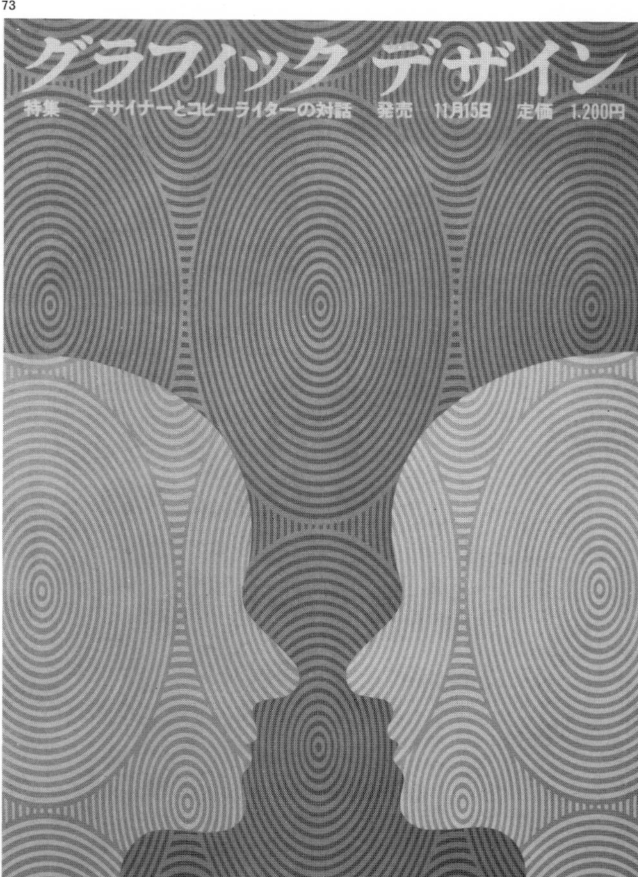

76

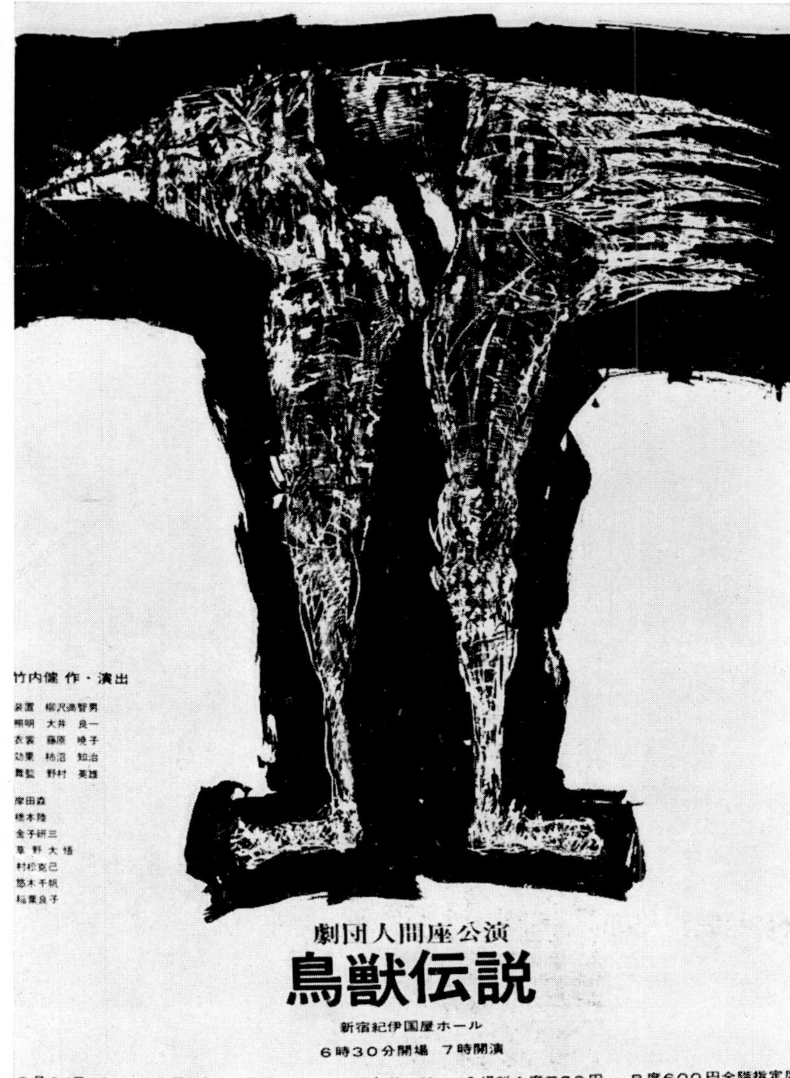

77

Artist / Künstler / Artiste:

71) HELFRIED HAGENBERG
72) JOHN RIEBEN
73) HIROSHI TANAKA
74) 75) JEAN MICHEL FOLON
76) FRITZ+SIBYLLE HAASE-KNELS
77) AKIHIDE IMAMURA

Art Director / Directeur artistique:

71) HELFRIED HAGENBERG
73) HIROSHI TANAKA
74) 75) FRANÇOIS MATHEY
76) FRITZ HAASE

Agency / Agentur / Agence – Studio:

76) ATELIER HAASE-KNELS, BREMEN

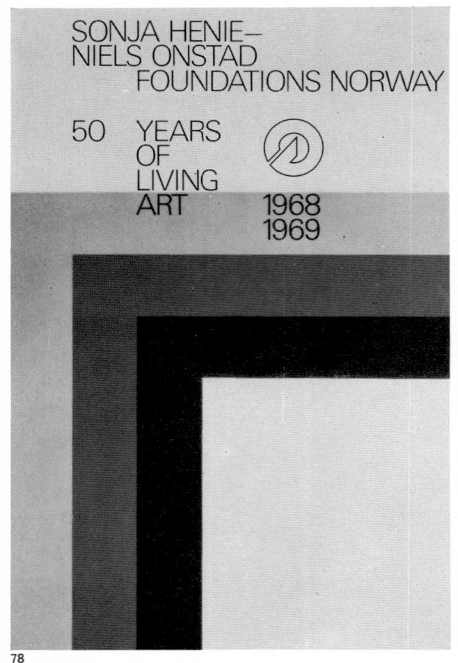

78

79

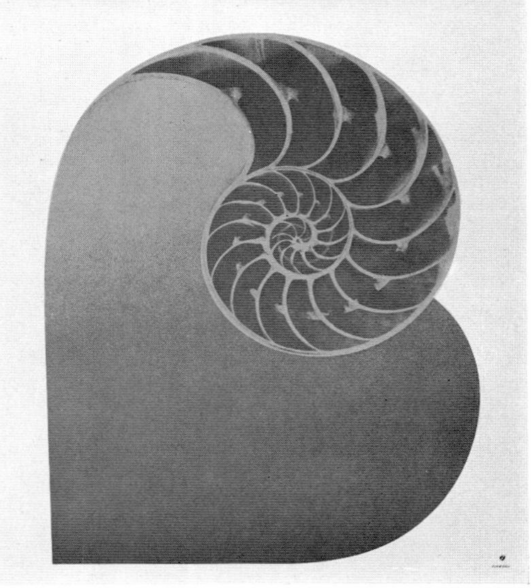

80

78) Poster for the opening of an art exhibition. (NOR)
79) Poster for a small theatre company in Denver. (USA)
80) Poster for a Bach Festival. Design silver grey. (USA)
81) Poster for a film programme at Colorado State University. Green and black on grey. (USA)
82) Poster for a programme of political discussions at a university. Ochre, blue and red. (USA)
83) Poster for a Shakespeare play. (USA)
84) Poster for a campus poster exhibition. Blue and black. (USA)
85) Poster for a lecture on Westerns. Two colours. (USA)
86) Poster for a Pirandello play. Black and silver. (USA)
87) Poster for a lecture, magenta and black. (USA)
88) Poster for an exhibition of modern prints. (GB)
89) For an exhibition by five illustrators. (GB)

78) Plakat zur Eröffnung einer Kunstausstellung. (NOR)
79) Plakat für eine Theatergruppe. (USA)
80) Plakat für ein Bach-Musikfest. (USA)
81) Plakat für die Aufführung von Filmklassikern an einer Universität. (USA)
82) Plakat für eine Reihe politischer Diskussionen an einer Universität. Ocker, blau und rot. (USA)
83) Plakat für die Aufführung eines Lustspiels von Shakespeare. Schwarz und magentarot. (USA)
84) Plakat für eine Plakatausstellung. (USA)
85) Plakat für eine Vorlesung über Wildwestfilme. (USA)
86) Plakat für ein Schauspiel von Pirandello. (USA)
87) Plakat für eine Vorlesung. (USA)
88) Plakat für die *Curwen*-Galerie in London. (GB)
89) Ausstellungsplakat des Royal College of Art. (GB)

78) Affiche pour le vernissage d'une exposition. (NOR)
79) Affiche pour une petite compagnie théâtrale. (USA)
80) Affiche pour un festival de musique. (USA)
81) Affiche pour une soirée cinématographique dans une université. Vert et noir sur gris. (USA)
82) Affiche pour une soirée de discussions politiques dans une université. Ocre, bleu et rouge. (USA)
83) Affiche pour une comédie de Shakespeare. Noir et fuchsia. (USA)
84) Affiche pour une exposition d'affiches. (USA)
85) Affiche pour une conférence sur le western. (USA)
86) Affiche pour une pièce de Pirandello. (USA)
87) Affiche pour une conférence. (USA)
88) Affiche pour une exposition. (GB)
89) Pour une exposition dans une école d'art. (GB)

82

83

85

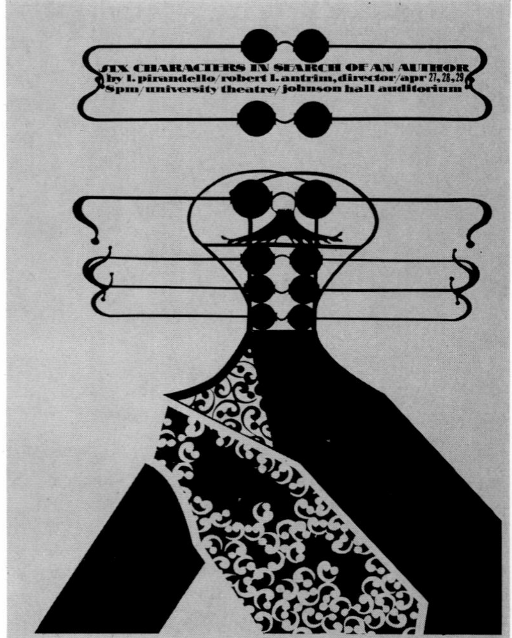

86

Artist / Künstler / Artiste:

78) SIEGFRIED ODERMATT
79) EUGENE HOFFMAN
80) DOUGLAS BAKER/EDWARD STRONG
81) 83) 85)–87) PHILIP E. RISBECK
82) ALLAN W. MILLER
84) JOHN J. SORBIE
88) BOB GILL
89) GARY BLAKE

Art Director / Directeur artistique:

78) SIEGFRIED ODERMATT
79) EUGENE HOFFMAN
80) DOUGLAS BAKER
81) 83) 85–87) PHILIP E. RISBECK
82) ALLAN W. MILLER
88) BOB GILL
89) GARY BLAKE

Agency / Agentur / Agence – Studio:

79) EUGENE HOFFMAN
82) VISUAL DESIGN PROGRAMS, SAN DIEGO

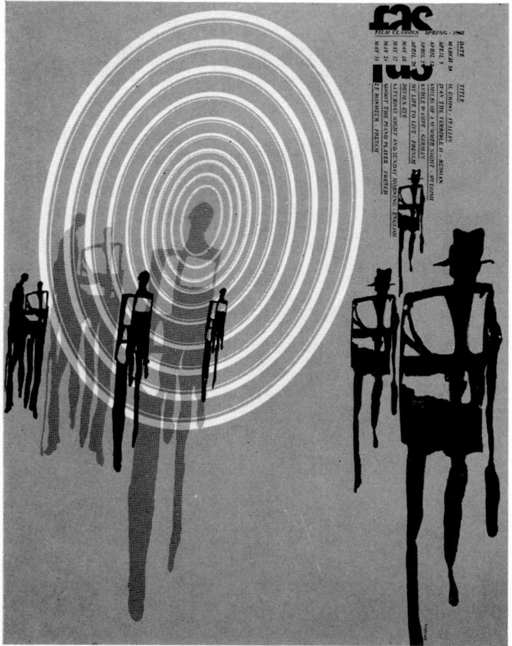

81

84

87

88

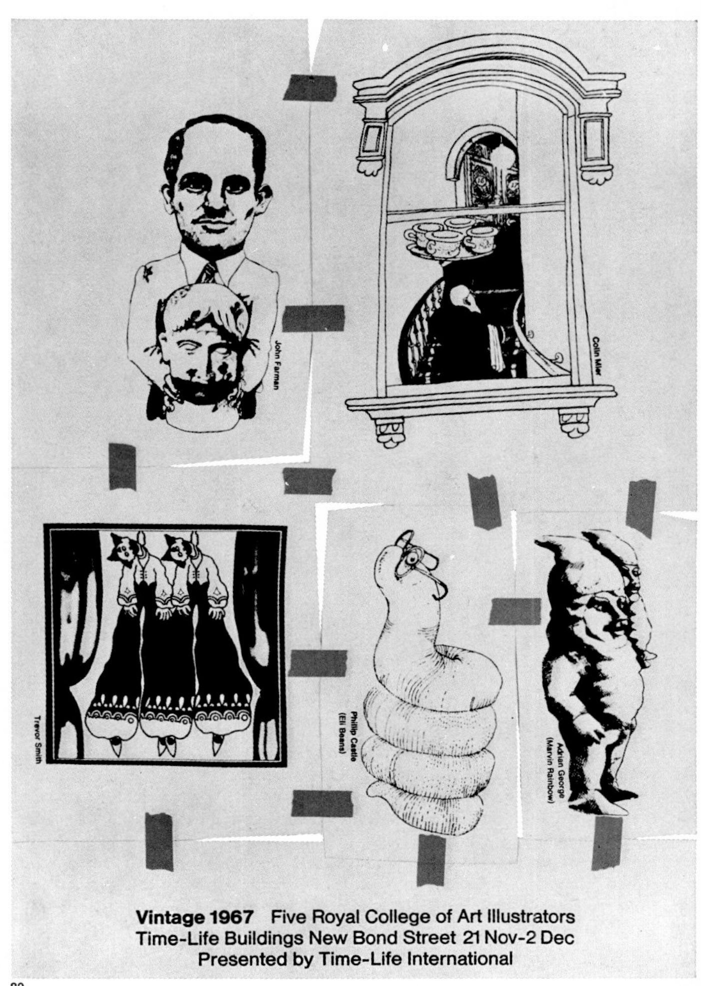

89

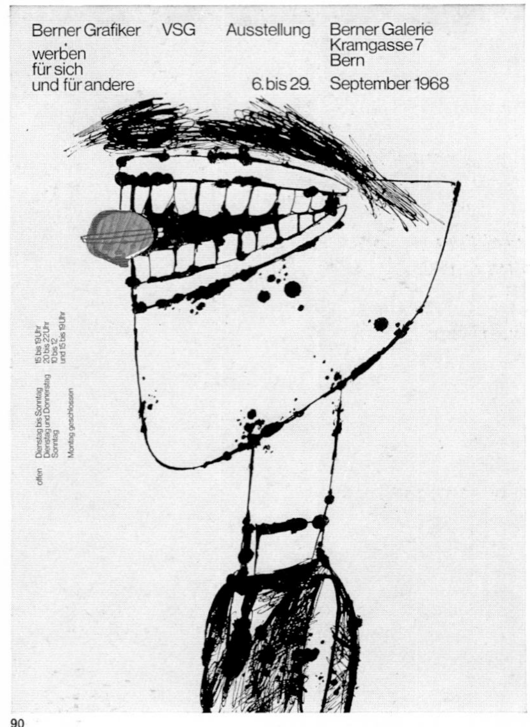

90

91

92

Stadttheater Bern

WEILL BRECHT

AUFSTIEG UND FALL DER STADT

MAHAGONNY

Oper in drei Akten von Kurt Weill Text von Bertolt Brecht
Berner Erstaufführung Première: 4. März 1969
Musikalische Leitung: Ewald Körner
Inszenierung: Edgar Kelling Bühnenbild: Rolf Christiansen

93

94

95

90) Poster for an exhibition of Bernese graphic design. (SWI)
91) For discussions on architecture. Black and white. (GER)
92) Poster for an exhibition of drawings by Searle. (FRA)
93) Poster for a performance of a Brecht opera in Berne. Black, white and beige. (SWI)
94) Poster for a Czech theatre festival. Gold with red and blue, black lettering. (CSR)
95) Poster for an exhibition of Russian industrial design. Five colours. (POL)
96) Poster for an exhibition of the artist's work. Two blues on silver. (USA)
97) Poster for an exhibition of Japanese posters from the last hundred years. (JAP)

90) Plakat für eine Ausstellung von Arbeiten von Berner Graphikern. Schwarz und braun auf weissem Grund. (SWI)
91) Plakat für eine Diskussionstagung der Vereinigung Freischaffender Architekten Deutschlands. (GER)
92) Plakat für eine Ausstellung der Zeichnungen von Ronald Searle. Schwarzweiss. (FRA)
93) Plakat für eine Opernaufführung im Stadttheater Bern. (SWI)
94) Festspielplakat «50 Jahre Tschechisches Theater». (CSR)
95) Plakat für eine Ausstellung russischer industrieller Formgebung. Mehrfarbig. (POL)
96) Plakat zur Ausstellung der Werke von Hundertwasser. (USA)
97) Plakat für eine Ausstellung japanischer Plakate der letzten hundert Jahre. (JAP)

90) Affiche pour une exposition d'œuvres de graphistes bernois. Noir et brun sur fond blanc. (SWI)
91) Affiche en noir pour un colloque d'architecture. (GER)
92) Affiche pour exposition de dessins de Ronald Searle. (FRA)
93) Affiche pour la représentation d'une pièce de Kurt Weill et Bertolt Brecht au théâtre de Berne. (SWI)
94) Affiche pour un festival de théâtre tchèque. (CSR)
95) Affiche pour une exposition de dessin industriel russe. Cinq couleurs. (POL)
96) Affiche pour une exposition des œuvres de l'artiste. Deux tons de bleu sur argent. (USA)
97) Affiche pour une exposition d'affiches japonaises de ces dernières cent années. (JAP)

Artist/Künstler/Artiste:

90) KURT WIRTH
91) D. + H. SCHLÜTER-CASSE
92) RONALD SEARLE
93) HEINZ JOST
94) JAROSLAV SŮRA
95) HUBERT HILSCHER
96) BRUCE MONTGOMERY
97) KENJI INOUE

Art Director/Directeur artistique:

90) KURT WIRTH
91) D. + H. SCHLÜTER-CASSE
95) GUSTAW MAJEWSKI
96) BRUCE MONTGOMERY
97) HIROMU HARA

Agency/Agentur/Agence – Studio:

95) WAG, WARSCHAU
96) BRUCE MONTGOMERY & ASSOC., SAN FRANCISCO
97) MATSUYA SENDENKA, TOKYO

96

日本のポスター100年展
編集=東京アートディレクターズクラブ 後援=美術出版社 1月5日金-16日火 8階 銀座 松屋
へうく坊

97

98

99

演劇座公演十一回
爆裂弾記
喜劇四幕
未来社版
作＝花田清輝　演出＝高山図南雄
六本木　俳優座劇場
一月三十日→二月四日　毎夕六時十五分開演
入場料 千円・前売券八百円・団体七百円
二月三日マチネ＝一時十五分・六時十五分　二月四日マチネ＝一時十五分のみ

100

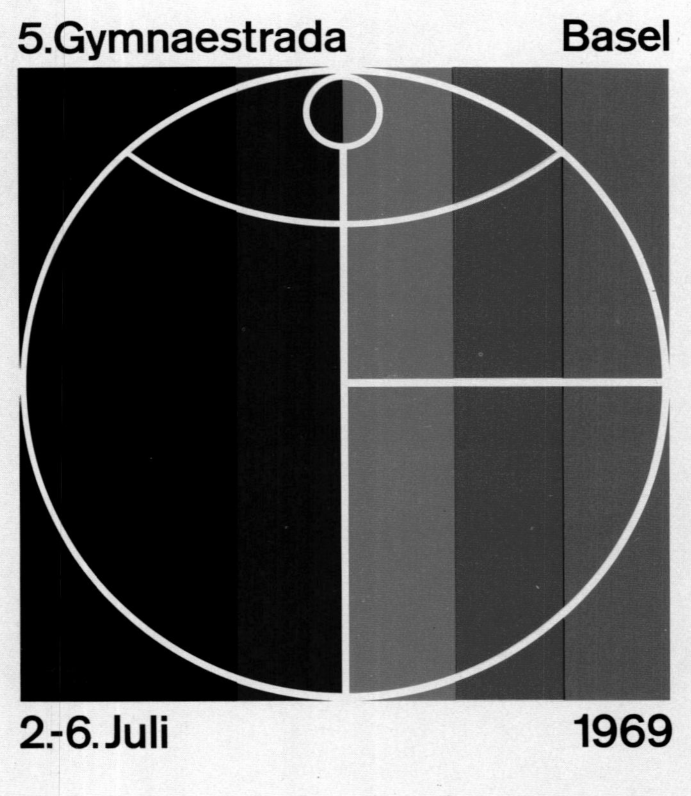

101

Posters / Plakate / Affiches

102

103

104

105

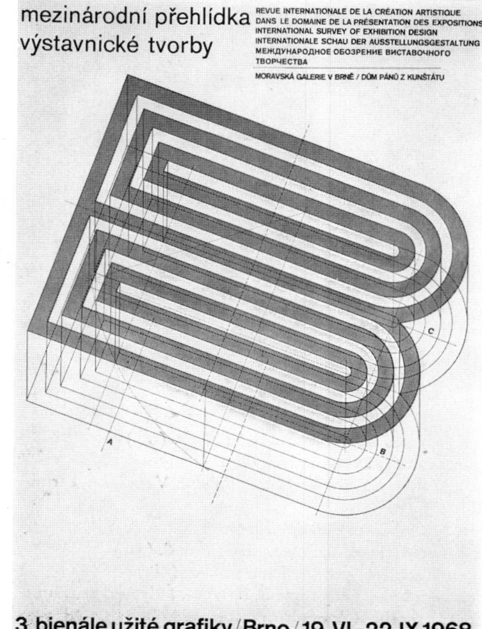

106

107

98) Poster for plays in four languages. (SWI)
99) Poster for a showing of American pop posters. (GER)
100) Poster for a play. (JAP)
101) Poster for a gymnastics display. (SWI)
102) Poster for an exhibition. Black and white. (SWI)
103) Poster for student housing schemes. Blue, white. (FIN)
104) Poster for a student meeting. Green and white. (FIN)
105) Poster for an awards dinner of the National Society of Interior Designers. Black and brown. (USA)
106) Poster for an international survey of exhibition design in Brno. Black and gold. (CSR)
107) Poster for a Tinguely machine sculpture exhibited in Basle. (SWI)

98) Plakat für Theateraufführungen in vier Sprachen, anlässlich der Junifestwochen in Zürich. (SWI)
99) Plakat für eine Ausstellung von Pop-Plakaten. (GER)
100) Plakat für ein Theaterstück, aufgeführt von der *Engeki-za*-Truppe. (JAP)
101) Plakat anlässlich der 5. Gymnaestrada in Basel. (SWI)
102) Plakat zur Ausstellung der Werke von Julius Bissier im Argauer Kunsthaus. Schwarzweiss. (SWI)
103) Plakat für Studentenheim-Projekte in Turku. (FIN)
104) Plakat für ein Studententreffen. Grün und weiss. (FIN)
105) Plakat zum Jahresfest einer Vereinigung von Innenarchitekten mit Preisverteilung. (USA)
106) Plakat für die Internationale Schau der Ausstellungsgestaltung in Brünn. (CSR)
107) Plakat zur Ausstellung einer Plastik von Tinguely. (SWI)

98) Affiche pour les représentations en quatre langues données à Zurich dans le cadre du Festival de juin. (SWI)
99) Affiche pour une exposition d'affiches pop. (GER)
100) Affiche pour une pièce de théâtre. (JAP)
101) Affiche pour une fête de gymnastique. (SWI)
102) Affiche en noir pour une exposition. (SWI)
103) Affiche pour un projet de cité universitaire. (FIN)
104) Affiche pour une réunion d'étudiants. Vert, blanc. (FIN)
105) Affiche pour le dîner annuel, avec remise de prix, d'une association d'ensembliers. Noir, brun. (USA)
106) Affiche pour une présentation internationale de dessin d'exposition à Brno. Noir et or. (CSR)
107) Affiche pour l'exposition d'une sculpture «mécanique» de Tinguely à Bâle. (SWI)

Artist | Künstler | Artiste:

108)–110) ANDRZEJ KRAJEWSKI
111) MARIA IHNATOWICZ
112) 113) WALDEMAR SWIERZY
114) 115) ASSEM STAREICHINSKI

Agency | Agentur | Agence – Studio:

113) WYDAWNICTWO WAG, POZNÁN/POL

108

109

111

112

108) Poster for a Japanese film. Two reds and black. (POL)
109) Poster for an American play. Polychrome. (POL)
110) Poster for a Hungarian film shown in Poland. Vermilion, carmine, violet and black. (POL)
111) Poster for a Spanish film. Full colour. (POL)
112) Poster for a theatrical performance. Blue ground. (POL)
113) Poster for a play. Black, grey, red and yellow. (POL)
114) Poster for a Lorca play performed in Plovdiv. Polychrome. (BUL)
115) Poster for a play entitled 'Vampire' performed in Pernik. Red, green, yellow and black. (BUL)

108) Plakat für einen japanischen Film. Zwei Rottöne, Schwarz. (POL)
109) Plakat für die Aufführung eines amerikanischen Schauspiels. (POL)
110) Plakat für einen ungarischen Film. Mehrfarbig. (POL)
111) Plakat für einen spanischen Film. Mehrfarbig. (POL)
112) Plakat für eine Theateraufführung. Blauer Grund. (POL)
113) Plakat für ein Schauspiel. Schwarz, grau, rot und gelb. (POL)
114) Plakat für die Aufführung eines Schauspiels von Garcia Lorca. Grün, blau, rot und schwarz. (BUL)
115) Plakat für das Schauspiel «Vampir», aufgeführt in Pernik. Rot, grün, gelb und schwarz. (BUL)

110

114

113

115

108) Affiche pour un film japonais. Deux tons de rouge et noir. (POL)
109) Affiche pour une pièce américaine. (POL)
110) Affiche en couleur pour un film hongrois. (POL)
111) Affiche pour un film espagnol. Polychrome. (POL)
112) Affiche pour une représentation théâtrale. Fond bleu. (POL)
113) Affiche pour une pièce de théâtre. Polychrome. (POL)
114) Affiche pour la représentation d'une pièce de Garcia Lorca dans un théâtre de Plovdiv. Polychrome. (BUL)
115) Affiche pour une pièce de théâtre intitulée « Le vampire ». Rouge, vert, jaune et noir. (BUL)

Posters / Plakate / Affiches

116) Poster for the *Fasching* in Munich. (GER)
117) Poster for a performance of Handel's Messiah. Black and white. (GER)
118) Poster for a crafts exhibition. Red, black. (GER)
119) Poster for a band playing soul and pop music. Blue, red and green. (FIN)
120) Poster for an orchestral concert. (JAP)
121) Poster for three concerts of modern music. (GER)
122) Poster for a dance at the University of Illinois. Yellow, green, black, with red lettering. (USA)
123) Poster for a Kafka play. (HUN)
124) Poster for a film festival at Locarno. Black, white and violet. (SWI)
125) Poster for a play. (SWE)
126) Poster for a theatrical performance. (JAP)

116) Plakat für den Fasching in München. (GER)
117) Plakat für eine Aufführung des *Messias* von G.F. Händel. Schwarzweiss. (GER)
118) Ausstellungsplakat der Arbeitsgruppe Kunsthandwerk in Hildesheim. (GER)
119) Plakat für eine Band, die Soul- und Popmusik spielt. Blau, rot und grün. (FIN)
120) Plakat für ein Orchesterkonzert. (JAP)
121) Plakat für drei Konzerte von Musik der Gegenwart in Berlin. (GER)
122) Plakat für einen Universitätsball. (USA)
123) Plakat für ein Schauspiel nach Kafka. (HUN)
124) Plakat für das Filmfestival von Locarno. (SWI)
125) Plakat für ein Schauspiel. (SWE)
126) Plakat für eine Theateraufführung. (JAP)

116) Affiche pour le carnaval de Munich. (GER)
117) Affiche pour une présentation du *Messie* de Hændel. Noir et blanc. (GER)
118) Affiche pour une exposition d'artisanat à Hildesheim. Rouge et noir. (GER)
119) Affiche pour un orchestre de musique soul et pop. Bleu, rouge et vert. (FIN)
120) Affiche pour un concert. (JAP)
121) Affiche pour trois concerts de musique moderne, à Berlin. (GER)
122) Affiche pour un bal universitaire. (USA)
123) Affiche pour une pièce d'après Kafka. (HUN)
124) Affiche pour le Festival du film de Locarno. Noir, blanc et violet. (SWI)
125) Affiche pour une pièce de théâtre. (SWE)
126) Affiche pour une représentation théâtrale. (JAP)

122

116

117

119

120

123

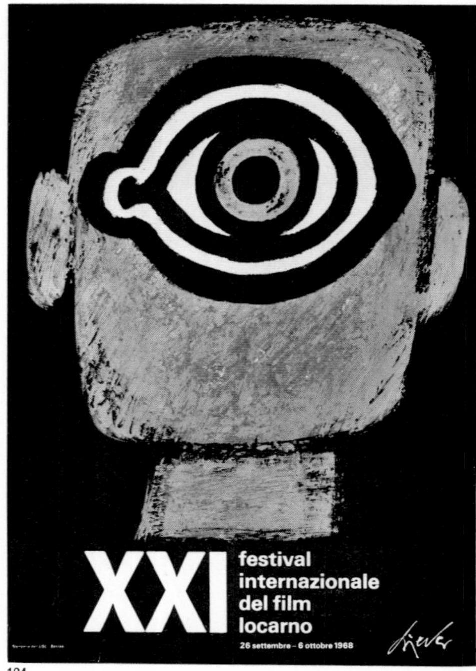

124

118

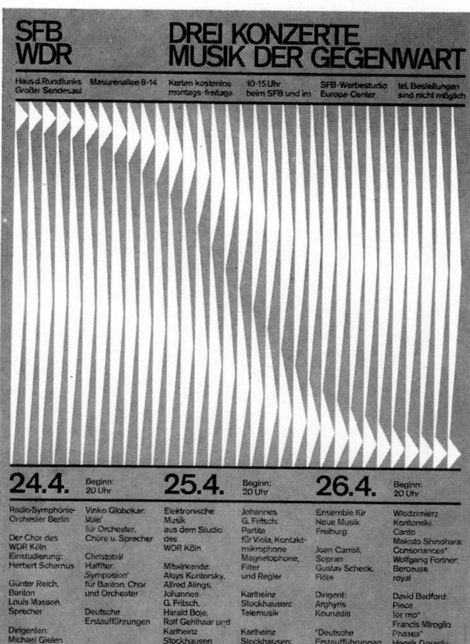

121

125

126

Artist | Künstler | Artiste:

116) ERNST STROM
117) WOLFGANG BÄUMER
118) PAUL KÖNIG
119) HEIKKI KASTEMAA
120) TOSHIRO MATSUMI
121) HANS FÖRTSCH/SIGRID VON BAUMGARTEN
122) LANNY SOMMESE
123) NÁNDOR SZILVÁSY
124) WALTER GRIEDER
125) P.O. NYSTRÖM
126) TADANORI YOKOO

Art Director | Directeur artistique:

117) WOLFGANG BÄUMER
118) PAUL KÖNIG
119) HEIKKI KASTEMAA
121) HANS FÖRTSCH/SIGRID VON BAUMGARTEN
122) LANNY SOMMESE
124) DR. SANDRO BIANCONI
125) P.O. NYSTRÖM
126) TADANORI YOKOO

Agency | Agentur | Agence – Studio:

121) HANS FÖRTSCH/SIGRID VON BAUMGARTEN, BERLIN
122) LANNY SOMMESE, URBANA, ILL.

Artist | Künstler | Artiste:

127) 128) WIKTOR GÓRKA
129) WALDEMAR SWIERZY
130) WOJCIECH ZAMECZNIK
131) TADEUSZ GRABOWSKI
132) WITOLD JANOWSKI
133) ČESTMÍR PECHR
134) KAREL VACA

Art Director | Directeur artistique:

127) 128) 132) GUSTAW MAJEWSKI
129) WALDEMAR SWIERZY
131) TADEUSZ GRABOWSKI

Agency | Agentur | Agence – Studio:

127) 128) 132) WAG, WARSCHAU
130) WDA 2, WARSCHAU
131) WAG, KATOWICE/POL
134) STAATSFILM PRAG

127

128

130

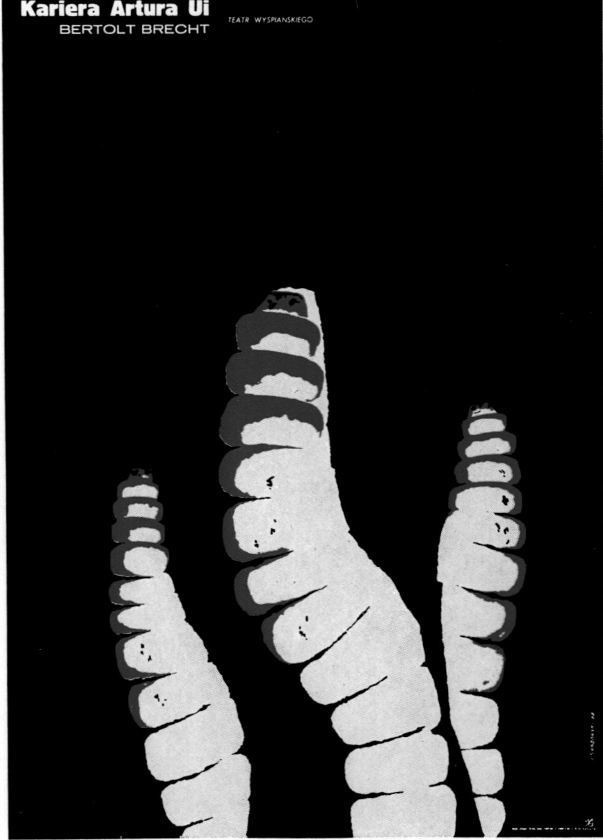

131

127) 128) Posters from a series for the Polish Circus. (POL)
129) Poster for a Polish film. (POL)
130) Poster for a cabaret performance. (POL)
131) Theatre poster for a play by Bertolt Brecht (The Stoppable Rise of Arturo Ui). (POL)
132) Poster from a series for the Polish Circus. Polychrome, red background, white lettering. (POL)
133) Poster for a play about the Ascension performed in Bratislava. (CSR)
134) Poster for a German film. (CSR)

127) 128) Aus einer Serie von Plakaten für den polnischen Zirkus. (POL)
129) Plakat für einen polnischen Film. (POL)
130) Plakat für das polnische Kabarett «Vagabund». (POL)
131) Plakat für das Schauspiel *Der aufhaltsame Aufstieg des Arturo Ui* von Bertold Brecht. (POL)
132) Aus einer Serie von Plakaten für den polnischen Zirkus. (POL)
133) Plakat für ein Schauspiel, «Die Himmelfahrt Christi», aufgeführt im Slowakischen Nationaltheater in Bratislava. (CSR)
134) Plakat für einen deutschen Film. (CSR)

Dancing w Kwaterze Hitlera filmowy dramat miłosny wg. opowiadania A. Brychta, Reżyseria: Jan Batory, Zdjęcia: W. Sobociński, w głównych rolach: Maja Wodecka, Andrz... Łapicki, Olgierd Łukaszewicz i inni. ... Prod. ZRF „Syrena"

129

133

132

134

127) 128) Affiches tirées d'une série pour le cirque polonais. (POL)
129) Affiche pour un film polonais. (POL)
130) Affiche pour le cabaret polonais «Vagabond». (POL)
131) Affiche pour une pièce de Bertold Brecht. (POL)
132) D'une série d'affiches pour le cirque polonais. Polychrome sur fond rouge, texte en blanc. (POL)
133) Affiche pour une représentation du Théâtre national slovaque (L'Ascension de Jésus-Christ). (CSR)
134) Affiche pour un film allemand. (CSR)

135

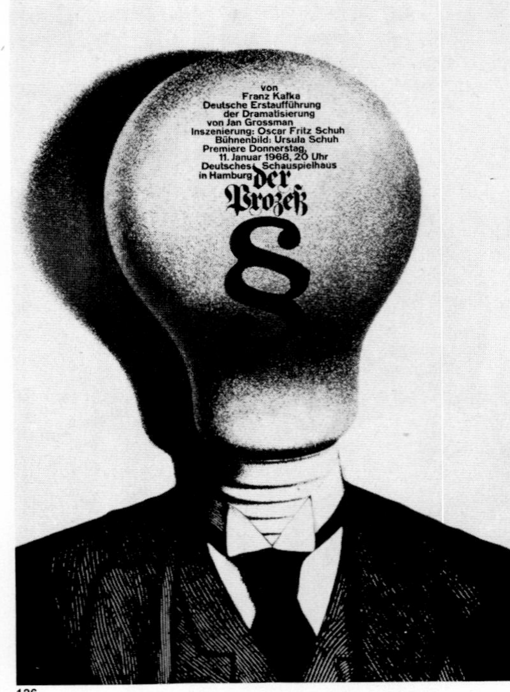

136

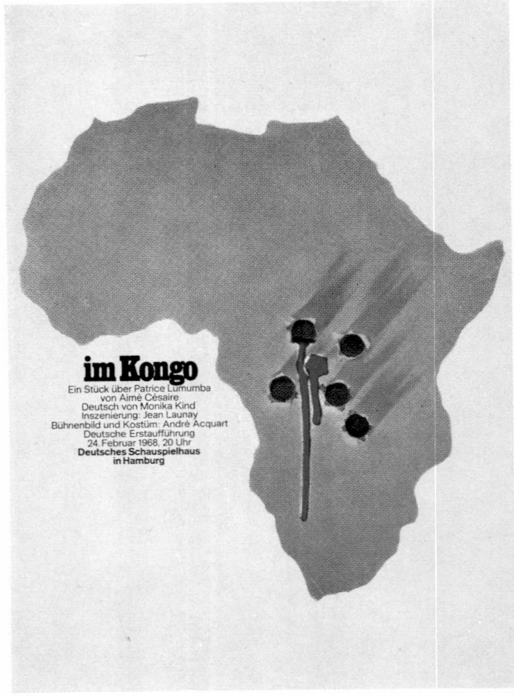

139

135) Tourist poster for Hakata, Fukuoka City. (JAP)
136) Poster for the première of a play based on Kafka's *The Trial*. Brown and black. (GER)
137) Poster for a ballet performance in the Dusseldorf opera house. Purple, magenta, blue and green. (GER)
138) Poster for the showing of prize-winning films in Berlin. Red, beige, black and white. (GER)
139) Poster for the first German performance of a play about Patrice Lumumba (In the Congo). (GER)
140) Poster for a play performed by the *Engeki-za* troupe. Black, white and two greys. Silk screen. (JAP)
141) Theatre poster for two new plays about Viet Nam performed by The Depot Theatre Group in Urbana. Black and white. (USA)
142) Poster for a Finnish film. Polychrome. (FIN)

137

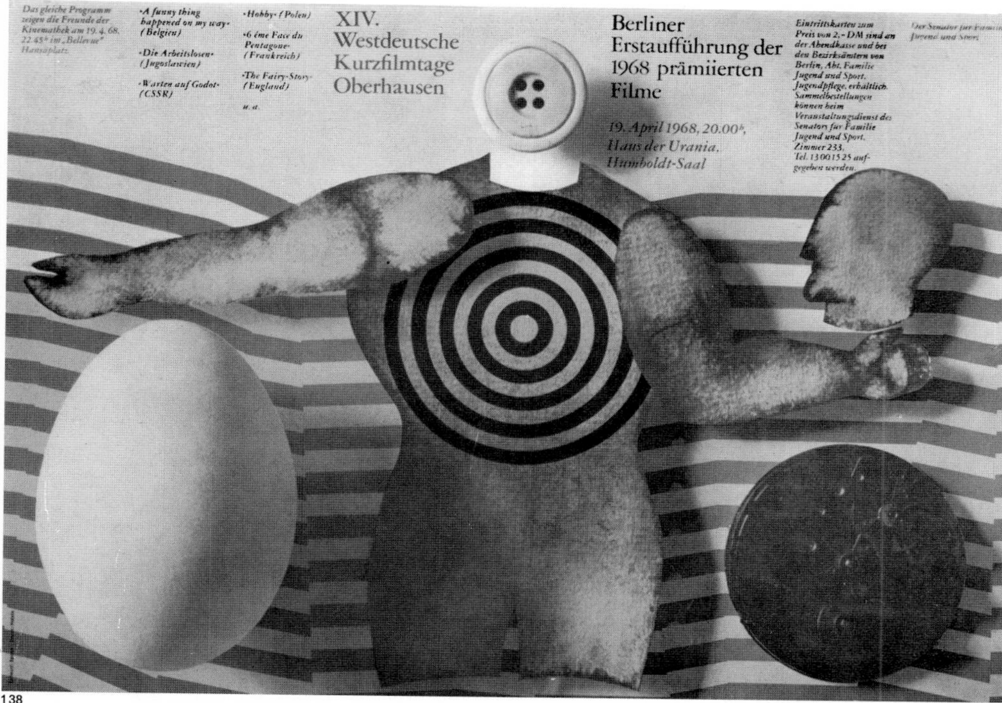

138

140

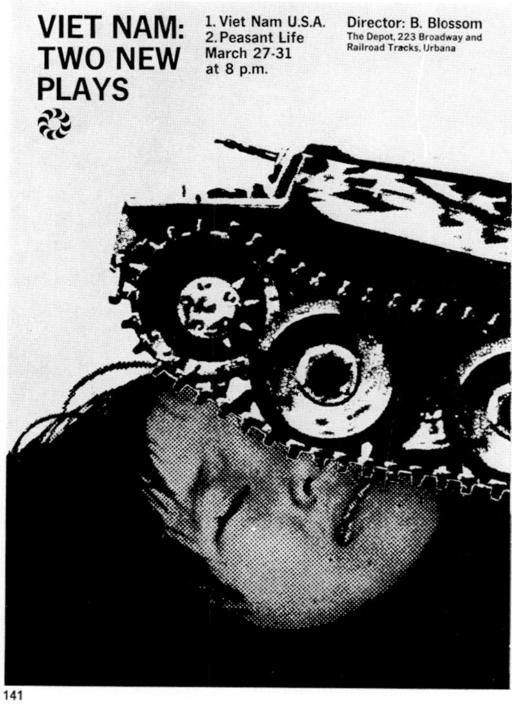

141

Artist / Künstler / Artiste:

135) ISAO NISHIJIMA
136) 139) HOLGER MATTHIES
137) WALTHER BERGMANN
138) HANS-JÜRGEN SPOHN
140) TADASHITO NADAMOTO
141) GARY VISKUPIC
142) P. O. NYSTRÖM

Art Director / Directeur artistique:

136) 139) HOLGER MATTHIES
137) DR. GRISCHA BARFUSS
138) HANS-JÜRGEN SPOHN
141) GARY VISKUPIC
142) P. O. NYSTRÖM

Agency / Agentur / Agence – Studio:

138) HANS-JÜRGEN SPOHN, BERLIN

142

135) Touristikplakat für Hakata, Fukuoka. (JAP)
136) Plakat für die deutsche Erstaufführung des Schauspiels *Der Prozess* nach Franz Kafka im Deutschen Schauspielhaus, Hamburg. Braun und schwarz. (GER)
137) Plakat für Ballettaufführungen in der Deutschen Oper am Rhein, Düsseldorf. Purpurrot, magentarot, verschiedene Blautöne. (GER)
138) Plakat für eine Aufführung von preisgekrönten Kurzfilmen in Berlin. Mehrfarbig. (GER)
139) Plakat für die Erstaufführung im Deutschen Schauspielhaus, Hamburg, des Stückes *Im Kongo*, das von Patrice Lumumba handelt. (GER)
140) Plakat für eine Aufführung einer *Engeki-za*-Truppe. (JAP)
141) Plakat für zwei Schauspiele über Vietnam. (USA)
142) Plakat für einen finnischen Film. Mehrfarbig. (FIN)

135) Affiche touristique pour la ville de Fukuoka. (JAP)
136) Affiche pour la première d'une pièce tirée du *Procès*, de Kafka. Brun et noir. (GER)
137) Affiche pour une soirée de ballets à l'Opéra de Dusseldorf. Pourpre, fuchsia, bleu et vert. (GER)
138) Affiche pour la présentation de courts-métrages primés, à Berlin. Rouge, beige, noir et blanc. (GER)
139) Affiche pour la première allemande, à Hambourg, d'une pièce s'inspirant de la vie de Patrice Lumumba, intitulée «Au Congo». (GER)
140) Affiche pour une pièce de théâtre. Noir, blanc et deux tons de gris. Sérigraphie. (JAP)
141) Affiche en noir pour deux nouvelles pièces de théâtre s'inspirant de la guerre du Viet-nam. (USA)
142) Affiche pour un film finlandais. Polychrome. (FIN)

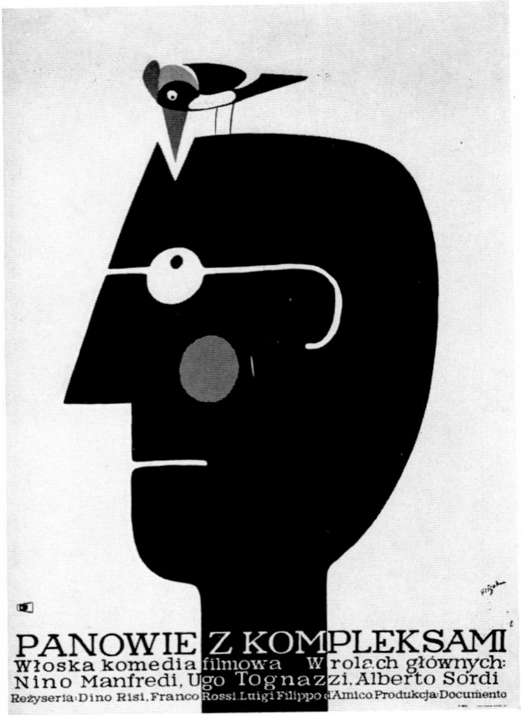

143

144

145

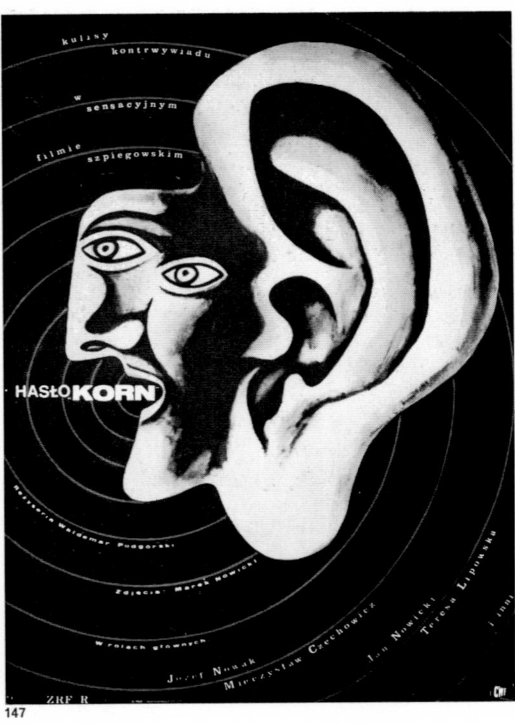

147

148

149

143) Film poster for an Italian satirical comedy. Black head with red cheek, red, green and black bird. (POL)
144) Poster for a Czech-Italian film comedy. Red shades. (POL)
145) Poster for an English film based on Agatha Christie's *Ten Little Niggers*. Black and white. (POL)
146) Poster for a Christmas exhibition at the National Museum in Prague. Brown and black on white. (CSR)
147) For a Polish spy film. Black and white, red rings. (POL)
148) Poster for a Czech-German film (The Terrible Wife). (POL)
149) Poster for a Swiss film. Black, brown and green. (POL)
150) Poster for a French film. (POL)
151) Poster for a Brazilian film tragedy. (POL)

143) Plakat für eine italienische Filmkomödie. Schwarzer Kopf auf weissem Grund, Vogel rot, grün und schwarz. (POL)
144) Plakat für einen italienisch-tschechischen Film. (POL)
145) Plakat für den englischen Kriminalfilm «10 kleine Negerlein» nach einem Buch von Agatha Christie. Schwarzweiss. (POL)
146) Plakat für eine Weihnachtsausstellung im Nationalmuseum Prag. Braun und schwarz auf weissem Grund. (CSR)
147) Plakat für einen polnischen Spionagefilm. (POL)
148) Plakat für einen deutsch-tschechischen Film. (POL)
149) Plakat für einen Schweizer Film. (POL)
150) Plakat für einen französischen Film. (POL)
151) Plakat für eine brasilianische Filmtragödie. (POL)

143) Affiche pour une comédie satirique italienne. Visage noir, joues rouges, oiseau rouge, vert et noir. (POL)
144) Affiche pour une co-production tchéco-italienne. (POL)
145) Affiche pour un film anglais, tiré du roman d'Agatha Christie «Les dix petits nègres». Noir et blanc. (POL)
146) Affiche pour une exposition de Noël au Musée national de Prague. Brun et noir sur fond blanc. (CSR)
147) Affiche pour un film d'espionage polonais. (POL)
148) Affiche en couleur pour un film. (POL)
149) Affiche pour un film suisse. (POL)
150) Affiche pour un film français. (POL)
151) Affiche pour un film brésilien. (POL)

146

Artist / Künstler / Artiste:

143)–145) JERZY FLISAK
146) JOSEF FLEJSAR
147) ERYK LIPINSKI
148) 149) MARIAN STACHURSKI
150) 151) FRANCISZEK STAROWIEYSKI

Art Director / Directeur artistique:

147) JERZY WITTECK

Agency / Agentur / Agence – Studio:

150) 151) WAG, WARSCHAU

150

151

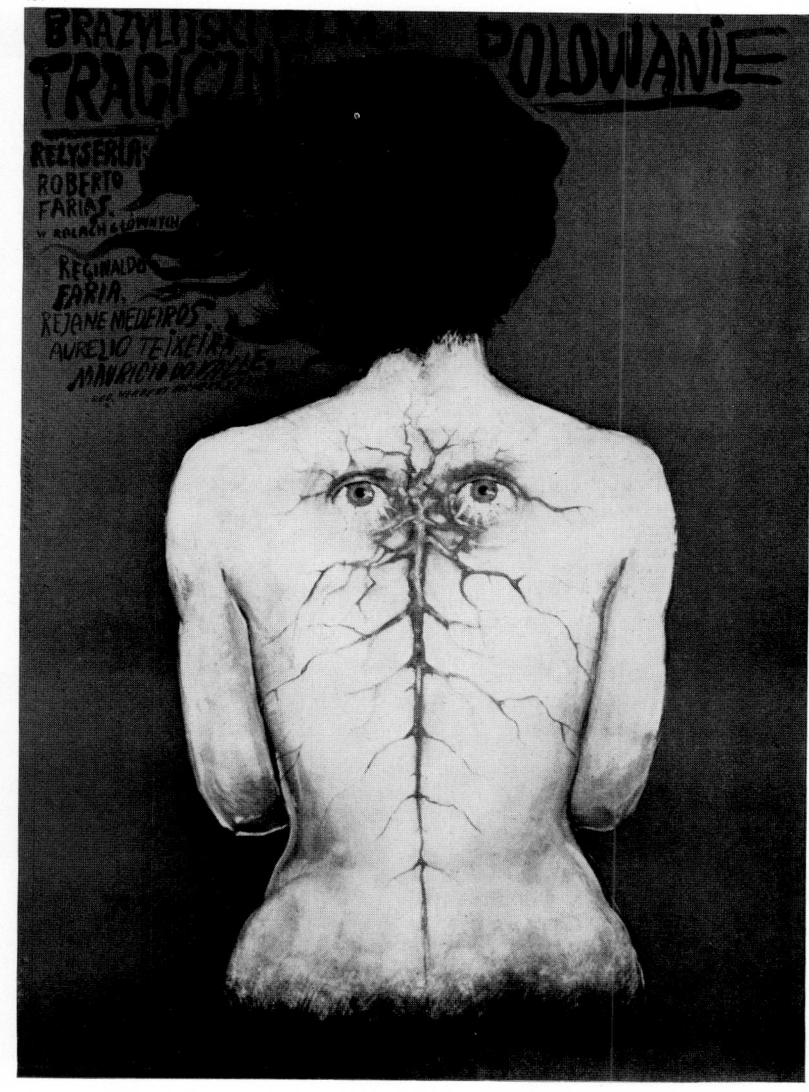

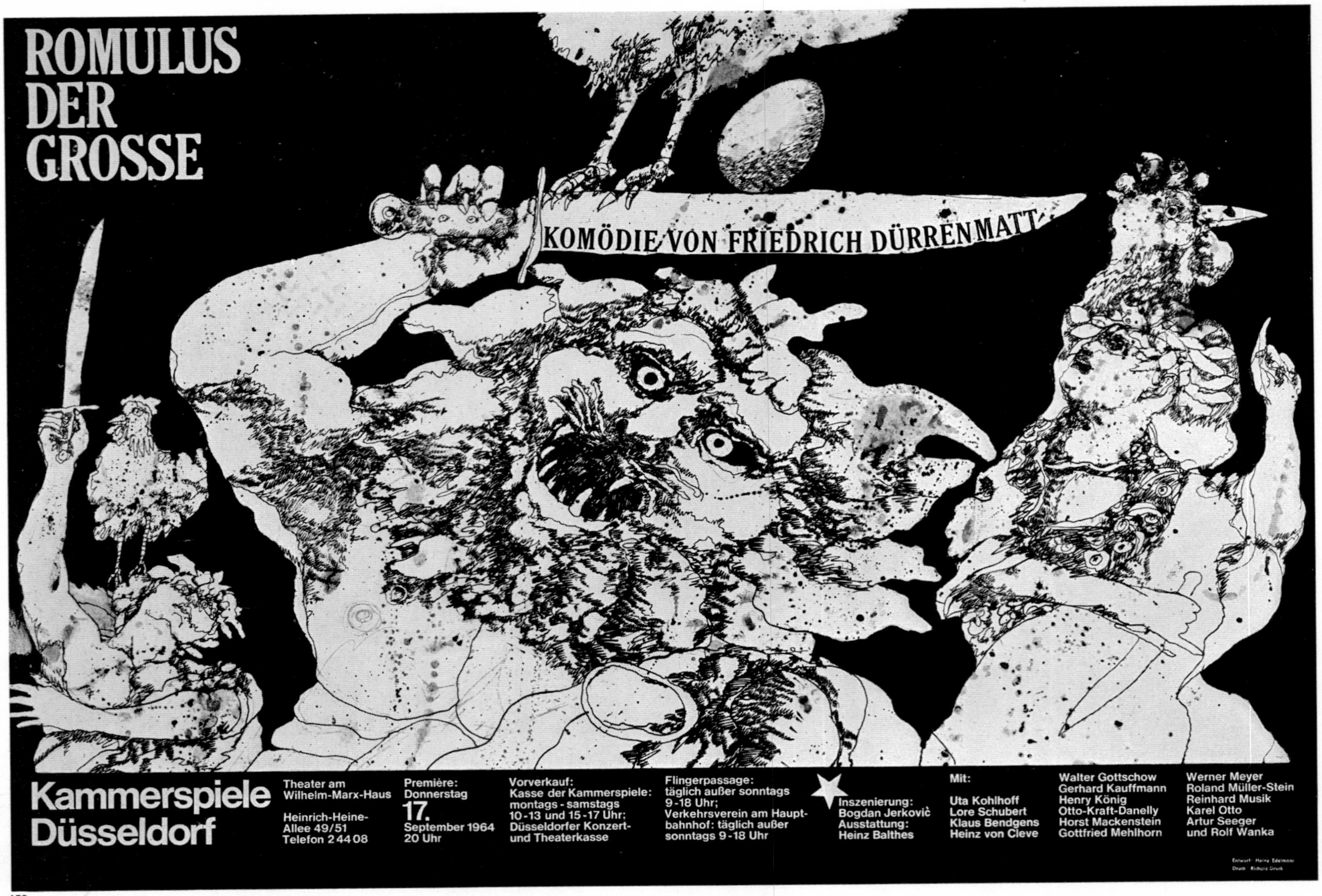

ROMULUS
DER
GROSSE

KOMÖDIE VON FRIEDRICH DÜRRENMATT

Kammerspiele Düsseldorf

Theater am Wilhelm-Marx-Haus

Heinrich-Heine-Allee 49/51
Telefon 2 44 08

Première:
Donnerstag
17.
September 1964
20 Uhr

Vorverkauf:
Kasse der Kammerspiele:
montags - samstags
10 - 13 und 15 - 17 Uhr;
Düsseldorfer Konzert- und Theaterkasse

Flingerpassage:
täglich außer sonntags
9 - 18 Uhr;
Verkehrsverein am Hauptbahnhof: täglich außer sonntags 9 - 18 Uhr

Inszenierung:
Bogdan Jerkoviċ
Ausstattung:
Heinz Balthes

Mit:

Uta Kohlhoff
Lore Schubert
Klaus Bendgens
Heinz von Cleve
Walter Gottschow
Gerhard Kauffmann
Henry König
Otto-Kraft-Danelly
Horst Mackenstein
Gottfried Mehlhorn
Werner Meyer
Roland Müller-Stein
Reinhard Musik
Karel Otto
Artur Seeger
und Rolf Wanka

152

Artist | Künstler | Artiste:

152) HEINZ EDELMANN
153) IKKO TANAKA
154) 156) 157) TOMI UNGERER
155) ROGER EXCOFFON

Art Director | Directeur artistique:

152) HEINZ EDELMANN
153) IKKO TANAKA
154) TOMI UNGERER

Agency | Agentur | Agence – Studio:

153) IKKO TANAKA, TOKYO
155) GEORGES CRAVENNE, PARIS
156) 157) TOMI UNGERER

155

152) Black-and-white poster for a comedy by Friedrich Dürrenmatt. (GER)
153) Poster for a *bunraku* performance in the National Theatre, Tokyo. (JAP)
154) 157) From a series of children's fairy-tale posters. Here *Little Red Riding Hood* and *Snow White's Seven Dwarfs*. Distributed by Darien House, Inc., New York. (USA)
155) Poster for a French film. Black chain, magenta mouth on white ground. (FRA)
156) Poster for *Truc*, a poster shop in Cambridge, Massachusetts. Polychrome. (USA)

152) Plakat für eine Komödie von Friedrich Dürrenmatt, aufgeführt im Theater Kammerspiele Düsseldorf. (GER)
153) Plakat für eine *Bunraku*-Aufführung im Nationaltheater Tokio. (JAP)
154) 157) Aus einer Serie von Kindermärchenplakaten, hier *Rotkäppchen* und *Schneewittchen und die sieben Zwerge*. (USA)
155) Plakat für den französischen Film «Die Gefangene». (FRA)
156) Plakat für eine Galerie, die Plakate verkauft. Mehrfarbig. (USA)

152) Affiche en noir pour une comédie de Dürrenmatt, présentée par une troupe de Dusseldorf. (GER)
153) Affiche pour une représentation *bunraku* au Théâtre national de Tokyo. (JAP)
154) 157) D'une série d'affiches inspirées par des contes de fées, ici *Le petit chaperon rouge* et *Blanche-Neige et les sept nains*. (USA)
155) Affiche pour le film *La prisonnière*, distribué par les Films Corona, Paris. (FRA)
156) Affiche en couleur pour une galerie de posters. (USA)

153

154

156

157

158

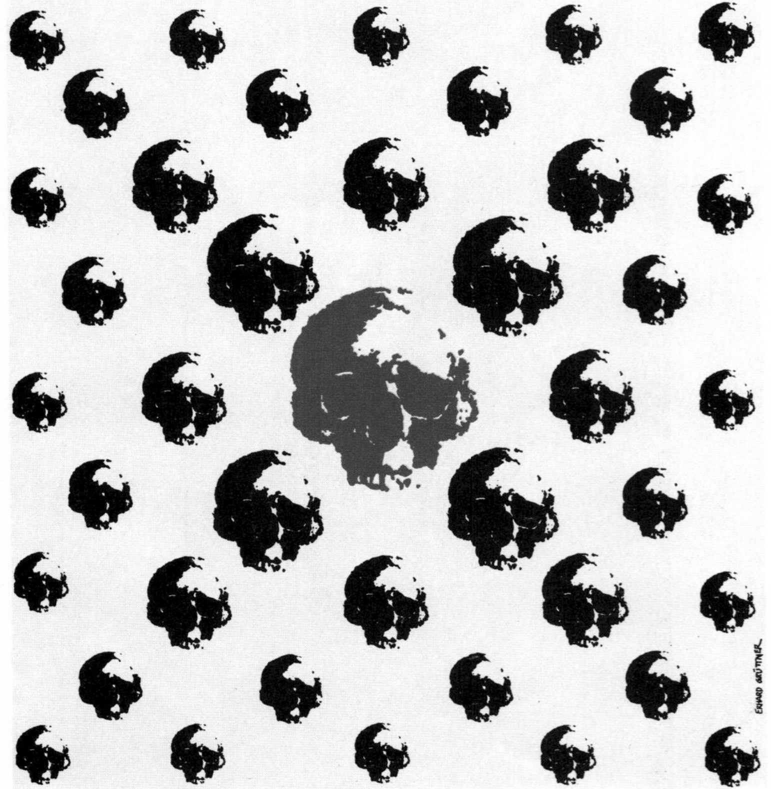

159

160

163

OŚWIĘCIM BRZEZINKA 1967

PAMIĘTAMY

166

161

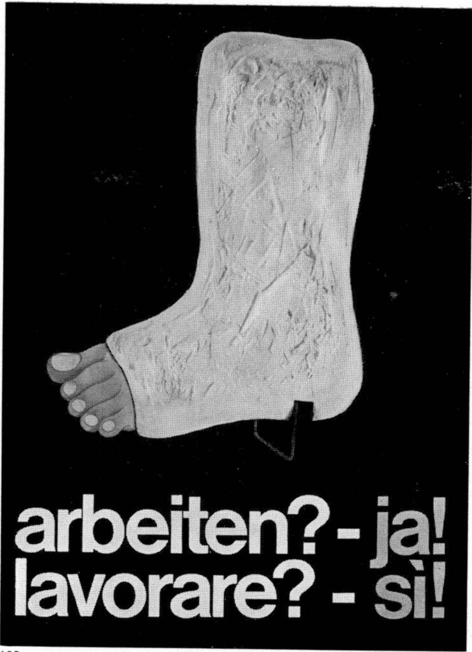

162

164

165

167

168

158) Anti-war poster. Silk screen. (JAP)
159) Anti-war poster for the magazine AVANT-GARDE. (USA)
160) 'Give and help.' Dutch church poster encouraging Easter donations. (NLD)
161) Poster for a child adoption campaign. Red house, green heart and lettering. (SPA)
162) Poster for a Swiss firm to encourage an early return to work after accidents. Black, white and yellow. (SWI)
163) Poster against nationalism and xenophobia. (FRA)
164) Poster against heart disease. Red heart. (FIN)
165) Poster for an election campaign. (SWI)
166) Poster for a commemorative museum at Auschwitz. (POL)
167) Poster protesting against a building project in Basle. Red, green and black. (SWI)
168) Peace poster. Red background, black lettering. (USA)

158) «Kein zweites Hiroshima», Plakat gegen den Krieg. (JAP)
159) Plakat gegen den Krieg. (USA)
160) «Gib und hilf», Plakat für die Osterkollekte der holländischen Kirche. (NLD)
161) Plakat für eine nationale Kampagne für Kinderadoption. Rot und grün auf weissem Grund. (SPA)
162) Plakat für den Unfallverhütungsdienst der Gebrüder Sulzer AG, Winterthur. (SWI)
163) Plakat für den Kampf gegen den Chauvinismus. (FRA)
164) Plakat einer medizinischen Institution, für den Kampf gegen Herzkrankheiten. (FIN)
165) Plakat für die Vereinigung evangelischer Wähler. (SWI)
166) Plakat für das Museum in Auschwitz. (POL)
167) Plakat für das Referendumskomitee gegen das Projekt für ein neues Gerichtsgebäude in Basel. (SWI)
168) Plakat für den Frieden. Rot, weiss, schwarz. (USA)

158) Affiche sérigraphique contre la guerre. (JAP)
159) Affiche antimilitariste pour la revue AVANT-GARDE. (USA)
160) «Donnez et aidez». Pour une collecte pascale. (NLD)
161) Affiche pour une campagne nationale en faveur de l'adoption. Maison rouge, cœur et texte verts. (SPA)
162) Affiche encourageant les accidentés à reprendre rapidement le travail. Polychrome. (SWI)
163) Affiche pour la lutte contre le chauvinisme. (FRA)
164) Affiche pour la lutte contre les affections cardiaques. Cœur rouge. (FIN)
165) Affiche en couleur de l'Association des élécteurs protestants. (SWI)
166) Affiche pour le Musée d'Auschwitz. (POL)
167) Affiche protestant contre la construction d'un nouveau palais de justice à Bâle. Polychrome. (SWI)
168) Affiche pour la paix. Rouge, blanc, noir. (USA)

Artist / Künstler / Artiste:

158) HIROKATSU HIJIKATA
159) ERHARD GRÜTTNER
160) MAX VELTHUIJS
161) ELIAS & SANTAMARINA
162) WILHELM RIESER
163) BERNARD MIOT
164) MARTTI A. MYKKÄNEN
165) 167) CELESTINO PIATTI
166) WOJCIECH ZAMECZNIK
168) STAN BROD

Art Director / Directeur artistique:

158) HIROKATSU HIJIKATA
160) MAX VELTHUIJS
161) ELIAS & SANTAMARINA
163) PHILIPPE GRIGNON
164) MARTTI A. MYKKÄNEN
168) STAN BROD

Agency / Agentur / Agence – Studio:

160) N.P.O., DEN HAAG
163) BRUN LAVAINE, PARIS
164) MARTTI A. MYKKÄNEN, HELSINKI
168) LIPSON-JACOB ASSOC., CINCINNATI

169) Poster to help sell British goods. Polychrome. (GB)
170) 174) From a series of children's fairy-tale posters, here for *Puss-in-Boots* and *The Frog Prince*. Polychrome. (SWI)
171) Poster for an M.I.T. programme of marine study. Blue and green design, black lettering. (USA)
172) Poster for a series of films by new directors. (USA)
173) Poster soliciting financial aid for Viet Nam. Black and brown, yellow moon. (SWI)
175) Poster for a boutique. Black lettering, magenta, red, black and pink. (SWI)
176) Poster against illiteracy for The International Year of Human Rights. (ARG)
177) Peace poster. (SPA)

169) Plakat für die Kampagne «Back Britain». Mehrfarbig. (GB)
170) 174) Aus einer Serie von Kindermärchenplakaten für Victor Dobàl, Zürich. Mehrfarbig. (SWI)
171) Plakat für Seminarien über Ozeanographie an einer Universität. Illustration in blau und grün. (USA)
172) Plakat für ein Kino in New York. Mehrfarbig. (USA)
173) Plakat für Hilfe an Vietnam, für Caritas, Bern. Schwarz, grau und braun, gelber Mond. (SWI)
175) Plakat für die Modeboutique Red Steps, Luzern. Mehrere Rottöne und Schwarz. (SWI)
176) Plakat für das Jahr der Menschenrechte, das auf das Problem des Analphabetentums aufmerksam macht. (ARG)
177) Plakat für den Frieden. (SPA)

169) Affiche pour la vente des produits britanniques. (GB)
170) 174) D'une série d'affiches s'inspirant de contes de fées. Polychrome. (SWI)
171) Affiche pour des séminaires d'océanographie dans une université américaine. Polychrome. (USA)
172) Affiche en couleur pour un cinéma de New York. (USA)
173) Affiche de Caritas, Berne, en faveur de l'aide au Viet-nam. Noir et brun, lune jaune. (SWI)
175) Affiche pour une boutique. Texte en noir, fuchsia, rouge et rose. (SWI)
176) Affiche pour la lutte contre l'analphabétisme, parue dans le cadre de l'Année des Droits de l'Homme. (ARG)
177) Affiche pour la paix. (SPA)

169

170

171

173

174

175

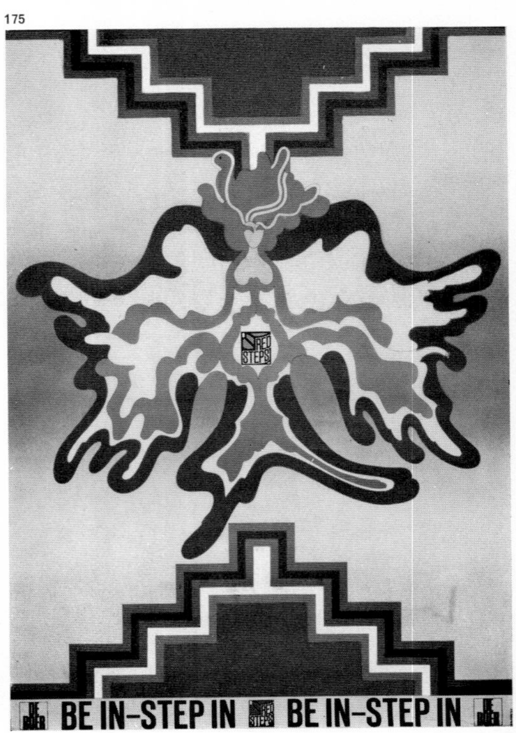

172

176

177

Artist / Künstler / Artiste:

169) ALAN ALDRIDGE/DAVID HOLMES
170) 174) UTE OSTERWALDER
171) DIETMAR R. WINKLER
172) JAMES MCMULLAN
173) HANS ERNI
175) DIETER NOTZ
176) A. PÁEZ TORRES
177) LUIS IGNACIO DE HORNA GARCIA

Art Director / Directeur artistique:

169) DAVID HOLMES
172) GENE PAVEY
176) A. PÁEZ TORRES

Agency / Agentur / Agence – Studio:

169) KINGSLEY, MANTON & PALMER, LONDON
172) RUGOFF THEATRES, INC., NEW YORK

178) Tourist poster for the Polish Airline LOT. Polychrome. (POL)
179) 182) Posters for a series of exhibitions on countries organized by the Seibu Railway Company, here for Canada and Mexico. (JAP)
180) Tourist poster for Scotland. Polychrome. (GB)
181) Poster for *Air France* encouraging travel to India. Polychrome. (FRA)
183) Poster for the Helsinki Tourist Office commemorating the founding of Helsinki. (FIN)
184) Sightseeing poster from a series for London Transport. (GB)
185) Poster for *Olympic Airways*. Polychrome. (FRA)

178) Touristikplakat für die Fluggesellschaft LOT. Mehrfarbig. (POL)
179) 182) Plakate für Ausstellungen über Canada und Mexico, veranstaltet von Seibu Railway Co. Ltd. (JAP)
180) Plakat, das auf Schottland als Ferienland aufmerksam macht. (GB)
181) Plakat für die Fluggesellschaft *Air France*. Mehrfarbig. (FRA)
183) Plakat für das Touristenbüro Helsinki. (FIN)
184) Aus einer Serie von Plakaten für die Londoner Transportgesellschaft, hier zum Besuch der Sehenswürdigkeiten Londons anregend. (GB)
185) Touristikplakat für die *Olympic Airways*. (FRA)

Artist / Künstler / Artiste:

178) WIKTOR GÓRKA
179) YUZO YAMASHITA/KAZUO AOKI
180) ANDRÉ AMSTUTZ
181) BERNARD VILLEMOT
182) YUZO YAMASHITA
183) MARTII A. MYKKÄNEN
184) ABRAM GAMES
185) ANDRÉ FRANÇOIS

Art Director / Directeur artistique:

178) GUSTAW MAJEWSKI
179) 182) YUZO YAMASHITA
180) JOHN ALLAN
185) JACQUES SEGUELA

Agency / Agentur / Agence – Studio:

178) WAG, WARSCHAU
185) AXE PUBLICITÉ, PARIS

178

179

181

182

Posters / Plakate
Affiches

178) Affiche de la compagnie aérienne polonaise Lot. (POL)
179) 182) Affiches pour une série d'expositions consacrées à différents pays, ici le Canada et le Mexique. (JAP)
180) Affiche touristique en faveur de l'Ecosse. Polychrome. (GB)
181) Affiche en couleur d'*Air France*. (FRA)
183) Affiche de l'Office du tourisme de Helsinki, commémorant la fondation de la capitale finlandaise. (FIN)
184) D'une série d'affiches en faveur des transports londoniens. (GB)
185) Affiche pour la compagnie grecque *Olympic Airways*. (FRA)

180

183

184

185

186

SPEND YOUR HOLIDAYS IN **POLAND**
in Mazury, the land of ten thousand lakes

187

189

Artist|Künstler|Artiste:

186) HISAMI KUNITAKE
187) WALDEMAR SWIERZY
188) ZIRALDO PINTO
189) RUDOLF DIRATZOUYAN
190) ERNST KELLER
191) PERIN + RALLI JACOB
192) ANDRÉ PASTURE

Art Director|Directeur artistique:

187) GUSTAW MAJEWSKI
189) M. ALVINERIE
191) J. B. COWASJI

Agency|Agentur|Agence – Studio:

187) WAG, WARSCHAU
189) INTERNATIONAL PUBLICITÉ, PARIS

Posters / Plakate / Affiches

188

186) Tourist poster for the Iki-Tsushima Tourist Association. Silk screen. (JAP)
187) Poster for the Polish Tourist Information Centre. (POL)
188) Poster for a popular film comedy entitled 'Every Girl Fears a Father Who's a Wild Beast'. Polychrome. (BRA)
189) Poster about car hire arranged through French National Railways. Polychrome. (FRA)
190) Poster for an international rowing regatta in Zurich. Blue, red and black. (SWI)
191) Poster for *Air India*. Red, yellow and black. (IND)
192) Poster for the Trans-Europ-Express from Brussels to Paris. (BEL)

186) Touristikplakat für das Reisebüro Iki-Tsushima. (JAP)
187) «Verbringen Sie Ihre Ferien in Polen, in Mazuria, dem Land der zehntausend Seen». Touristikplakat. (POL)
188) Plakat für eine volkstümliche Filmkömodie. (BRA)
189) Plakat für die französische Eisenbahngesellschaft, die auf ihren Mietwagendienst aufmerksam macht. (FRA)
190) Plakat für eine internationale Ruderregatta in Zürich. Blau, rot, schwarz. (SWI)
191) Plakat für *Air India*. Mehrfarbig. (IND)
192) Plakat für die neue Zugsverbindung Brüssel–Paris des Trans-Europ-Express. Mehrfarbig. (BEL)

186) Affiche touristique. Sérigraphie. (JAP)
187) Affiche de l'Office polonais du tourisme. (POL)
188) Affiche pour un film tiré d'une comédie populaire. Polychrome. (BRA)
189) Affiche pour les voitures de location de la Société nationale des chemins de fer français. Polychrome. (FRA)
190) Affiche pour les régates internationales d'aviron à Zurich. Bleu, rouge et noir. (SWI)
191) Affiche d'*Air India*. Rouge, jaune et noir. (IND)
192) Affiche de la Société nationale des chemins de fer belges, Bruxelles. Polychrome. (BEL)

190

191

192

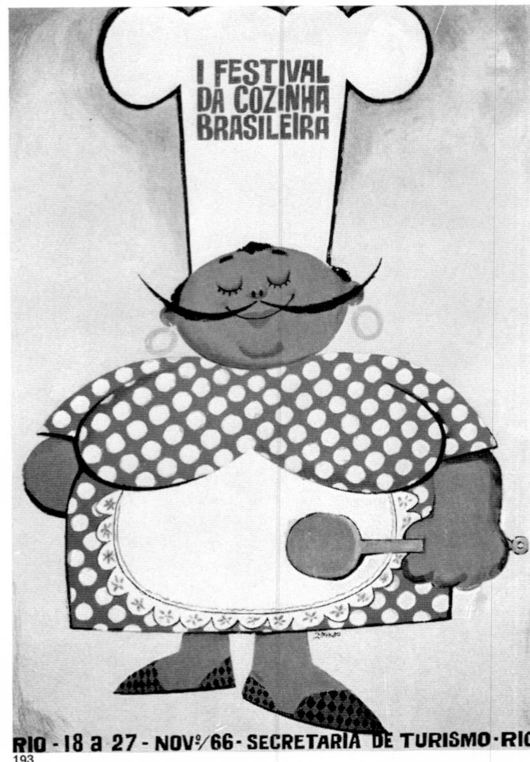

193

194

196

197

193) Poster for a festival of Brazilian cooking. Yellow, red, blue and black. (BRA)
194) Poster for Westinghouse Broadcasting Co. advertising Pittsburgh as the world's busiest inland port. Black and white. (USA)
195) Poster advertising Denver as a possible site for the 1976 Winter Olympics. Red, white and blue. (USA)
196) Poster for the Shimabara Hot Springs in Nagasaki Prefecture. Polychrome. (JAP)
197) Tourist poster for Biwako Lake in Shiga Prefecture. Violet birds, gold water. (JAP)
198) Tourist poster for the Ise-Shima National Park. Grey, pink, yellow and black. (JAP)
199) Poster for the Winter Olympics to be held in Japan in 1972. Black and white, red circle, coloured rings. (JAP)

193) Plakat für ein Festival der brasilianischen Küche. Gelb, rot, blau und schwarz. (BRA)
194) Plakat der Westinghouse Broadcasting Co., N.Y., das für Pittsburgh, den grössten Inlandhafen der Welt, wirbt. (USA)
195) Plakat für Denver als möglichen Schauplatz der Olympischen Winterspiele 1976. Rot und blau auf weissem Grund. (USA)
196) Touristikplakat für die Thermalquellen von Shimabara. (JAP)
197) Touristikplakat, das zum Besuch des Biwako-Sees anregt. Gold, violett und schwarz auf weissem Grund. (JAP)
198) Touristikplakat für den Ise-Shima Nationalpark. Grau, rosa, gelb und schwarz. (JAP)
199) Plakat für Sapporo, den Schauplatz der Olympischen Winterspiele im Jahre 1972. Schwarzweiss mit rotem Kreis und farbigen Ringen. (JAP)

195

198

Artist / Künstler / Artiste:

193) ZIRALDO PINTO
194) TOM WOODWARD
195) GUNTHER TETZ
196) 197) ISAO NISHIJIMA
198) UKICHI MATSUMOTO
199) IKKO TANAKA

Art Director / Directeur artistique:

194) TOM WOODWARD
195) GUNTHER TETZ
198) UKICHI MATSUMOTO
199) IKKO TANAKA

Agency / Agentur / Agence – Studio:

195) UNIMARK INTERNATIONAL, CHICAGO
198) NIPPON ADCONSULT CO. LTD., OSAKA

199

193) Affiche pour un festival de cuisine brésilienne. Jaune, rouge, bleu et noir. (BRA)
194) Affiche d'un émetteur radiophonique, présentant Pittsburgh comme le plus grand port intérieur du monde. (USA)
195) Affiche en faveur du choix de Denver pour les Jeux olympiques d'hiver en 1976. Rouge, blanc et bleu. (USA)
196) Affiche pour les sources chaudes de Shimabara, dans la préfecture de Nagasaki. Polychrome. (JAP)
197) Affiche touristique en faveur d'un lac de la préfecture de Shiga. Mauve, or et noir sur fond blanc. (JAP)
198) Affiche touristique pour le Parc national d'Ise-Shima. Gris, rose, jaune et noir. (JAP)
199) Affiche pour les Jeux olympiques d'hiver à Sapporo, en 1972. Noir et blanc, anneaux polychromes. (JAP)

2

Newspaper Advertisements
Magazine Advertisements

Zeitungs-Inserate
Zeitschriften-Inserate

Annonces de presse
Annonces de revues

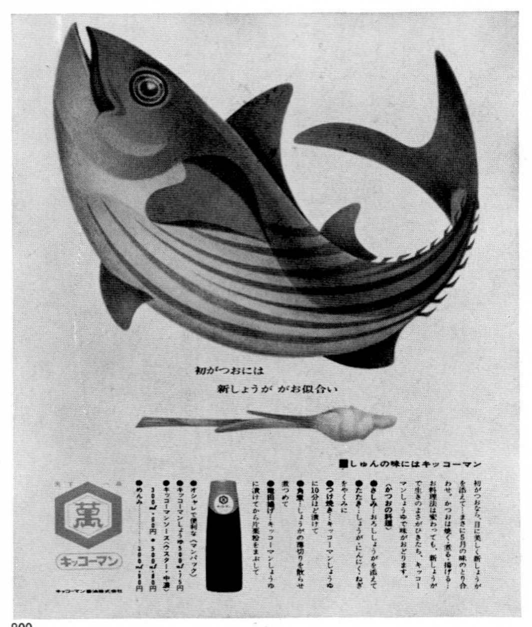

200

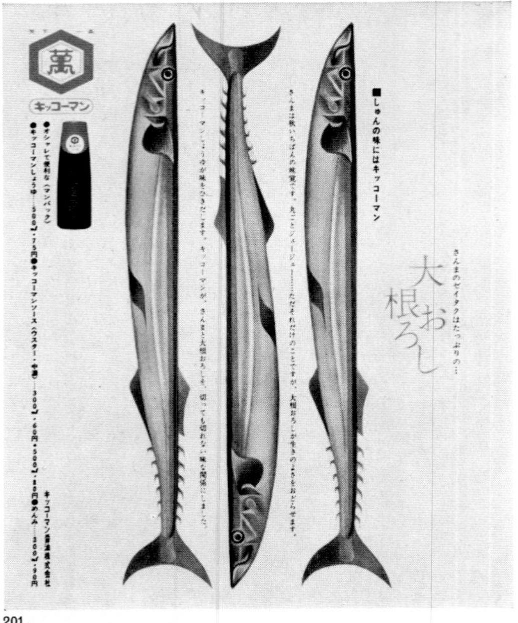

201

202

203

204

205

207

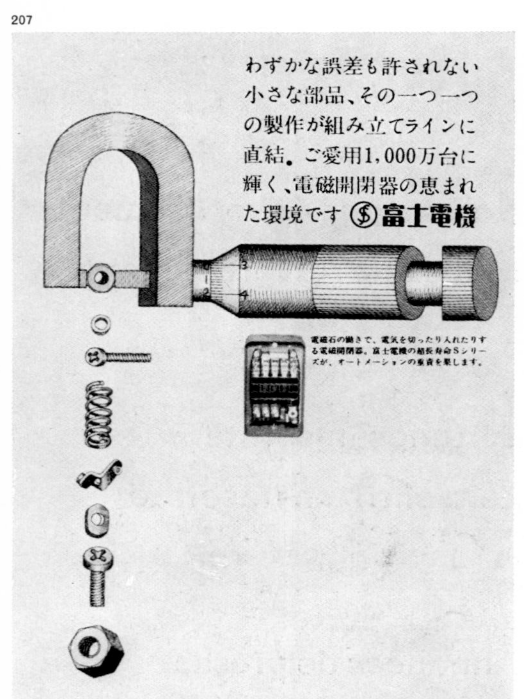

208

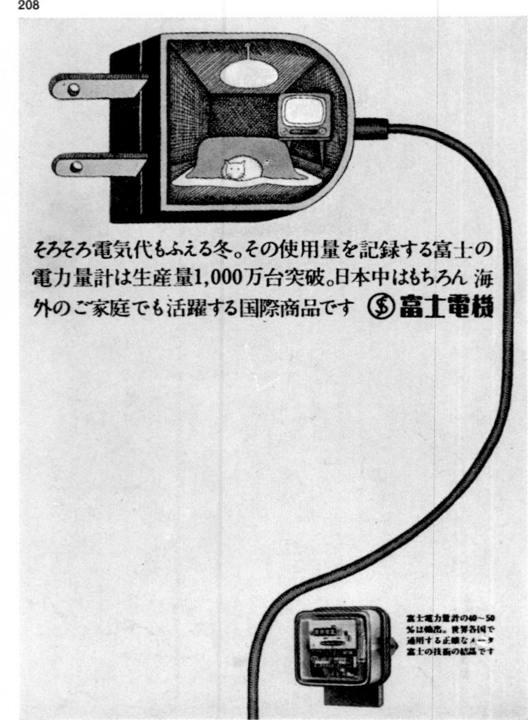

209

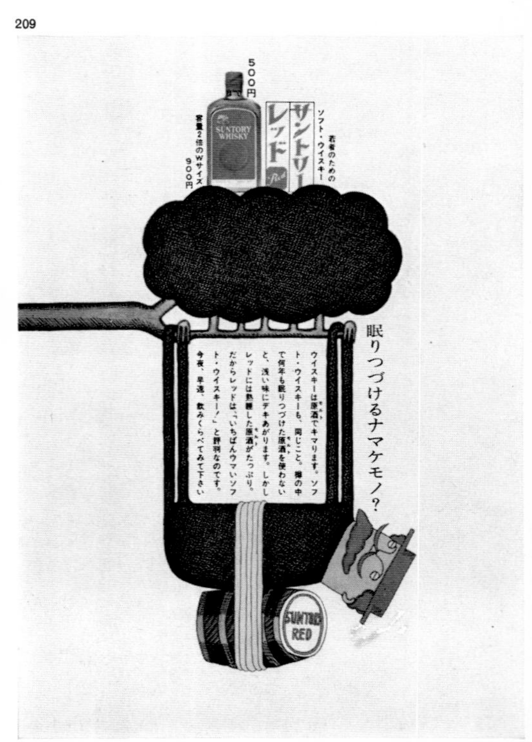

200)–202) Magazine advertisements for a soy sauce made by Kikkoman Shoyu Co. Ltd. Full colour. (JAP)
203)–205) From a series of black-and-white advertisements for *Lion* toothpaste. (JAP)
206) Magazine advertisement in colour for three books of mathematical theory (project). (JAP)
207) 208) Colour magazine ads for Fuji Electric Co. (JAP)
209)–212) From a series of magazine advertisements in colour for *Suntory* whisky. (JAP)

200)–202) Zeitschrifteninserate für eine Soya-Sauce. (JAP)
203)–205) Aus einer Serie von Inseraten für die Zahnpasta *Lion*. Schwarzweiss. (JAP)
206) Zeitschrifteninserat für drei Bücher über Mathematik (Entwürfe). Mehrfarbig. (JAP)
207) 208) Zeitschrifteninserate für Fuji Electric Co. (JAP)
209)–212) Aus einer Serie Zeitschrifteninserate für *Suntory*-Whisky. Mehrfarbig. (JAP)

200)–202) Annonces de revues en couleur pour une marque de sauces au soja. (JAP)
203)–205) D'une série d'annonces de revues pour une pâte dentifrice. Noir et blanc. (JAP)
206) Annonce de revues en couleur pour trois ouvrages de mathématiques (maquette). (JAP)
207) 208) Annonces pour la Fuji Electric Co. (JAP)
209)–212) D'une série d'annonces pour du whisky. (JAP)

Artist / Künstler / Artiste:

200)–202) TADASHI OHASHI
203)–205) EINOSUKE YAMAZAKI/SHOHEI KOJIMA
206) TADAO KITANO
207) 208) KENICHI MATSUNAGA/YOSHIO NANBA
209)–212) KENICHI MATSUNAGA

Art Director / Directeur artistique:

200)–202) TADASHI OHASHI
203)–205) EINOSUKE YAMAZAKI
206) TADAO KITANO
207) 208) KOICHI GOTO/MAMORU ISSHI
209)–212) MASAO SUGIMURA

206

Advertisements / Inserate / Annonces

210

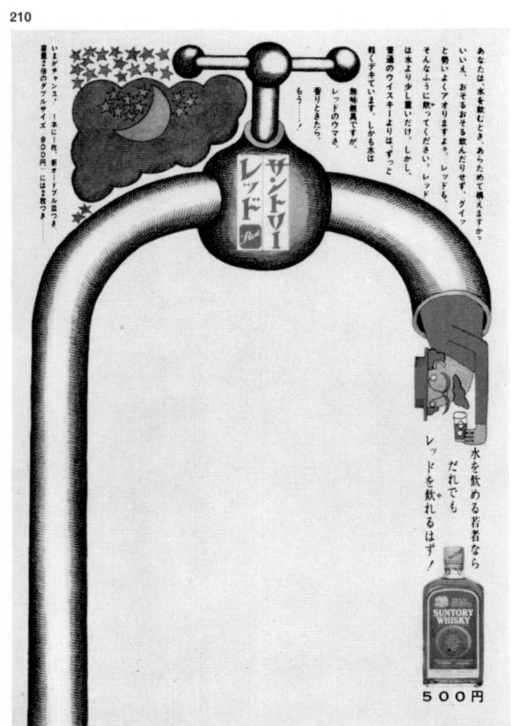

211

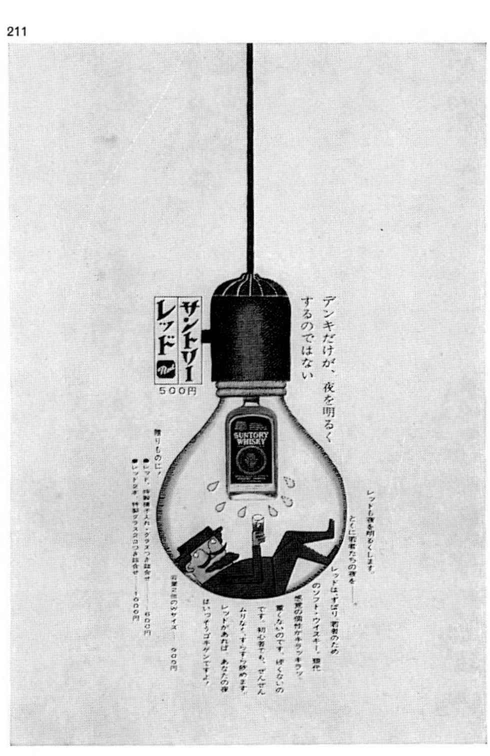

212

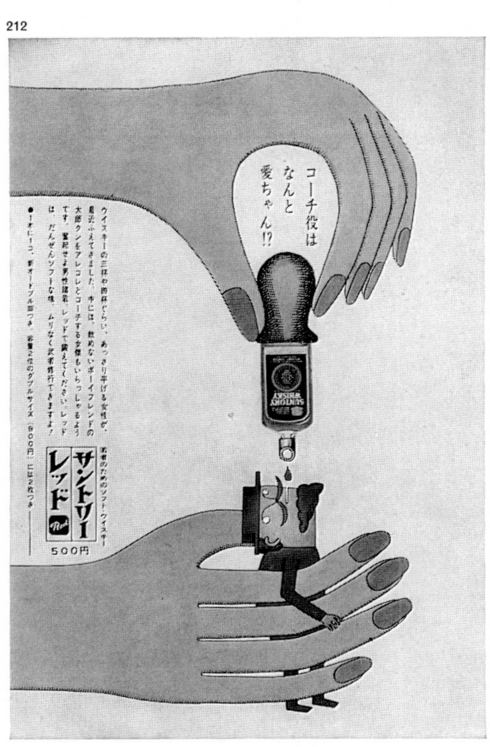

213

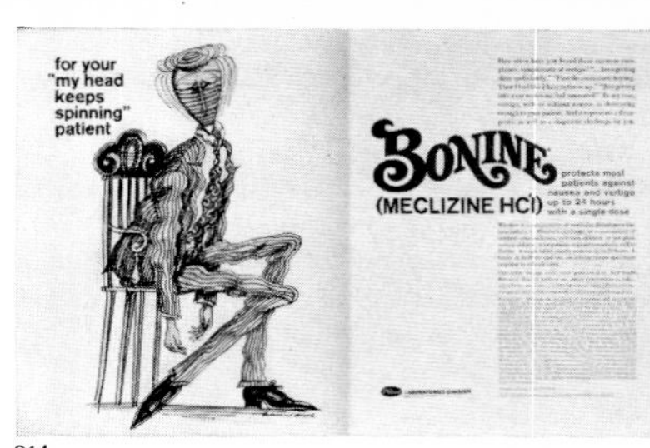

214

213) 214) Illustration and complete double-spread ad for a *Pfizer* drug against vertigo. (USA)
215) Trade magazine advertisement in full colour for a nylon that dyes well. (USA)
216) Magazine ad for CIBA, who develop thousands of drugs but market only the best. (USA)
217) 218) Complete double-spread trade magazine advertisement and illustration for an antibiotic made by Bristol Laboratories. (USA)

213) 214) Illustration und Inserat für ein Mittel gegen Schwindelgefühle. (USA)
215) Fachzeitschrifteninserat für ein Nylongewebe, das sich gut einfärben läßt. (USA)
216) Zeitschrifteninserat für CIBA, die viele Arzneimittel erprobt, aber nur die allerbesten auf den Markt bringt. (USA)
217) 218) Vollständiges Inserat und Illustration für ein Antibiotikum. (USA)

213) 214) Illustration et annonce correspondante, pour un médicament contre les vertiges. (USA)
215) Annonce de revues professionnelles pour du nylon facile à teindre. Polychrome. (USA)
216) Annonce de revues pour CIBA, qui teste des milliers de préparations, mais ne met en vente que les meilleures d'entre elles. (USA)
217) 218) Annonce de revues professionnelles et son illustration, pour un antibiotique. (USA)

215

216

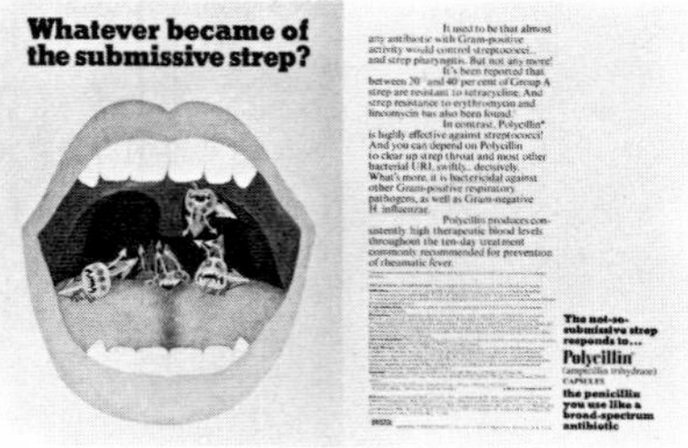

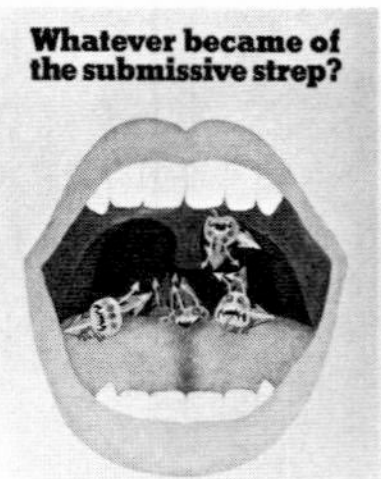

217

Art Director/Directeur artistique:

213) 214) ARTHUR LUDWIG
215) DAN MACDONOUGH
216) PETER BELLAVAU
217) 218) STEVEN BROTHERS

Agency/Agentur/Agence – Studio:

213) 214) 217) 218) SUDLER & HENNESSEY, INC., NEW YORK
215) BENTON & BOWLES LTD., LONDON
216) WILLIAM DOUGLAS MCADAMS, NEW YORK

Advertisements/Inserate Annonces

Artist/Künstler/Artiste:

213) 214) EDWARD SOREL
215) ANDRÉ AMSTUTZ/DAN MACDONOUGH
216)–218) ETIENNE DELESSERT

218

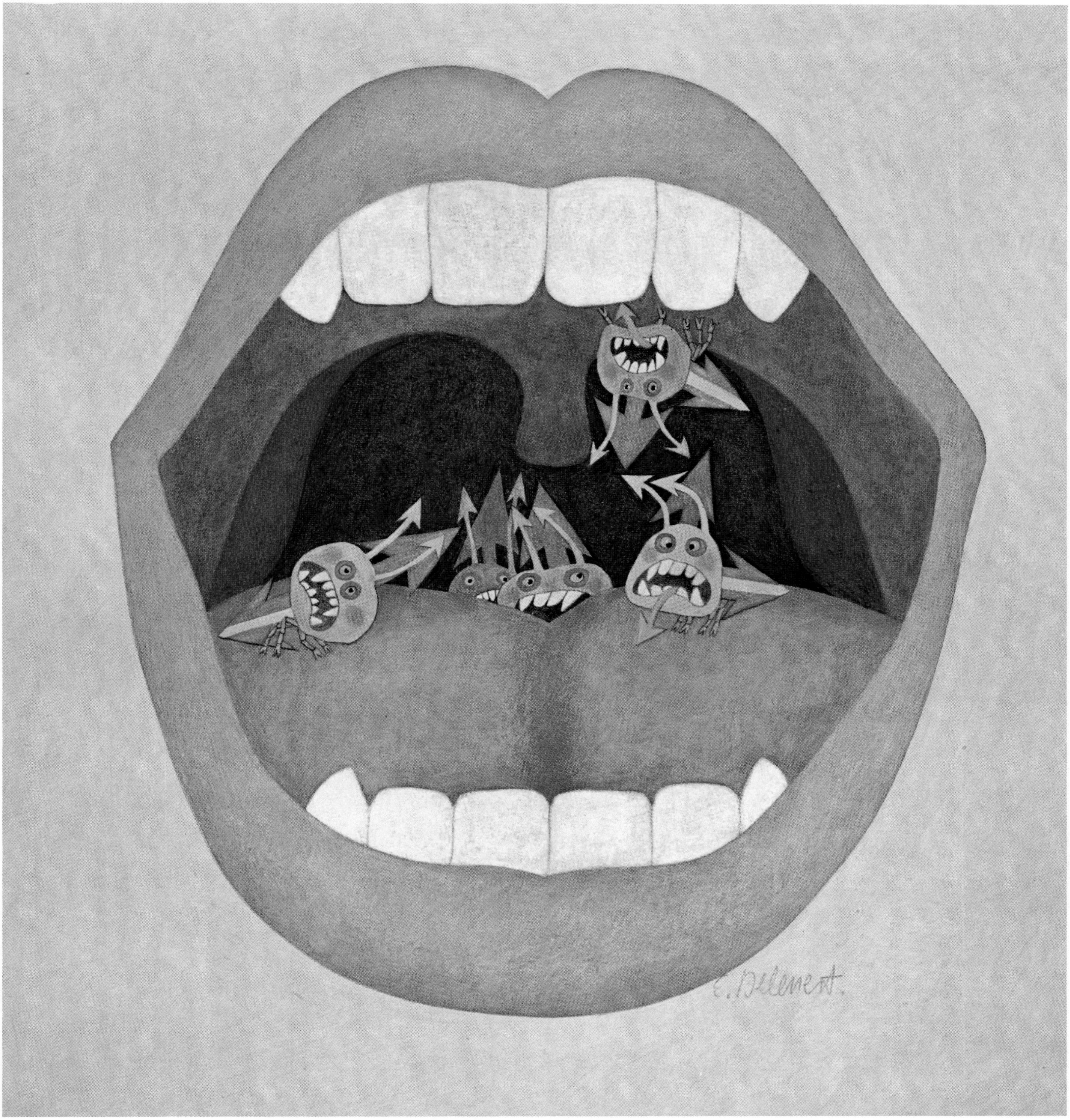

219

220

Artist/Künstler/Artiste:

219) 220) FREDRIC KURTZ
221) DAN BRIDY/PETER J. MURPHY
222) ROBERT O. BLECHMANN/ALLAN BEAVER
223) ROBERT GROSSMANN/FRANK FRISTACHI
224) MAX VELTHUIJS
225) SEYMOUR CHWAST

219) 220) Illustration and complete advertisement for *DuPont* dyes and chemicals. (USA)
221) Trade magazine advertisement for *Alcoa* alumina used in paper for added brightness. (USA)
222) 223) Magazine ads in two colours for *Talon* zippers to prevent painful situations. (USA)
224) Magazine advertisement for summer fashion fabrics. Full colour. (NLD)
225) Double-spread magazine ad for a range of snacks made by General Mills. Full colour. (USA)

219) 220) Illustration und vollständiges Inserat für Farbstoffe und chemische Präparate von *Du Pont*. (USA)
221) Inserat für Tonerde, die in der Papierherstellung verwendet wird. (USA)
222) 223) Zeitschrifteninserate für den Reissverschluss *Talon*. (USA)
224) Zeitschrifteninserat für Sommerstoffe. Mehrfarbig. (NLD)
225) Doppelseitiges Zeitschrifteninserat für Salzgebäck. Mehrfarbig. (USA)

219) 220) Illustration et annonce pour les colorants et les produits chimiques *DuPont*. (USA)
221) Annonce de revues pour l'alumine *Alcoa*, utilisée dans la fabrication du papier. (USA)
222) 223) Annonces de revues en deux couleurs, pour les fermetures à glissière *Talon*. (USA)
224) Annonce de revues pour des étoffes d'été. Polychrome. (NLD)
225) Annonce de revue pour des biscuits salés. Double page en couleur. (USA)

221

Art Director / Directeur artistique:

219) 220) WILLIAM HOGATE
221) PETER J. MURPHY
222) ALLAN BEAVER
223) FRANK FRISTACHI
225) JERRY ANDRIOZZI

Agency / Agentur / Agence – Studio:

221) KETCHUM, MAC LEOD & GROVE, INC., PITTSBURGH
222) 223) DELEHANTY, KURNIT & GELLER ADV. CO., NEW YORK
224) N.P.O., DEN HAAG
225) WELLS, RICH, GREENE, INC., NEW YORK

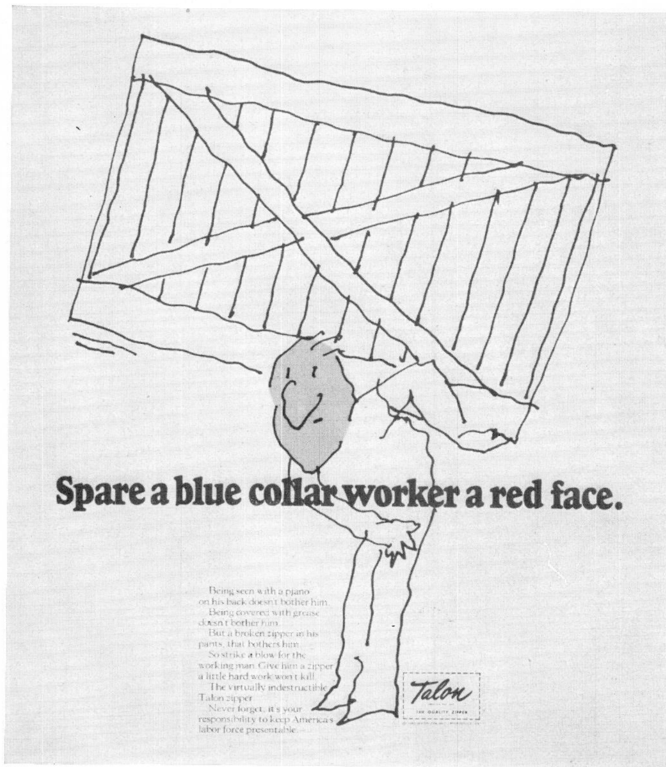

222

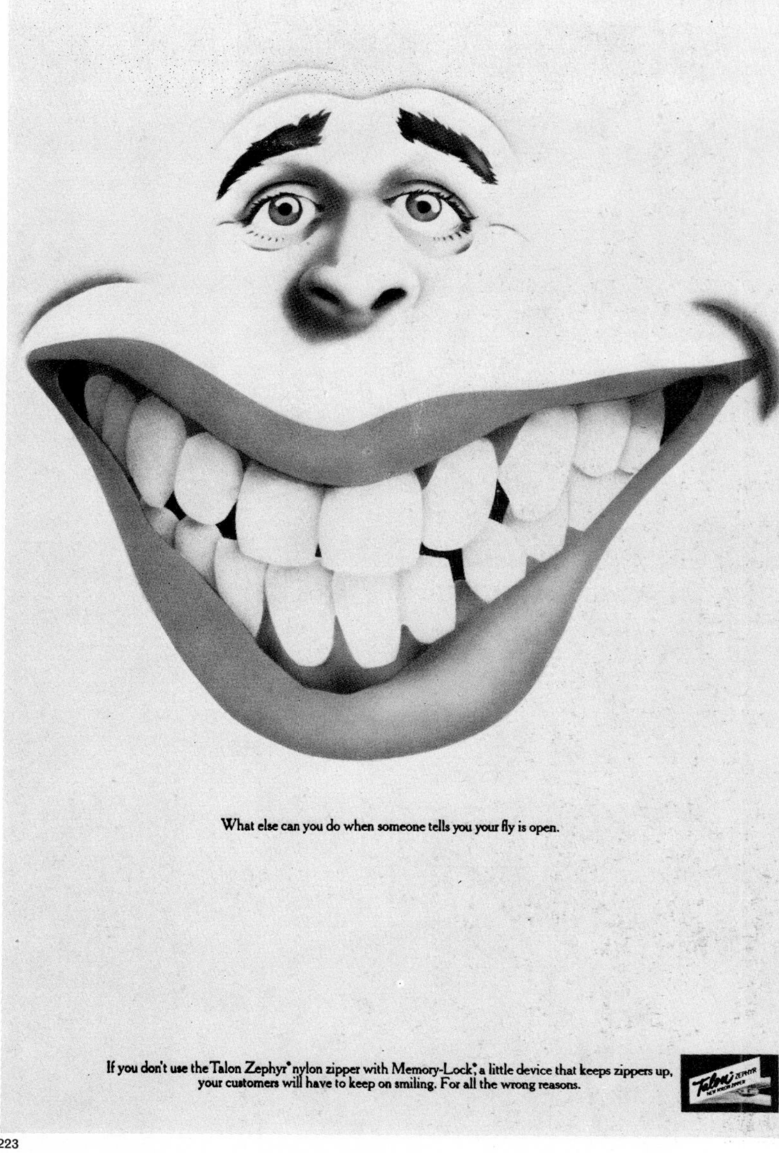

223

Het zomerse dag en nacht modeplezier van de Ploeg

Zojuist verschenen: de kleuren van chianti en champagne, van kreeft en olijven, van Mediterrannée en Acropolis, van pijnbossen en malse weiden, van felle sportwagens en luie schommelbanken, van vuurwerk in Stockholm en parasols op Capri . . . kortom de kleuren die de blijheid van zomer en vakantie zijn. Kom al dat modemoois kijken * - gauw, gauw, gauw.

Ploegstoffen: Bergeyk/ Londen/Düsseldorf/Brussel

* Wilt u weten waar u Ploegstoffen kunt kopen? Een kaartje aan weverij de Ploeg, afdeling voorlichting, Bergeyk, en u krijgt omgaand antwoord.

224

"I'd love a salted corn snack."

"Well... maybe a cheddar cheese snack."

"Wait, I'll make that a buttery popcorn taste."

"In fact I'll stick to a grilled cheese on toast taste."

"Oh, I don't know– maybe something else altogether!"

The Big G has a snack you'll like, no matter what you like.

225

Advertisements / Inserate / Annonces

Advertisements

Art Director / Directeur artistique:

226) 229) BERNIE ZLOTNICK
230) 231) ROLLIN S. BINZER

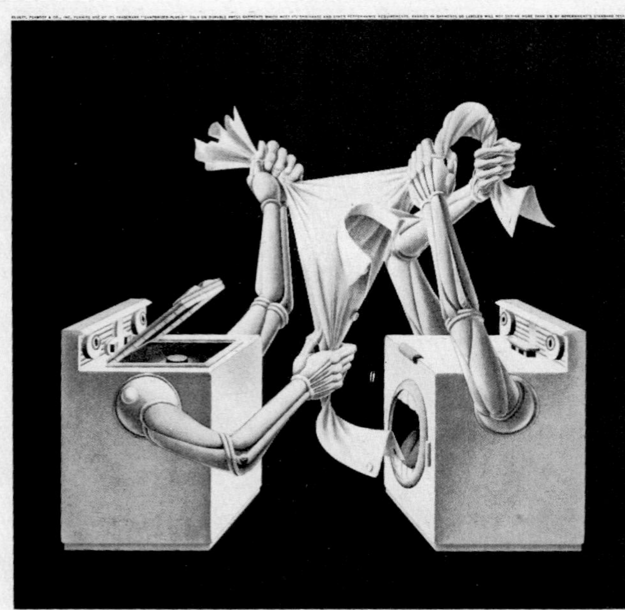

226

227

228

229

226) 229) Black-and-white magazine advertisements for the *Sanforized* process. (USA)
227) 228) Black-and-white magazine ads for a non-shrink textile treatment. (SWI)
230) 231) Complete advertisement and illustration for a race course. (USA)

226) 229) Zeitschrifteninserate für das Sanforisieren von Textilien. (USA)
227) 228) Zeitschrifteninserate für den *Sanfor*-Dienst, Schweiz. (SWI)
230) 231) Vollständiges Inserat und Illustration für eine Rennbahn. (USA)

226) 229) Annonces de revues en noir pour le procédé *Sanforized.* (USA)
227) 228) Annonce pour un procédé de traitement des textiles. (SWI)
230) 231) Annonce et son illustration pour un champ des courses. (USA)

Artist / Künstler / Artiste:

226) DON PUNCHATZ/BERNIE ZLOTNICK
227) 228) WILHELM RIESER
229) PAUL DAVIS/BERNIE ZLOTNICK
230) 231) MILTON GLASER/ROLLIN S. BINZER

Agency / Agentur / Agence – Studio:

226) 229) YOUNG & RUBICAM, INC., NEW YORK
227) 228) ADOLF WIRZ AG, ZÜRICH
230) 231) HURVIS, BINZER & CHURCHILL, INC., CHICAGO

230

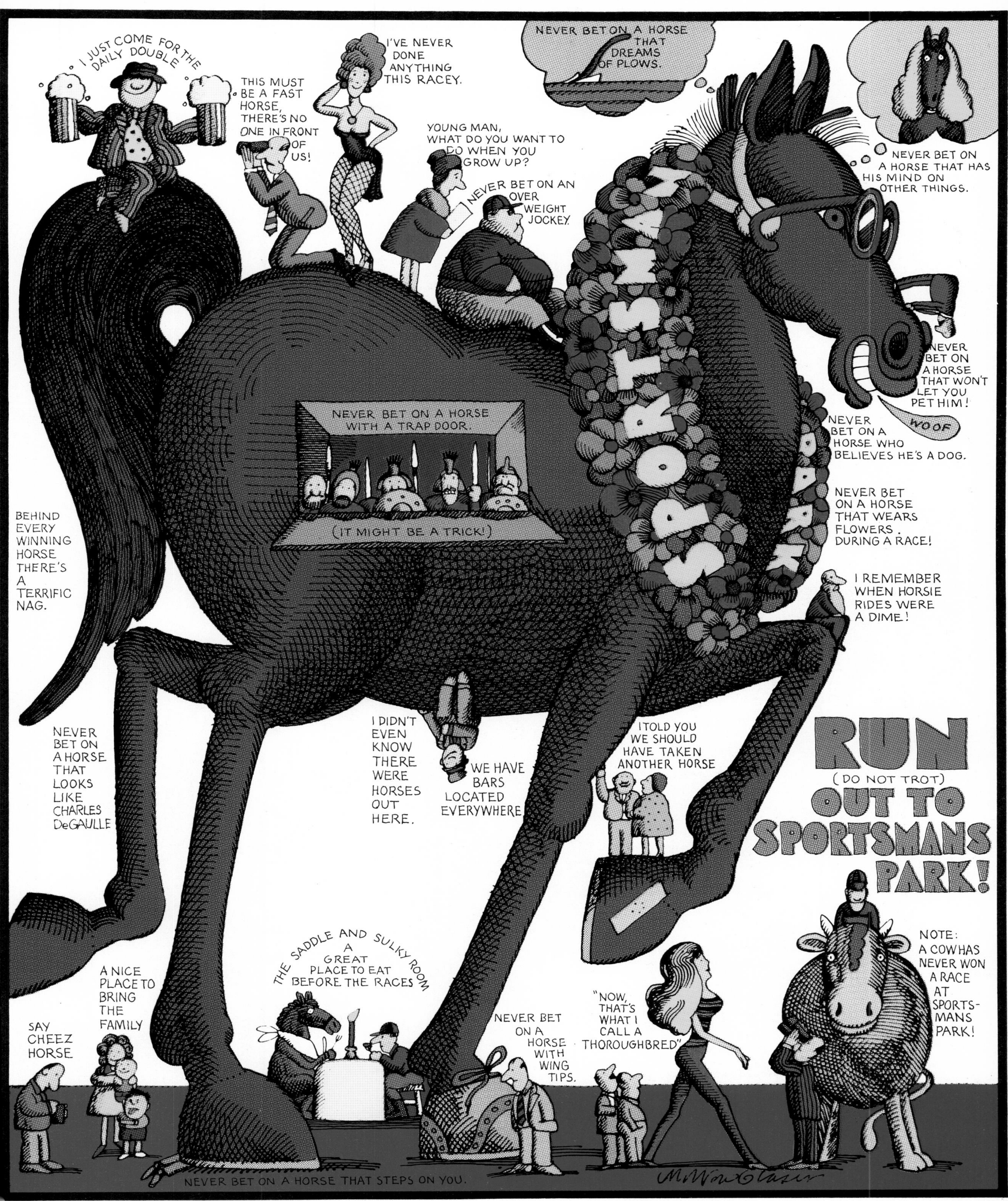
I JUST COME FOR THE DAILY DOUBLE
THIS MUST BE A FAST HORSE, THERE'S NO ONE IN FRONT OF US!
I'VE NEVER DONE ANYTHING THIS RACEY.
YOUNG MAN, WHAT DO YOU WANT TO DO WHEN YOU GROW UP?
NEVER BET ON AN OVER WEIGHT JOCKEY.
NEVER BET ON A HORSE THAT DREAMS OF PLOWS.
NEVER BET ON A HORSE THAT HAS HIS MIND ON OTHER THINGS.
SPORTSMAN PARK
NEVER BET ON A HORSE THAT WON'T LET YOU PET HIM!
WOOF
NEVER BET ON A HORSE WHO BELIEVES HE'S A DOG.
NEVER BET ON A HORSE WITH A TRAP DOOR.
(IT MIGHT BE A TRICK!)
BEHIND EVERY WINNING HORSE THERE'S A TERRIFIC NAG.
NEVER BET ON A HORSE THAT WEARS FLOWERS. DURING A RACE!
I REMEMBER WHEN HORSIE RIDES WERE A DIME!
NEVER BET ON A HORSE THAT LOOKS LIKE CHARLES DeGAULLE
I DIDN'T EVEN KNOW THERE WERE HORSES OUT HERE.
WE HAVE BARS LOCATED EVERYWHERE
I TOLD YOU WE SHOULD HAVE TAKEN ANOTHER HORSE
RUN (DO NOT TROT) OUT TO SPORTSMANS PARK!
NOTE: A COW HAS NEVER WON A RACE AT SPORTS-MANS PARK!
SAY CHEEZ HORSE
A NICE PLACE TO BRING THE FAMILY
THE SADDLE AND SULKY ROOM A GREAT PLACE TO EAT BEFORE THE RACES
NEVER BET ON A HORSE WITH WING TIPS.
"NOW, THAT'S WHAT I CALL A THOROUGHBRED"
NEVER BET ON A HORSE THAT STEPS ON YOU.

Aufgeschrieben!!

Name: Klein
Beruf: Halsfeger
Arbeitsort: Im Hals
Seit wann: Seit Generationen
Besondere Merkmale: Gegen Husten, Heiserkeit und Katarrh
Wirklich, mit dem ersten Halsfeger auf der Zunge beginnt die Besserung. Und wie köstlich! Ein altes Heilkräuter-Rezept, unverändert überliefert und angewandt. Darum auch diese Wohltat bei Rachen- und Raucherkatarrh. Eine willkommene Erleichterung für alle, die von Berufes wegen ihre Stimme viel brauchen.

Sie merken den Unterschied sofort: Klein's Halsfeger sind die mit der honigweichen Füllung.

KLEIN'S HALS FEGER

232

232) 233) Complete magazine advertisement and illustration for coughdrops. (SWI)
234)–236) Magazine advertisements to encourage advertising in the magazine TIPS. (BEL)
237)–239) Trade magazine advertisements for a Milanese printing house. Fig. 237 conveys Christmas wishes, fig. 239 uses the firm's trade mark. (ITA)
240) 241) Trade magazine advertisements for a process engraver. The references are to Braille and the experiments of William Leggo. Black and white. (ITA)

232) 233) Zeitschrifteninserat und Illustration für *Klein's Halsfeger*. (SWI)
234)–236) Zeitschrifteninserate zur Anzeigenwerbung in der Zeitschrift TIPS. (BEL)
237)–239) Fachzeitschrifteninserate für eine Druckerei in Mailand. Abb. 237 übermittelt Weihnachtswünsche, Abb. 239 verwendet das Firmenzeichen. (ITA)
240) 241) Fachzeitschrifteninserate für eine graphische Anstalt, mit Hinweisen auf Braille und die Experimente von William Leggo. Schwarzweiss. (ITA)

232) 233) Annonce de revues et son illustration pour des bonbons contre la toux. (SWI)
234)–236) Annonces de revues pour la publicité dans la revue TIPS. (BEL)
237)–239) Annonces de revues professionnelles pour l'imprimerie Alfieri & Lacroix, Milan: 237) vœux de Noël; 239) utilisation de l'emblème de la firme. (ITA)
240) 241) Annonces de revues professionnelles pour l'atelier de photogravure G. Colombi S.p.A., Milan, évoquant Braille et les expériences de William Leggo. Noir et blanc. (ITA)

233

Donald Brun

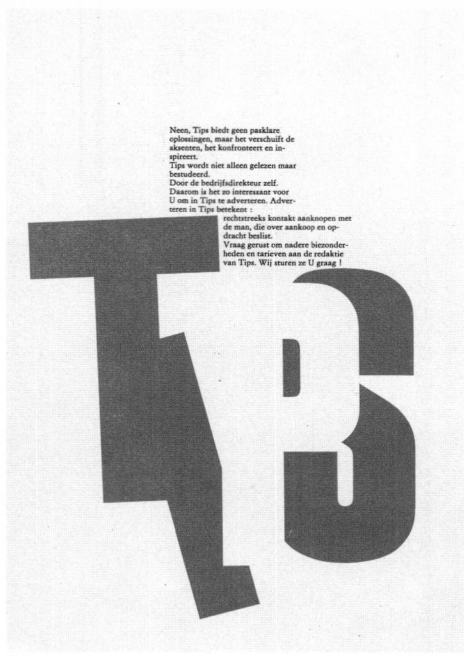

234

235

236

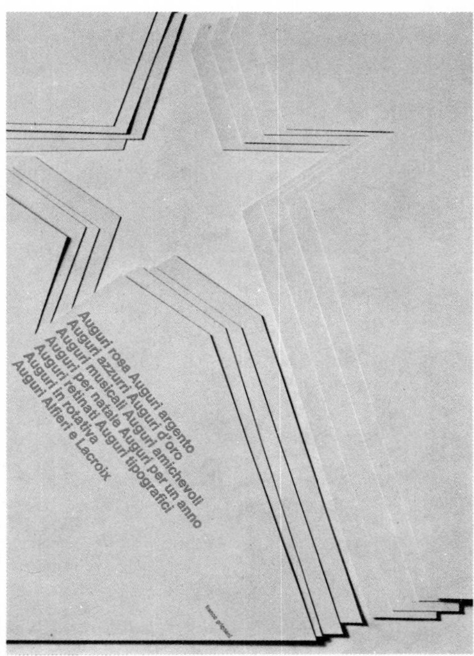

237

238

239

B R A I L L E

La luce del segno nel buio

Luigi Braille insegnante francese, colpito da cecità non volle arrendersi al buio nè rinunziare alla luce più vitale e più alta della cultura.

L'alfabeto per ciechi ideato da Braille è un sistema di scrittura a punti in rilievo: scorrendo sui caratteri sensibilissime dita, i ciechi rivedono il mondo delle idee e dei pensieri, ristabiliscono il ponte tra sé e l'universo della civiltà trascritta.

I caratteri tattili sono la pista d'emergenza attraverso la quale pensiero e cultura riconquistano l'anima al di là della tenebra. La funzione mediatrice del segno tipografico è in questo caso vittoria dell'uomo sulla sofferenza.

Fedele allo spirito dei grandi maestri Stabilimento Poligrafico
G. Colombi S.p.A.
20016 Pero (Milano)

Studio Boggeri

240

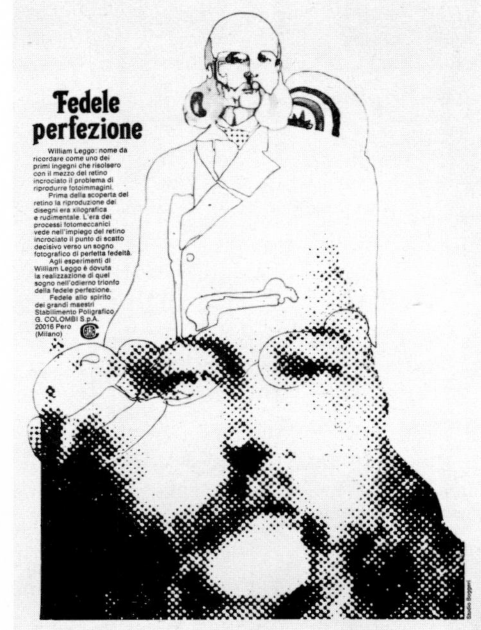

241

Artist/Künstler/Artiste:

232) 233) DONALD BRUN
234)–236) ROSMARIE TISSI
237)–239) FRANCO GRIGNANI
240) 241) H. + U. OSTERWALDER

Art Director/Directeur artistique:

232) 233) DONALD BRUN
234)–236) SIEGFRIED ODERMATT
237)–239) FRANCO GRIGNANI
240) 241) ANTONIO BOGGERI

Agency/Agentur/Agence – Studio:

234)–236) ATELIER ODERMATT, ZÜRICH
237)–239) STUDIO GRIGNANI, MILAN
240) 241) STUDIO BOGGERI, MILAN

Edward Sorel

242

243

246

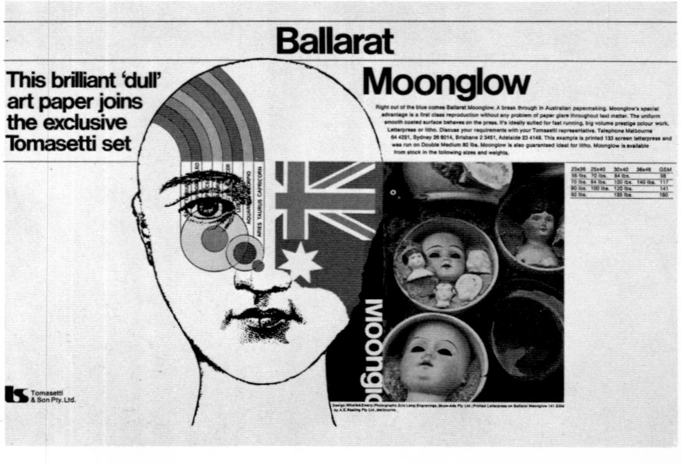

Ballarat

This brilliant 'dull' art paper joins the exclusive Tomasetti set

Moonglow

Right out of the blue comes Ballarat Moonglow. A break through in Australian papermaking. Moonglow's special advantage is a first class reproduction without any problem of paper glare throughout text matter. The uniform smooth coated surface behaves on the press. It's ideally suited for fast running, big volume prestige colour work. Letterpress or litho. Discuss your requirements with your Tomasetti representative. Telephone Melbourne 64 4221, Sydney 26 6014, Brisbane 2 3451, Adelaide 23 4149. This example is printed 133 screen letterpress and was run on Double Medium 80 lbs. Moonglow is also guaranteed ideal for litho. Moonglow is available from stock in the following sizes and weights.

23x36	25x40	30x40	36x46	GSM
56 lbs.	70 lbs.	84 lbs.		98
70 lbs.	84 lbs.	100 lbs.	140 lbs.	117
80 lbs.	100 lbs.	120 lbs.		141
93 lbs.		135 lbs.		160

ARIES TAURUS CAPRICORN AQUARIUS

Moonglow

Tomasetti & Son Pty. Ltd.

Advertisements/Inserate/Annonces

Artist / Künstler / Artiste:

242) 243) EDWARD SOREL/ALLAN BEAVER
244) 245) EDWARD SOREL/PETER HIRSCH
246) WHAITE & EMERY
247) TSUNEHISA KIMURA
248) SHIGEO FUKUDA
249) TEIJI NAKADE

Art Director / Directeur artistique:

242) 243) ALLAN BEAVER
244) 245) PETER HIRSCH
249) MASAOMI UNAGAMI

Agency / Agentur / Agence – Studio:

242)–245) DELEHANTY, KURNIT & GELLER ADV. CO., NEW YORK
246) HAYES ADVERTISING PTY. LTD., MELBOURNE

242)–245) Illustration and complete magazine advertisements for TAP Portuguese Airways. (USA)
246) Trade advertisement announcing a new paper by Tomasetti & Son Pty. Ltd. Full colour. (AUL)
247) 248) Magazine advertisements for Oji Paper Co. Ltd. and Toyo Printing Co. Ltd. (JAP)
249) Double-spread magazine advertisement for *Dainichi Seika* colours and chemicals. (JAP)

242)–245) Illustration und vollständige Inserate für die portugiesische Fluglinie TAP. (USA)
246) Fachzeitschrifteninserat, das auf eine neue Papierqualität aufmerksam macht. (AUL)
247) Fachzeitschrifteninserat für eine Papierfabrik. (JAP)
248) Fachzeitschrifteninserat für eine Druckerei. (JAP)
249) Doppelseitiges Zeitschrifteninserat für Farbstoffe und chemische Präparate. (JAP)

242)–245) Illustration et annonces pour la compagnie aérienne portugaise TAP. (USA)
246) Annonce de revues professionnelles pour une nouvelle qualité de papier. Polychrome. (AUL)
247) 248) Annonces de revues pour une fabrique de papier et une imprimerie. (JAP)
249) Annonce de revues sur double page pour des colorants et des produits chimiques. (JAP)

244

245

247

248

249

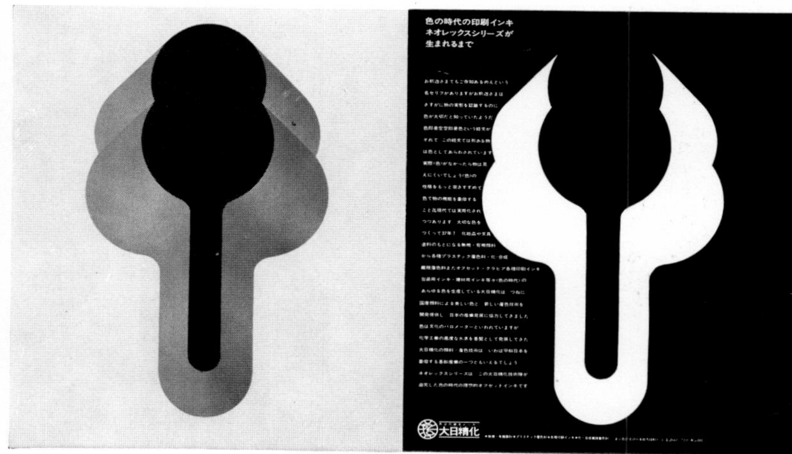

Artist | Künstler | Artiste:

250) 251) NICOLE CLAVELOUX
252) BURT BLUM/PAUL RUBINSTEIN
253) URS FURRER
254) TOMI UNGERER
255) GEORGE SCHWENK
256) DANTE VERNICE
257) JON FISHER

250

252

Nous ne sommes pas les plus beaux...

...mais nous sommes de loin les plus exquis, les plus futés, les plus talentueux, les plus inventifs... et aussi les plus serviables, les plus enjoués, les mieux informés, les plus constructifs, les plus efficaces (ouf!)... Personne ne s'étonnera si nous devenons sous peu la première Agence européenne !

HAVAS-CONSEIL

251

253

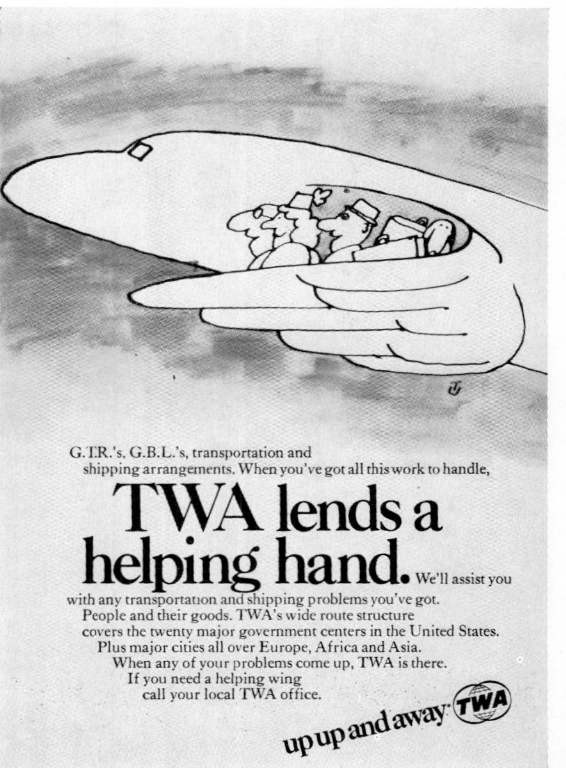

254

Art Director | Directeur artistique:

250) 251) DE MOULIN
252) PAUL RUBINSTEIN
253) URS FURRER
254) RICHARD BECK
255) MYRTLE JOHNSON
256) DANTE VERNICE
257) JON FISHER

Agency | Agentur | Agence – Studio:

250) 251) HAVAS CONSEIL, PARIS
252) YOUNG & RUBICAM, INC., NEW YORK
253) URS FURRER, ZÜRICH
254) FOOTE, CONE & BELDING, INC., NEW YORK
255) SUDLER & HENNESSEY, INC., NEW YORK
256) C.P.V. ITALIANA S.P.A., MILAN
257) CAMPBELL-EWALD CO., INC., NEW YORK

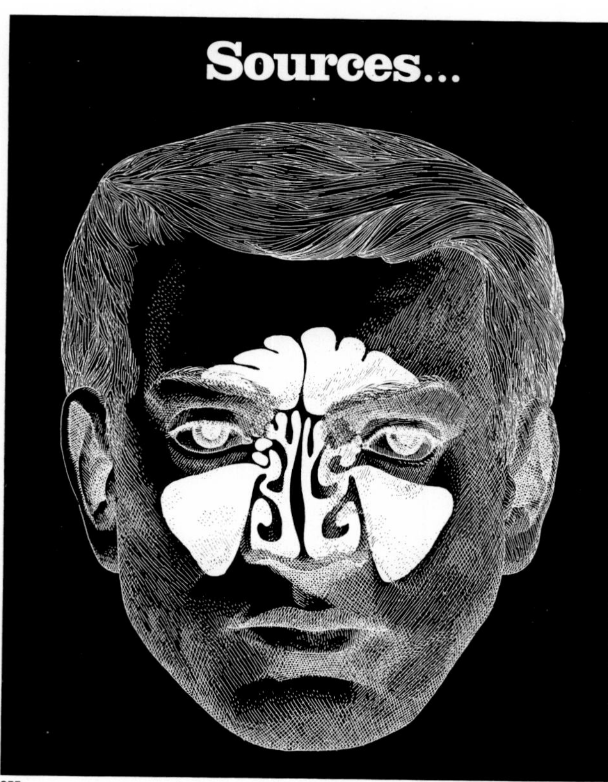

255

256

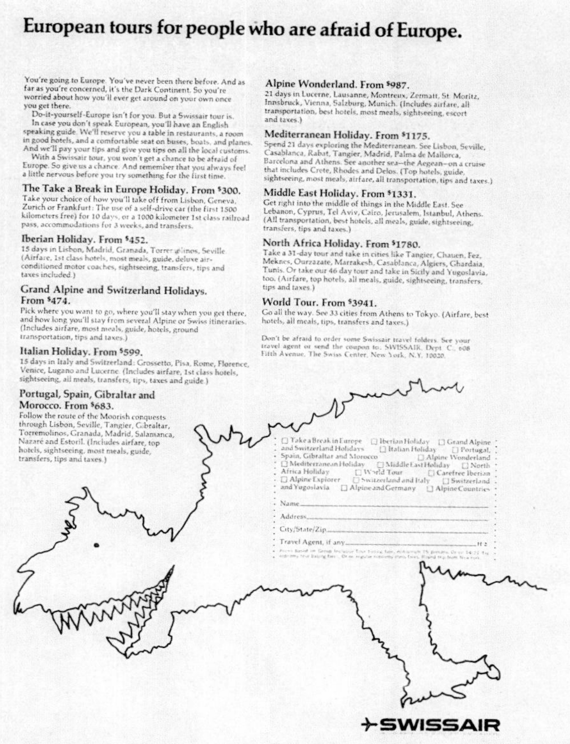

257

250) 251) Illustration and complete advertisement for the advertising agency Havas Conseil. Black and white. (FRA)
252) Magazine ad for *Young & Rubicam* TV commercials. (USA)
253) Black-and-white advertisement for a fashion shop. (SWI)
254) Trade magazine advertisement for the transportation services of the TWA airline. Black and white. (USA)
255) First page of a three-page trade magazine ad about a *Warner-Chilcott* drug against sinus headaches. (USA)
256) Magazine advertisement for an advertising agency. (ITA)
257) Magazine ad about European tours by *Swissair*. (USA)

250) 251) Illustration und vollständiges Inserat für die Werbeagentur Havas Conseil, Paris. Schwarzweiss. (FRA)
252) Zeitschrifteninserat für Werbefilme einer Agentur. (USA)
253) Zeitschrifteninserat für die *Naphtaly*-Boutique in Zürich. Schwarzweiss. (SWI)
254) Fachzeitschrifteninserat für den Transport-Dienst der Fluggesellschaft TWA. Schwarzweiss. (USA)
255) Erste Seite aus einer dreiseitigen Zeitschriftenanzeige für ein Arzneimittel gegen Kopfschmerzen. (USA)
256) Zeitschrifteninserat für eine Werbeagentur. (ITA)
257) Zeitschrifteninserat für *Swissair*-Europareisen. (USA)

250) 251) Illustration et annonce pour l'agence de publicité Havas Conseil, Paris. Noir et blanc. (FRA)
252) Annonce de revues pour des films publicitaires. (USA)
253) Annonce en noir pour une boutique de mode. (SWI)
254) Annonce de revues professionnelles en noir pour les services de transport de la compagnie aérienne TWA. (USA)
255) Premier volet d'une annonce sur trois pages pour un médicament contre les maux de tête. (USA)
256) Annonce pour l'agence C.P.V. Italiana, Milan. (ITA)
257) Annonce de revues pour *Swissair*. (USA)

Advertisements / Inserate / Annonces

258)–261) Illustration and complete magazine advertisements for a *Minolta* camera. (USA)
262) 263) Detail and complete magazine advertisement about a new case for *Teacher's* whisky. (USA)
264) Magazine advertisement in colour for sportswear. (FRA)
265) 266) Magazine advertisement and illustration from a *Shell* series about places worth visiting. (GB)

258)–261) Illustration und vollständige Fachzeitschrifteninserate für die Kamera *Minolta*. (USA)
262) 263) Ausschnitt und vollständiges Zeitschrifteninserat über eine neue Flaschenschutzhülle für einen Whisky. (USA)
264) Zeitschrifteninserat für Sportbekleidung. (FRA)
265) 266) Zeitschrifteninserat und Illustration aus einer Serie für *Shell* über touristische Sehenswürdigkeiten. (GB)

258)–261) Illustration et annonces de revues pour un appareil photographique. (USA)
262) 263) Détail et annonce de revues pour un whisky. (USA)
264) Annonce de revues en couleur pour les vêtements de sport de *Mossant Sport*, Nice. (FRA)
265) 266) Annonce de revues et son illustration, tirée d'une série touristique *Shell*. (GB)

Art Director / Directeur artistique:
258)–261) ROBERT BODENSTEIN
262) 263) BOB WATERSON
264) JACQUES SÉGUELA/GIBBERT SOULIÉ

Agency / Agentur / Agence – Studio:
258)–261) E.T. HOWARD ADVERTISING, NEW YORK
262) 263) SULLIVAN, STAUFFER, COLWELL & BAYLES, INC., NEW YORK
264) AXE PUBLICITÉ, PARIS
265) 266) COLMAN, PRENTIS & VARLEY LTD., LONDON

262

258

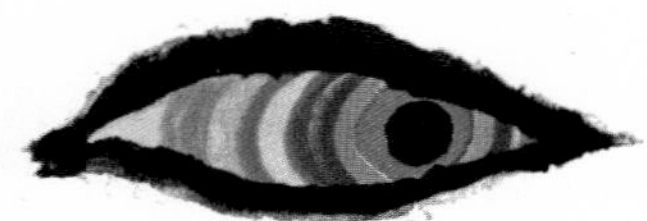

259

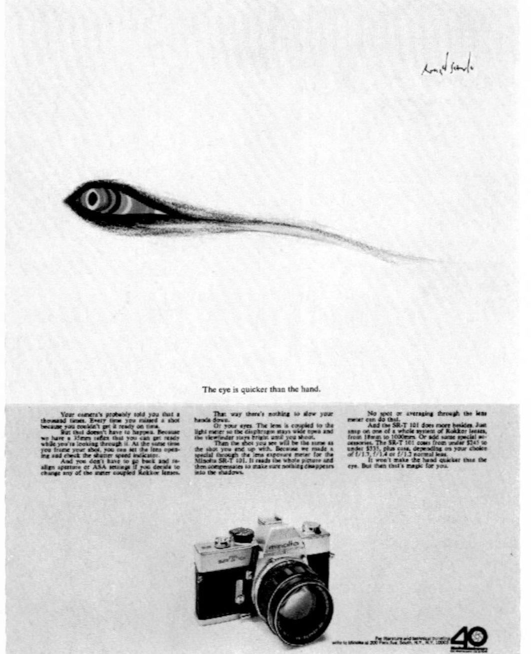

260

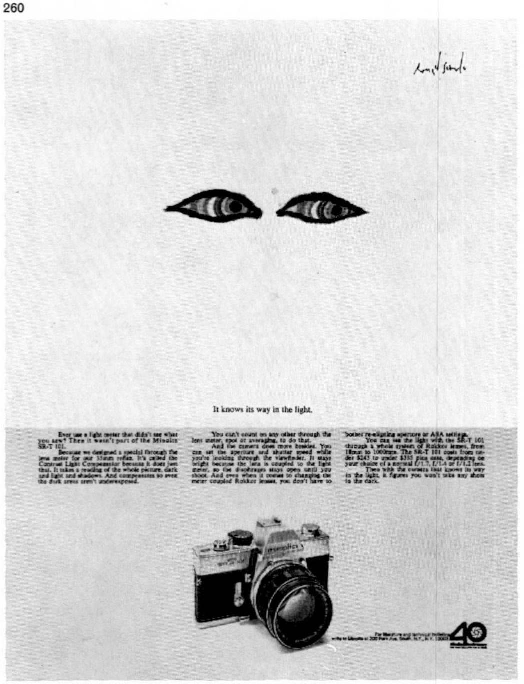

261

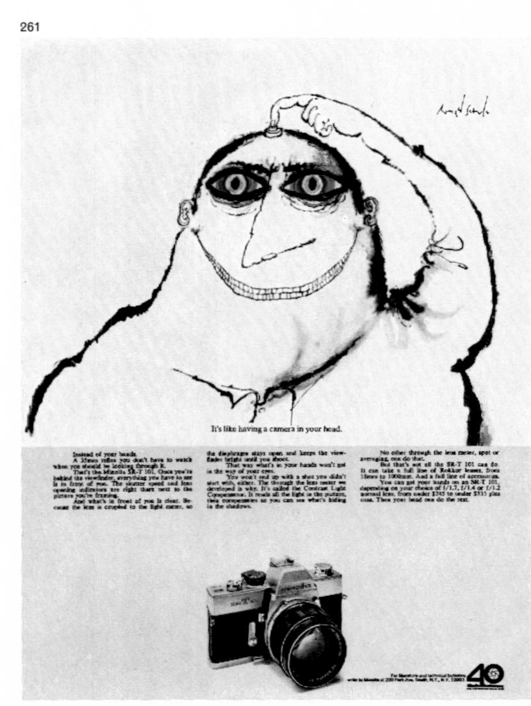

263

264

265

Artist | Künstler | Artiste:

258)–261) RONALD SEARLE
262) 263) SEYMOUR CHWAST
264) ALAIN BRANDALISE
265) 266) GRAHAM A. CLARKE

266

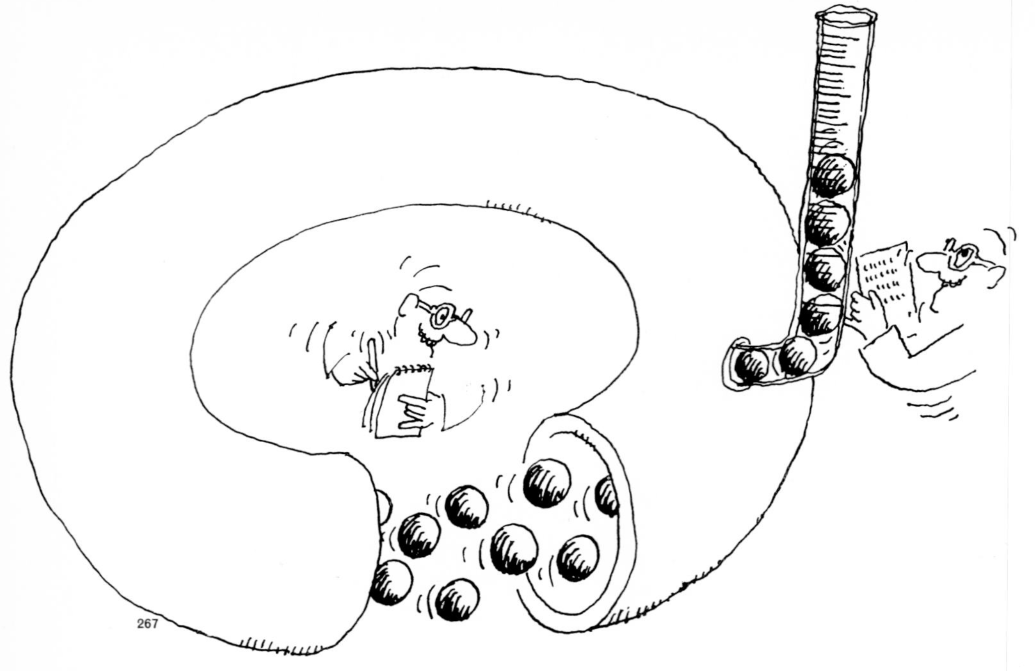

267

Die Leistung im Blutkreislauf erfährt...
... wer Fluß und Druck des Blutes mißt und zugleich rechnet. Oder – einfacher – wer sein Biotronex Blutfluß-Meßsystem mit Blutdruck- und Computer-Einschüben ergänzt.
Mit dieser platzsparenden, einfach zu bedienenden Meßanordnung lassen sich laufend Leistung, Schlagvolumen und Schlagarbeit ermitteln.
Weitere Biotronex-Geräte: Leichte-Flow-Transducer verschiedenster Ausführungen, für akute Versuche und chronische Implantationen.
Extrakorporales Blutfluß-Meßgerät: handliches Gerät zur elektromagnetischen Messung in einem externen Kreislauf (z. B. Herz-Lungen-Maschine, künstliche Nieren usw.).
Blutdruck-Meßgerät für verschiedene Druckbereiche mit dazugehörigen Druckgebern nach dem Prinzip des Differential-Transformators.
Heart Motion Video Tracker. Signalabtaster zur Bewegungsanalyse von Herz und anderen internen Organen.
Biotronex
Elmetra
Biotronex Laboratory Inc., Silver Spring, Maryland, vertreten durch Elmetra AG, Geißacher 6, 8126 Zumikon bei Zürich Tel. 051 89 38 77
Verkaufsbüro in Deutschland: 5256 Hommerich, Kalkofen, Tel. 02207 1111
Detaillierte Unterlagen, Beratung und Offerten durch spezialisierte Mitarbeiter der Elmetra.
Elmetra ist auch zuständig für die medizinischen Geräte der Firmen: National Cylinder Gas, Chicago/Illinois Cordis Corp., Miami/Florida, und Gulton Medical Instruments, Willow Grove/Pennsylvania.

268

272

269

270

271

273

274

275

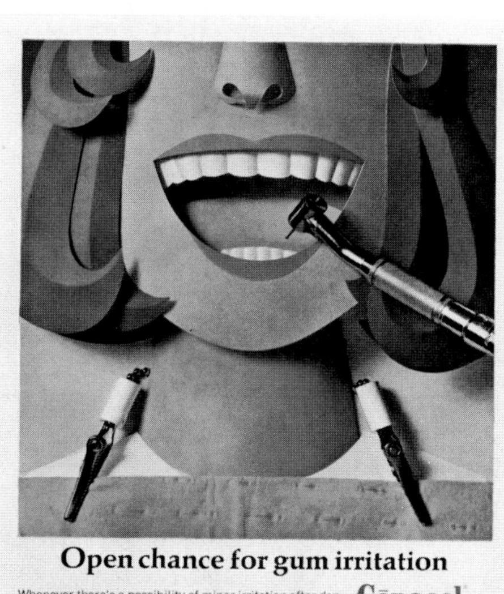

276

267) 268) Illustration and trade magazine ad for instruments to measure blood pressure. (SWI)
269) 270) Trade magazine ads for *Pirelli* cables and underwater pipelines. Full colour. (ITA)
271) Trade ad about a firm's 'constant evolution'. (ITA)
272)–275) Illustration and advertisements for the Container Corporation of America. (USA)
276) Magazine ad for a *Merrell* mouthwash. (USA)

267) 268) Illustration und Inserat für Blutmessgeräte, von Elmetra AG, Zumikon. (SWI)
269) 270) Fachzeitschrifteninserate für Kabel und Unterwasser-Rohrleitungen von *Pirelli*. (ITA)
271) Fachzeitschrifteninserat für De Cardenas. (ITA)
272)–275) Illustration und Inserate für ein Unternehmen der Kartonnage-Branche. (USA)
276) Zeitschrifteninserat für ein Mundwasser. (USA)

267) 268) Illustration et annonce de revues professionnelles pour un sphygmomanomètre. (SWI)
269) 270) Annonces pour produits *Pirelli*. (ITA)
271) Annonce pour De Cardenas S.p.A., Milan. (ITA)
272)–275) Illustration et annonces pour une entreprise de cartonnage. (USA)
276) Annonce pour une eau dentifrice. (USA)

Artist / Künstler / Artiste:

267) 268) RENÉ FEHR
269) UNIMARK INTERNATIONAL
270) FRANÇOIS ROBERT
271) ILIO NEGRI
272)–274) JOHN MASSEY
275) JOHN R. RIEBEN
276) BLAKE HAMPTON/IRV BAHRT

Art Director / Directeur artistique:

267) 268) RUEDI KÜLLING
269) 270) TERESITA CAMAGNI HANGELDIAN
271) ILIO NEGRI
272)–274) JOHN MASSEY
276) JIM MCFARLAND

Agency / Agentur / Agence – Studio:

267) 268) ADVICO AG, ZÜRICH
269) 270) CENTRO S.R.L., MILAN
271) STUDIO NEGRI, MILAN
272)–275) N.W. AYER & SONS, INC., CHICAGO
276) SUDLER & HENNESSEY, INC., NEW YORK

Advertisements / Inserate
Annonces

277) Newspaper advertisement from a campaign for IBM computers. (SWI)
278) Colour newspaper ad for *Utica Club* beer inviting visitors to the brewery. (USA)
279) 280) Black-and-white advertisements from a campaign for *Alka-Seltzer*. (USA)
281) 282) Magazine ad with illustration in actual size for *Suntory* whisky. (JAP)

277) Zeitungsinserat aus einer Kampagne für IBM-Rechenzentren. (SWI)
278) Zeitungsinserat für das *Utica Club* Bier, das zum Besuch der Brauerei einlädt. Mehrfarbig. (USA)
279) 280) Aus einer Inseratenkampagne für *Alka-Seltzer*. Schwarzweiss. (USA)
281) 282) Zeitschrifteninserat und Illustration für eine Whisky-Marke. (JAP)

277) Annonce de presse d'une campagne en faveur des ordinateurs IBM. (SWI)
278) Annonce de presse en couleur pour la bière *Utica Club*, invitant les amateurs à visiter la brasserie. (USA)
279) 280) Annonces en noir d'une campagne en faveur de l'*Alka-Seltzer*. (USA)
281) 282) Annonce de revues et illustration pour une marque de whisky. (JAP)

277

Keinen Computer zu haben, mag gemütlich sein. Aber irgendwann hört die Gemütlichkeit auf.

Gemütlichkeit ist gemütlich. Aber sie bringt manchen Unternehmer mit seiner Zeit in Rückstand.

Datenverarbeitung meint Fortschritt für das Unternehmen. Gleich, wie alt das Unternehmen ist. Gleich, wie geartet das Unternehmen ist. Gleich, wie gross das Unternehmen ist.

Als multinationales Unternehmen kennen wir die Unternehmen vieler Länder. Und damit können wir jedem Unternehmen seine ihm angemessene Datenverarbeitung anbieten.

Wir haben grosse und kleine Computer. Wir haben Allround-Computer und Spezial-Computer. Wir haben Programme und vor allem Spezialisten für die Computer.

Sie können Datenverarbeitung mieten oder kaufen. Sie können Ihre Arbeiten von IBM Rechenzentren erledigen lassen oder mittels Datenfernverarbeitung mit einem Computer des Rechenzentrums arbeiten. Sie können einen eigenen Computer haben und ausserdem ins Rechenzentrum gehen.

Der Möglichkeiten gibt es viele. Wenn Sie gerne wissen möchten, wie Sie am besten von der Datenverarbeitung profitieren können, dann lassen Sie sich von Ihrem IBM Beratungszentrum beraten. Gleich, ob es darum geht, den Lagerbestand für einen Lebensmittelgrosshandel zu minimieren.

Oder die Kapazität für eine Motorenfabrik zu terminieren.

Oder die Touren für eine Brauerei zu planen.

Oder die kranke Verwaltung eines Krankenhauses zu heilen.

Oder die Statik eines Ingenieurbüros zu berechnen.

Oder Computerschaltungen für die IBM zu entwickeln.

Oder das Material für eine Kartonagenfabrik zu disponieren.

Oder die Fertigung für eine Automobilfirma zu steuern. Oder Tagesauszüge für eine Bank zu erstellen.

Oder die Lohnkonten für eine Schuhfabrik zu führen. Oder oder oder.

Fänden Sie das ungemütlich?

IBM

278

Come lift a stein with us over the holidays.

We're delighted to show you around our brewery any time. But we're especially glad to have you during the holidays. It's a sentimental time and we're sentimental people. In fact, when it comes to making beer, we're probably the most determinedly sentimental people you'll ever meet.

We age Utica Club for months to get exactly the kind of beer we want. Its taste is mellow. There is absolutely no bitterness. The foam is rich and creamy, with fine bubbles—the kind you get in champagne. Natural bubbles.

Can you tell we're proud of our beer? Well, we are. And we're equally proud of our brewery. Like a good cook's kitchen, it's spotless and filled with gleaming copper and stainless steel and tile. We think it's beautiful. Especially during the holidays. So drop in and see us anytime between 10 a.m. and 5 p.m. Monday through Friday. The drinks are on the house.

And by the way, if you like our illustration, we'll gladly send you a color poster version of it (without all these words). Just drop a note to me, Walter Matt, President, Utica Club Beer, Utica, New York 13503. Happy Holiday.

281

279

Alka-Seltzer.®
When you and your stomach don't agree.

Picture, if you will, a salami-pepper-and-onion sandwich entering your stomach.

It arrives, un-announced, and upsets your stomach.

Blindly striking back, your stomach upsets you and you get heartburn.

That's his way of saying "*Watch it*, Mac."

It's a pity you can't get together with your stomach, and decide what foods you can both agree on.

There is a communications problem.

Therefore, you must speak to your stomach in a language he understands, like Alka-Seltzer.

Alka-Seltzer is your way of saying "Forgive me."

It has alkalizers which will soothe your upset stomach and reduce excess acidity.

You take care of your stomach.

Your stomach won't bother you.

280

Our First National Ailment, The Blahs.

You don't get the Blahs, the Blahs get you. They come from our fast pace. The pressures and tensions we live with.

The Blahs. The feeling that heartburn is approaching... A headache is sneaking up... A cold coming on... An upset stomach closing in.

When the Blahs get you, take Alka-Seltzer.

You get a little something for all the little things that bother you. A pain reliever for your head. Alkalizers for your stomach. Alka-Seltzer... for the Blahs.

Alka-Seltzer®

Artist / Künstler / Artiste:
277) GERSTNER, GREDINGER + KUTTER AG
278) MILTON GLASER/WARREN MARGULIES
279) ROBERT BLECHMAN/ JOHN DANZA
280 WARRY KING/SAL AUDITORE
281) 282) SHIGEKAZU YAMAGUCHI

Art Director / Directeur artistique:
277) GERSTNER, GREDINGER + KUTTER AG
278) WARREN MARGULIES
279) JOHN DANZA
280) SAL AUDITORE
281) 282) MASAO SUGIMURA

Agency / Agentur / Agence – Studio:
277) GERSTNER, GREDINGER + KUTTER AG, BASEL
278) WELLS, RICH, GREENE, INC., NEW YORK
279) 280) JACK TINKER & PARTNERS, INC., NEW YORK

OLD VATTED AND FINE FLAVOUR
PURE MALT

SUNTORY
WHISKY
White
CHOICEST PRODUCT
MATURED AT OUR OWN YAMAZAKI WHISKY
THE QUALITY NEVER VARIES
OSAKA SUNTORY LTD.

AND FINE FLAVOUR
POT STILL

NTORY
HISKY
White
CHOICEST PRODUCT
OWN YAMAZAKI WHISKY DISTILLERY
QUALITY NEVER VARIES
UNTORY LTD. TOKYO

282

Artist / Künstler / Artiste:

283) RICHARD SAWERS / BOB MARCHANT
284) WALTER GRIEDER
285) KURT WIRTH
286) EUGENIE ARCH
287) 288) DAN BRIDY / RONALD A. LAYPORT

Agency / Agentur / Agence – Studio:

283) MARCHANT, WEINREICH, LONDON
284) WALTER GRIEDER, BASEL
285) KURT WIRTH, BERN
287) 288) FAHLGREEN & ASSOCIATES, PITTSBURGH

283

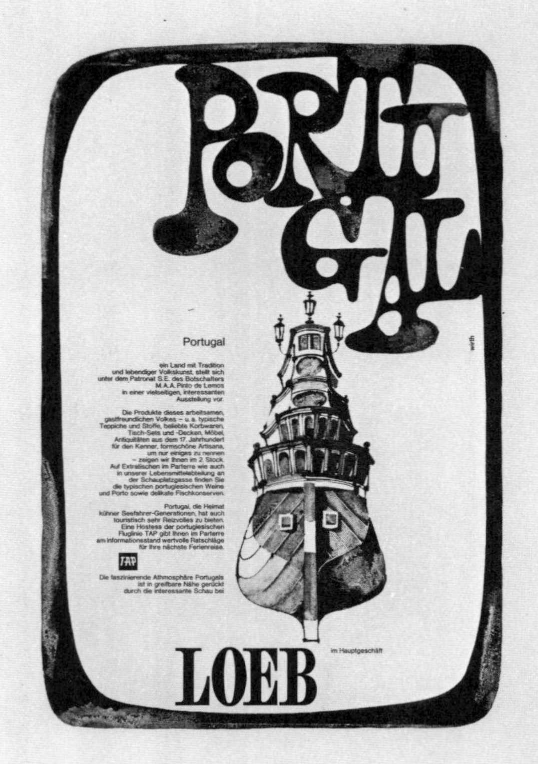

285

284

286

283) Newspaper advertisement offering a *Debenham & Freebody* catalogue as a means of avoiding the Christmas rush. (GB)
284) Black-and-white ad for an autumn church bazaar. (SWI)
285) Newspaper ad for a display of Portuguese goods in a Bernese department store. (SWI)
286) Colour newspaper ad for fashions from *Eaton's* stores. (CAN)
287) 288) Newspaper advertisement and illustration for *Wheeling Dollar* loans. (USA)

283) Inserat für ein Warenhaus, das auf seinen Katalog hinweist, der den Kunden die Weihnachtseinkäufe erleichtern soll. (GB)
284) Inserat für den Herbst-Markt-Bazar der Heilig-Geist-Kirche in Basel. Schwarzweiss. (SWI)
285) Zeitungsinserate für eine Ausstellung portugiesischer Produkte im Warenhaus *Loeb*, Bern. (SWI)
286) Ganzseitiges Zeitungsinserat eines Warenhauses. (CAN)
287) 288) Inserat und Illustration für ein Finanzinstitut. (USA)

283) Annonce de presse suggérant d'utiliser le catalogue d'un grand magasin pour faciliter les achats de Noël. (GB)
284) Annonce en noir pour une vente de charité. (SWI)
285) Annonce de presse pour une exposition de produits portugais dans un grand magasin de Berne. (SWI)
286) Annonce de presse en couleur pour un grand magasin. (CAN)
287) 288) Annonce de presse et illustration pour une société de financement. (USA)

287

Art Director / Directeur artistique:
283) BOB MARCHANT
284) WALTER GRIEDER
285) KURT WIRTH
286) NEIL WHITWORTH
287) 288) RONALD A. LAYPORT

288

Advertisements / Inserate / Annonces

Artist / Künstler / Artiste:

289) MUNENORI KAWAZOE / KAZUKO WATANABE
290) SHIGENORI TANAKA
291) GAIL MITCHEM / MARLON CHAPMAN
292) 293) LUIGI GRENDENE
294) CAROL GANGEMI / LOUISE REEVES

Art Director / Directeur artistique:

290) SHIGENORI TANAKA
291) MARLON CHAPMAN
292) 293) RUEDI KÜLLING
294) ROYSTON T. EVANS

Agency / Agentur / Agence – Studio:

292) 293) ADVICO AG, ZÜRICH

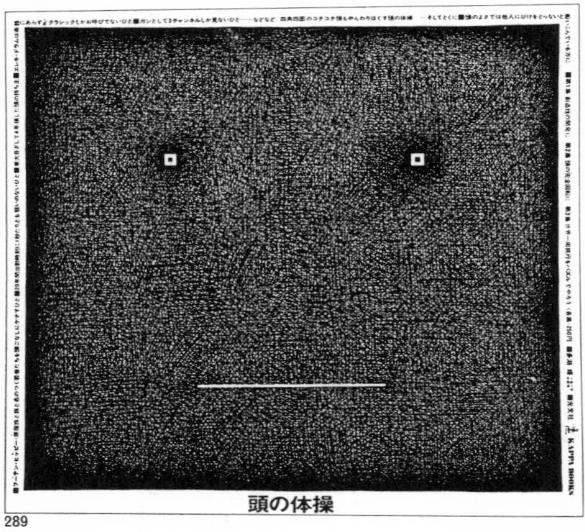

289

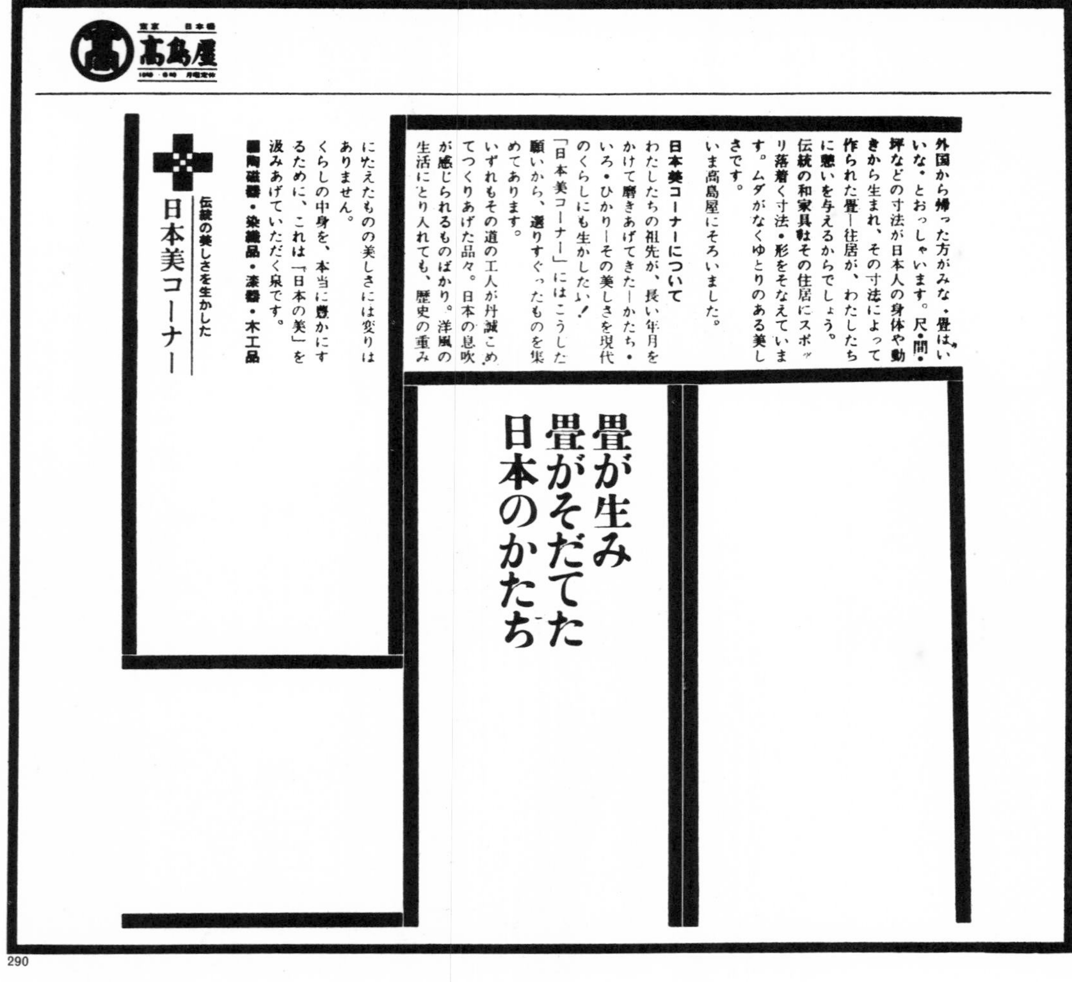

290

289) Black-and-white advertisement for a book of puzzles. (JAP)
290) Newspaper advertisement for a department store. (JAP)
291) Newspaper advertisement for tortoiseshell accessories from *Joseph Magnin* fashion stores. (USA)
292) 293) Newspaper advertisements for modern furniture. (SWI)
294) Newspaper advertisement in colour for *Buster Brown* children's shoes. (USA)

289) Inserat für ein Buch mit Rätselspielen. Schwarzweiss. (JAP)
290) Zeitungsinserat für ein Warenhaus. (JAP)
291) Zeitungsinserat für Mode-Accessoires aus Schildpatt aus den Modehäusern *Joseph Magnin.* (USA)
292) 293) Zeitungsinserate für die *Wohnhilfe,* ein Geschäft für moderne Wohnungseinrichtungen in Zürich. (SWI)
294) Zeitungsinserat für Kinderschuhe. Mehrfarbig. (USA)

289) Annonce pour un recueil de jeux et devinettes. (JAP)
290) Annonce de presse pour un grand magasin. (JAP)
291) Annonce de presse pour des accessoires en carapace de tortue. (USA)
292) 293) Annonces de presse pour un magasin d'ameublement moderne. Noir et blanc. (SWI)
294) Annonce de presse pour des chaussures d'enfants. (USA)

291

292

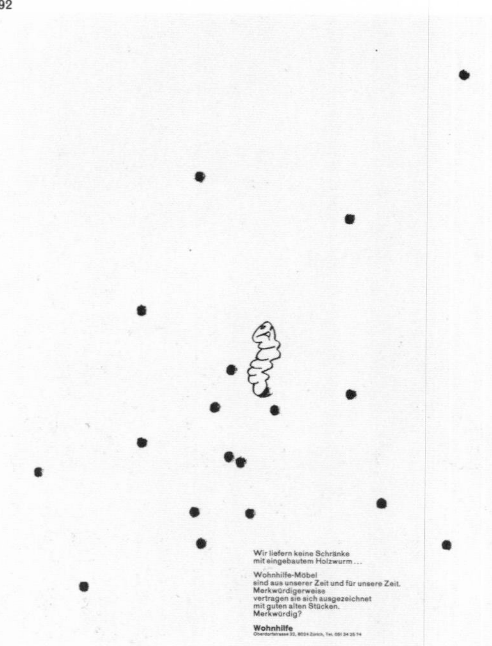

293

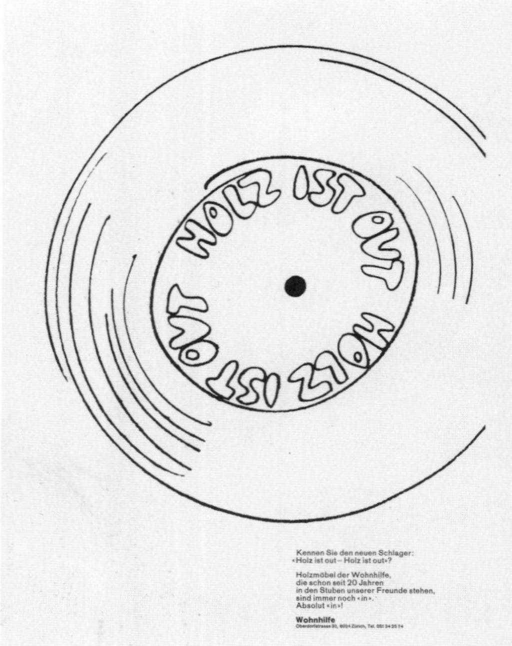

I'M FOR
BUSTER BROWN
We'd campaign for you anytime, Buster Brown.
Your platform of comfortable, great
looking leather shoes with gleaming metal
touches keeps all the girls (and their mothers)
on your side. Oh, Buster Brown, you're the
groovy one. Let's put Tige on the ticket, too!
A. Justine, brassy plate with kiltie trim,
in burning bush brown, 10.50.
B. I.D., chained casual in antique brown tone, 10.50.
C. Carmen, brushed leather step-in, metal buckle
trim, gold, green, or rust, 10.99 and 11.99.
D. Dianne, T-strap pattern with brass-type nail
heads, brown or black, 9.50 to 11.99.
Children's Shoes, Fourth Floor; all stores.
John Wanamaker
294

Artist | Künstler | Artiste:

295) 296) PINO TOVAGLIA
297) ROBERT OSBORN
298) WARREN PFAFF
299)–301) ED RENFRO
302) STEWART BIRBROWER / DON BATTERSHALL

Art Director | Directeur artistique:

295) 296) TERESITA CAMAGNI HANGELDIAN
297) DOUG MAXWELL
298) JOHN LUCCI
299)–301) JOHN DIGNAM
302) DON BATTERSHALL

Agency | Agentur | Agence – Studio:

295) 296) CENTRO S.R.L., MILAN
297) DOYLE, DANE, BERNBACH LTD., LONDON
299)–301) J. WALTER THOMPSON CO., NEW YORK
302) PAPERT, KŒNIG, LOIS, INC., NEW YORK

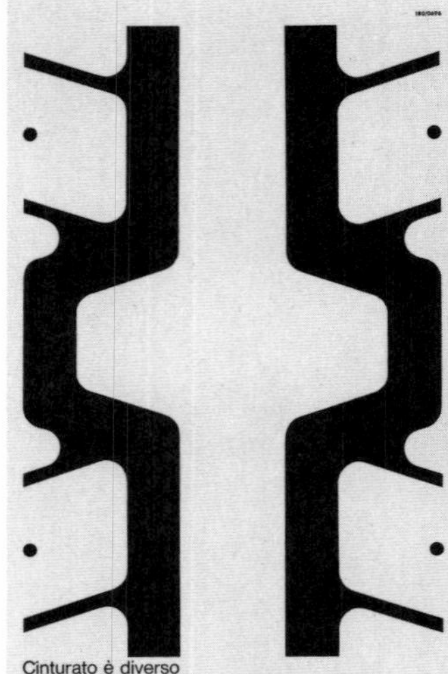

Cinturato è diverso
è un pneumatico radiale interamente tessile
una cintura stringe il pneumatico, ne impedisce le deformazioni dovute alla forza centrifuga
Cinturato è morbido, elastico
i fianchi sono flessibili ma la zona d'impronta è rigida per la massima aderenza al terreno
un battistrada aggressivo, spesso, lamellato
Cinturato aderisce di più, scorre di più, dura di più
Cinturato è sicuro sempre:
in curva, in rettilineo, in velocità, in frenata, sull'asciutto, sul bagnato

per vetture e ora anche per autocarri

il radiale a struttura interna tessile è brevetto Pirelli

CINTURATO
è solo PIRELLI

295

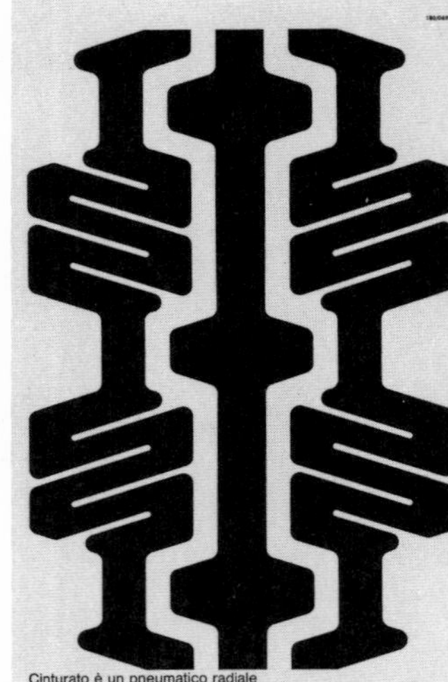

Cinturato è un pneumatico radiale
la geometria della sua struttura, caratterizzata da una cintura inestensibile, lo rende indeformabile fuori della zona d'impronta sulla strada, lo protegge dalle sollecitazioni della forza centrifuga, lo fa durare più a lungo, lo rende più scorrevole, risparmiando carburante
Cinturato è un pneumatico radiale interamente tessile
i fianchi e la cintura sono morbidi e flessibili verticalmente, il pneumatico durante lo schiacciamento è più confortevole e sicuro, assorbe senza danni gli ostacoli della strada
Cinturato è un pneumatico radiale con un battistrada aggressivo; il suo disegno assicura a qualunque velocità una perfetta aderenza in curva, in frenata, in accelerazione, sull'asciutto, sul bagnato, sulla neve
le lamelle orientate in tutte le direzioni danno la massima tenuta di strada; l'alto spessore consente un'elevata resa chilometrica; gli elementi arrotondati danno un consumo regolare

per vetture e ora anche per autocarri

il radiale a struttura interna interamente tessile è brevetto Pirelli

CINTURATO
è solo PIRELLI

296

299

300

301

297

298

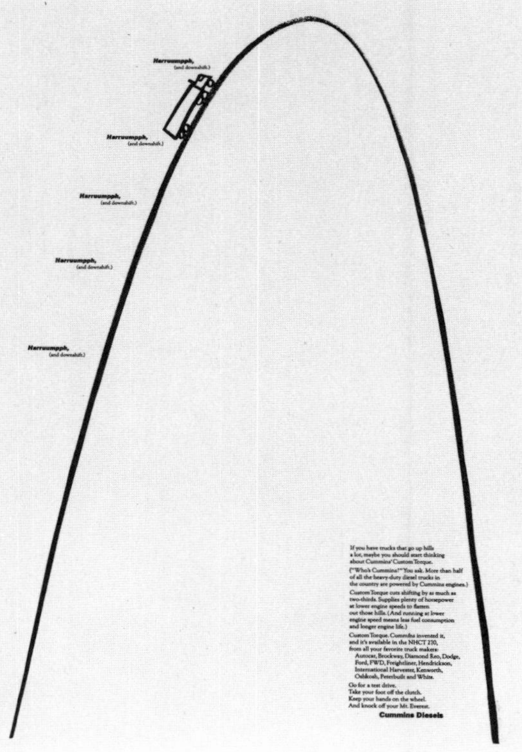

302

295) 296) Newspaper advertisements from a series for *Pirelli* tyres. (ITA)
297) Newspaper advertisement for *Dhobi* raincoats with tear-out linings. Red lining. (USA)
298) Newspaper advertisement for a TV jingle agency. (USA)
299)–301) Illustration and complete advertisements for a car leasing service. (USA)
302) Trade advertisement for a *Cummins* gear torque system for heavy trucks. (USA)

295) 296) Aus einer Serie von Zeitungsinseraten für *Pirelli* Pneus. (ITA)
297) Zeitungsinserat für Regenmäntel mit auswechselbarem Futter. (USA)
298) Zeitungsinserat für eine Agentur, die Musik für Fernsehwerbung produziert. (USA)
299)–301) Illustration und vollständige Inserate für einen Mietwagendienst. (USA)
302) Fachzeitungsinserat für ein Schaltgerät für Lastwagen. (USA)

295) 296) Annonces de presse tirées d'une série pour les pneus *Pirelli*. (ITA)
297) Annonce de presse pour des manteaux de pluie à doublure amovible. Doublure en rouge. (USA)
298) Annonce de presse pour une agence spécialisée dans la musique pour la télévision. (USA)
299)–301) Illustration et annonces pour une agence de location de voitures. (USA)
302) Annonce de revues professionnelles en faveur d'un changement de vitesses spécial pour les poids lourds. (USA)

How to tell if a girl caterpillar is happy...
she's wearing all her Alexis Originals shoes at once! Red and green and yellow and navy and brown and black and grey and wheeeeeeeee – they're tied, buckled and some are made to jump into on the run. There's soft calf. Suede. Suede-and-calf. Shiny patent too! The only place to find them (10.00 to 13.00) is N-M. Children's Shoes, fifth floor, Downtown; NorthPark, mall level and Fort Worth.
Neiman-Marcus
303

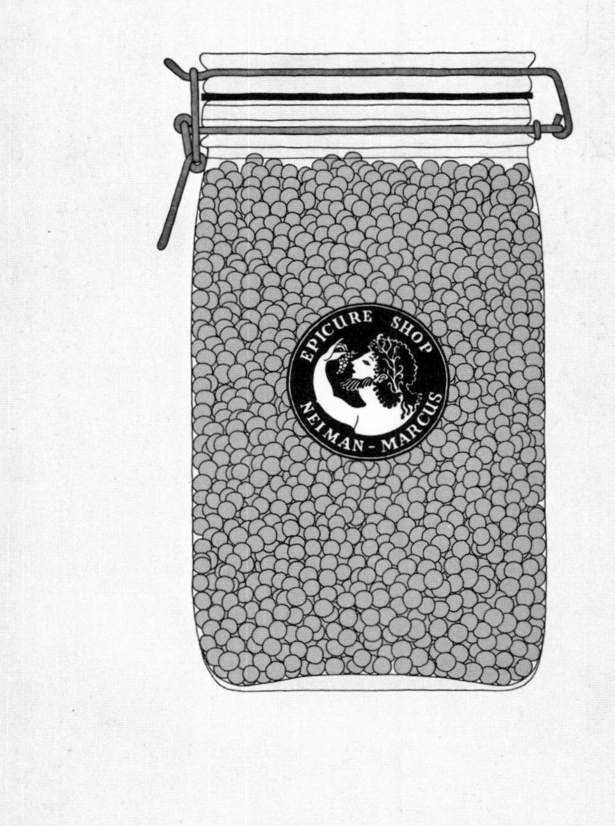

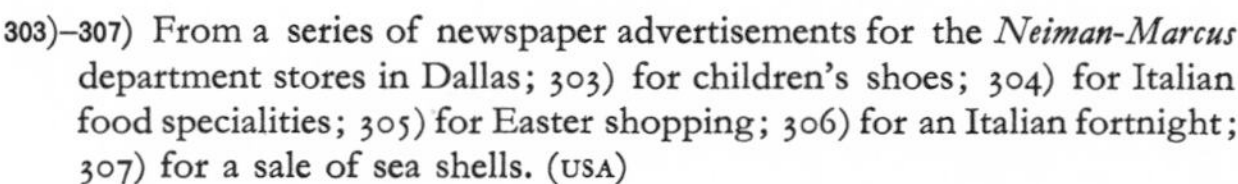

304

NEIMAN-MARCUS

Some of our best customers are big, fuzzy, friendly and have long pink ears. Watch for them.

What better place for Easter bunnies to shop than N-M? Where tomorrow azaleas will blaze and a million enchanting ideas are ready to pop into our new blue butterfly bag. Where giant bonnets float down the escalator to remind you that this is the Easter hats return in a big way. Bunnies are multiplying everywhere in Italian glass, solid brass, Godiva chocolate and marvelous fuzzy stuff to cuddle. Our windows are giant panorama eggs—you peek inside and see the darlingest little girl looks. And how do you like your eggs—spun sugar, porcelain, or marble? Come see for yourself tomorrow; we're twitching with Easter excitement, Downtown and Northpark and Ft. Worth!

305

303)–307) From a series of newspaper advertisements for the *Neiman-Marcus* department stores in Dallas; 303) for children's shoes; 304) for Italian food specialities; 305) for Easter shopping; 306) for an Italian fortnight; 307) for a sale of sea shells. (USA)

303)–307) Aus einer Serie von Zeitungsinseraten für ein Warenhaus in Dallas; 303) für Kinderschuhe; 304) für italienische Delikatessen; 305) für Ostereinkäufe; 306) für eine italienische Verkaufsausstellung; 307) für den Verkauf von Muscheln. (USA)

303)–307) Annonces de presse pour un grand magasin de Dallas: 303) pour les chaussures d'enfants; 304) pour les spécialités culinaires italiennes; 305) pour les achats de Pâques; 306) pour une Quinzaine italienne; 307) pour une vente de coquillages. (USA)

Artist / Künstler / Artiste:

303) DOROTHY MICHAELSON / PATTY KIRTLEY
304) TONY EUBANKS / MARTHA BARRETT
305) TONY EUBANKS
306) DAVID RENNING
307) DOROTHY MICHAELSON / MARTHA BARRETT

Art Director / Directeur artistique:

303)–307) RON FIREBAUGH

Advertisements / Inserate / Annonces

306

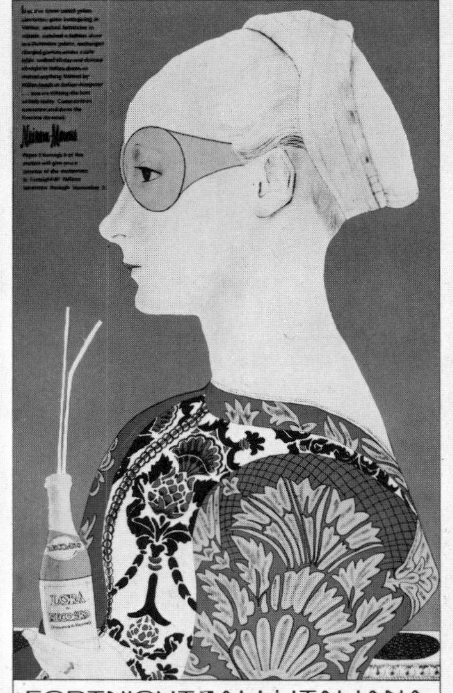

307

The story of two men...one quite small and young, the other quite large and old. They knew each other for about a year. You'll know them forever.
the two of us.
Judith Crist, NBC: "An overwhelming experience. I love 'The Two Of Us'."

309

308

Artist / Künstler / Artiste:

308) 309) STANISLAV ZAGORSKI / ED BRODKIN
310) CHARLES SCHULZ / MICHAEL URIS
311) LOU DORFSMAN
312) JEROME MARTIN / BOB PASQUALINA
313) 314) TOMI UNGERER / BERNIE ZLOTNICK

Art Director / Directeur artistique:

308) 309) JAMES PEARSALL
310) MORT RUBENSTEIN / DAVID NOVEMBER
311) LOU DORFSMAN
312) TONY MANDARINO

Advertisements / Inserate Annonces

You're in Love, Charlie Brown

Good old Charlie Brown has always managed to survive the abuse heaped upon him by his "Peanuts" friends. But can even Charlie hope to survive spring, a certain cute little red-haired girl and (good grief!) falling head over heels in love?

8:30pm, in color CBS©2

310

311

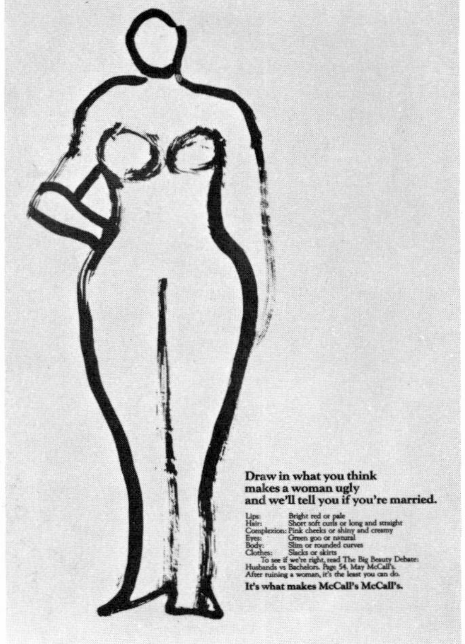

312

Agency / Agentur / Agence – Studio:

308) 309) DIENER, HAUSER, GREENTHAL CO., INC., NEW YORK
312) GREY ADVERTISING, INC., NEW YORK
313) 314) YOUNG & RUBICAM, INC., NEW YORK

313

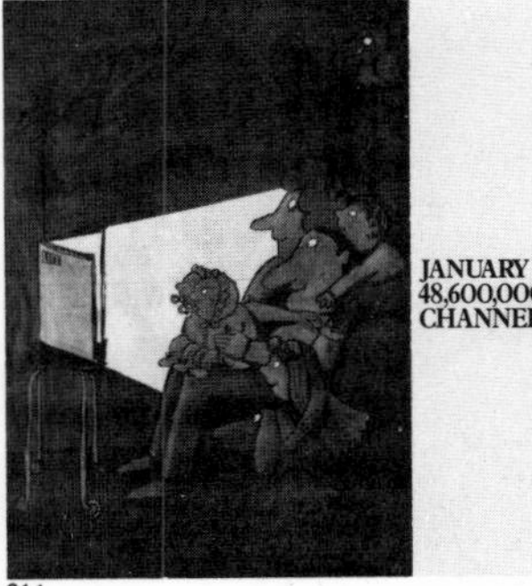

314

308) 309) Illustration and full-page newspaper advertisement for the film *The Two of Us.* (USA)
310) Newspaper ad for a CBS TV programme. (USA)
311) Newspaper advertisement for CBS News. (USA)
312) Newspaper ad for McCALL's magazine. (USA)
313) 314) Illustration and double-page newspaper advertisement for LIFE magazine. (USA)

308) 309) Illustration und ganzseitiges Zeitungsinserat für den Film *Der alte Mann und das Kind.* (USA)
310) Zeitungsinserat für ein Fernsehprogramm. (USA)
311) Zeitungsinserat für die CBS-Nachrichten. (USA)
312) Zeitungsinserat für die Zeitschrift McCALL's. (USA)
313) 314) Illustration und doppelseitiges Zeitungsinserat für die Zeitschrift LIFE. (USA)

308) 309) Illustration et annonce de presse sur page entière pour le film *Le vieil homme et l'enfant.* (USA)
310) Annonce pour un programme à la TV. (USA)
311) Annonce pour les actualités télévisées. (USA)
312) Annonce de presse pour la revue McCALL's. (USA)
313) 314) Illustration et annonce de presse sur double page pour l'hebdomadaire LIFE. (USA)

Advertisements / Inserate / Annonces

Artist / Künstler / Artiste:

315) MASAMITSU YAMANAKA
316) HISAKI HIRAMATSU / TOSHIHARU TABUCHI / HISASHI KONOE
317) MUNENORI KAWAZOE / MITANI KAZUKO WATANABE
318) JOHN ALCORN / PETE NOTO
319) ED RENFRO
320) ROY CARRUTHERS / JOHN HEGARTY
321) SUSAN MAXWELL / JOHN HEGARTY

315) Newspaper advertisement for poetry books. (JAP)
316) Black-and-white advertisement for a book of fairy tales. (JAP)
317) Advertisement for a series of books on the history of thought. (JAP)
318) Newspaper ad to encourage trade advertising in FOOTWEAR NEWS. (USA)
319) Full-page newspaper ad for the *Pan American* airline. (USA)
320) 321) Newspaper advertisements for *El Al* Israel Airlines. (ISR)

315) Zeitungsinserat für Gedichtbände. (JAP)
316) Inserat für ein Märchenbuch. Schwarzweiss. (JAP)
317) Inserat für eine Bücherreihe über die Geschichte des Denkens. (JAP)
318) Zeitungsinserat zur Anzeigenwerbung in einer Fachzeitschrift. (USA)
319) Ganzseitiges Zeitungsinserat für die Fluggesellschaft *Pan American.* (USA)
320) 321) Zeitungsinserate für die Fluggesellschaft *El Al.* (ISR)

315) Annonce de presse pour des recueils de poèmes. (JAP)
316) Annonce en noir pour un recueil de légendes. (JAP)
317) Annonces pour une collection d'ouvrages sur l'histoire de la pensée. (JAP)
318) Annonce pour la publicité dans une revue professionnelle. (USA)
319) Annonce de presse sur page entière pour la compagnie aérienne *Pan American.* (USA)
320) 321) Annonces de presse pour la compagnie israélienne *El Al.* (ISR)

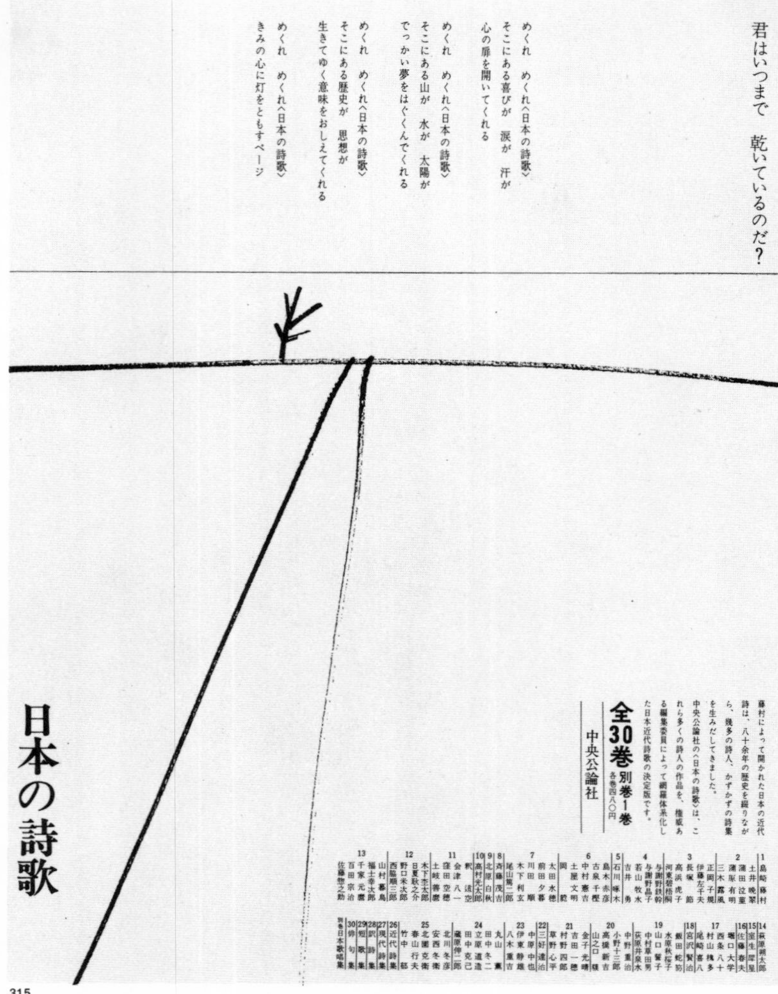

315

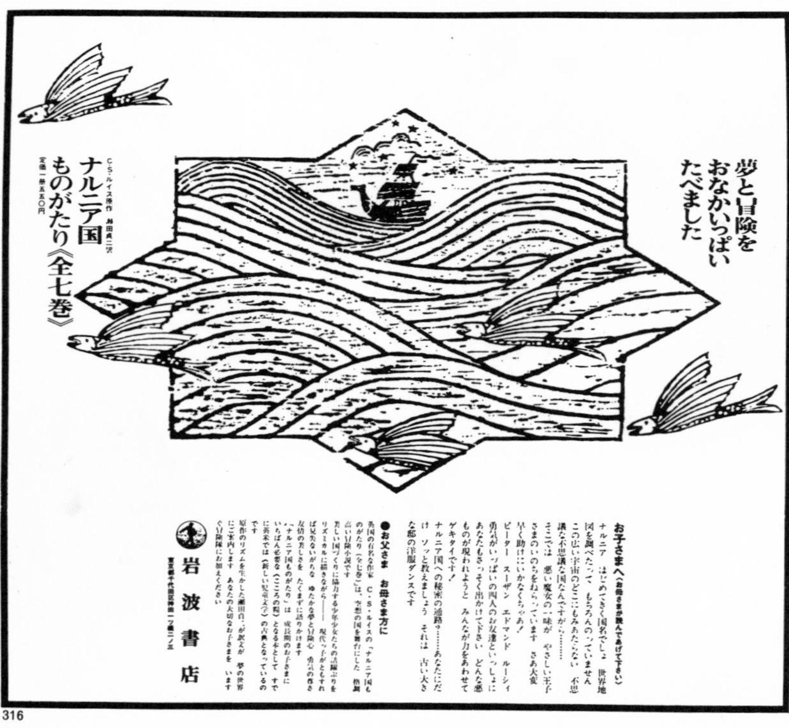

316

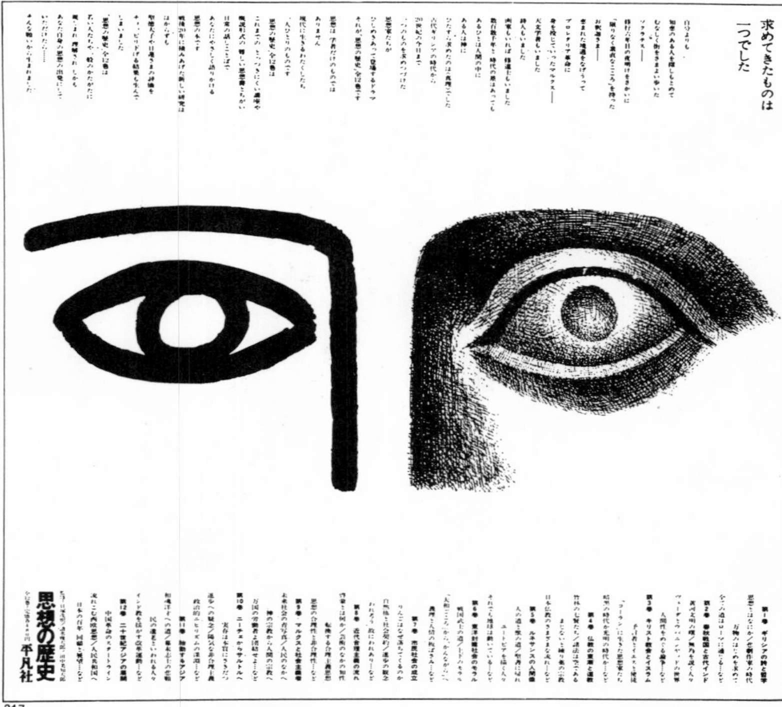

317

Art Director / Directeur artistique:

315) MASAMITSU YAMANAKA
316) TOSHIHARU TABUCHI
318) LEO KAYE
319) RICHARD TARCZYNSKI
320) 321) JOHN HEGARTY

Agency / Agentur / Agence – Studio:

315) ASASHI SHINBUNSHIA, TOKYO
316) IWANAMI SHOTEN, KOBE
318) FAIRCHILD PUBLICATIONS, NEW YORK
319) J. WALTER THOMPSON CO., NEW YORK
320) 321) JOHN COLLINGS & PARTNERS, LONDON

anatomy of a salesman

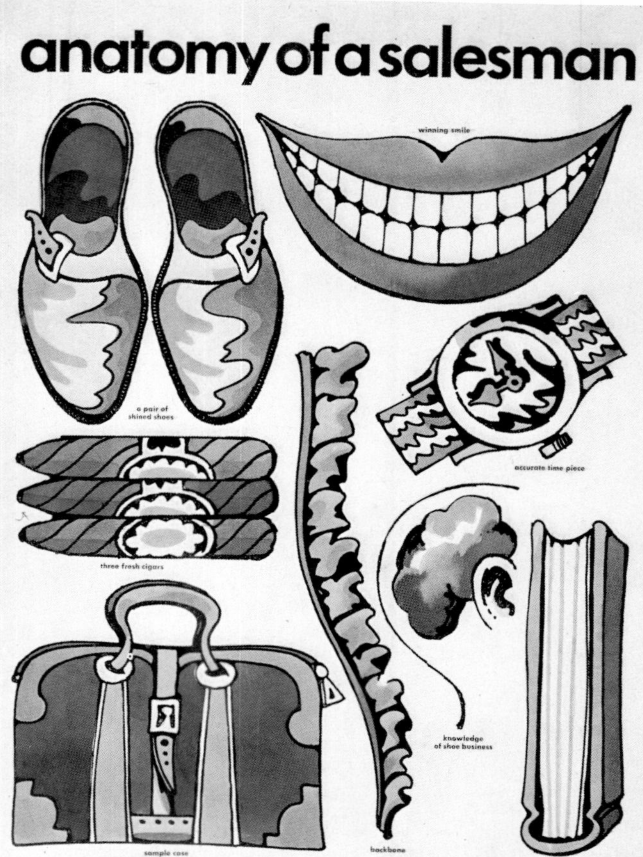

The salesman's job is to sell. These are the tools he uses to make the contact . . . present the line, get in and out fast and on to the next customer. His job is to get the order and frankly, he is not much interested in anything else.

If you are depending on him to build company reputation, discuss promotions and merchandising, tell your company's success and growth story . . . chances are it is not getting done.

The biggest mistake you can make is to just assume that everyone knows your company . . . who you are, what you stand for, your ideas. Or to assume your salesmen are telling the story for you.

Your customers and prospects don't know much about you unless you communicate with them . . . and in the footwear industry the one sure way to talk to them is through advertising in Footwear News. Plan an advertising campaign in FN and you will find everyone who is anyone will see it . . . and will know what your company and your product is all about.

That leaves your salesmen free to sell which is what you hired them for in the first place.

Footwear News
Fairchild Publications inc.

318

Regálele un lugar del mundo.

Nueva York. California. Miami. Europa. Oriente. Alrededor del mundo.

Un viaje con Pan American no sólo recompensará los esfuerzos del estudiante sino que aumentará sus conocimientos. Le mostrará nuevos horizontes y quizás hasta le inspire una especialización.

Las impresiones de un viaje duran toda la vida. Además es un regalo fácil de pagar. ¡Una módica suma inicial . . . y a volar!

Al saberse en manos de Pan American, su estudiante tendrá la íntima satisfacción de haber recibido lo mejor.

Llame a su Agente de Viajes Pan Am® o a nuestras oficinas: Caracas: Puente Urapal y Avenida Urdaneta, Tel. 55-81-01. También oficinas en Maracaibo, Valencia, Barquisimeto, Puerto La Cruz y Puerto Ordaz.

PAN AM®
La línea aérea de mayor experiencia en el mundo

Lo grande es ir con Pan Am

319

Yes, it has been known to rain in Israel.

Once upon a time we had quite a lot of it. Forty days and forty nights by all accounts.

Since then, the weather seems to have cleared up quite a bit. The old millibars, isobars and anti-cyclones etc. are all in our favour.

Most of the country can rely on 9 months uninterrupted sunshine a year. And Eilat, a lush resort on the Red Sea, only gets 5 days rain out of 365.

If you want to bake gently till a golden brown you'll find plenty of beaches to do it on.

We have four seas (Med., Dead, Red and Galilee), scores of sandy beaches and modern resorts like Nathanya, Ashkelon and Herzlia.

When you get browned-off sunbathing there are plenty of other things to see and do.

There are three thousand years of history to browse through. Biblical place names to bring to life. Colourful street markets and fashionable shops. Classical concerts in Roman amphitheatres. Wining, dining and dancing in bars, bistros and discotheques.

And all this is only 4½ hours away from London by EL AL's non-stop Boeings. Any day of the week.

Talk to your local travel agent. He says the nicest things.

Like, 'Yes, sir. Of course you can afford it. Even after devaluation. There are special low cost holidays which include 14 days in a hotel as well as return air fare. Sign here.'

Sign there. And go.

And don't worry about the rain. If it ever happens again everyone will be in the same boat, anyway.

EL AL

EL AL. The Airline of the People of Israel.

320

This year, why not spend Hanukah with the folks at home?

They'll be glad to see you.

Because, this year, Hanukah in Israel is rather special. There hasn't been one like it since the Maccabeans regained the Temple and inaugurated the Festival of Lights.

For 2,108 years Hanukah has been a festival of commemoration. This year it's more a festival of celebration.

Share it with the folks at home. It's not far away.

Board one of EL AL's Boeings, any day of the week, at London. After 4½ hours of comfortable, cosseted flight you'll be in Tel Aviv.

You'll know you're home when you see the lights.

EL AL

EL AL. The Airline of the People of Israel.

321

3

Booklets
Folders
Catalogues
Invitations
Programmes
Annual Reports

Broschüren
Faltprospekte
Kataloge
Einladungen
Programme
Jahresberichte

Brochures
Dépliants
Catalogues
Invitations
Programmes
Rapports annuels

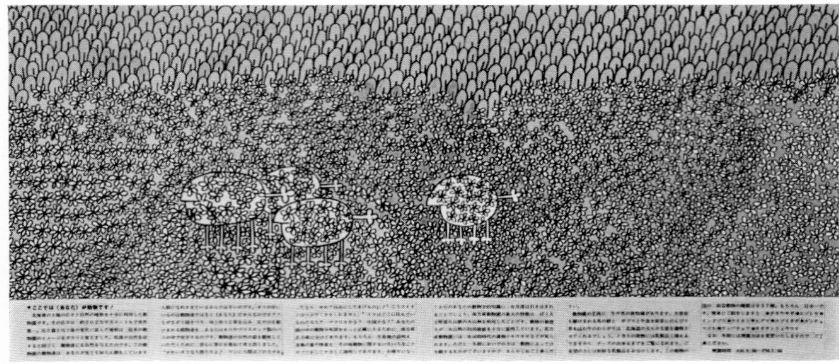

322

323

324

325

322) 323) Pages from a booklet on the Northern National Park. Project. (JAP)
324) Inside of a folder for a paper mill that distributes pin-ups to its customers. (BEL)
325) From a folder about a *Westvaco* book paper. Arabic and Cyrillic characters in colour. (USA)
326) From a folder for International Paper Co. Each panel on a different paper grade. (USA)
327) 328) 328a) Cover and pages of a booklet about *Shell* for new employees. (FIN)
329) Bundle of small folders about various collections of *Armstrong* rugs. (CAN)
330) Cover of a booklet about a *Honeywell* data processing system. (USA)

326

322) 323) Seiten aus einer Broschüre für einen Nationalpark. Entwurf. (JAP)
324) Aus einem Prospekt für eine Papierfabrik, die ihren Kunden auch Pin-ups verschenkt. (BEL)
325) Aus einem Prospekt für *Westvaco* Buchpapier. Arabische und kyrillische Schrift farbig. (USA)
326) Prospekt für eine Papierfabrik. Für jedes Feld wurde ein anderes Papier verwendet. (USA)
327) 328) 328a) Umschlag und Seiten aus einer Broschüre über *Shell* für Neueintretende. (FIN)
329) Bund kleiner Prospekte für die verschiedenen Teppichkollektionen von *Armstrong*. (CAN)
330) Umschlag einer Broschüre für eine Datenverarbeitungsmaschine von *Honeywell*. (USA)

322) 323) Pages d'une brochure en faveur d'un parc national. Maquette. (JAP)
324) Vue d'un dépliant des Papeteries de Virginal SA, Virginal. (BEL)
325) D'un dépliant en faveur d'un papier pour livre. Caractères en couleur. (USA)
326) D'un dépliant pour une fabrique de papier. Papier différent pour chaque volet. (USA)
327) 328) 328a) Couverture et pages d'une brochure *Shell* à l'intention des nouveaux employés. (USA)
329) Liasse de petits dépliants pour les différentes collections de tapis *Armstrong*. (CAN)
330) Couverture d'une brochure décrivant un nouvel ordinateur *Honeywell*. (USA)

328a

327

328

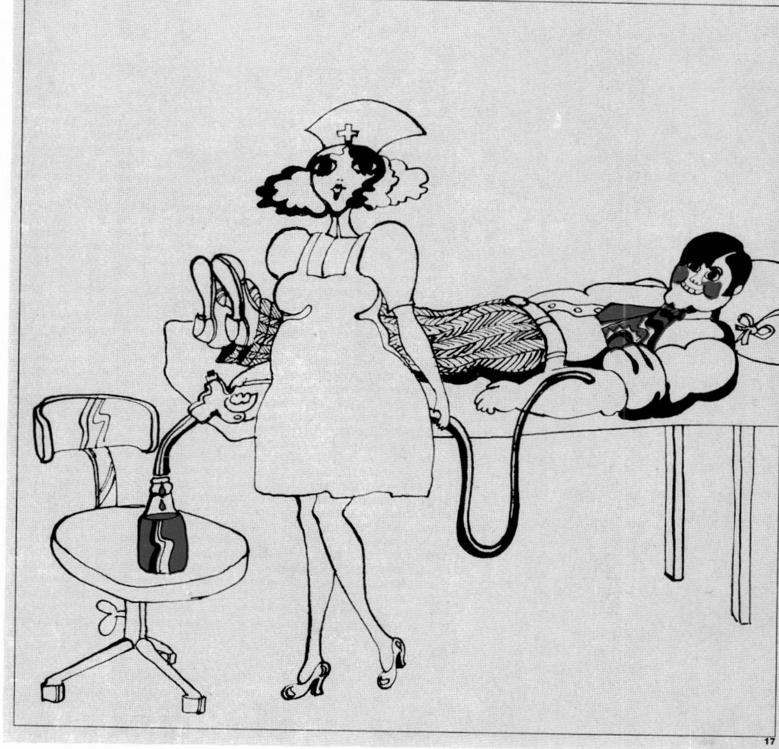

329

330

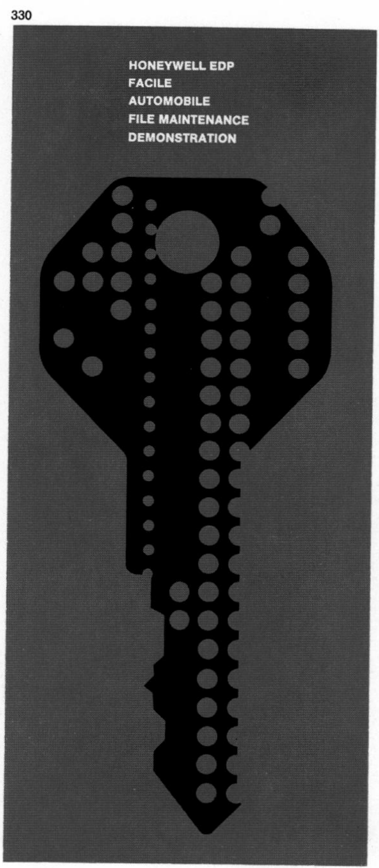

Artist / Künstler / Artiste:

322) 323) TOSHIHIKO TAKAHASHI / KATSUO KUBOTA
324) CHARLES ROHONYI
325) ALVIN EISENMAN / BRADBURY THOMPSON
326) STANLEY GLAUBACH / I. D. MILLER
327) 328) 328a) HEIKKI KASTEMAA
329) STUART ASH
330) ROBERT CIPRIANI

Art Director / Directeur artistique:

322) 323) TOSHIHIKO TAKAHASHI
324) CARLOS TIMSONNET
325) BRADBURY THOMPSON
326) IRVING D. MILLER
329) STUART ASH
330) GAEL BURNS

Agency / Agentur / Agence – Studio:

326) IRVING D. MILLER, NEW YORK
327) 328) 328a) SEK ADVERTISING, HELSINKI
329) GOTTSCHALK + ASH LTD., MONTREAL
330) GUNN ASSOC., BOSTON

Booklets / Prospekte
Prospectus

331

Artist / Künstler / Artiste:

331) ROBERT V. PAGANUCCI
332) 334) 335) ARTHUR BODEN
333) CARL MILLER
336) IAN BRADBERY
337) RICHARD ROGERS
338) JACK REICH
339) 340) GAVIN HEALEY

Art Director / Directeur artistique:

331) ROBERT V. PAGANUCCI
332) 334) 335) ARTHUR BODEN
333) CARL MILLER
336) IAN BRADBERY
337) 338) RICHARD ROGERS
339) 340) GAVIN HEALEY

Agency / Agentur / Agence – Studio:

339) 340) HEALEY MILLS ASSOC., LONDON

332

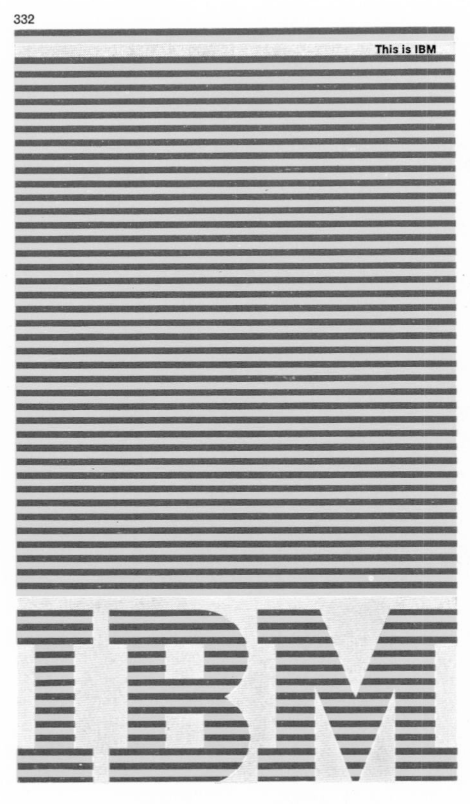

333

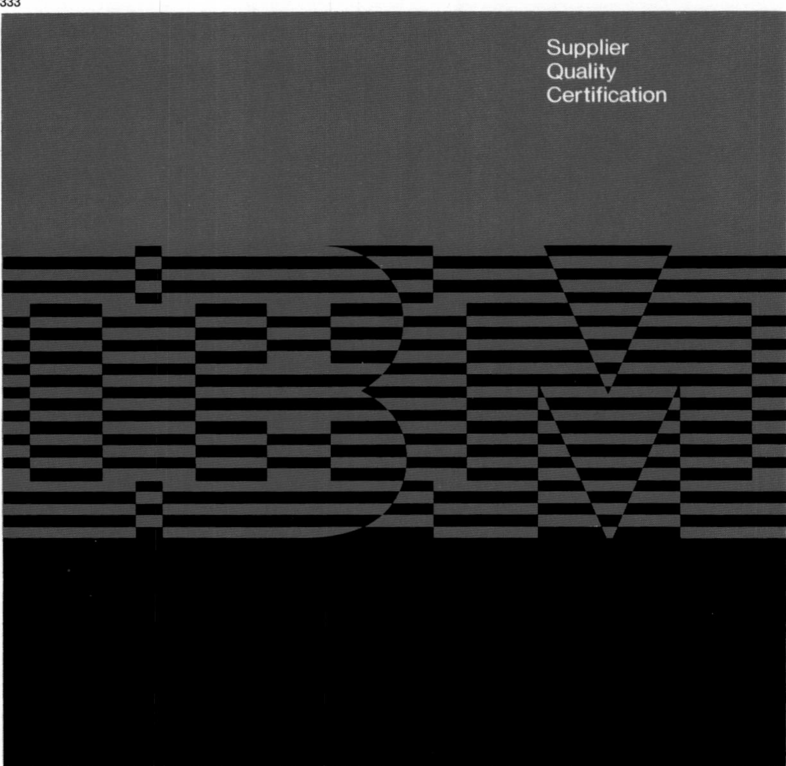

335

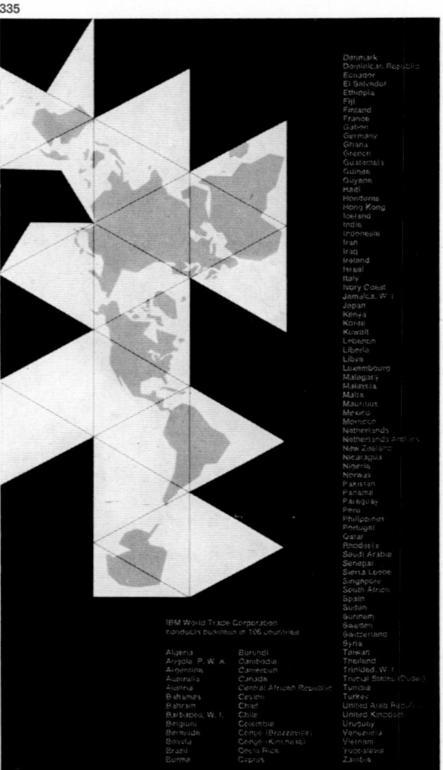

336

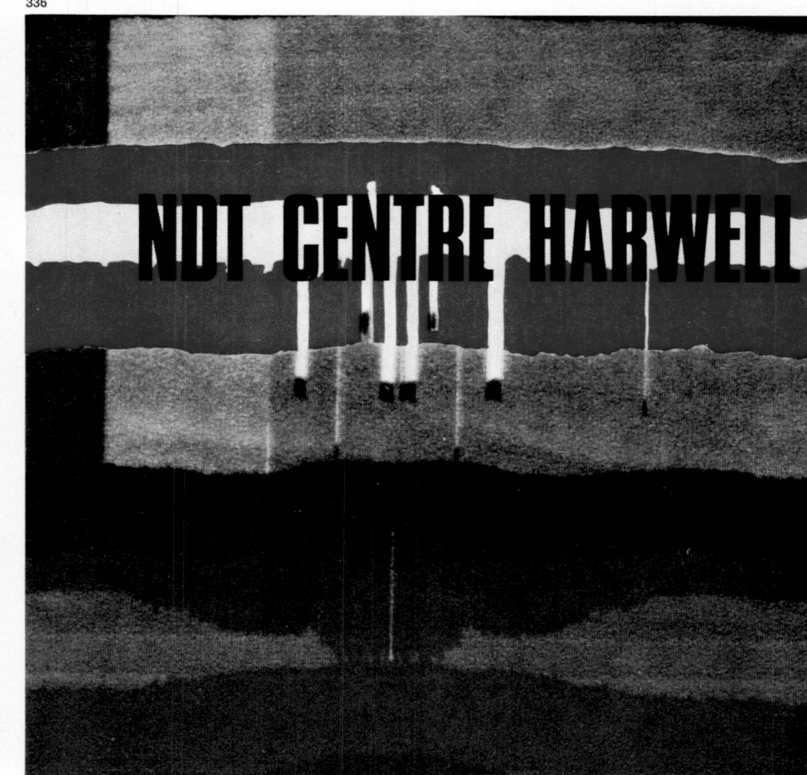

331) From the cover of an IBM booklet. (USA)
332) 335) Cover and page of a brochure about IBM for new employees. (USA)
333) Cover of an IBM brochure about supplier quality control. (USA)
334) Cover of a folder about an IBM dinner. White on orange. (USA)
336) Cover of a brochure about a test centre of the U.K.A.E.A. (GB)
337) 338) Two of a set of cards announcing an IBM exhibition. (USA)
339) 340) Spreads from a series of IBM booklets about computers. (USA)

331) Ausschnitt aus dem Umschlag einer Broschüre für IBM. (USA)
332) 335) Umschlag und Seite aus einer Broschüre über IBM. (USA)
333) Umschlag einer Broschüre für IBM über Qualitätsüberwachung. (USA)
334) Umschlag einer Menukarte für eine IBM-Einladung. (USA)
336) Umschlag einer Broschüre über ein Testzentrum der Atombehörde. (GB)
337) 338) Aus einer Serie von Einladungskarten für eine Ausstellung. (USA)
339) 340) Seiten aus einer Serie von IBM-Broschüren. (USA)

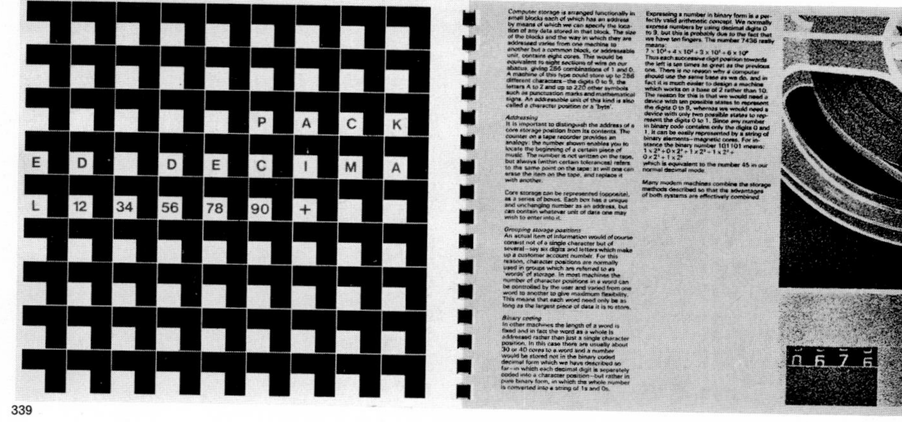

339

334

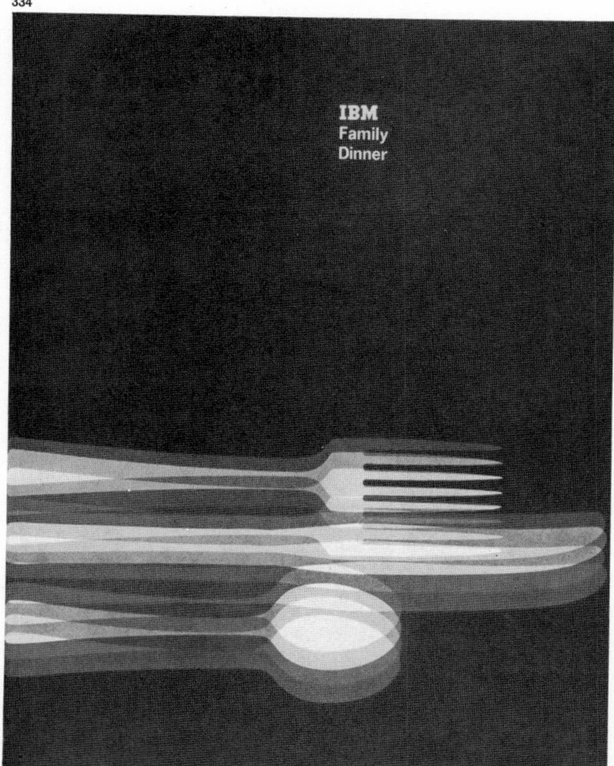

340

337

338

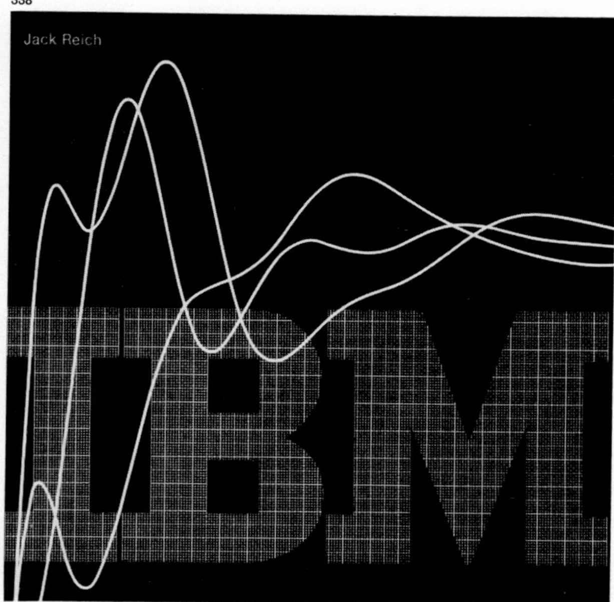

331) 333) Couvertures de brochures IBM. (USA)
332) 335) D'une brochure IBM à l'intention des nouveaux employés. (USA)
334) Couverture du menu d'un banquet IBM. Blanc sur orange. (USA)
336) Couverture d'une brochure sur un centre de recherches atomiques. (GB)
337) 338) D'une série d'invitations à une exposition IBM. (USA)
339) 340) Pages d'une série de brochures IBM. (USA)

Artist | Künstler | Artiste:

341) 342) TOM GEISMAR
343) RALPH COBURN
344) ANDRÉ DAHAN
345) JOE A.WATSON
346) JOHN DOLBY
347) 349) ROBERT CIPRIANI
348) HENRY WOLF
350) FRANCESCO MILANI
351) JOAN & BRYCE BROWNING

Art Director | Directeur artistique:

341) 342) TOM GEISMAR
344) ALAIN MOUNIER
345) ROCCO YVERVASI
346) JOHN DOLBY
347) 349) GAEL BURNS
348) JAMES MIHO
350) FRANCESCO MILANI
351) JOAN & BRYCE BROWNING

Agency | Agentur | Agence – Studio:

341) 342) CHERMAYEFF & GEISMAR ASSOC., NEW YORK
344) EDITIONS PUBLICIS, PARIS
345) FALLON, WATSON & GIURLANDO, INC., NEW YORK
346) UNIMARK INTERNATIONAL, CHICAGO
347) 349) GUNN ASSOC., BOSTON
348) NEEDHAM, HARPER & STEERS, INC., NEW YORK
350) FRANCESCO MILANI, BELLINZONA

341

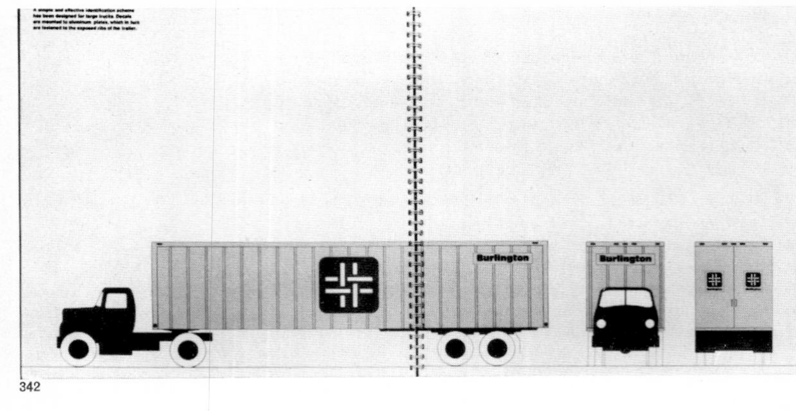

342

343

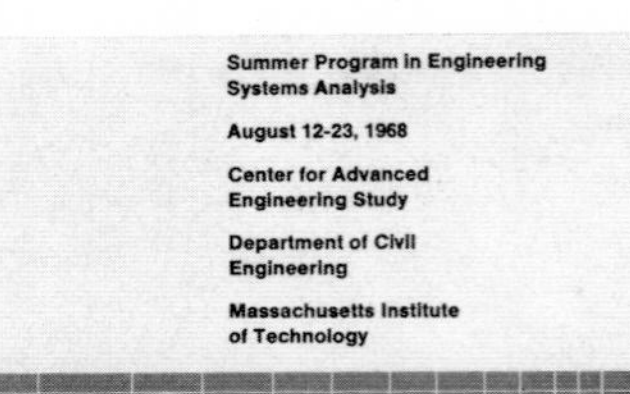

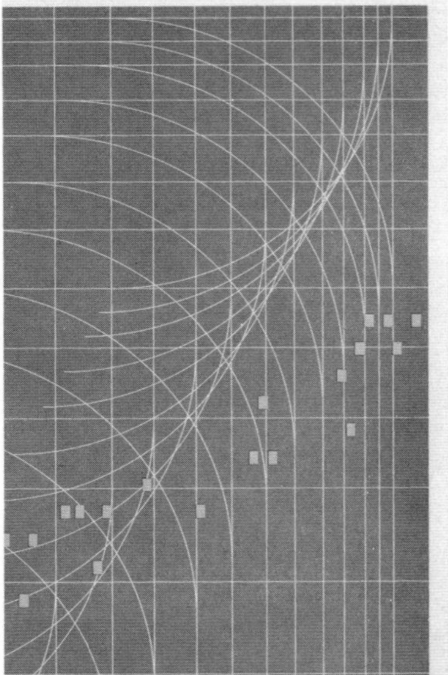

344

347

349

348

341) 342) Cover and double spread of a design manual for Burlington Industries, textile manufacturers. (USA)
343) Cover of a folder about an M.I.T. engineering programme. Green, vermilion and black. (USA)
344) Cover of a brochure about a new residential estate. Green shades. (FRA)
345) Cover of a *Xerox* instruction booklet. (USA)
346) Mailer to introduce a new furniture line of the Corry Jamestown Corporation to dealers. (USA)
347) 349) Spread and page in black and silver from a *Honeywell* booklet on a computer system. (USA)
348) Spread from *Inspiration*, a booklet issued regularly by Champion Papers, here devoted to the circus. (USA)
350) Cover of a folder about sales stands. (SWI)
351) Folder for the insurance company Industrial Indemnity Co. Full colour. (USA)

345

346

350

351

341) 342) Umschlag und Doppelseite aus einem Gestaltungshandbuch für Burlington Industries. (USA)
343) Prospekt über Kurse an einer Hochschule. (USA)
344) Umschlag einer Broschüre über Wohnbauten. (FRA)
345) Umschlag einer Broschüre von *Xerox*. (USA)
346) Werbesendung für eine Möbelfabrik. (USA)
347) 349) Doppelseite und Seite in Schwarz und Silber aus einem Prospekt für *Honeywell*-Rechenmaschinen. (USA)
348) Doppelseite aus einer Broschüre, die von einer Papierfabrik herausgegeben wird. (USA)
350) Prospekt für Verkaufsständer von Plastifil SA, Mendrisio. (SWI)
351) Prospekt für eine Versicherungsgesellschaft. (USA)

341) 342) Couverture et double page d'un répertoire du groupe industriel textile Burlington. (USA)
343) Couverture en couleur d'un prospectus pour un cours de vacances dans une université. (USA)
344) Couverture d'une brochure Gefic, Paris. (FRA)
345) Couverture d'une brochure *Xerox*. (USA)
346) Publicité directe d'une fabrique de meubles. (USA)
347) 349) D'un prospectus pour des ordinateurs. (USA)
348) Double page d'une brochure publiée par une fabrique de papier, numéro consacré au cirque. (USA)
350) Dépliant pour des comptoirs en plastique. (SWI)
351) Dépliant pour une compagnie d'assurance. (USA)

352

352) Invitation to the stand of an electrotechnical company at Milan Fair. (ITA)
353) 354) Cover and spread from a booklet about a Nuffield Mathematics Teaching Project in which children report on how they built a duckpond. (GB)
355) Cover of an album of twelve early posters. Dark brown and pale blue on beige. (ITA)
356) 357) Brochure with cut-outs and full-colour illustration, using Botticelli's *Birth of Venus* to introduce a new *Reed* coated paper. (GB)

352) Einladung zum Besuch des Verkaufsstandes eines elektrotechnischen Unternehmens an der Mailändermesse. (ITA)
353) 354) Umschlag und Doppelseite aus einer Broschüre über einen Lehrplan für Mathematik, worin Schulkinder beschreiben, wie sie einen Ententeich bauten. (GB)
355) Umschlag eines Plakatalbums. Dunkelbraun und hellblau auf beigem Grund. (ITA)
356) 357) Broschüre mit ausgeschnittenen Quadraten. Unter Verwendung von Botticellis *Geburt der Venus* wird ein neues Kunstdruckpapier lanciert. (GB)

352) Invitation à visiter le stand d'une société électro-technique à la Foire de Milan. (ITA)
353) 354) Couverture et double page d'une brochure sur une méthode d'enseignement des mathématiques: les élèves expliquent comment ils ont construit une mare pour les canards. (GB)
355) Couverture d'un album renfermant douze vieilles affiches, publié par Arti Grafiche Ricordi, Milan. Marron et bleu clair sur beige. (ITA)
356) 357) Brochure présentant un nouveau papier couché avec une reproduction de la *Naissance de Vénus* de Botticelli. Découpes en carrés et illustration en couleur. (GB)

353

354

355

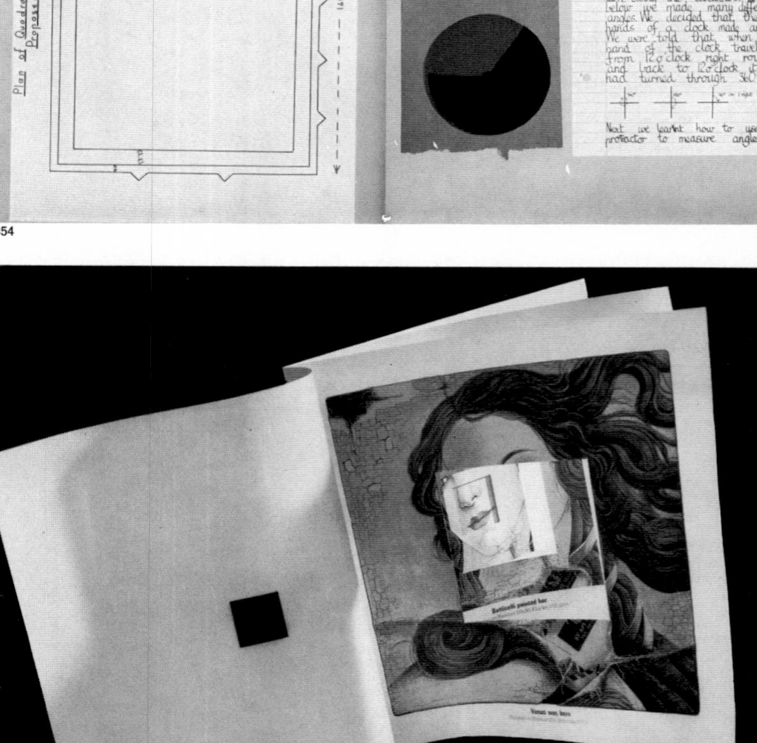
356

Artist / Künstler / Artiste:

352) VENIERO BERTOLOTTI
353) 354) THE CHILDREN OF LADY MARGARET SCHOOL
355) GIANCARLO BUONFINO
356) LOU KLEIN
357) ILENE ASTRAHAN/LOU KLEIN

Art Director / Directeur artistique:

352) VENIERO BERTOLOTTI
353) 354) IVAN DODD
355) GIANCARLO BUONFINO
356) 357) LOU KLEIN

Agency / Agentur / Agence – Studio:

352) STUDIO 4, MILAN
353) 354) DODD+DODD, LONDON
355) STUDIO BUONFINO, MILAN
356) 357) CHARLES HOBSON & GREY, LONDON

357

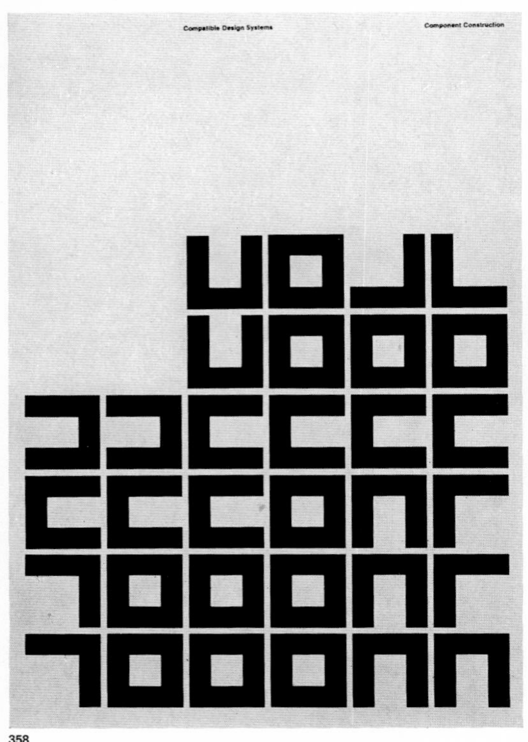

358

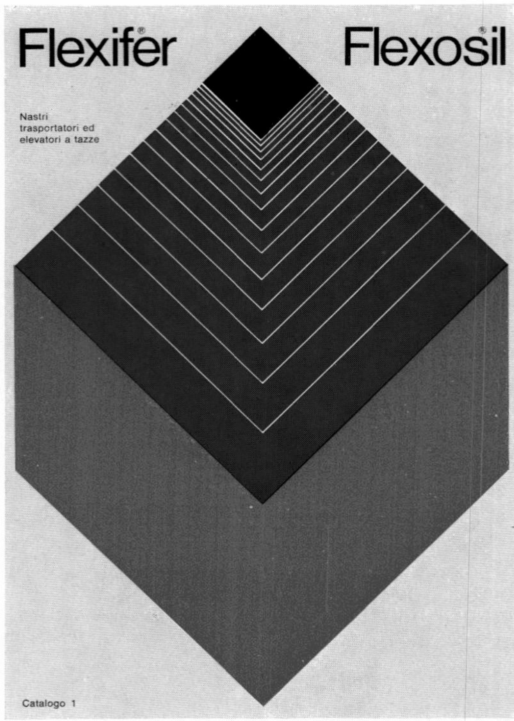

359

360

Artist | Künstler | Artiste:

358) BRUCE MONTGOMERY
359) HANS KNOPFLI
360) ERNST ROCH / ROLF HARDER
361) CROSBY / FLETCHER / FORBES
362)–364) SIMMS TABACK
365) IAN PERCIVAL
366) BARRY O'DWYER
367) 368) DAVE HOLT / JAMES VAN NOY

Art Director | Directeur artistique:

358) BRUCE MONTGOMERY
359) TERESITA CAMAGNI HANGELDIAN
360) ERNST ROCH / ROLF HARDER
361) CROSBY / FLETCHER / FORBES
362)–364) NORM SEIGEL
365) JOHN BLACKBURN
366) BARRY O'DWYER
367) 368) DENNIS S. JUETT

362

363

365

366

Booklets / Prospekte / Prospectus

361

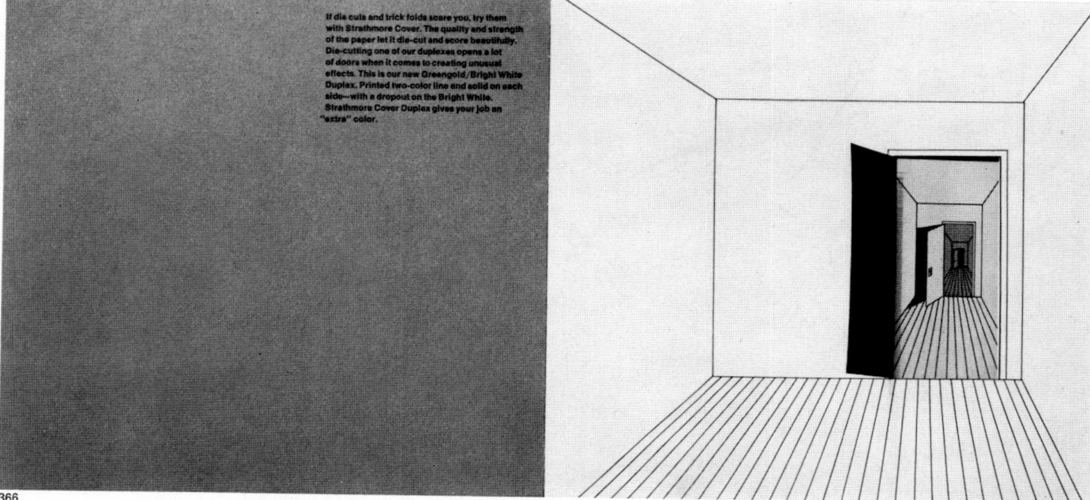

366

368

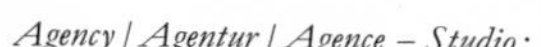

Agency / Agentur / Agence – Studio:

358) BRUCE MONTGOMERY & ASSOC., SAN FRANCISCO
359) CENTRO S.R.L., MILAN
360) DESIGN COLLABORATIVE, MONTREAL
361) CROSBY/FLETCHER/FORBES, LONDON
362)–364) LAMPERT ADV., NEW YORK
365) SMITH & JULIUS PTY. LTD., SYDNEY
367) 368) DENNIS S. JUETT, LA CANADA, CALIF.

358) Cover of a folder about the modular building components of Compatible Design Systems. (USA)
359) Booklet on *Pirelli* conveyor belts. (ITA)
360) Cover of a booklet about the pulp and paper industry, for distribution to students. (CAN)
361) Cover of a brochure on *Pirelli* cables. (ITA)
362)–364) Cover (with holes), page and spread (open door) of a booklet on *Strathmore* papers. (USA)
365) Cover of a folder about an appetite suppressant made by Smith, Kline & French. (AUL)
366) Folder about a vitamin product of British Drug Houses Ltd. Green lettering. (GB)
367) 368) Inside and outside spread of a full-colour folder on *Franciscan Masterpiece* china. (USA)

358) Umschlag eines Prospektes für vorfabrizierte Bauelemente. (USA)
359) Broschüre für Förderbänder von *Pirelli*. (ITA)
360) Broschüre über die Papierindustrie. (CAN)
361) Umschlag einer Broschüre für *Pirelli*-Kabel. (ITA)
362)–364) Umschlag (mit Perforierungen), Seite und Doppelseite für eine Papierfabrik. (USA)
365) Umschlag eines Prospektes für ein appetithemmendes Mittel. (AUL)
366) Prospekt für ein Vitamin-Präparat. (GB)
367) 368) Faltprospekt für Porzellan. (USA)

358) Couverture d'un dépliant pour des éléments de construction préfabriqués. (USA)
359) Brochure pour les bandes transporteuses de la Pirelli S.p.A., Milan. (ITA)
360) Brochure sur l'industrie du papier. (CAN)
361) Prospectus pour les câbles *Pirelli*. (ITA)
362)–364) Brochure pour une fabrique de papier. (USA)
365) Dépliant pour une préparation destinée à réduire l'appétit. (AUL)
366) Dépliant pour un produit vitaminé. (GB)
367) 368) Dépliant pour de la vaisselle. (USA)

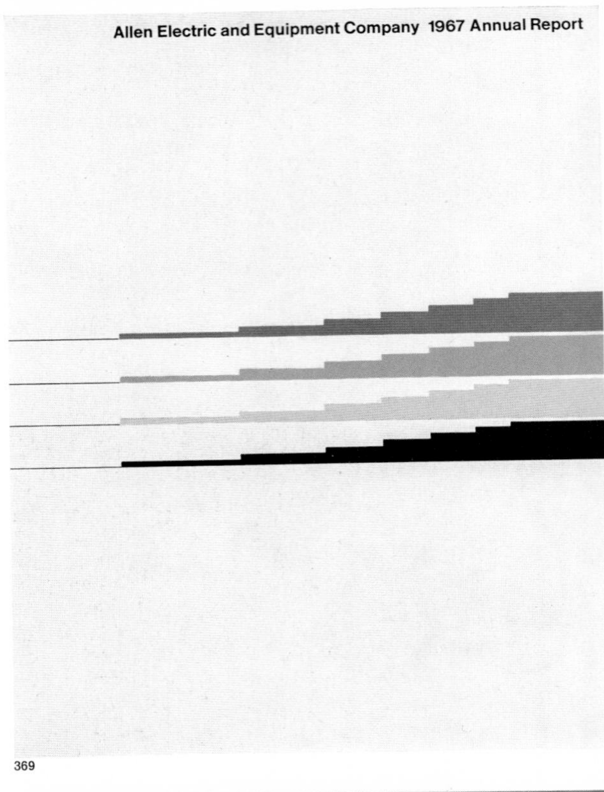

369

370

372

373

369) Annual report of the Allen Electric and Equipment Co., Chicago. Four colours. (USA)
370) Folder for reports of the Univision Corp., film producers. (USA)
371) 375) Cover and double spread from a report on the RCA annual meeting. Black and white. (USA)
372) Report on Canadian publishing for John Deyell Ltd. (USA)
373) Annual report of the French *Esso* company. Blue lettering. (FRA)
374) 376) Illustration in two colours and spread from the annual report of the National Boulevard Bank of Chicago. (USA)
377) Spread from an annual report of Broadway-Hale Stores, Inc. (USA)

369) Jahresbericht für eine elektrotechnische Fabrik. Mehrfarbig. (USA)
370) Umschlag für Berichte der Univision Corp., einer Filmproduktionsgesellschaft in Boston. (USA)
371) 375) Umschlag und Doppelseite aus einem Bericht über die Jahresversammlung der Radio Corporation of America. Schwarzweiss. (USA)
372) Bericht über das Verlagswesen in Kanada. Grau, rot und schwarz. (USA)
373) Jahresbericht für Esso Standard S.A.F. Blaue Schrift. (FRA)
374) 376) Zweifarbige Illustration und Doppelseite aus dem Jahresbericht einer Bank. (USA)
377) Doppelseite aus dem Jahresbericht eines Modehauses. (USA)

371

375

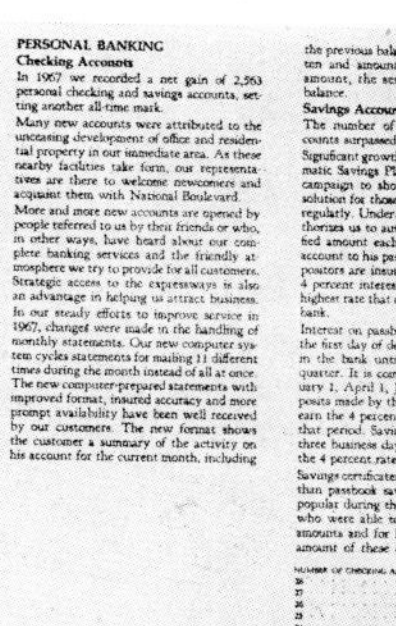

PERSONAL BANKING
Checking Accounts

In 1967 we recorded a net gain of 2,563 personal checking and savings accounts, setting another all-time mark.

Many new accounts were attributed to the unceasing development of office and residential property in our immediate area. As these nearby facilities take form, our representatives are there to welcome newcomers and acquaint them with National Boulevard.

More and more new accounts are opened by people referred to us by their friends or who, in other ways, have heard about our complete banking services and the friendly atmosphere we try to provide for all customers. Strategic access to the expressways is also an advantage in helping us attract business.

In our steady efforts to improve service in 1967, changes were made in the handling of monthly statements. Our new computer system cycles statements for mailing 11 different times during the month instead of all at once. The new computer-prepared statements with improved format, insured accuracy and more prompt availability have been well received by our customers. The new format shows the customer a summary of the activity on his account for the current month, including the previous balance, number of checks written and amount, number of deposits and amount, the service charge, and current balance.

Savings Accounts

The number of new passbook savings accounts surpassed any previous year.

Significant growth was also noted in the Automatic Savings Plan following a promotional campaign to show this method as an easy solution for those who have difficulty saving regularly. Under this plan, the customer authorizes us to automatically transfer a specified amount each month from his checking account to his passbook savings account. Depositors are insured up to $15,000. We pay 4 percent interest on passbook savings, the highest rate that can be paid by a commercial bank.

Interest on passbook savings is earned from the first day of deposit if the savings remain in the bank until the end of the calendar quarter. It is compounded and paid on January 1, April 1, July 1, and October 1. Deposits made by the tenth day of the quarter earn the 4 percent rate from the first day of that period. Savings withdrawn in the last three business days of any quarter still earn the 4 percent rate for that period.

Savings certificates, which pay higher interest than passbook savings, became increasingly popular during the past year among persons who were able to commit money in larger amounts and for longer periods. The dollar amount of these certificates outstanding at

376

374

Artist | Künstler | Artiste:

369) EDWARD HUGHES
370) DIETMAR R. WINKLER
371) 375) MARK ENGLISH/SHELDON SEIDLER
372) A. NORMAN LAW, JR.
373) BRUNO LE SOURD
374) 376) PITT GROUP/DON TROUSDELL
377) MAURICE YANEZ

Art Director | Directeur artistique:

369) EDWARD HUGHES
370) DIETMAR R. WINKLER
371) 375) SHELDON SEIDLER
372) A. NORMAN LAW, JR.
373) J. B. BRUANT
377) ROBERT MILES RUNYAN

Agency | Agentur | Agence – Studio:

369) EDWARD HUGHES DESIGN, CHICAGO
371) 375) SHELDON SEIDLER, NEW YORK
372) ARTHUR D. LITTLE, INC., CAMBRIDGE, MASS.
377) ROBERT MILES RUNYAN & ASSOC., LOS ANGELES

377

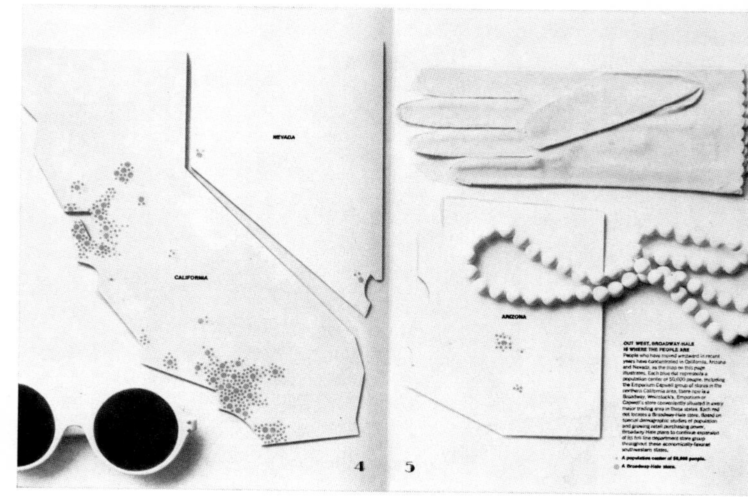

369) Compte rendu d'exercice d'une fabrique d'équipement électrique. (USA)
370) Pochette pour les rapports de l'Univision Corp., une société de production cinématographique de Boston. (USA)
371) 375) Couverture et double page d'un rapport sur l'assemblée annuelle d'une société de radiodiffusion. Noir et blanc. (USA)
372) Rapport sur l'édition au Canada. Gris, rouge et noir. (USA)
373) Compte rendu d'exercice de l'Esso Standard, Courbevoie. Texte en bleu. (FRA)
374) 376) Illustration en deux couleurs et double page du compte rendu d'exercice d'une banque de Chicago. (USA)
377) Double page du rapport annuel d'une maison de confection. (USA)

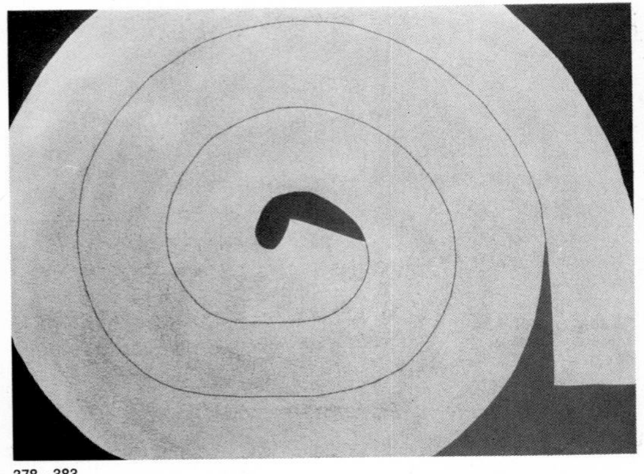

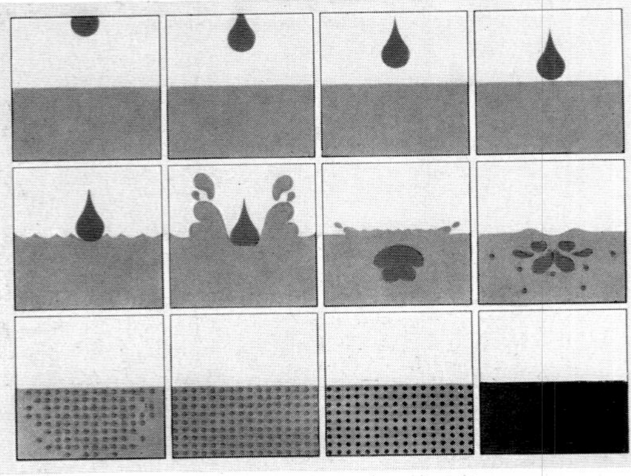

378–383

Artist / Künstler / Artiste:

378)–385) APPELBAUM & CURTIS, INC.
386) MARKUS J. LÖW
387) RANDALL HOFFELD
388) 389) GIULIO CITTATO
390) SEYMOUR CHWAST/MILTON GLASER

Art Director / Directeur artistique:

378)–385) HARVEY HERMAN
386) MARKUS J. LÖW
387)–389) JOHN MASSEY
390) HAL JOSEPHS

Agency / Agentur / Agence – Studio:

378)–385) COMPLAN, INC., NEW YORK
386) GEIGY CORPORATE ART SERVICES, ARDSLEY, N.Y.
390) HENDERSON & ROLL, INC., NEW YORK

386

388

389

Banners, traditionally one of the most exciting forms of public art, are also the most eloquent spokesmen of the human condition. Like man himself, the banner is both rooted to the earth and inclined freely toward the heavens.
Banners express the continual dynamic between physical and spiritual. Grounded, they float free in kinetic excitement from their point of static mooring.

Center designers created a series of banners for Chicago's Civic Center Plaza. They transform the plaza into a multi-use environment, humanizing the seat of government, converting a neutral expanse of steel, stone, and glass into a fanciful playground.
The banners soar with the wind, evolving a litany of shapes, carving out of the sky the aspirations of a city self-consciously in quest of its destiny.
Chicago's banners celebrate the loftiness of human ambition, grounded in human experience. The proud declarative, "I Will," billows with each gust that sweeps the Civic Center Plaza.

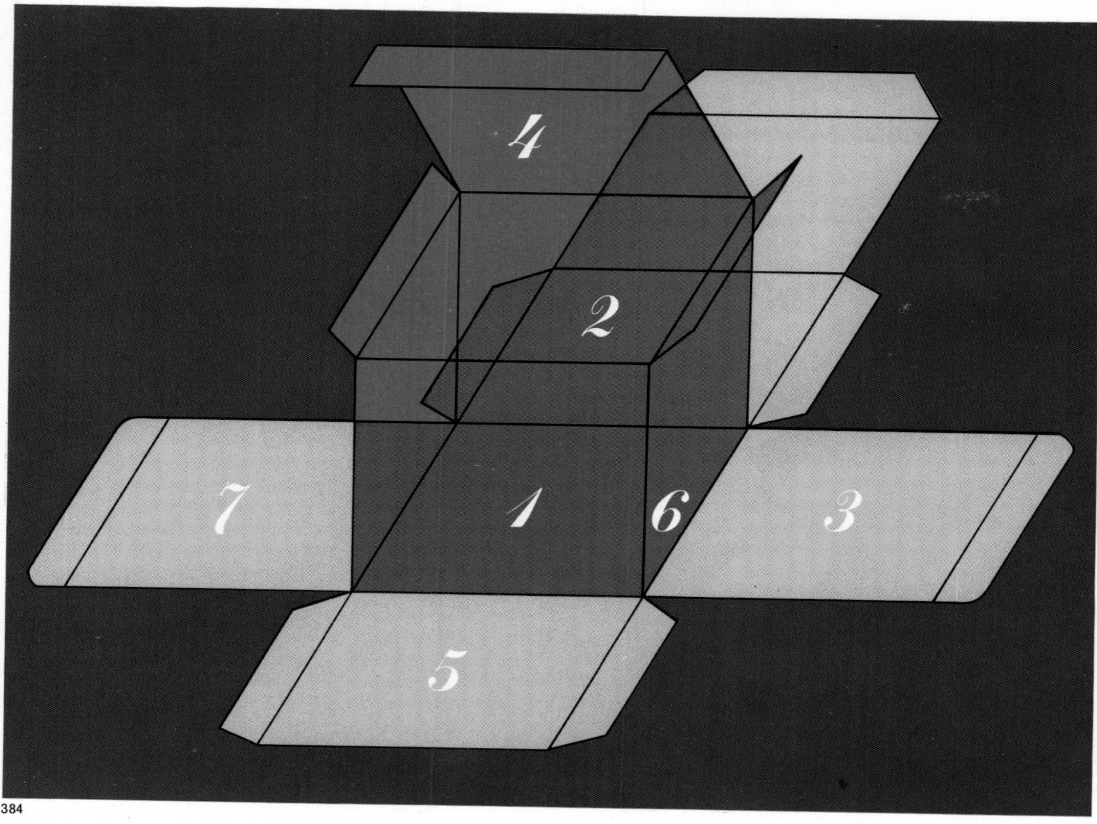

384

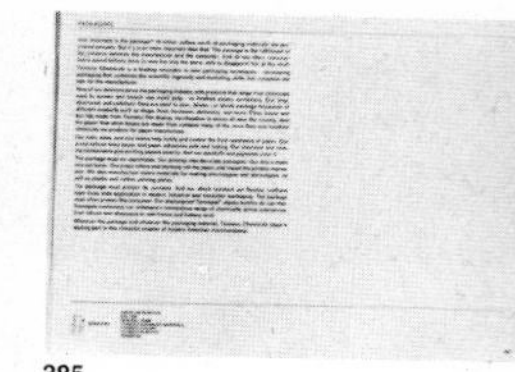

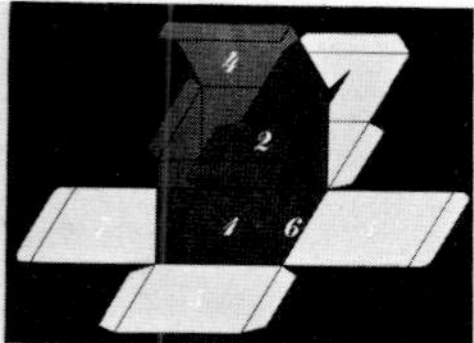

385

378)–385) Colour pages and spread from a booklet about Tenneco Chemicals, Inc. Each illustration relates to a different division of the company. (USA)
386) Cover for a binder containing information on *Geigy* dyes. Three-colour silkscreen on plastic. (USA)
387) Double spread from the catalogue of an exhibition of paper artifacts sponsored by the Container Corp. (USA)
388) 389) Cover and double spread from a booklet about the Centre for Advanced Research in Design, Chicago. (USA)
390) Inside of a folder from a series about famous personalities printed on *Union Camp* papers – here on Fiorello La Guardia, sometime mayor of New York. (USA)

378)–385) Seiten und Doppelseite aus einer Broschüre für Tenneco Chemicals, Inc. Jede Illustration bezieht sich auf eine Abteilung des Unternehmens. (USA)
386) Umschlag für Drucksachen über *Geigy*-Farbstoffe. (USA)
387) Doppelseite aus dem Katalog einer Ausstellung von kunsthandwerklichen Arbeiten aus Papier, veranstaltet von einer Verpackungsfirma. (USA)
388) 389) Umschlag und Doppelseite aus einer Broschüre für ein Gestaltungszentrum in Chicago. (USA)
390) Geöffneter Prospekt aus einer Serie über bekannte Persönlichkeiten, gedruckt auf *Union-Camp*-Papier. (USA)

378)–385) Pages en couleur et double page d'une brochure pour une usine de produits chimiques. Chaque illustration se rapporte à une division de la société. (USA)
386) Pochette pour de la documentation sur les colorants *Geigy*. Sérigraphie en trois couleurs sur plastique. (USA)
387) Double page du catalogue d'une exposition d'objets artisanaux en papier. (USA)
388) 389) Couverture et double page d'une brochure pour un centre de recherches graphiques. (USA)
390) Dépliant tiré d'une série consacrée à des personnages célèbres, en faveur d'une fabrique de papier. (USA)

387

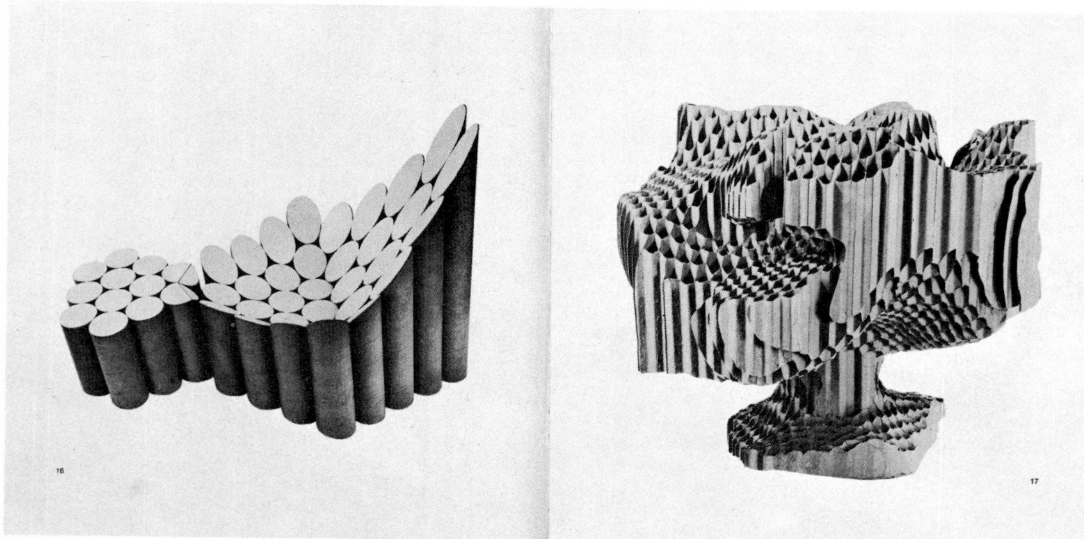

390

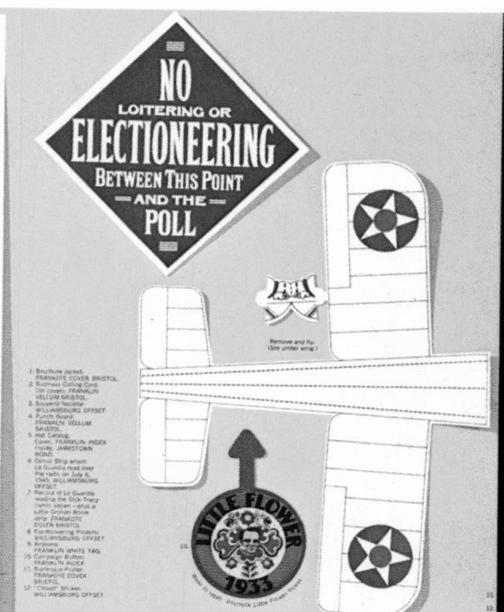

391

Artist/Künstler/Artiste:

391) GRAPHICTEAM
392) KOJI ITO/ HIROSHI WATANABE
393)–398) DICK HESS
399) SEYMOUR CHWAST/ MILTON GLASER

Art Director:

392) KOJI ITO
393)–398) DICK HESS
399) GIORGIO SOAVI

Agency/Agentur:

391) GRAPHICTEAM, KÖLN
393)–398) RICHARD HESS, INC., NEW YORK

393-398

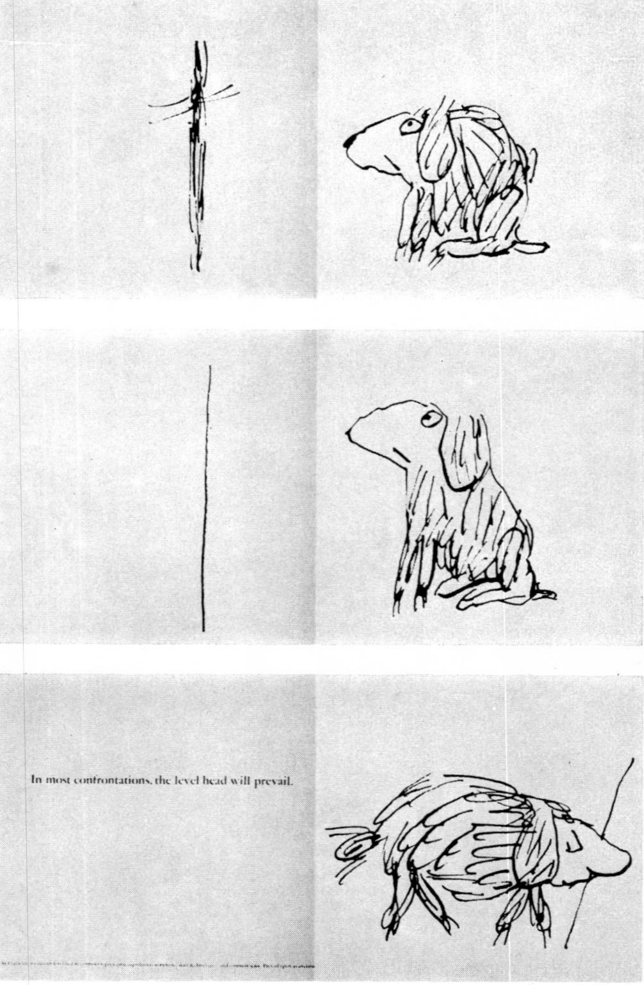

392

Booklets / Prospekte / Prospectus

391) One of a series of mailers for a printing house. (GER)
392) Mailer on the *Seibu* store's 1968 gift pack. (JAP)
393)-398) Double spreads from a booklet for Franklin Typographers, Inc. Black and white. (USA)
399) Selection of stationery, masks, buttons and various informational pieces issued by *Olivetti* to reporters at the 1968 Olympic Games in Mexico. (USA)

391) Aus einer Serie von Werbefaltkartons der Druckerei Bagel, Düsseldorf. (GER)
392) Prospekt über das Geschenk eines Warenhauses. (JAP)
393)-398) Doppelseiten aus dem Werbeprospekt einer amerikanischen Druckerei. Schwarzweiss. (USA)
399) Propagandamaterial, das von *Olivetti* an Journalisten an den Olympischen Spielen in Mexico verteilt wurde. (USA)

391) Dépliant tiré d'une série pour une imprimerie. (SWI)
392) Prospectus pour les emballages cadeaux des grands magasins *Seibu*. (JAP)
393)-398) Doubles pages d'une brochure en faveur d'une imprimerie. Noir et blanc. (USA)
399) Matériel publicitaire distribué par *Olivetti* aux reporters des jeux Olympiques de Mexico. (USA)

399

Artist|Künstler|Artiste:

400) MAX SCHMID
401) KEITH POTTS
402) 403) BECKER-VON FRANSECKY
404) JOSSE GOFFIN
405) HARRY SEHRING
406) ROLAND AESCHLIMANN
407) PAOLO GUIDOTTI/GIAMBATTISTA ZACCO
408) MAY NÉAMA

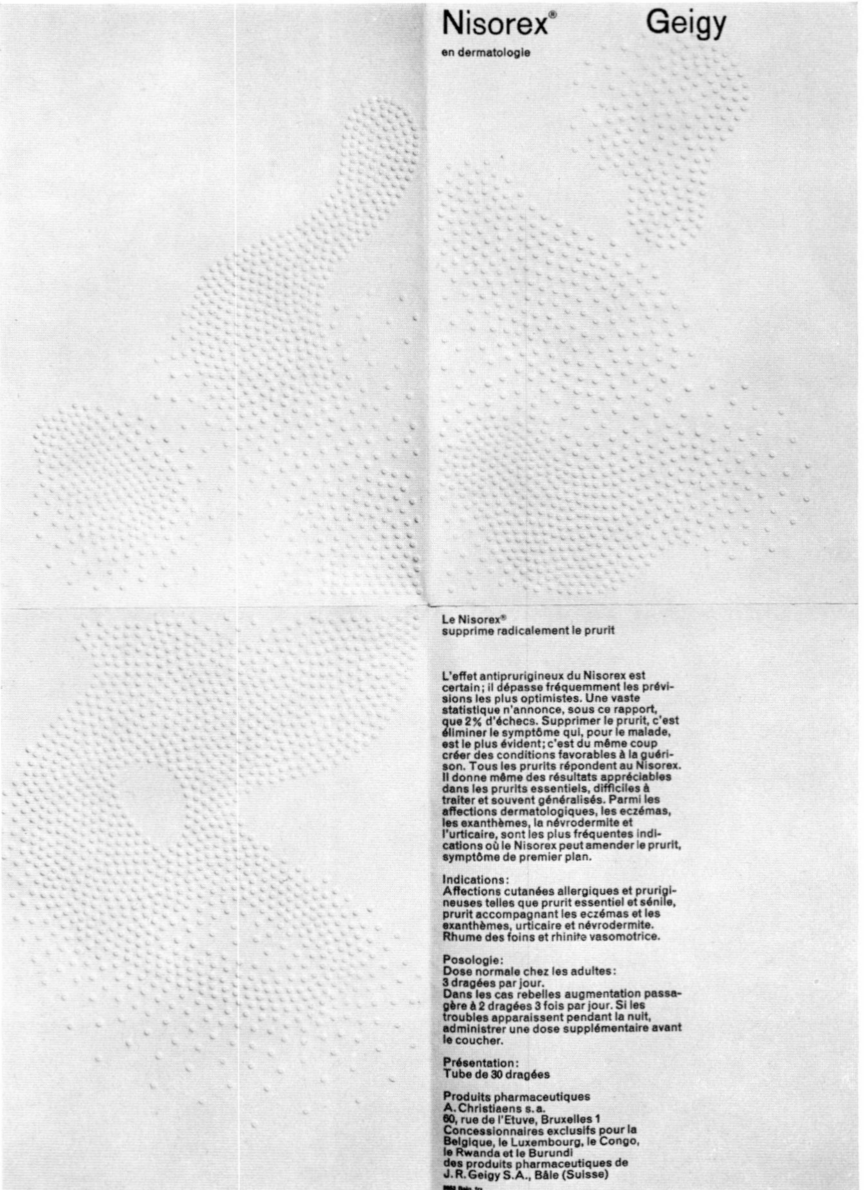

400

401

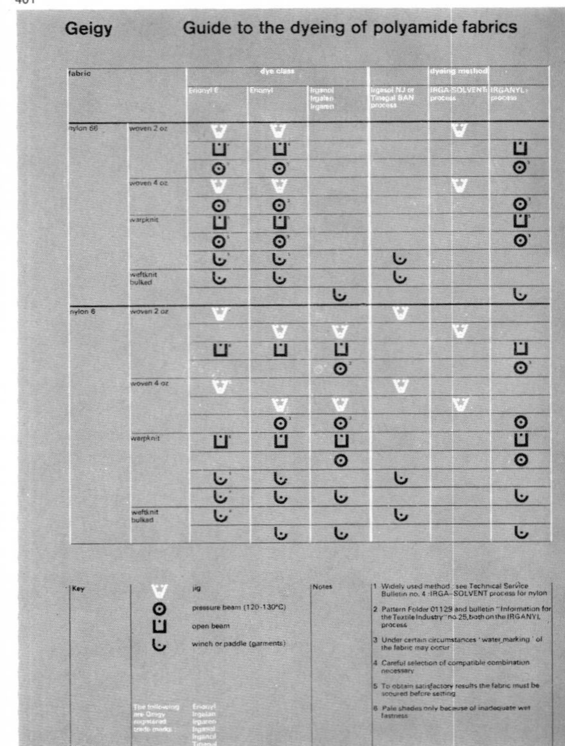

405

400) Folder for a *Geigy* pharmaceutical against skin complaints, shown fully open. Black and white with embossed design. (SWI)
401) Wall card for use as a guide to *Geigy* dyeing processes. Symbols in colour. (GB)
402) 403) Colour covers of folders about a *Merck* digestive aid. (GER)
404) Mailing card for a *Vedim* tonic. Full colour. (BEL)
405) Cover of a folder containing information on a *Roche* tranquillizer. (USA)
406) Page from a brochure on a *Geigy* drug. Tubes in colour. (SWI)
407) Mailing card for a *Roche* analgesic. Full colour. (ITA)
408) Cover of a brochure about *Roche* tranquillizers. Blue, red and black. (BEL)

400) Prospekt (ganz geöffnet) für ein *Geigy*-Medikament gegen Hautleiden. (SWI)
401) Gebrauchsanleitung für das Färben von Polyamid-Textilien mit *Geigy*-Farbstoffen. (GB)
402) 403) Umschläge von Prospekten für ein Verdauungsmittel von E. Merck. (GER)
404) Werbekarte für ein Tonikum von *Vedim*. Mehrfarbig. (BEL)
405) Umschlag eines Prospektes für ein Beruhigungsmittel von *Roche*. (USA)
406) Seite aus einer Broschüre für ein Medikament von *Geigy*. Reagenzgläser farbig. (SWI)
407) Werbekarte für *Saridon* von *Roche*. Mehrfarbig. (ITA)
408) Umschlag einer Broschüre für Beruhigungsmittel von *Roche*. Blau, rot und schwarz. (BEL)

400) Vue ouverte d'un dépliant pour une préparation dermatologique *Geigy*. (SWI)
401) Mode d'emploi des colorants *Geigy* pour la teinture des textiles polyamides. (GB)
402) 403) Dépliants polychromes pour une préparation *Merck* favorisant la digestion. (GER)
404) Carte publicitaire pour un tonique des laboratoires Vedim SA, Bruxelles. Polychrome. (BEL)
405) Couverture d'un dépliant pour un tranquillisant *Roche*. (USA)
406) Page d'une brochure pour un médicament *Geigy*. Eprouvettes en couleur. (SWI)
407) Carte publicitaire pour un analgésique des laboratoires Roche S.p.A., Milan. (ITA)
408) Brochure pour des tranquillisants des laboratoires Roche S.A., Bruxelles. (BEL)

Art Director/ Directeur artistique:

400) 406) MAX SCHMID
401) PHILIP SMYTHE
402) 403) BECKER-VON FRANSECKY
404) HENRY VAN HOOF
405) HARRY SEHRING/ALICE KATZ
407) GIAMBATTISTA ZACCO
408) LUCIEN LEPPERT

Agency/ Agentur/ Agence – Studio:

400) GEIGY WERBEABTEILUNG, BASEL
401) GEIGY (U.K.) LTD., MANCHESTER
402) 403) BECKER-VON FRANSECKY, FRIEDRICHSDORF/GER
405) WM. D. MCADAMS, ADV., NEW YORK
407) UFFICIO PUBBLICITÀ ROCHE, MILAN

402

403

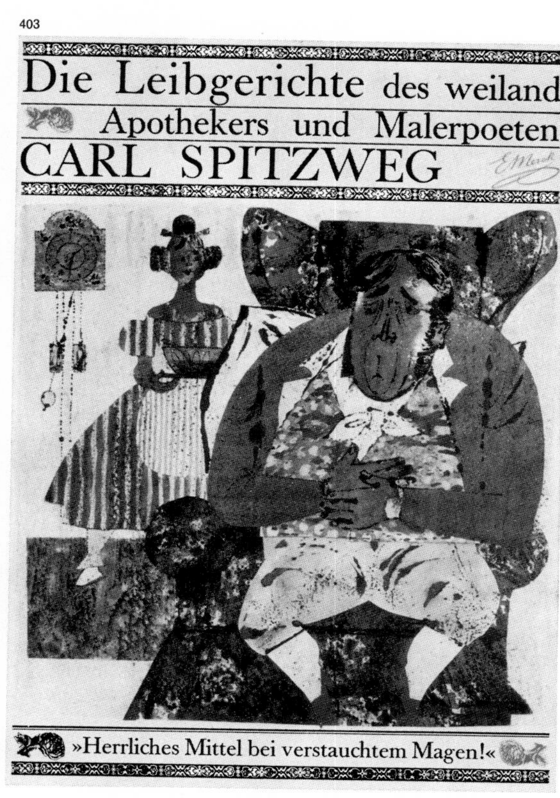

404

406

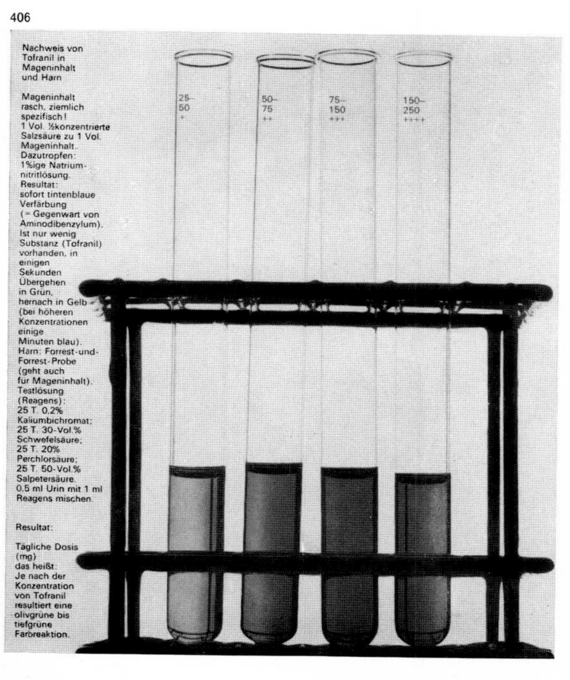

407

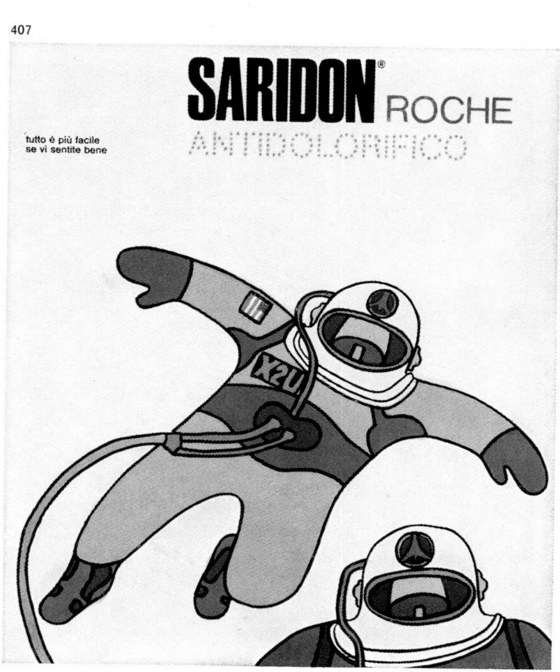

408

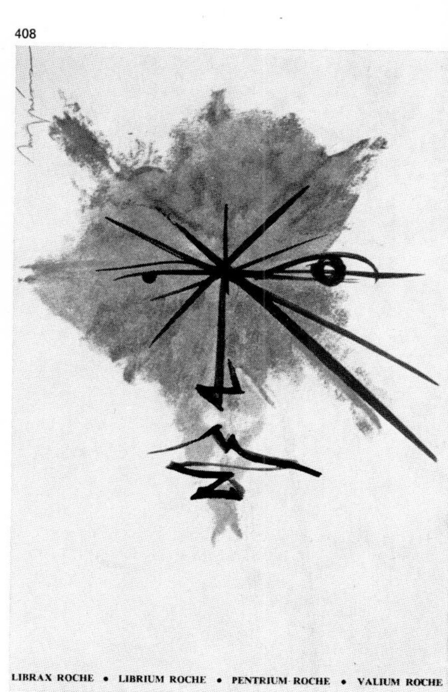

409) 410) Double spread and illustration from a booklet issued by Smith, Kline & French Laboratories. (USA)
411) 412) Page and spread with colour illustrations from a booklet explaining diabetes. (SWI)
413) 414) Mailing card and illustration for a *Galup* abdominal sedative. (SPA)
415) Mailing card for a *Sarva* antibiotic. (BEL)
416) Mailer for a *Salvoxyl* cough cure. Full colour. (FRA)

409) 410) Doppelseite und Illustration aus einer Broschüre für pharmazeutische Produkte. (USA)
411) 412) Seite und Doppelseite mit Farbillustrationen aus einer Broschüre, herausgegeben von der Schweizerischen Diabetes-Gesellschaft. (SWI)
413) 414) Werbekarte und Illustration für ein Beruhigungsmittel. (SPA)
415) Werbekarte für ein Antibiotikum. (BEL)
416) Werbekarte für ein Hustenmittel. (FRA)

409) 410) Double page et illustration tirées d'une brochure pour des produits pharmaceutiques. (USA)
411) 412) Page et double page illustrées en couleur, tirées d'une brochure explicative sur le diabète. (SWI)
413) 414) Carte publicitaire et illustration pour un tranquillisant des laboratoires Galup, Barcelone. (SPA)
415) Carte publicitaire pour un antibiotique de l'Union chimique belge, Bruxelles. (BEL)
416) Carte publicitaire pour un médicament contre la toux des laboratoires Salvoxyl S.à.r.l., Paris. (FRA)

410

THE FACE IS FAMILIAR

409

411

Was ist Zuckerkrankheit?

Durch eine angeborene «Minderwertigkeit» der Bauchspeicheldrüse (Pankreas) wird beim Zuckerkranken zu wenig oder wenig wirksames Insulin gebildet. Insulin ist ein Wirkstoff (Hormon), der in den Inselzellen der Bauchspeicheldrüse aufgebaut wird. Ohne diesen gibt es *keine Verbrennung* und Verwertung der verschiedenen Zuckerarten *der menschlichen Nahrung* (Stärke, Rohr-, Malz-, Milch-, Fruchtzucker usw.) und der Zuckergehalt des Blutes steigt an (normal 0,80 bis 1,20 g in 1 Liter Blut). Wenn der Blutzucker stark erhöht ist (über 1,70 g/l), wird Zucker im Urin ausgeschieden.

2

412

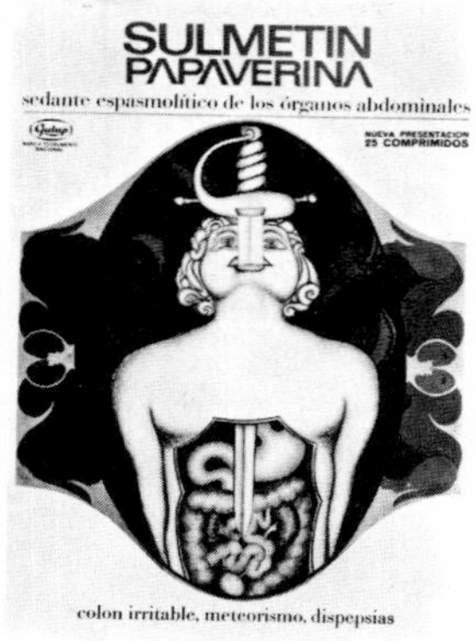

413

Artist/Künstler/Artiste:

409) 410) DONALD PUNCHATZ/A. NEAL SIEGEL
411) 412) BALZ BAECHI
413) 414) JUAN ROMEU
415) RAYMOND CÔME
416) MICHEL GUIRÉ-VAKA/BERNARD GAULIN

Art Director/Directeur artistique:

409) 410) A. NEAL SIEGEL
411) 412) BALZ BAECHI
413) 414) ENRIC HUGUET
415) HENRY VAN HOOF
416) BERNARD GAULIN

Agency/Agentur/Agence – Studio:

416) EDITIONS ARGON, NEUILLY-SUR-SEINE

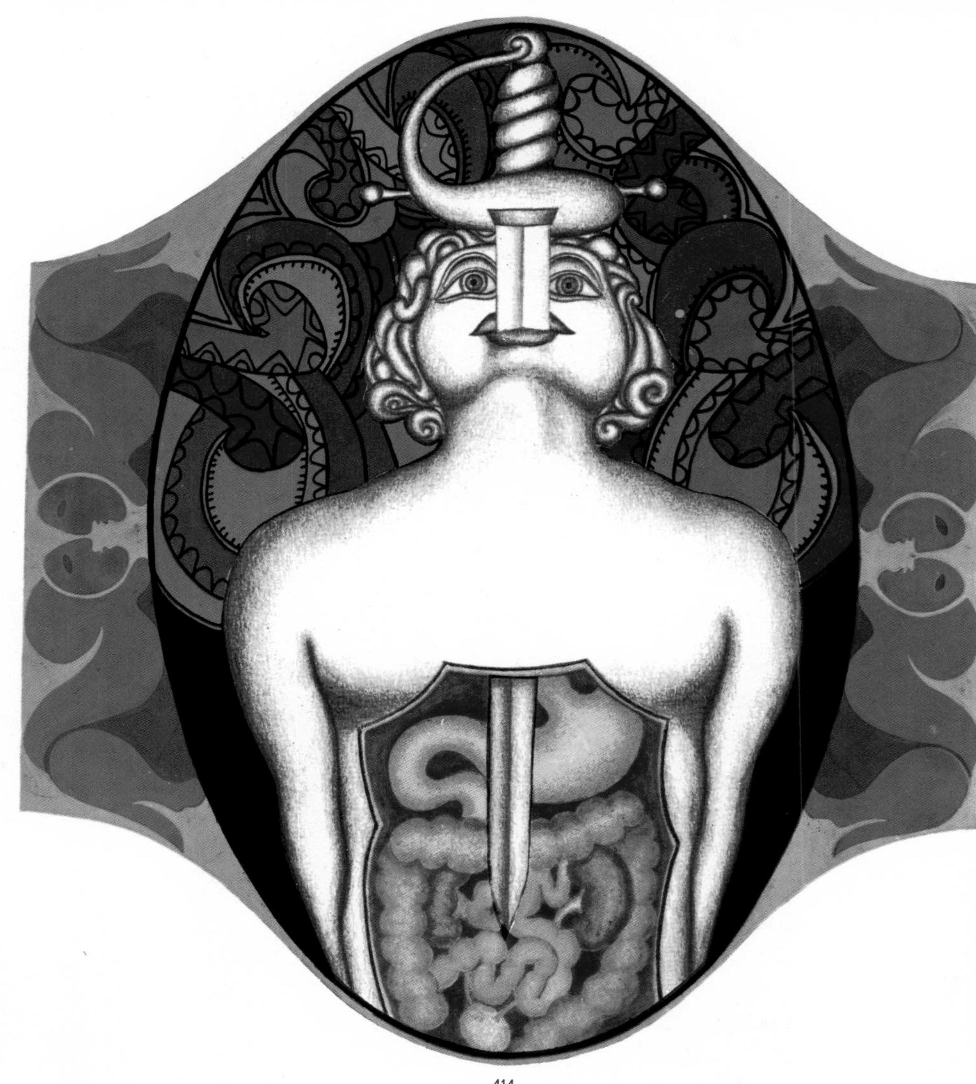

414

415

416

417

418

421

422
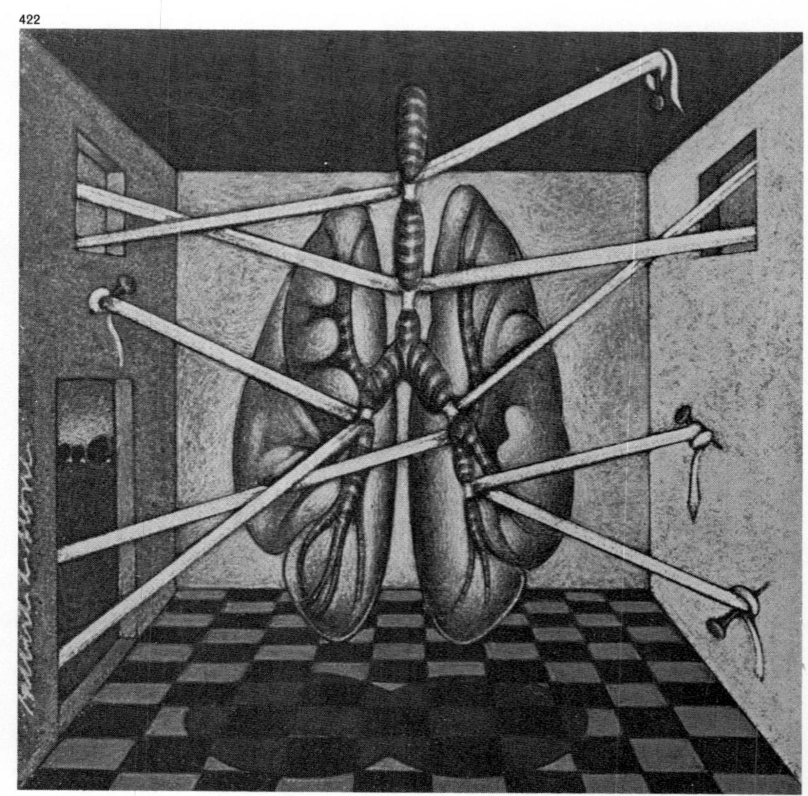

Booklets / Prospekte / Prospectus

IS DANDRUFF CATCHING? WILL IT MAKE YOU BALD?

The answers to both questions are, "No." Seborrhea is not catching—not even from a comb. It doesn't cause baldness, although it may contribute to hair loss when people have an inherited tendency to baldness.

Some, however, are more prone to dandruff than others. Certain groups (the English, for instance) have it more often than others. You have a greater chance of getting seborrhea if your complexion is more oily than dry. There also appears to be an inherited tendency to dandruff, and we sometimes hear of "dandruff families."

Dandruff seems to have a seasonal pattern. You may notice it more—or have it worse—in the Spring or Fall.

Strangely enough, summer can be both a good time and a bad one for people with seborrhea. While ultraviolet rays often help alleviate the disease, high heat and humidity can aggravate symptoms.

The world's great beauties
Could be even more fair
If they dyed their dandruff
To match their hair.
ANONYMOUS

9

419

HOW MUCH OF A PROBLEM IS IT?

Generally, not too much of one. If left unchecked, though, scales can remain on the scalp indefinitely. And sooner or later, seborrhea may occur in other areas about the face that are also rich in oil glands.

Of course, this doesn't happen to everyone. And when it does, not every area is necessarily affected. Seborrhea, however, can occur in many sites about the body, and the more areas affected, the greater the chance for starting infection. When this occurs, the condition may become generalized—not just limited to areas of increased oil gland production.

Dr. Paul Unna gave the first scientific description of seborrhea in 1887. He described three types—dry scaling of the scalp, oily scaling, and scattered scaling about the body. Now, all three kinds are considered to be the same disorder—the differences being the degree of oil gland function and possible complications due to infection.

It's as easy to cure dandruff
as it is to count the flakes.
FOLK SAYING

11

420

417) Cover of a self-promotion publication. (DEN)
418) Cover of a *Hoffmann-La Roche* brochure on the use of ascorbic acid in foods. (SWI)
419) 420) Double spreads with colour illustrations from a book about dandruff published by Abbott Laboratories. (USA)
421) Cover of a brochure about a *Roche* pharmaceutical for use against eczema. Full colour. (SWI)
422)–424) Full-colour cover, two-colour illustration (Marcel Proust) and spread from a *Roche* booklet about asthma. (USA)

417) Umschlag einer Broschüre. Eigenwerbung des Künstlers. (DEN)
418) Umschlag einer Broschüre von Hoffmann-La Roche, Basel, über die Verwendung von Ascorbinsäure in Nahrungsmitteln. (SWI)
419) 420) Doppelseiten mit farbigen Illustrationen aus einem Buch über Schuppenbildung, von Abbott Laboratories. (USA)
421) Umschlag einer Broschüre für ein Psychopharmakon von F. Hoffmann-La Roche & Co. AG, Basel. Mehrfarbig. (SWI)
422)–424) Mehrfarbiger Umschlag, Illustration (Marcel Proust) und Doppelseite aus einer *Roche*-Broschüre über Asthma. (USA)

417) Couverture d'une plaquette autopublicitaire. (DEN)
418) Couverture d'une brochure décrivant les usages de l'acide ascorbutique dans l'industrie alimentaire. (SWI)
419) 420) Doubles pages illustrées en couleur, tirées d'un ouvrage sur la formation des pellicules. (USA)
421) Couverture d'une brochure pour une préparation *Roche* utilisée dans le traitement de l'eczéma. Polychrome. (SWI)
422)–424) Couverture en couleur, illustration (Marcel Proust) et double page d'une brochure *Roche* sur l'asthme. (USA)

423

424

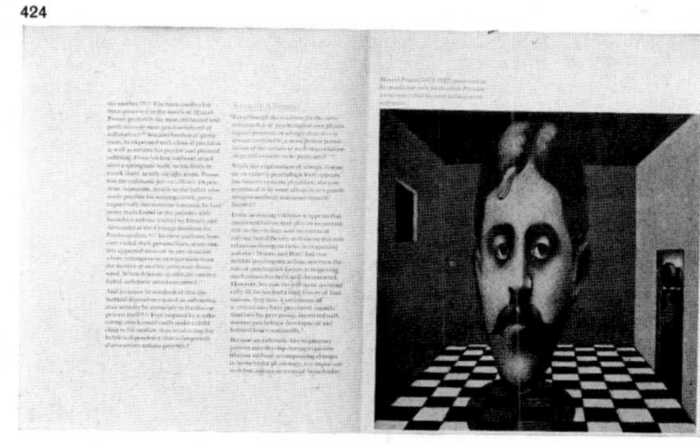

Artist / Künstler / Artiste:

417) OVE SPÄTH
418) SYLVIA GOESCHKE
419) 420) JOHN EVERDS/PETER GRUBE
421) HUGO WETLI/PH. LARGIADÈR
422)–424) GILBERT STONE/HARRY SEHRING

Art Director / Directeur artistique:

417) OVE SPÄTH
418) 421) JACQUES HAUSER
419) 420) CHARLES WALZ
422)–424) HARRY SEHRING/MORT RUBENSTEIN

Agency / Agentur / Agence – Studio:

417) OVE SPÄTH, KOPENHAGEN
419) 420) BERT RAY STUDIO, CHICAGO
422)–424) WM. D. MCADAMS INC., NEW YORK

425

426

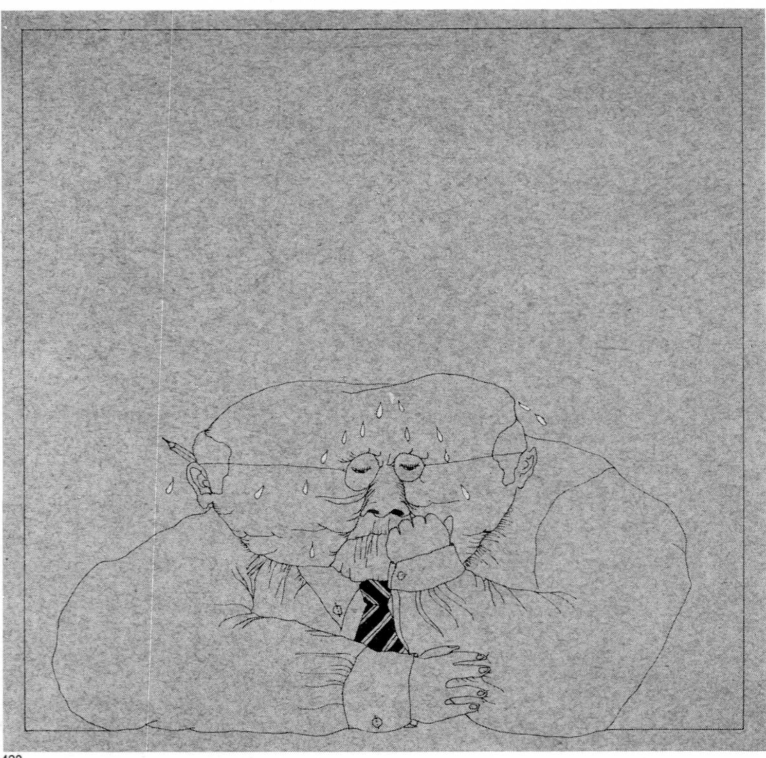

429

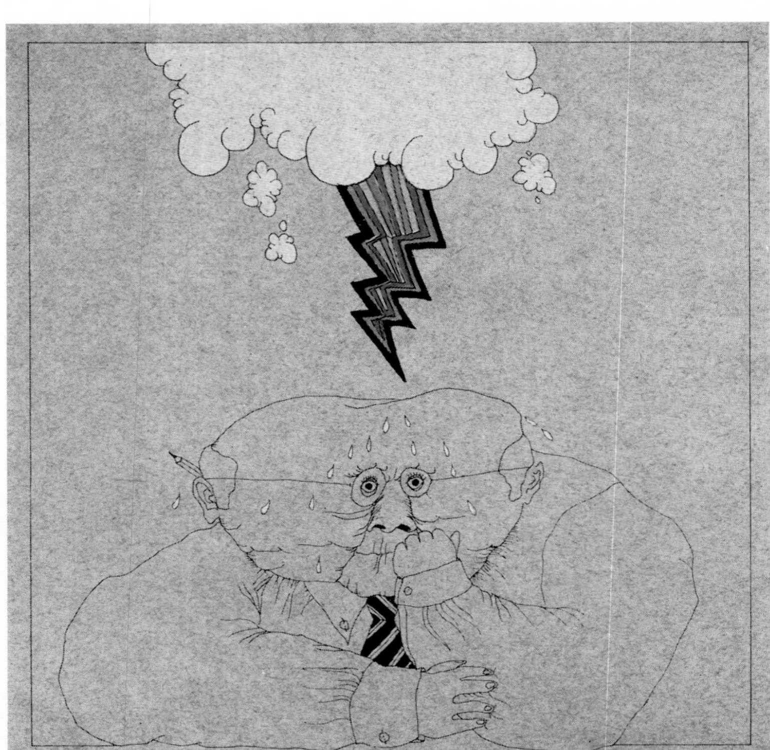

430

425) Cover of an invitation to the opening of the first Spanish supermarket. Black, blue and red. (SPA)
426) Polychrome cover of a brochure about Davis, Delaney's printing plant. (USA)
427) 431) Illustrations from an artist's self-promotion booklet. Black and white. (USA)
428) Folder about a type face, mailed by a type foundry. (SPA)
429) 430) Cover and page from a call for entries for the annual exhibition of the Western Art Directors Club. Black on grey paper, coloured lightning. (USA)
432) Cover of a booklet about programmed teaching for Behavioral Research Labs. (USA)

425) Umschlag einer Einladung zur Eröffnung des ersten spanischen Supermarktes. Schwarz, blau und rot. (SPA)
426) Mehrfarbiger Umschlag einer Broschüre für eine Druckerei. (USA)
427) 431) Illustrationen aus dem Eigenwerbungsprospekt eines Künstlers. (USA)
428) Faltprospekt für eine neue Schrift, der von einer Schriftgiesserei versandt wird. (SPA)
429) 430) Umschlag und Seite aus der Einladung zu der alljährlich stattfindenden Ausstellung eines Art Directors Clubs. Schwarz auf grauem Papier. Blitz mehrfarbig. (USA)
432) Umschlag einer Broschüre über den programmierten Unterricht. (USA)

425) Couverture d'une invitation à l'inauguration du premier super-marché espagnol. Noir, bleu et rouge. (SPA)
426) Couverture polychrome d'une brochure en faveur d'une imprimerie. (USA)
427) 431) Illustrations tirées d'une brochure autopublicitaire. Noir et blanc. (USA)
428) Dépliant pour les caractères de la Fundición Typografica Neufville SA, Barcelone. (SPA)
429) 430) Couverture et page d'une invitation à soumettre des spécimens pour l'exposition annuelle du Western Art Directors Club. Noir sur papier gris, éclair polychrome. (USA)
432) Couverture d'une brochure décrivant un programme d'enseignement. (USA)

427

Agency / Agentur / Agence – Studio:

425) ESTUDIO GRÁFICO MORILLAS, BARCELONA
426) CHERMAYEFF & GEISMAR ASSOC., NEW YORK
427) 431) HUTCHINS ADV. CO., INC., NEW YORK
429) 430) OSBORN / WAX DESIGNERS, PALO ALTO, CALIF.
432) BEVERIDGE & ASSOC., INC., WASHINGTON, D.C.

428

431

432

Artist / Künstler / Artiste:

425) ANTONIO MORILLAS
426) IVAN CHERMAYEFF / GENE SERCANDER
427) 431) JOHN KUCHERA
428) K.L. ROTHENBERGER
429) 430) STEPHEN OSBORN
432) TED ZEIGLER

Art Director / Directeur artistique:

425) ANTONIO MORILLAS
426) IVAN CHERMAYEFF
427) 431) JOHN KUCHERA
428) K.L. ROTHENBERGER
429) 430) STEPHEN OSBORN
432) EDDIE BYRD

Booklets / Prospekte Prospectus

433

434

438

439

Artist / Künstler / Artiste:

433) LOUIS SILVERSTEIN
434) MILTON GLASER
435)–437) PAUL FLORA
438) JAMES MCMULLAN / RICHARD NAVA
439) PAUL DAVIS / RICHARD NAVA
440) RON CHERESKIN
441) 442) TOMI UNGERER

Art Director / Directeur artistique:

433) LOUIS SILVERSTEIN
434) SILAS RHODES
435)–437) PAUL FLORA
438) 439) RICHARD NAVA
440) DIONE M. GUFFEY / FRED KITTEL

Agency / Agentur / Agence – Studio:

434) PUSH PIN STUDIOS, INC., NEW YORK
438) 439) DELEHANTY, KURNIT & GELLER, INC., NEW YORK
440) J. WALTER THOMPSON & CO., NEW YORK

433) Cover of a folder containing selections from THE NEW YORK TIMES. (USA)
434) Invitation to a sculpture exhibition in the gallery of the School of Visual Arts. (USA)
435)–437) Spreads and illustration from a book on the readership of a magazine. (GER)
438) 439) Illustrations from a campaign for Westinghouse Broadcasting Co. (USA)
440) Cover of a newspaper supplement about The Salvation Army. Full colour. (USA)
441) 442) Invitation, with black-and-white illustration, to a publisher's ball. (SWI)

433) Umschlag einer Broschüre mit Auszügen aus der NEW YORK TIMES. (USA)
434) Einladung zu einer Ausstellung mit Plastiken in einer Kunstschule. (USA)
435)–437) Doppelseiten und Illustration eines Buches über den Leserkreis einer Zeitschrift. (USA)
438) 439) Illustrationen aus einer Kampagne für eine Radiogesellschaft. (USA)
440) Umschlag einer Zeitungsbeilage über die Heilsarmee. Mehrfarbig. (USA)
441) 442) Einladung zum *Diogenes*-Ball 1968 in Zürich. (SWI)

433) Couverture d'un dépliant contenant des extraits du NEW YORK TIMES. (USA)
434) Invitation à une exposition de sculpture dans la galerie d'une école d'art. (USA)
435)–437) Doubles pages et illustration, tirées d'un ouvrage consacré aux lecteurs d'une revue. (GER)
438) 439) Illustrations d'une campagne publicitaire en faveur d'un émetteur radiophonique. (USA)
440) Couverture du supplément d'un quotidien consacré à l'Armée du salut. (USA)
441) 442) Invitation et son illustration en noir, pour le bal d'une maison d'édition. (SWI)

In addition to an overall report on the interest values for the West German population, for regular DAS BESTE readers, and for a group of regular magazine readers the results are shown in respect of the following sub-groups:

a) Sex

b) Phases of life

c) Groups of classes

The concept of phases of life has already been briefly introduced in the inquiry about the mode of life of DAS BESTE readers. The phases of life relate to characteristic stages in human life, which are determined by age, family status, and the phase of development of the household.

Generally a distinction is made between six phases of life:

Phase 1 Young single people

Phase 2 Young married couples without children

Phase 3 Young married couples with small children

Phase 4 Older married couples with fairly grown-up children

Phase 5 Older adults without dependent children in their households

Phase 6 Elderly single or widowed people

For the sake of a clearer synopsis and to avoid excessively small sub-groups, we shall combine Groups 2 and 3 and Groups 5 and 6 respectively when considering the phases of life. This procedure is justified because each of the groups so combined shows in between it reactions more similar than when compared with those of all other groups.

In our classification by social classes we have followed the recommendations of ZAW for media research and used the so-called point-group method in order to allow, if possible, for all significant factors that could influence a person's belonging to a given class. With this point-group method, education, occupational status, and family income are considered as class characteristics. In our report, point-groups I and II are combined as upper classes, group III is the middle class, and groups IV and V are shown as lower classes.

1. DESIRE FOR SAFETY— HOME AND HOUSEHOLD

The product sphere forming one of the consumers' strongest interests comprises all things connected with home in the widest sense. The following table lists all the items out of the 78 products examined which were combined in the group of domestic and household goods by means of the factors analysis*.

* Cf. appendix, loading of the products with factor I.

96

435

436

440

437

441

442

443

444

443) Mailing piece about a holiday competition sponsored by *Tetley* tea bags. (GB)
444) Cover of an artist's self-promotion brochure. (BEL)
445) Annual report cover for VSI Corp., makers of metal and plastic goods. (USA)
446) Cover of a booklet about a firm manufacturing office equipment. (FRA)
447) 448) Detail of lettering in the original size and complete cover of a brochure offering space at *Northprint 69*, a printing exhibition. The conception of the cover is an optical gimmick: the lettering is only readable when held at arm's length. (USA)

443) Drucksache für einen von einem Tee-Importeur veranstalteten Wettbewerb. (GB)
444) Umschlag für die Eigenwerbungsbroschüre eines Künstlers. (BEL)
445) Jahresbericht für einen Hersteller von Metall- und Plastikartikeln. (USA)
446) Umschlag einer Broschüre für einen Hersteller von Büroeinrichtungen. (FRA)
447) 448) Detail der Beschriftung in Originalgrösse und vollständiger Umschlag einer Broschüre, die für die Platzvermietung an einer Ausstellung graphischer Betriebe wirbt. Die Konzeption des Umschlags besteht in einem optischen Trick: die Schrift wird erst lesbar, wenn man sie mit gestrecktem Arm vor sich hält. (USA)

443) Imprimé publicitaire annonçant un concours de récréation organisé par un importateur de thé. (GB)
444) Couverture d'une brochure autopublicitaire. (BEL)
445) Couverture du compte rendu d'exercice d'une fabrique d'articles en métal et en plastique. (USA)
446) Couverture d'une brochure de la Société Dupré & Cie., Paris, fournitures et machines de bureau. (FRA)
447) 448) Détail du texte en grandeur originale et couverture d'une brochure annonçant une exposition de travaux d'imprimerie. La couverture est conçue en un jeu optique: l'écriture n'est lisible qu'en tenant la couverture à longueur de bras. (USA)

446

445

Artist/Künstler/Artiste:

443) GINGER TILLEY
444) CHARLES ROHONYI
445) WILLIAM P. HAINES
446) ROGER EXCOFFON
447) 448) JOHN GIBBS

Art Director/Directeur artistique:

443) DICK O'BRIEN
445) CURRIE W. HAINES
446) ROGER EXCOFFON
447) 448) JOHN GIBBS

Agency/Agentur/Agence – Studio:

443) CATO O'BRIEN ASSOC., LONDON
444) KEUSTERMANS, BRUXELLES
445) HAINES ART STUDIO, LOS ANGELES
447) 448) UNIT FIVE DESIGN LTD., LONDON

448

447

449

450

449) Programme cover for sponsored plays in a Brussels theatre. (BEL)
450) Invitation to a Lautrec exhibition. Red, two greens, black. (CAN)
451) 452) Cover and side of a programme for a museum week in Basle. (SWI)
453)-455) Cover, page and illustration (for the publishers Mondadori) from a brochure about a jazz festival. Black and white. (ITA)
456) Invitation to an exhibition on the history of collage. (SWI)
457) Cover for the catalogue of a contemporary art exhibition. (USA)

449) Programmumschlag für Aufführungen in einem Brüsseler Theater. (BEL)
450) Einladung zu einer Lautrec-Ausstellung. Mehrfarbig. (CAN)
451) 452) Programm (geschlossen und offen) der Basler Museumswochen. (SWI)
453)-455) Umschlag, Seite und Illustration (für den Verlag Mondadori) aus einer Broschüre für ein Jazzfestival. (ITA)
456) Einladung zu einer Ausstellung im Kunstgewerbemuseum Zürich. (SWI)
457) Katalogsumschlag für eine Kunstausstellung in Chicago. (USA)

449) Programme des représentations du Théâtre 140, Bruxelles. (BEL)
450) Invitation à une exposition d'œuvres de Toulouse-Lautrec. (CAN)
451) 452) Vues du programme de la Semaine des musées, Bâle. (SWI)
453)-455) Couverture, page et illustration (en faveur des Editions Mondadori) sur le Festival international de jazz de Lecco. (ITA)
456) Invitation à une exposition de l'histoire du collage. (SWI)
457) Couverture du catalogue d'une exposition d'art contemporain. (USA)

453

454

455

Basler Museumswochen 11.–24. November 1968

UNSERE MUSEEN EINMAL ANDERS

451

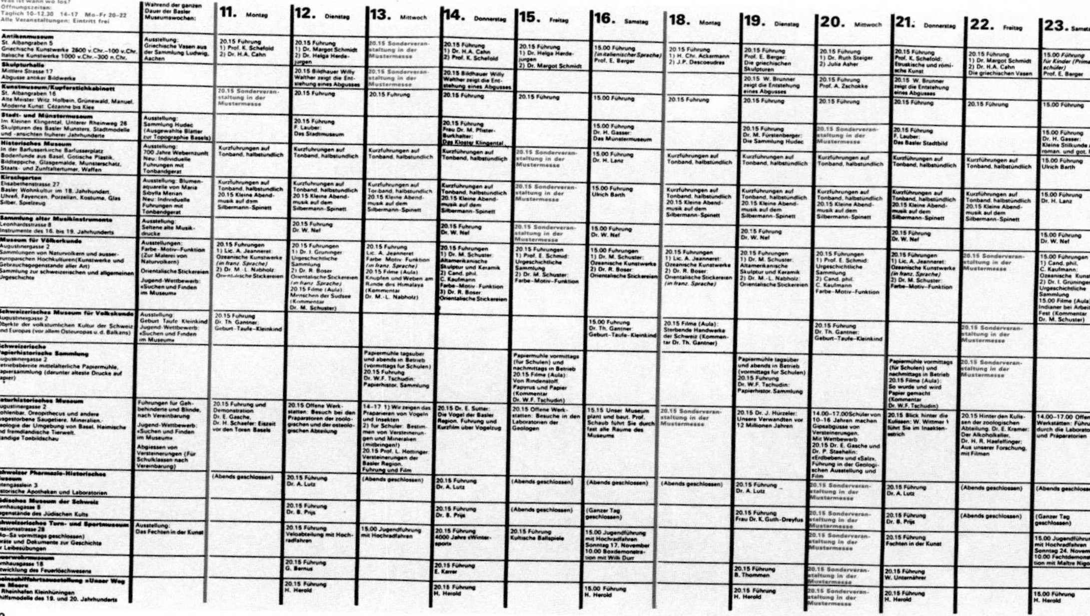

Was ist wann wo los?
Öffnungszeiten:
Täglich 10–12.30 14–17 Mo–Fr 20–22
Alle Veranstaltungen: Eintritt frei

	Während der ganzen Dauer der Basler Museumswochen:	11. Montag	12. Dienstag	13. Mittwoch	14. Donnerstag	15. Freitag	16. Samstag	18. Montag	19. Dienstag	20. Mittwoch	21. Donnerstag	22. Freitag	23. Samstag
Antikenmuseum St. Albangraben 5 Griechische Kunstwerke 2600 v.Chr.–100 v.Chr. Italische Kunstwerke 1000 v.Chr.–300 n.Chr.	Ausstellung: Griechische Vasen aus der Sammlung Ludwig, Aachen	20.15 Führung 1) Prof. K. Schefold 2) Dr. H.A. Cahn	20.15 Führung 1) Dr. Margot Schmidt 2) Dr. Helga Herdejürgen	20.15 Sonderveranstaltung in der Mustermesse	20.15 Führung 1) Dr. H.A. Cahn 2) Prof. K. Schefold	20.15 Führung 1) Dr. Helga Herdejürgen 2) Dr. Margot Schmidt	15.00 Führung *(in italienischer Sprache)* Prof. E. Berger	20.15 Führung 1) H. Chr. Ackermann 2) J.P. Descoeudres	20.15 Führung Prof. E. Berger: Die griechischen Skulpturen	20.15 Führung 1) Dr. Ruth Steiger 2) Julia Asher	20.15 Führung Prof. K. Schefold: Etruskische und römische Kunst	20.15 Führung 1) Dr. Margot Schmidt 2) Dr. H.A. Cahn Die griechischen Vasen	15.00 *Führung für Kinder (Primarschüler)* Prof. E. Berger
Skulpturhalle Mittlere Strasse 17 Abgüsse antiker Bildwerke			20.15 Bildhauer Willy Walther zeigt die Entstehung eines Abgusses	20.15 Sonderveranstaltung in der Mustermesse	20.15 Bildhauer Willy Walther zeigt die Entstehung eines Abgusses				20.15 W. Brunner zeigt die Entstehung eines Abgusses	20.15 Führung Prof. A. Zschokke	20.15 W. Brunner zeigt die Entstehung eines Abgusses		
Kunstmuseum/Kupferstichkabinett St. Albangraben 16 Alte Meister: Witz, Holbein, Grünewald, Manuel. Moderne Kunst: Cézanne bis Klee		20.15 Sonderveranstaltung in der Mustermesse	20.15 Führung	20.15 Führung	20.15 Führung	20.15 Führung	15.00 Führung	20.15 Führung	20.15 Führung	20.15 Führung	20.15 Führung	20.15 Führung	15.00 Führung
Stadt- und Münstermuseum Im Kleinen Klingental, Unterer Rheinweg 26 Skulpturen des Basler Münsters, Stadtmodelle und -ansichten früherer Jahrhunderte	Ausstellung: Sammlung Hudec (Ausgewählte Blätter zur Topographie Basels)		20.15 Führung F. Lauber: Das Stadtmuseum		20.15 Führung Frau Dr. M. Pfister-Burkhalter: Das Kloster Klingental		15.00 Führung Dr. H. Gasser: Das Münstermuseum		20.15 Führung Dr. M. Fürstenberger: Die Sammlung Hudec	20.15 Sonderveranstaltung in der Mustermesse	20.15 Führung F. Lauber: Das Basler Stadtbild		15.00 Führung Dr. H. Gasser: Kleine Stilkunde an roman. und got. Plastik
Historisches Museum In der Barfüsserkirche Barfüsserplatz Bodenfunde aus Basel, Gotische Plastik, Bildteppiche, Glasgemälde, Münsterschatz, Staats- und Zunftaltertümer, Waffen	Ausstellung: 700 Jahre Webernzunft Neu: Individuelle Führungen mit Tonbandgerät	Kurzführungen auf Tonband, halbstündlich	Kurzführungen auf Tonband, halbstündlich	Kurzführungen auf Tonband, halbstündlich	Kurzführungen auf Tonband, halbstündlich	20.15 Sonderveranstaltung in der Mustermesse	15.00 Führung Dr. H. Lanz	Kurzführungen auf Tonband, halbstündlich	Kurzführungen auf Tonband, halbstündlich	Kurzführungen auf Tonband, halbstündlich	Kurzführungen auf Tonband, halbstündlich	Kurzführungen auf Tonband, halbstündlich	15.00 Führung Ulrich Barth
Kirschgarten Elisabethenstrasse 27 Basler Wohnkultur im 18. Jahrhundert, Uhren, Fayencen, Porzellan, Kostüme, Glas, Silber, Spielzeug	Ausstellung: Blumenaquarelle von Maria Sibylla Merian Neu: Individuelle Führungen mit Tonbandgerät	Kurzführungen auf Tonband, halbstündlich 20.15 Kleine Abendmusik auf dem Silbermann-Spinett	Kurzführungen auf Tonband, halbstündlich 20.15 Kleine Abendmusik auf dem Silbermann-Spinett	Kurzführungen auf Tonband, halbstündlich 20.15 Kleine Abendmusik auf dem Silbermann-Spinett	Kurzführungen auf Tonband, halbstündlich 20.15 Kleine Abendmusik auf dem Silbermann-Spinett	20.15 Sonderveranstaltung in der Mustermesse	15.00 Führung Ulrich Barth	Kurzführungen auf Tonband, halbstündlich 20.15 Kleine Abendmusik auf dem Silbermann-Spinett	Kurzführungen auf Tonband, halbstündlich 20.15 Kleine Abendmusik auf dem Silbermann-Spinett	Kurzführungen auf Tonband, halbstündlich 20.15 Kleine Abendmusik auf dem Silbermann-Spinett	Kurzführungen auf Tonband, halbstündlich 20.15 Kleine Abendmusik auf dem Silbermann-Spinett	Kurzführungen auf Tonband, halbstündlich 20.15 Kleine Abendmusik auf dem Silbermann-Spinett	15.00 Führung Dr. H. Lanz
Sammlung alter Musikinstrumente Leonhardsstrasse 8 Instrumente des 16. bis 19. Jahrhunderts	Ausstellung: Seltene alte Musikdrucke		20.15 Führung Dr. W. Nef		20.15 Führung Dr. W. Nef	20.15 Sonderveranstaltung in der Mustermesse	15.00 Führung Dr. W. Nef		20.15 Führung Dr. W. Nef		20.15 Führung Dr. W. Nef		15.00 Führung Dr. W. Nef
Museum für Völkerkunde Augustinergasse 2 Sammlungen von Naturvölkern und aussereuropäischen Hochkulturen (Kunstwerke und Gebrauchsgegenstände aller Art) Sammlung zur schweizerischen und allgemeinen Urgeschichte	Ausstellungen: Farbe–Motiv–Funktion (Zur Malerei von Naturvölkern) Orientalische Stickereien Jugend-Wettbewerb: «Suchen und Finden im Museum»	20.15 Führungen 1) Lic. A. Jeanneret: Ozeanische Kunstwerke *(in franz. Sprache)* 2) Dr. M.-L. Nabholz: Orientalische Stickereien	20.15 Führungen 1) Dr. I. Grüninger: Urgeschichtliche Sammlung 2) Dr. R. Boser: Orientalische Stickereien *(in franz. Sprache)* 20.15 Filme (Aula): Menschen der Südsee (Kommentar Dr. M. Schuster)	20.15 Führung Lic. A. Jeanneret: Farbe–Motiv–Funktion *(in franz. Sprache)* 20.15 Filme (Aula): Knüpfen und Weben am Rande des Himalaya (Kommentar Dr. M.-L. Nabholz)	20.15 Führungen 1) Dr. M. Schuster: Altamerikanische Skulptur und Keramik 2) Cand. phil. C. Kaufmann Farbe–Motiv–Funktion 3) Dr. R. Boser: Orientalische Stickereien	20.15 Führungen 1) Prof. E. Schmid: Urgeschichtliche Sammlung 2) Dr. M. Schuster: Farbe–Motiv–Funktion	15.00 Führungen 1) Dr. M. Schuster: Ozeanische Kunstwerke 2) Dr. R. Boser: Orientalische Stickereien	20.15 Führungen 1) Lic. A. Jeanneret: Ozeanische Kunstwerke 2) Dr. R. Boser: Orientalische Stickereien *(in franz. Sprache)*	20.15 Führungen 1) Dr. M. Schuster: Altamerikanische Skulptur und Keramik 2) Dr. M.-L. Nabholz: Orientalische Stickereien	20.15 Führungen 1) Prof. E. Schmid: Urgeschichtliche Sammlung 2) Cand. phil. C. Kaufmann Farbe–Motiv–Funktion	20.15 Führungen 1) Lic. A. Jeanneret: Ozeanische Kunstwerke *(in franz. Sprache)* 2) Dr. M. Schuster: Farbe–Motiv–Funktion	20.15 Sonderveranstaltung in der Mustermesse	15.00 Führungen 1) Cand. phil. C. Kaufmann: Ozeanische Kunstwerke 2) Dr. I. Grüninger: Urgeschichtliche Sammlung 15.00 Filme (Aula): Indianer bei Arbeit und Fest (Kommentar Dr. M. Schuster)
Schweizerisches Museum für Volkskunde Augustinergasse 2 Objekte der volkstümlichen Kultur der Schweiz und Europas (vor allem Osteuropas u.d. Balkans)	Ausstellung: Geburt–Taufe–Kleinkind Jugend-Wettbewerb: «Suchen und Finden im Museum»	20.15 Führung Dr. Th. Gantner: Geburt–Taufe–Kleinkind					15.00 Führung Dr. Th. Gantner: Geburt–Taufe–Kleinkind	20.15 Filme (Aula): Sterbende Handwerke der Schweiz (Kommentar Dr. Th. Gantner)		20.15 Führung Dr. Th. Gantner: Geburt–Taufe–Kleinkind		20.15 Sonderveranstaltung in der Mustermesse	
Schweizerische Papierhistorische Sammlung Augustinergasse 2 Betriebsbereite mittelalterliche Papiermühle, Papiersammlung (darunter älteste Drucke auf Papier)				Papiermühle tagsüber und abends in Betrieb (vormittags für Schulen) 20.15 Führung Dr. W.F. Tschudin: Papierhistor. Sammlung		Papiermühle vormittags (für Schulen) und nachmittags in Betrieb 20.15 Filme (Aula): Von Rindenstoff, Papyrus und Papier (Kommentar Dr. W.F. Tschudin)			Papiermühle tagsüber und abends in Betrieb (vormittags für Schulen) 20.15 Führung Dr. W.F. Tschudin: Papierhistor. Sammlung		Papiermühle vormittags (für Schulen) und nachmittags in Betrieb 20.15 Filme (Aula): So wurde und wird Papier gemacht (Kommentar Dr. W.F. Tschudin)	20.15 Sonderveranstaltung in der Mustermesse	
Naturhistorisches Museum Augustinergasse 2 Höhlenbär, Oreopithecus und andere ausgestorbene Säugetiere, Mineralien, Geologie der Umgebung von Basel, Heimische und fremdländische Tierwelt. Ständige Tonbildschau	Führungen für Gehbehinderte und Blinde, nach Vereinbarung Jugend-Wettbewerb: «Suchen und Finden im Museum» Abgiessen von Versteinerungen (Für Schulklassen nach Vereinbarung)	20.15 Führung und Demonstration Dr. E. Gasche, Dr. H. Schaefer: Eiszeit vor den Toren Basels	20.15 Offene Werkstätten: Besuch bei den Präparatoren der zoologischen und der osteologischen Abteilung	14–17 1) Wir zeigen das Präparieren von Vögeln und Insekten 2) für Schüler: Bestimmen von Versteinerungen und Mineralien (mitbringen!) 20.15 Prof. L. Hottinger: Versteinerungen der Basler Region, Führung und Film	20.15 Dr. E. Sutter: Die Vögel der Basler Region, Führung und Kurzfilm über Vogelzug	20.15 Offene Werkstätten: Besuche in den Laboratorien der Geologen	15.15 Unser Museum plant und baut. Prof. Schaub führt Sie durch fast alle Räume des Museums	20.15 Sonderveranstaltung in der Mustermesse	20.15 Dr. J. Hürzeler: Unsere Verwandten vor 12 Millionen Jahren	14.00–17.00 Schüler von 10–16 Jahren machen Gipsabgüsse von Versteinerungen. Mit Wettbewerb 20.15 Dr. E. Gasche und Dr. P. Staehelin: «Erdbeben» und «Salz». Führung in der Geologischen Ausstellung und Film	20.15 Blick hinter die Kulissen: W. Wittmer führt Sie im Insektenestrich	20.15 Hinter den Kulissen der zoologischen Abteilung. Dr. E. Kramer: Der Alkoholkeller, Dr. H. R. Haefelfinger: Aus unserer Forschung, mit Filmen	14.00–17.00 Offene Werkstätten: Führung durch die Laboratorien und Präparatorien
Schweizer Pharmazie-Historisches Museum Totengässlein 3 Historische Apotheken und Laboratorien		(Abends geschlossen)	20.15 Führung Dr. A. Lutz	(Abends geschlossen)	20.15 Führung Dr. A. Lutz	(Abends geschlossen)	(Abends geschlossen)	(Abends geschlossen)	20.15 Führung Dr. A. Lutz	20.15 Sonderveranstaltung in der Mustermesse	20.15 Führung Dr. A. Lutz	(Abends geschlossen)	(Abends geschlossen)
Jüdisches Museum der Schweiz Kornhausgasse 8 Gegenstände des Jüdischen Kults			20.15 Führung Dr. B. Prijs		20.15 Führung Dr. B. Prijs	(Abends geschlossen)	(Ganzer Tag geschlossen)		20.15 Führung Frau Dr. K. Guth-Dreyfus	20.15 Sonderveranstaltung in der Mustermesse	20.15 Führung Dr. B. Prijs	(Abends geschlossen)	(Ganzer Tag geschlossen)
Schweizerisches Turn- und Sportmuseum Missionsstrasse 28 (Mo–Sa vormittags geschlossen) Geräte und Dokumente zur Geschichte der Leibesübungen	Ausstellung: Das Fechten in der Kunst		20.15 Führung Veloabteilung mit Hochradfahren	15.00 Jugendführung mit Hochradfahren	20.15 Führung 4000 Jahre «Wintersport»	20.15 Führung Kultische Ballspiele	15.00 Jugendführung mit Hochradfahren Sonntag 17. November 10.00 Boxdemonstration mit Willi Durr			20.15 Sonderveranstaltung in der Mustermesse	20.15 Führung Fechten in der Kunst		15.00 Jugendführung mit Hochradfahren Sonntag 24. November 10.00 Fechtdemonstration mit Maître Nigon
Feuerwehrmuseum Kornhausgasse 18 Entwicklung des Feuerlöschwesens			20.15 Führung G. Bernus		20.15 Führung E. Karrer				20.15 Führung B. Thommen	20.15 Sonderveranstaltung in der Mustermesse	20.15 Führung W. Unternährer		
Rheinschiffahrtsausstellung «Unser Weg zum Meer» Im Rheinhafen Kleinhüningen Schiffsmodelle des 19. und 20. Jahrhunderts			20.15 Führung H. Herold		20.15 Führung H. Herold		15.00 Führung H. Herold		20.15 Führung H. Herold	20.15 Sonderveranstaltung in der Mustermesse	20.15 Führung H. Herold		15.00 Führung H. Herold

452

456

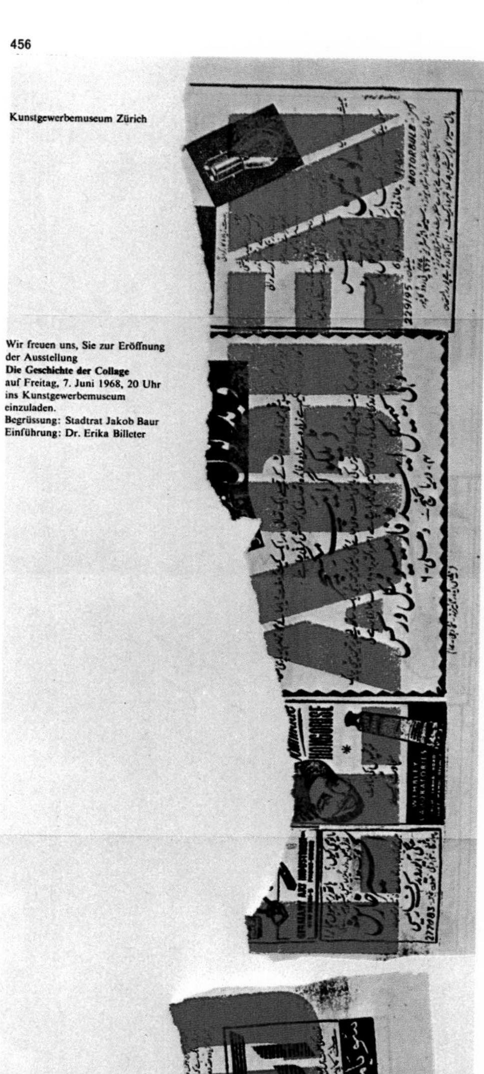

457

Artist/Künstler/Artiste:

449) MONIQUE BORLÉE-LOMBAL
450) FRITZ GOTTSCHALK
451) 452) F. + D. GYSSLER
453) TITTI FABIANI
454) 455) FERENC PINTER
456) FRIDOLIN MÜLLER
457) ROBERT LIPMAN

Art Director/Directeur artistique:

449) PAUL PATIGNY
451) 452) F. + D. GYSSLER
453) TITTI FABIANI
454) 455) BRUNO BINOSI
457) ROBERT LIPMAN

Agency/Agentur/Agence – Studio:

449) PUBLIART, BRUXELLES
450) GOTTSCHALK & ASH LTD., MONTREAL
451) 452) F. + D. GYSSLER, BASEL
453) STUDIO B, MILAN
454) 455) ARNOLDO MONDADORI EDITORE, MILAN
457) ROBERT LIPMAN DESIGN, CHICAGO

458

Das Ei in der Bibliothek
nach Agatha Christie

Hercule Poirot überblickte raschen Auges die Leute, die sich in der Bibliothek versammelt hatten. Da saß Miss Higgins, klein, zart und schon wieder mit einer Stickerei beschäftigt. Neben ihr lehnte Major Street. Sein vom Alkohol gerötetes Gesicht war finster. Im Club schon hatte er Poirot angeknurrt, weil die Suppe nicht heiß war; er hatte ihn für einen Kellner gehalten. Poirot erschauerte. Am Tag zuvor war er von Miss Higgins für einen Friseur gehalten worden. Es war nicht auszudenken. Ach, diese Engländer!

Poirots Augen ruhten nachdenklich auf Miss Rutherford, der Frau mit den fast männlichen Zügen. Tiefe Stille herrschte. Dann sagte Mrs. Wintersdoon in ihrer herausfordernden Art:

„Nun, Monsieur Poirot, man sagt Ihnen nach, Sie seien ein Genie und hätten bisher jeden Kriminalfall gelöst. Warum sagen Sie uns nicht, wer der Mörder ist!"

Poirot streichelte seinen Schnurrbart.

„Ich zögere nicht", sagte er selbstbewußt, „Ihnen mitzuteilen, daß ich vermittels meiner kleinen grauen Zellen auch diesen Fall gelöst habe. Ich werde Ihnen nun also den Mörder zeigen. Vorher jedoch werden Sie mir ein paar Worte gestatten. Sie wissen, Mr. Lampsman starb nach dem Genuß eines Spiegeleis. Der Rest, der noch in der Pfanne war, enthielt — wie Sie wissen — Arsen. Nun sagte ich zu mir selber: wenn Mr. Lampsman nach dem Genuß eines Spiegeleis an Arsenvergiftung starb und wenn im Rest des Eis noch Arsen zu finden war — dann muß dieses Spiegelei den Tod von Mr. Lampsman verursacht haben . . ."

Poirot schwieg einen Augenblick und sonnte sich im Raunen der Bewunderung, das sich erhob.

„Genial!" — „Großartig!" „Ganz einfach unglaublich!" wurde von allen Seiten geflüstert. Poirot fuhr fort: „Und da, meine Damen und Herren, fiel mir der kleine Kinderreim ein: 'Spiegelzwei, Spiegeldrei, Lampsman starb an 'nem Spiegelei!'

Wer aber, frage ich euch, hat dieses Lied ständig gesungen? — Sie, Miss Rutherford. Und darum sage ich Ihnen: sie hat es getan!

Das Hühnchen und Studer
nach Friedrich Glauser

Der Nebel war wie Watte. Dann kam etwas Helles daraus hervor und glitzerte. Es war ein Velo. Studer hielt die Hand in die Höhe. Richtig: es war Hurny. Das Knechtlein Hurny. „Steigen Sie ab, ich muß mit Ihnen reden", sagte Studer in seinem besten Hochdeutsch. „Und sind nid so kurlig, ich tue Euch nichts." Das Knechtlein war abgestiegen und zitterte.

„Jetzt los Köbi . . ." Studer seufzte. Mußte das Knechtlein ausgerechnet Jakob heißen wie er selber? Nun, vielleicht wirkte das Du.

„Los, Köbi, woher chunsch?"

„Von Bolligen. Habe mir zwei Nastücher gekauft."

Zwei mächtige rote Nastücher, wie auch Studer sie verwendete, wurden geschwenkt.

„Gut. Und jetzt seg mir: wer war gestern abend in der Küche?"

Schweigen.

„Na", brummte Studer, „wird's bald? So red schon."

Hurny bekam einen roten Kopf. „s' Ewsy."

„So so — s' Ewsy!" Studer schmunzelte. „Und wer het das Spiegelei gemacht?"

„De Aeby."

„Aebe, de Aeby." Und nachher hatte es Arsen darin, und der Hungerlott starb. Also doch der Aeby — Studer hatte es längst vermutet.

Auf einmal kam durch die dicke Watte des Nebels schrilles Heulen, verstummte, schrillte wieder, heulend und klagend, dann krachte es, und auf einmal war alles still. Studer und Hurny eilten zurück — mitten auf der Straße lag Aeby. Er stöhnte, und aus seinem Mund floß Blut.

Studer beugte sich über ihn. „Nun, Aeby", sagte er leise, fast zärtlich, „wollt Ihr noch gestehen, bevor Ihr sterben müßt? Sägid?"

„Ja, ich will gestehen. Ich habe das Arsen, oder wie der Gebildete sagt, das A-Es, in das Spiegelei getan. Ich hasse Spiegeleier. Es muß da ein Säuglingserlebnis . . ."

„Sid still, Aeby. Aber: wie habt Ihr das Arsen in die Küche gebracht?"

„Ich habe es in einem roten Schnupftuch getragen. Da fiel es nicht so auf." Aha, darum mußte sich der Knecht Hurny nachher neue Schnupftücher besorgen. „Als niemand hinsah, habe ich das Arsen in die Pfanne geschüttet, und das Schnupftuch versteckte ich. Ich dachte, wenn man es finde, werde man den Hurny verdächtigen."

Aeby schloß die Augen und war tot. Studer stand aufrecht, die breiten Schultern hochgezogen. Und er sagte, als rede er zu sich selber: „So kommt es, wenn man sich nicht entschließen kann, ob man Hochdeutsch oder Bernerdeutsch schreiben soll." Er wandte sich Hurny zu. „Gang hei, Köbi, und hürot's Ewsy!"

459

Artist/Künstler/Artiste:

458) 462)–464) RENÉ CREUX/PAUL PERRET
459)–461) 465) 466) HEINZ EDELMANN

462

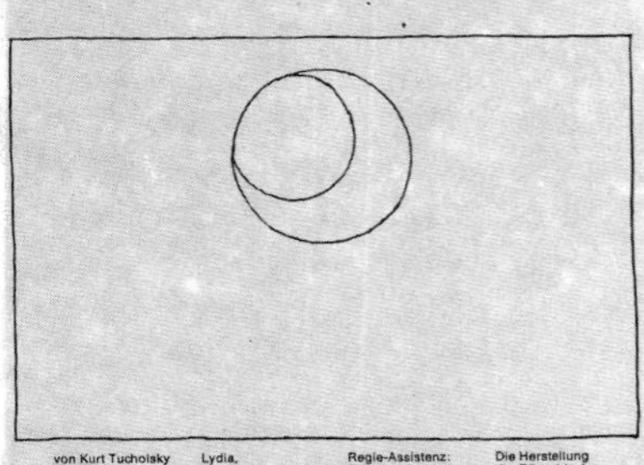

von Kurt Tucholsky
Nach der Bühnenfassung von Martin Trautwein für die Kammerspiele Düsseldorf bearbeitet von Herbert Hauck und Wolfgang Fentsch, Musik von David Kamien
Inszenierung: Herbert Hauck
Musikalische Leitung: David Kamien
Bühnenbild Wolfgang Fentsch

Lydia, genannt die Prinzessin: Renate Clair
Peter: Günter Wissemann
Billie: Helen von Münchhofen
Karlchen: Gottfried Mehlhorn
Walter Gottschow als: Taxifahrer, Gepäckträger, Zeitungsverkäufer, Speisewagenkellner, Polysander von Kuckers zu Thiessenhausen, Zollbeamter, Nervenarzt, Dolmetscher Bengtson, Schloßverwalter, Bahnhofsvorsteher in Mariefred, Tourist

Regie-Assistenz: Susanne Sexauer
Technische Leitung: Gerd Schooldermann
Ausstattungs-Assistenz: Marlene Baum
Bühnentechnik: Willi Fesser und Heinz Boschulte
Beleuchtung: Gerd Schooldermann.
Zwei Teile (16 Bilder) mit einem Vor- und einem Nachspiel
Pause nach dem ersten Teil
Aufführungsrechte: Rowohlt-Theaterverlag, Reinbek bei Hamburg

Die Herstellung der Düsseldorfer Fassung erfolgte unter Verwendung zahlreicher Originaltexte und Chansons Kurt Tucholskys, insbesondere: ‚Rheinsberg', ‚Lottchen beichtet einen Geliebten', ‚Deutsch für Amerikaner', ‚In der Hotelhalle', ‚Wie wird man Generaldirektor?', u.a.m.

460

Kammerspiele Düsseldorf Theater am Wilhelm-Marx-Haus Was ist an Tolen so sexy?

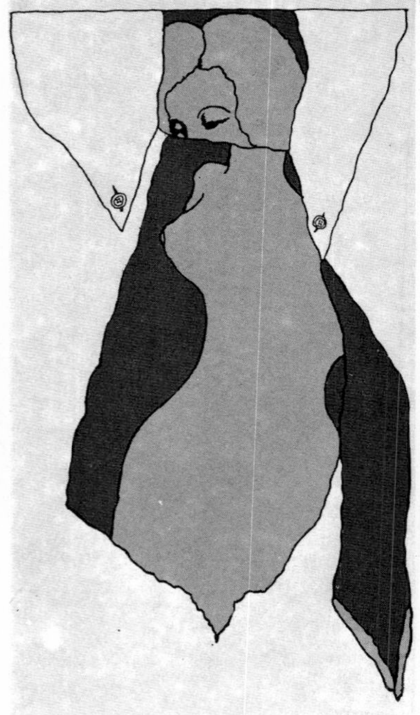

461

463

464

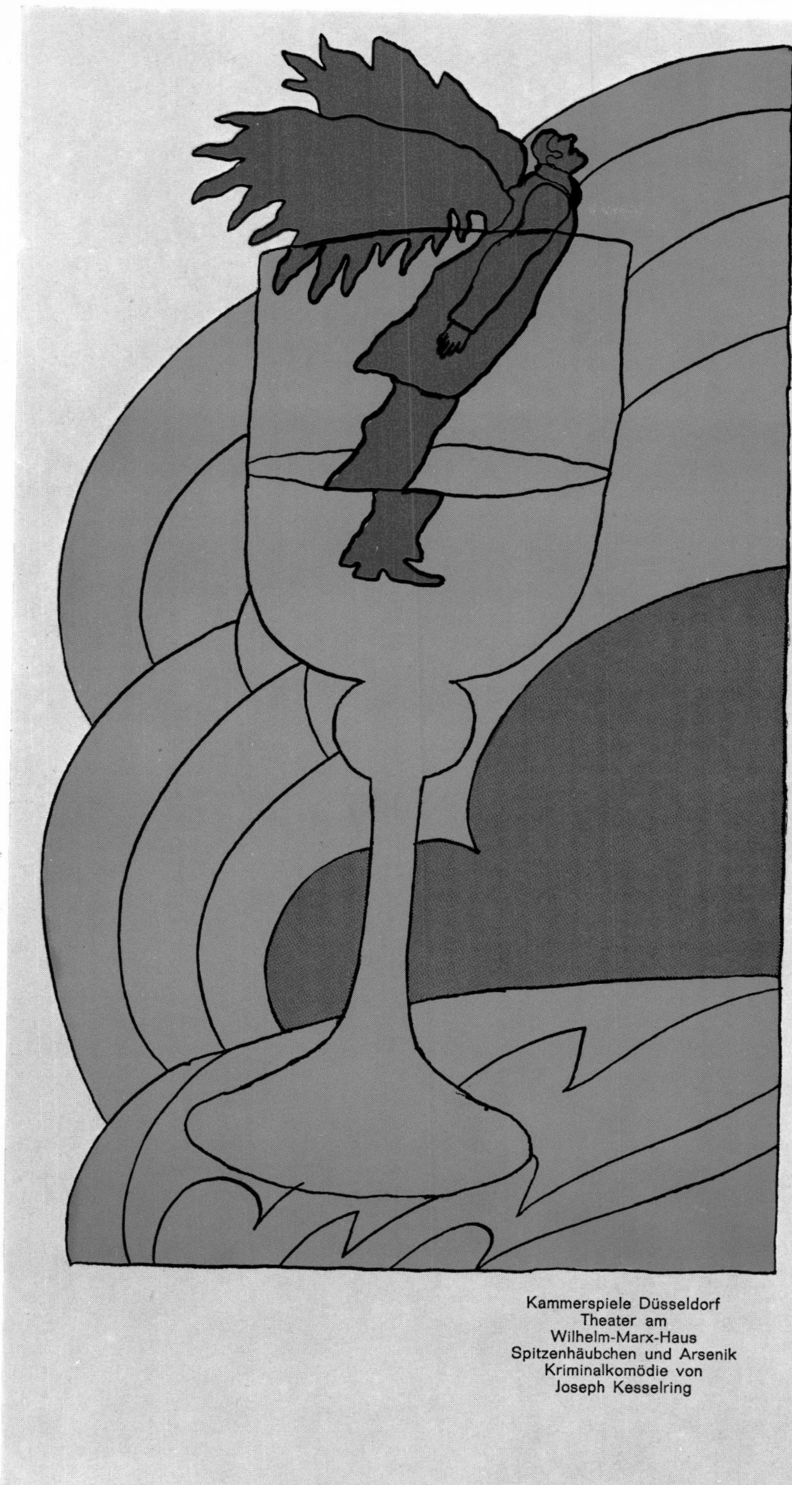

465

466

458) 462)–464) Illustrations and corresponding double spreads from a booklet about Switzerland handed out in the Swiss Pavilion at *Hemisfair 68*, San. Antonio, Tex. (SWI)
459)–461) 465) 466) Pages and cover from programmes for a Dusseldorf theatre (figs. 459 and 465 for *Arsenic and Old Lace*, figs. 460 and 466 for Tucholsky's *Gripsholm Castle* and fig. 461 for Anne Jellicoe's *The Knack*). (GER)

458) 462)–464) Illustrationen und Doppelseiten aus einer Broschüre über die Schweiz, herausgegeben von PRO HELVETIA für die *Hemisfair 68* in San Antonio, Tex. (SWI)
459)–461) 465) 466) Seiten und Umschlag von Programmheften der Kammerspiele Düsseldorf (Abb. 459 und 465 für *Spitzenhäubchen und Arsenik*, Abb. 460 und 466 für *Schloss Gripsholm* und Abb. 461 für *The Knack* von Anne Jellicoe). (GER)

458) 462)–464) Illustrations et doubles pages correspondantes, tirées d'une brochure sur la Suisse distribuée aux visiteurs du pavillon suisse à l'exposition *Hemisfair 68*, San Antonio, Tex. (SWI)
459)–461) 465) 466) Pages et couverture des programmes d'un théâtre de Dusseldorf: 459 et 465 pour *Arsenic et vieilles dentelles*, 460 et 466 pour *Château de Gripsholm*, de Tucholsky, et 461 pour *The Knack*, d'Anne Jellicoe. (GER)

467

468

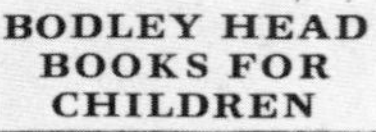

472

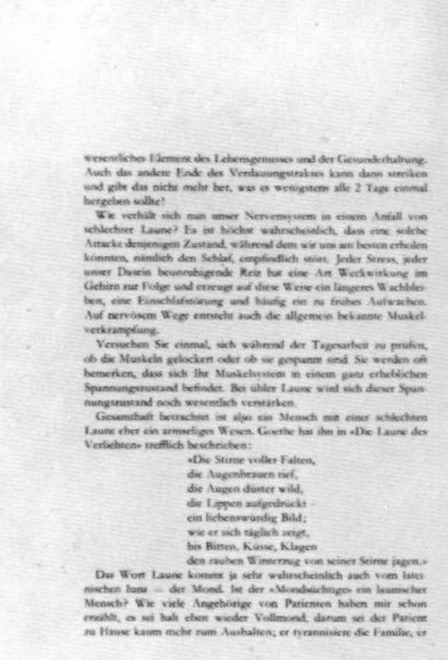

wesentliches Element des Lebensgenusses und der Gesunderhaltung. Auch das andere Ende des Verdauungstraktes kann dann streiken und gibt das nicht mehr her, was es wenigstens alle 2 Tage einmal hergeben sollte!

Wie verhält sich nun unser Nervensystem in einem Anfall von schlechter Laune? Es ist höchst wahrscheinlich, dass eine solche Attacke denjenigen Zustand, während dem wir uns am besten erholen könnten, nämlich den Schlaf, empfindlich stört. Jeder Stress, jeder unser Dasein beunruhigende Reiz hat eine Art Weckwirkung im Gehirn zur Folge und erzeugt auf diese Weise ein längeres Wachbleiben, eine Einschlafstörung und häufig ein zu frühes Aufwachen. Auf nervösem Wege entsteht auch die allgemein bekannte Muskelverkrampfung.

Versuchen Sie einmal, sich während der Tagesarbeit zu prüfen, ob die Muskeln gelockert oder ob sie gespannt sind. Sie werden oft bemerken, dass sich Ihr Muskelsystem in einem ganz erheblichen Spannungszustand befindet. Bei übler Laune wird sich dieser Spannungszustand noch wesentlich verstärken.

Gesamthaft betrachtet ist also ein Mensch mit einer schlechten Laune eher ein armseliges Wesen. Goethe hat ihn in «Die Laune des Verliebten» trefflich beschrieben:

«Die Stirne voller Falten,
die Augenbrauen tief,
die Augen düster wild,
die Lippen aufgedrückt –
ein liebenswürdig Bild;
wie er sich täglich zeigt,
bis Bitten, Küsse, Klagen
den rauhen Winterzug von seiner Stirne jagen.»

Das Wort Laune kommt ja sehr wahrscheinlich auch vom lateinischen luna – der Mond. Ist der «Mondsüchtige» ein launischer Mensch? Wie viele Angehörige von Patienten haben mir schon erzählt, es sei halt eben wieder Vollmond, darum sei der Patient zu Hause kaum mehr zum Aushalten; er tyrannisiere die Familie, er

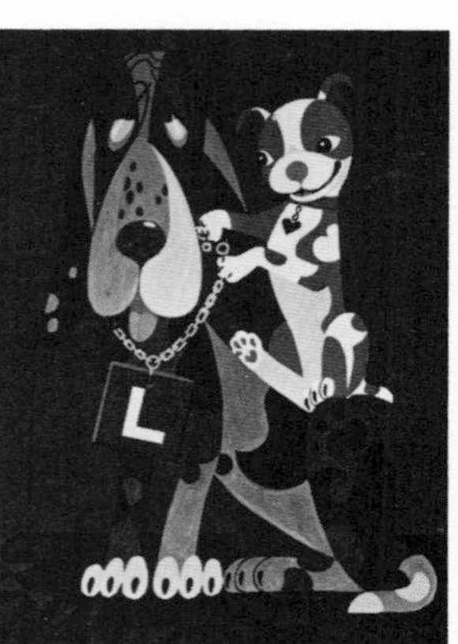

473

474

Artist/Künstler/Artiste:

467) 472) MAURICE SENDAK/JOHN RYDER
468) LUCIANO FRANCESCONI
469)–471) ROBERT O. BLECHMANN/LOUIS PORTUESI
473) 474) DONALD BRUN
475) RONALD SEARLE/ALAIN DIGARD
476) SEYMOUR CHWAST

Art Director/Directeur artistique:

467) 472) JOHN RYDER
469)–471) LOUIS PORTUESI
476) ARTHUR ROSENBLATT

470

469

471

475

Agency / Agentur / Agence – Studio:
468) STUDIO BOMPIANI, MILAN
469)-471) AMPERSAND, NEW YORK
476) PUSH PIN STUDIO, INC., NEW YORK

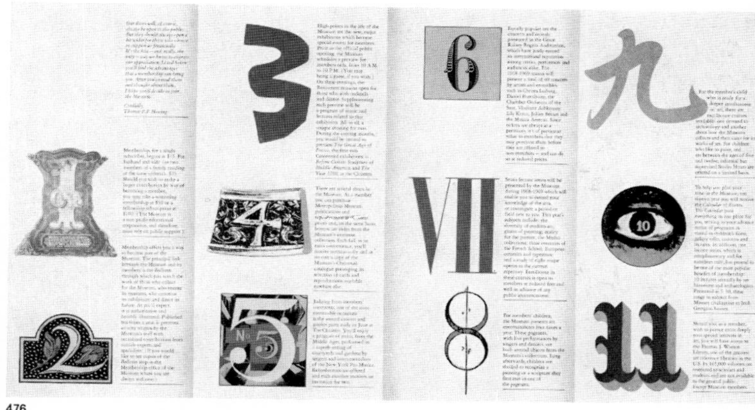
476

467) 472) Illustration and cover for a *Bodley Head* children's book catalogue. (GB)
468) Page introducing a new section in a publisher's catalogue. Black and white. (ITA)
469)-471) Illustrations and cover of a space promotion booklet for READER'S DIGEST. (USA)
473) 474) Spread and illustration from a jubilee booklet for an insurance company. (SWI)
475) Announcement by a bookshop of the inception of a book-of-the-month scheme. (FRA)
476) From a folder to encourage membership of the Metropolitan Museum of Art. (USA)

467) 472) Illustration und Umschlag für einen Kinderbücherkatalog. (GB)
468) Titelseite für einen Bücherkatalog. Schwarzweiss. (ITA)
469)-471) Illustrationen und Umschlag zur Inserentenwerbung in READER'S DIGEST. (USA)
473) 474) Aus der Jubiläumsschrift der *Coop* Lebensversicherungs-Genossenschaft, Basel. (SWI)
475) Ankündigung eines Buchhändlers über die künftige Bekanntgabe eines «Buches des Monats». (FRA)
476) Aus einem Faltprospekt zur Mitgliederwerbung für ein Museum. (USA)

467) 472) Illustration et couverture d'un catalogue de livres d'enfants. (GB)
468) Page d'un catalogue de livres des Editions Bompiani, Milan. (ITA)
469)-471) D'un prospectus pour la publicité dans le READER'S DIGEST. (USA)
473) 474) Double page et illustration tirées de la plaquette anniversaire de la section assurances d'une société coopérative. (SWI)
475) Imprimé publicitaire de la Galerie-Librairie La Pochade, Paris. (FRA)
476) D'un dépliant en faveur de l'adhésion à un musée de New York. (USA)

Artist/Künstler/Artiste:

477) FRITZ GOTTSCHALK
478) 479) WALTER TAFELMAIER
480) JOHN COPELAND
481) TOMI UNGERER
482) GÜNTHER KIESER
483) JAMES D. TAYLOR
484) HEINZ KRÖHL

477

478

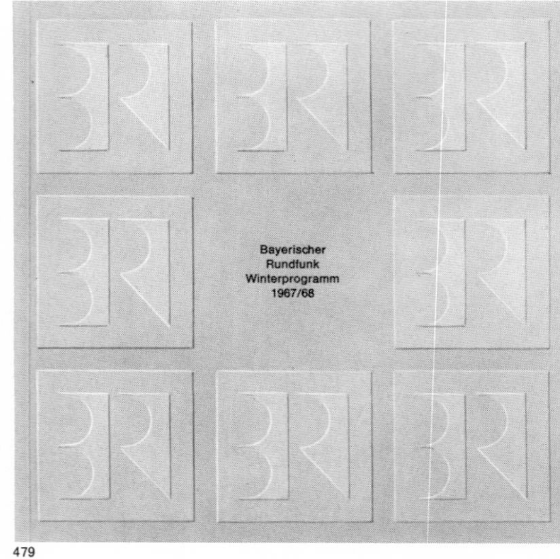

479

481

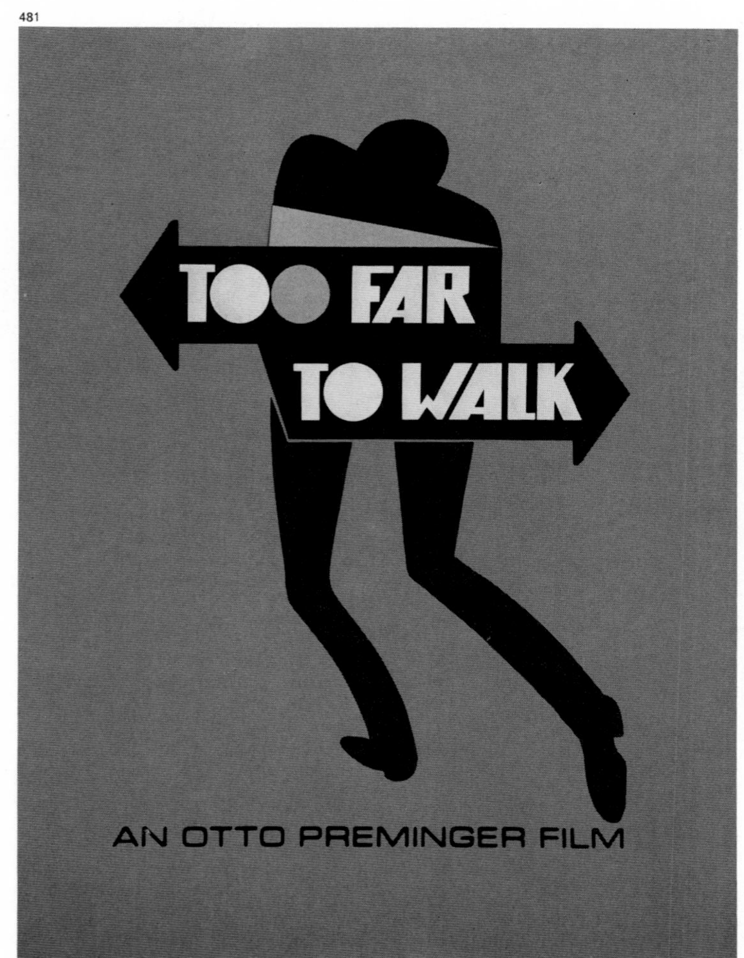

482

Booklets
Prospekte
Prospectus

Art Director/ Directeur artistique:

477) FRITZ GOTTSCHALK
483) JAMES D. TAYLOR
484) HEINZ KRÖHL

Agency/ Agentur/ Agence – Studio:

477) GOTTSCHALK+ASH LTD., MONTREAL
483) ROUS & MANN PRESS LTD., TORONTO

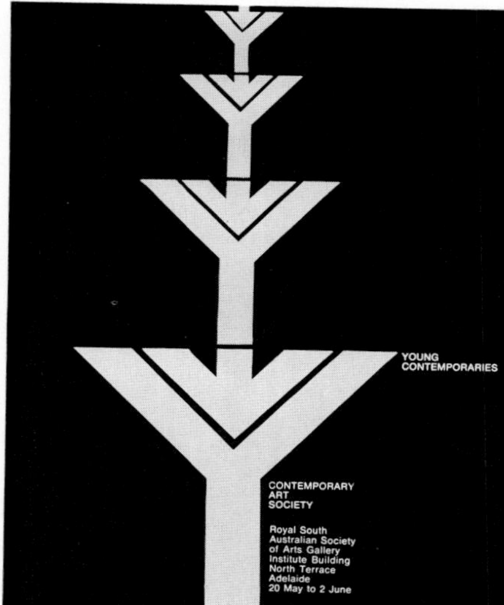

480

483

Einladung zum Johannisfest
im Gutenberg-Jahr 1968

484

477) Invitation to an exhibition of photographs by Karsh. (CAN)
478) 479) Spread and cover of a winter programme of the Bavarian radio. (GER)
480) Cover for the catalogue of a contemporary arts exhibition. (AUL)
481) Cover for a brochure on a new film. Black, green and white on blue. (USA)
482) Cover of a programme of the Hessian radio. Black and white. (GER)
483) Programme for a showing of films on art. Black and two browns. (CAN)
484) Cover of a programme for a Gutenberg Festival. (GER)

477) Einladung zu einer Photo-Ausstellung. (CAN)
478) 479) Seite und Umschlag eines Programmes des Bayerischen Rundfunks. (GER)
480) Katalogsumschlag für eine Ausstellung zeitgenössischer Kunst. (AUL)
481) Umschlag einer Broschüre über einen neuen Film. Mehrfarbig. (USA)
482) Programmumschlag für den Hessischen Rundfunk. Schwarzweiss. (GER)
483) Programm für eine Vorführung von Filmen über Kunst. (CAN)
484) Programmumschlag für die Gutenberg-Festaufführungen. (GER)

477) Invitation à une exposition de photographie. (CAN)
478) 479) Double page et couverture d'un programme de la Radio bavaroise. (GER)
480) Couverture du catalogue d'une exposition d'art contemporain. (AUL)
481) Couverture d'une brochure pour un film. Polychrome. (USA)
482) Couverture du programme d'un émetteur radiophonique. (GER)
483) Programme d'une présentation de films d'art. Noir et deux bruns. (CAN)
484) Couverture du programme d'un Festival Gutenberg. (GER)

Artist/Künstler/Artiste:

485) K. L. ROTHENBERGER
486) REYNOLD RUFFINS
487) 488) WILHELM BETTGES
489) MILTON GLASER
490) JOHN JANOS
491) GILBERT LESSER
492) PETER GAULD

Art Director/Directeur artistique:

485) K. L. ROTHENBERGER
486) JIM ADAIR
487) 488) ROBERT HIRSCHBERGER
489) SILAS H. RHODES
490) JOHN JANOS
491) GILBERT LESSER
492) BRIAN CONNON

Agency/Agentur/Agence-Studio:

486) GEER, DUBOIS, INC., NEW YORK
489) PUSH PIN STUDIOS, INC., NEW YORK
490) MONOGRAM, INC., NEW YORK

485

486

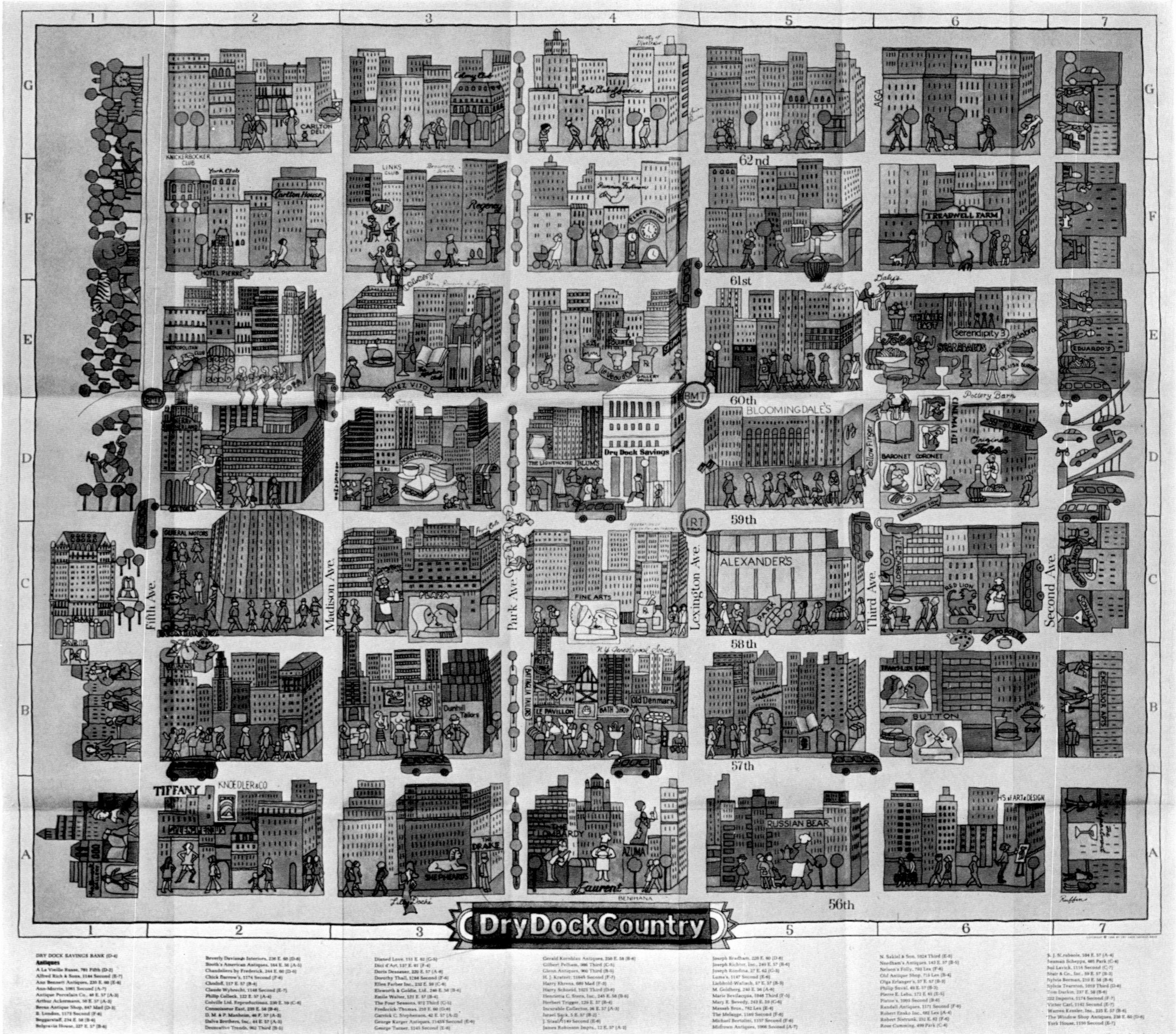

Wie sehen und erleben Sonntagsleser

Bild am Sonntag

Ein Intermedia-Vergleich

487

BILD am SONNTAG ist als Zeitung und Illustrierte in einem konzipiert. Daß sie von ihren Lesern entsprechend verstanden wird und wie die Nutzung im Vergleich zu Tageszeitungen und Illustrierten ist, schildert eine Untersuchung. Sie wurde im November und Dezember 1967 vom Institut infratest, München, durchgeführt. Zeitungs-, Illustrierten- und BILD-am-SONNTAG-Leser beantworteten gleichlautende Fragen. Die wichtigsten Antworten und Ergebnisse legen wir Ihnen hier vor.

488

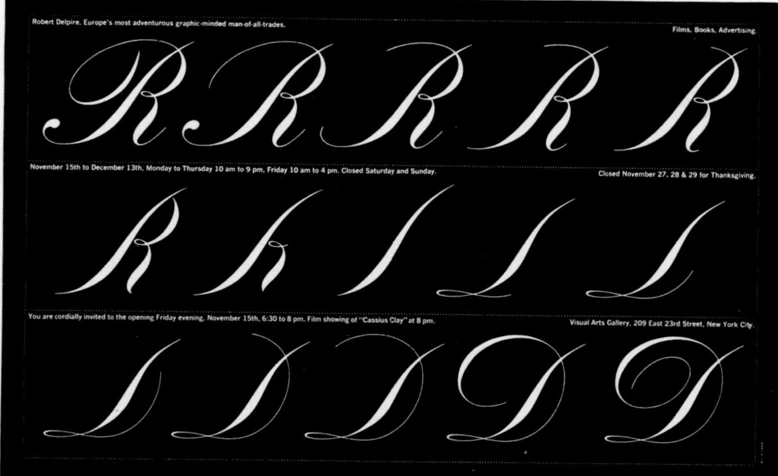

489

490

485) Cover of a type specimen book. Silver and black, embossed ground. (SPA)
486) Folder with map of the shopping area surrounding Dry Dock Saving Bank. Full colour. (USA)
487) 488) Cover and page from a space promotion booklet for a Sunday newspaper. (GER)
489) Invitation to a showing of a Robert Delpire film in the Visual Arts Gallery. (USA)
490) Cover of the Bureau of Advertising's choice of the best 1968 newspaper advertising. (USA)
491) Cover of a folder about the business magazine FORTUNE. (USA)
492) Cover of a folder for Westminster Bank addressed to students of a London college. (GB)

485) Umschlag eines Schriftenkatalogs. Silber und schwarz auf geprägtem Grund. (SPA)
486) Prospekt für eine Bank, die auf einer Karte zeigt, wie zentral sie gelegen ist. (USA)
487) 488) Umschlag und Seite einer Broschüre zur Inserentenwerbung in BILD AM SONNTAG. (GER)
489) Einladung zur Vorführung eines Films von Robert Delpire in einer Kunstgallerie. (USA)
490) Umschlag für eine Auswahl der besten Zeitungsinserate von 1968. (USA)
491) Umschlag eines Faltprospektes für die Finanzzeitschrift FORTUNE. (USA)
492) Faltprospekt für eine Bank, zur Verteilung an Studenten. (GB)

485) Couverture d'un catalogue de caractères de la fonderie Neufville SA, Barcelone. (SPA)
486) Dépliant pour une banque, contenant une carte du quartier où elle se trouve. (USA)
487) 488) Couverture et page d'une brochure pour la publicité dans un journal dominical. (GER)
489) Invitation à la présentation d'un film de Robert Delpire dans une galerie de New York. (USA)
490) Couverture d'une collection des meilleures annonces de presse de 1968. (USA)
491) Couverture d'un dépliant pour la revue FORTUNE. (USA)
492) Couverture d'un dépliant en faveur d'une banque, pour distribution aux étudiants. (GB)

491

492

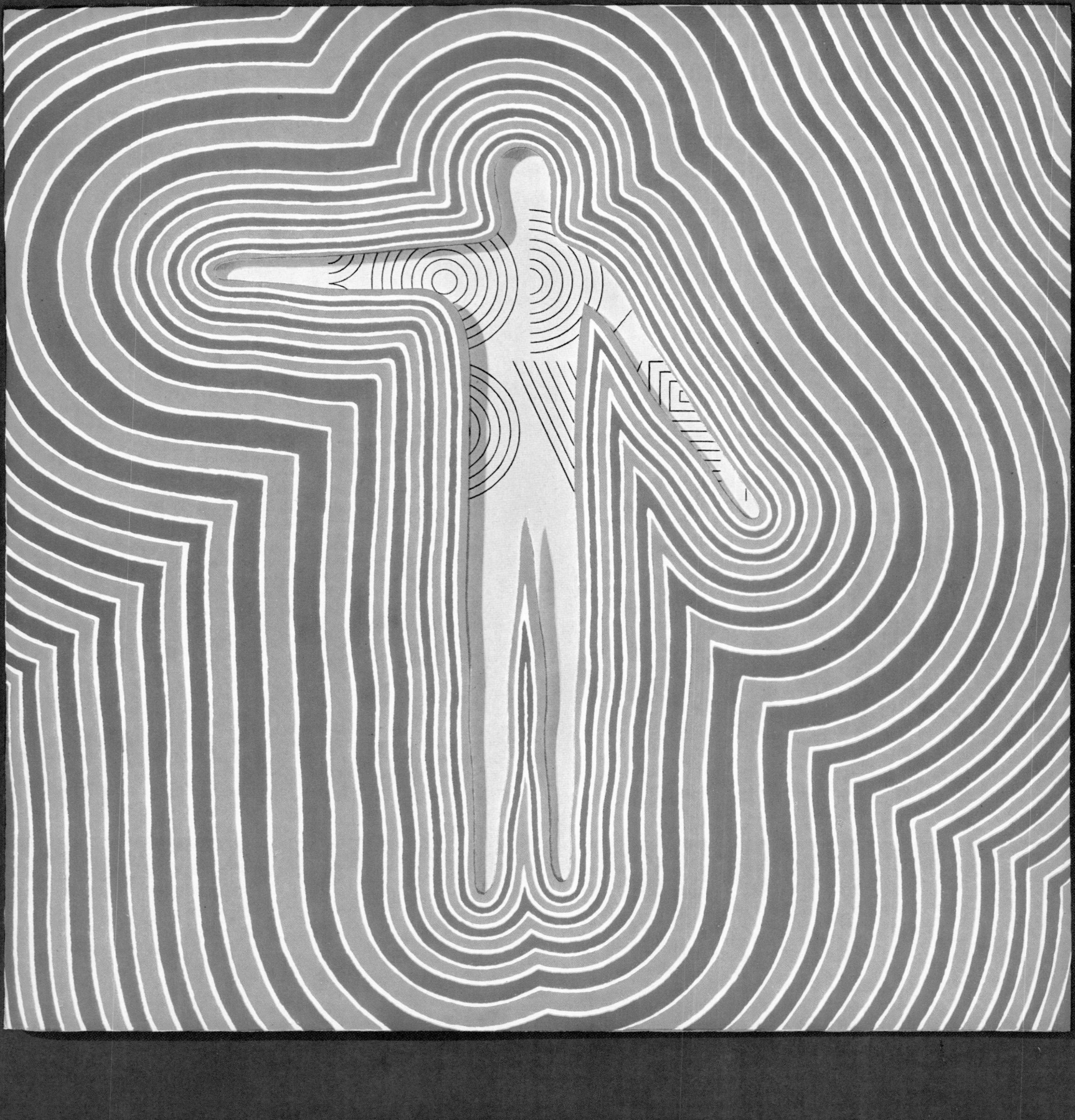

493

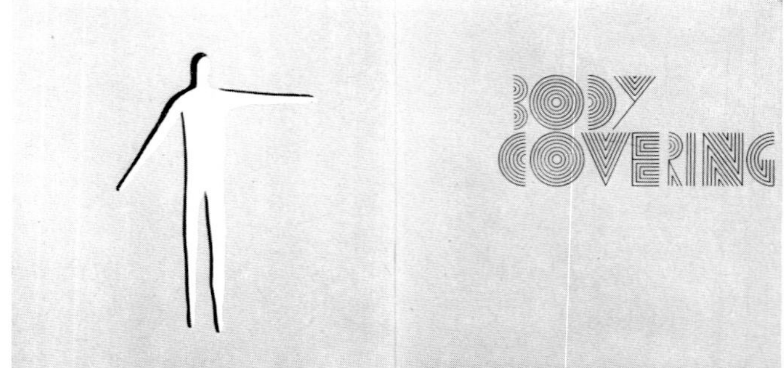

494

Artist / Künstler / Artiste:

493) 494) EMIL ANTONUCCI
495) HANS FÖRTSCH / SIGRID VON BAUMGARTEN
496) BERNARD MIOT
497) MONIQUE BORLÉE LOMBAL
498) DON WELLER / DON KANO

Booklets / Prospekte / Prospectus

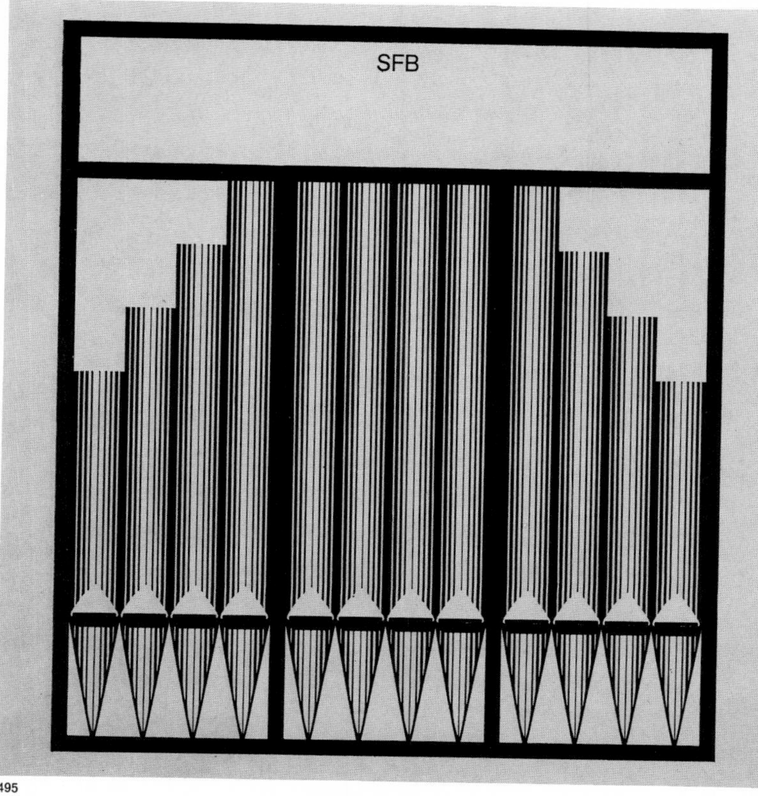

495

496

497

493) 494) Cover with cut-out and first inside spread of a catalogue for an exhibition entitled 'Body Covering' staged in New York. (USA)
495) Cover for a transmitting station's concert programme. (GER)
496) Catalogue cover for an exhibition of 'oleo-pneumatic' sculptures by Bernard Miot. (FRA)
497) Programme for a sponsored theatrical performance. Black, red and turquoise. (BEL)
498) Invitation to the annual student show of the UCLA Department of Art. (USA)

493) 494) Umschlag mit Ausschnitt und erste Doppelseite eines Katalogs für eine in New York veranstaltete Ausstellung über «Körperbekleidung». (USA)
495) Programmheft für Konzerte, die vom Sender Freies Berlin ausgestrahlt werden. (GER)
496) Katalogsumschlag für eine Ausstellung von Skulpturen. (FRA)
497) Programmheft für Aufführungen in einem Brüsseler Theater. Schwarz, rot und türkis. (BEL)
498) Einladung zur alljährlichen Ausstellung von Studentenarbeiten an einer Universität. (USA)

493) 494) Couverture et première double page du catalogue d'une exposition intitulée «Vêtements», organisée à New York. (USA)
495) Couverture du programme d'un concert retransmis par l'émetteur de Berlin libre. (GER)
496) Couverture du catalogue d'une exposition des œuvres «oléo-pneumatiques» du sculpteur Bernard Miot, à Paris. (FRA)
497) Programme d'une représentation au Théâtre 140, Bruxelles. Polychrome. (BEL)
498) Invitation à l'exposition annuelle de travaux d'étudiants dans une université. (USA)

Art Director/ Directeur artistique:

495) HANS FÖRTSCH/SIGRID VON BAUMGARTEN
496) BERNARD MIOT
497) PAUL PATIGNY
498) KATAOKA/DON KANO/DON WELLER

Agency/ Agentur/ Agence – Studio:

495) HANS FÖRTSCH/SIGRID VON BAUMGARTEN, BERLIN
497) PUBLIART, BRUXELLES
498) KATAOKA/KANO/WELLER, LOS ANGELES

UCLA DEPARTMENT OF ART ANNUAL STUDENT SHOW JUNE 10-JULY 28 1968

498

499

500

501

502

503

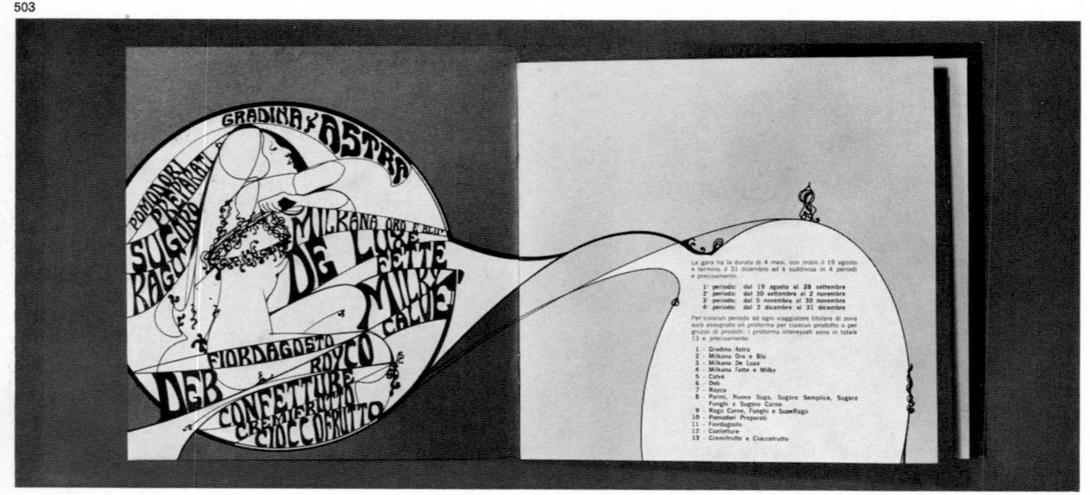

Booklets / Prospekte / Prospectus

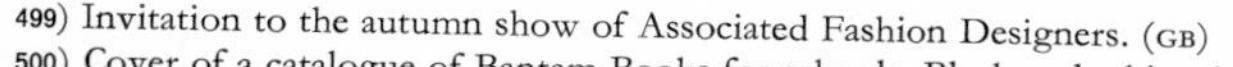

499) Invitation to the autumn show of Associated Fashion Designers. (GB)
500) Cover of a catalogue of Bantam Books for schools. Black and white. (USA)
501) Direct-mail piece in the form of a dress for TIME magazine. (USA)
502) Cover of a catalogue of new Swiss books. Red ground. (SWI)
503) Colour spread from a booklet about a contest among food salesmen. (ITA)
504) 505) Colour pages from a booklet about a make of zip fasteners. (FRA)
506) Cover of a brochure about diamonds. (FRA)
507) 508) Cover and spread from a catalogue of cosmetic products. (SWI)

499) Einladung zur Herbstausstellung einer Vereinigung von Modezeichnern. (GB)
500) Katalogumschlag für *Bantam*-Bücher für Schulen. Schwarzweiss. (USA)
501) Werbung für die Zeitschrift TIME in Form eines Kleides. (USA)
502) Umschlag des Katalogs *Neue Schweizer Bücher 1968*. Roter Grund. (SWI)
503) Doppelseite aus einer Broschüre über einen Wettbewerb für Verkäufer. (ITA)
504) 505) Farbseiten aus einer Broschüre für eine Reissverschlussmarke. (FRA)
506) Umschlag einer Broschüre über Diamanten. (FRA)
507) 508) Umschlag und Doppelseite eines Katalogs für *Elle + Lui*-Kosmetika. (SWI)

499) Invitation aux présentations d'automne d'une association de dessinateurs de mode. (GB)
500) Couverture d'un catalogue de livres scolaires. Noir et blanc. (USA)
501) Publicité en forme de vêtement pour la revue TIME. (USA)
502) Couverture d'un catalogue de nouveaux livres suisses. Fond rouge. (SWI)
503) Double page en couleur d'une brochure en faveur d'un concours pour les représentants en produits alimentaires, organisé par Van den Bergh, Milan. (ITA)
504) 505) Pages en couleur d'une brochure en faveur des fermetures *Eclair*. (FRA)
506) Couverture d'une brochure sur les diamants, publiée par De Beers Consolidated Mines Ltd., Londres. (FRA)
507) 508) Couverture et double page d'un catalogue de produits cosmétiques. (SWI)

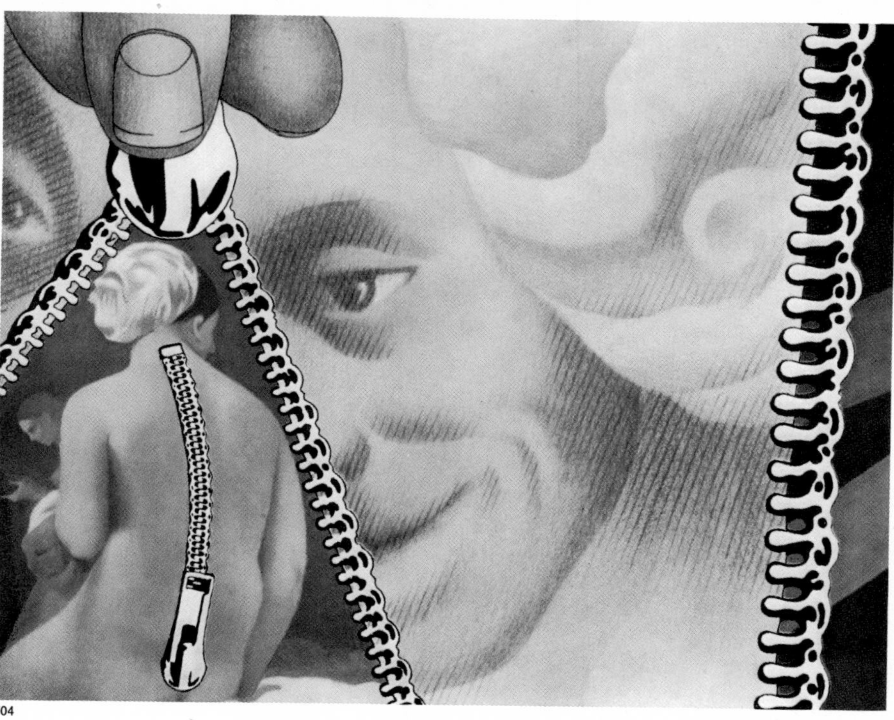

504

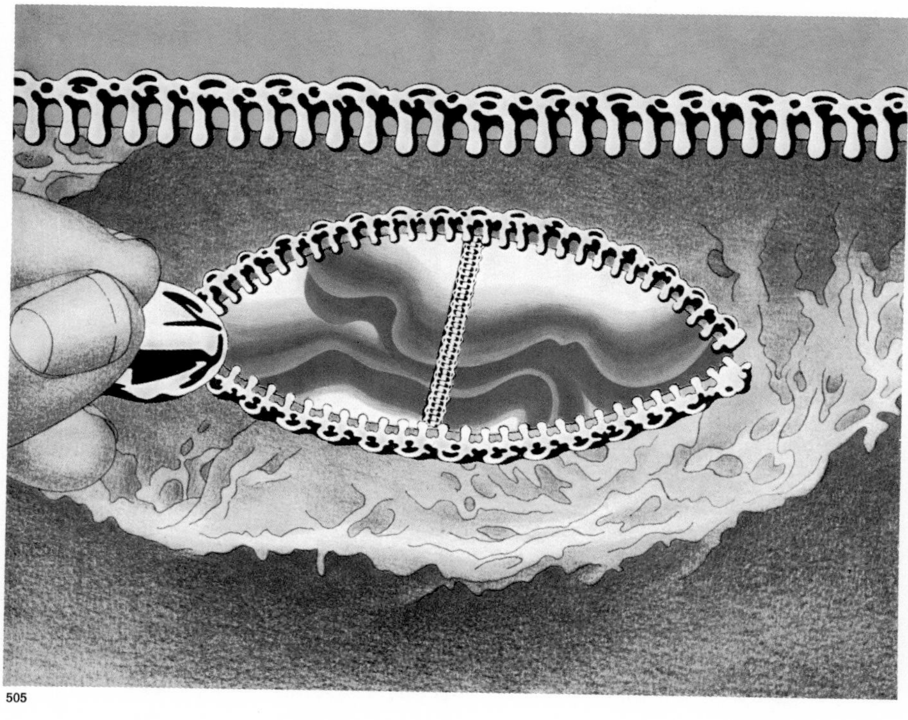

505

506

Artist/Künstler/Artiste:

499) REGINALD MOUNT/EILEEN EVANS
500) LISA CAYNE
501) RON DEVITO
502) JOSEF A. NIEDERBERGER
503) SERGIO DEGIPO
504) 505) MICHEL QUAREZ
506) JEAN FORTIN
507) 508) CIOMA SCHÖNHAUS

Art Director/Directeur artistique:

500) LISA CAYNE
501) WALTER LEFMANN
504) 505) ANTOINE KIEFFER
506) JEAN FORTIN

Agency/Agentur/Agence – Studio:

504) 505) MAFIA (MAIMÉ ARNODIN, FAYOLLE, INT. ASSOC.), PARIS
506) EDITIONS PUBLICIS, PARIS
507) 508) CIOMA SCHÖNHAUS, BASEL

507

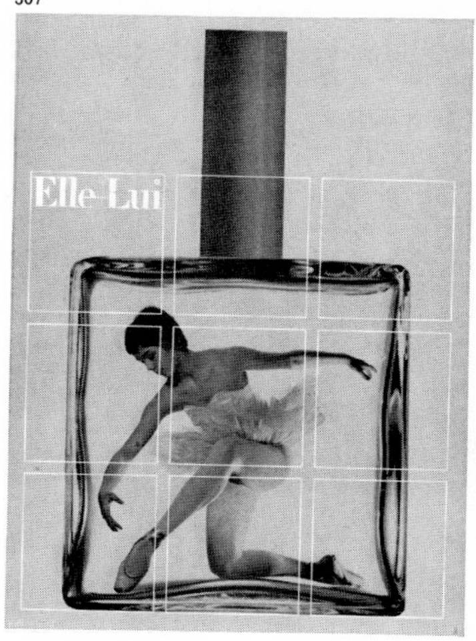

508

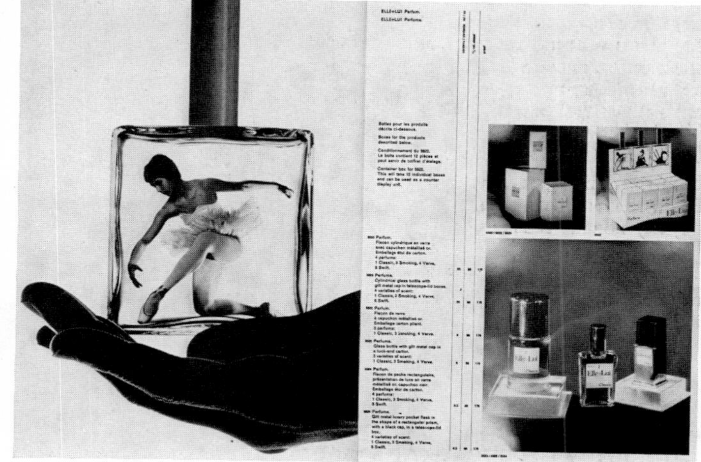

509

Artist/Künstler/Artiste:

509) NORMAN KOHN
510) JAMES DUNNE/WILLIAM J. BATTAGLIA
511) ARTHUR ZELGER
512) ANNEGRET BEIER
513)–516) PHILIPPE KAILHENN

Art Director/Directeur artistique:

509) RICHARD HENDERSON
510) WILLIAM J. BATTAGLIA
512)–516) ROBERT DELPIRE

Agency/Agentur/Agence – Studio:

509) BURTON-CAMPBELL ADV., INC., ATLANTA, GEORGIA
510) LEO BURNETT CO., INC., CHICAGO
512)–516) DELPIRE PUBLICITÉ, PARIS

510

511

Booklets / Prospekte / Prospectus

512

513

514

515

516

509) Cover of a booklet for the Great Southwest Corporation. (USA)
510) Mailing piece for United Air Lines. (USA)
511) Cover of a travel folder for the Southern Tyrol. Four colours. (ITA)
512) Complete cover for a brochure about a *Citroën* model. (FRA)
513)–516) Double spreads from an information bulletin issued by *Citroën*. (FRA)

509) Couverture d'une brochure pour la Great Southwest Corporation. (USA)
510) Imprimé publicitaire pour une compagnie aérienne. (USA)
511) Couverture d'un dépliant touristique pour le Tyrol du Sud. Polychrome. (ITA)
512) Couverture d'une brochure pour une voiture *Citroën*. (FRA)
513)–516) Doubles pages d'une brochure documentaire publiée par *Citroën*. (FRA)

509) Umschlag einer Broschüre für die Great Southwest Corporation. (USA)
510) Werbedrucksache für eine Fluggesellschaft. (USA)
511) Prospektumschlag für das Landesfremdenverkehrsamt für Südtirol, Bozen. (ITA)
512) Vollständiger Umschlag einer Broschüre über ein *Citroën*-Modell. (FRA)
513)–516) Doppelseiten aus einer von *Citroën* herausgegebenen Informationsbroschüre. (FRA)

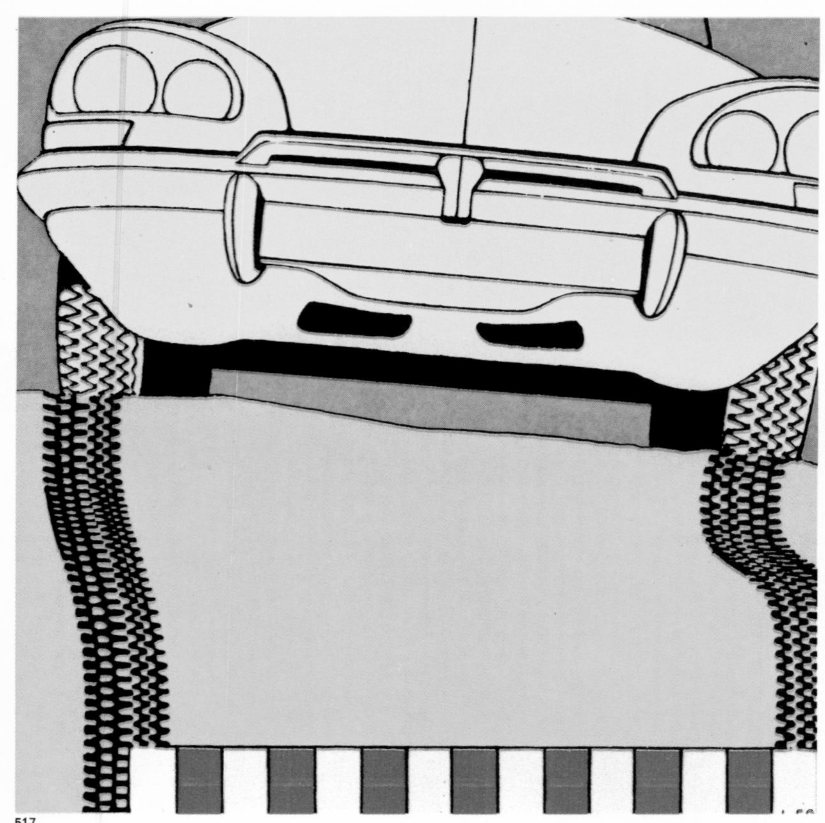

517

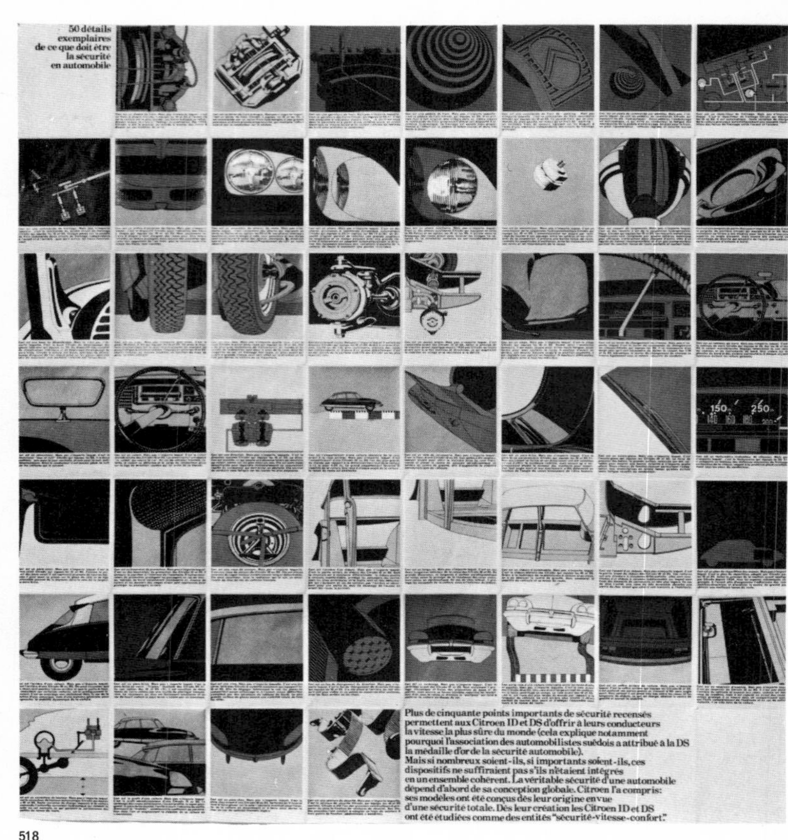

518

Booklets/Prospekte/Prospectus

521

519

520

522

LES GRANDES HEURES DE LA 2CV

Artist/Künstler/Artiste:

517) 518) HANS TROXLER
519) 520) MICHEL QUAREZ
521) 522) ALAIN LE FOLL

Art Director/Directeur artistique:

517)–521) ROBERT DELPIRE
522) ROBERT DELPIRE/ALAIN LE FOLL

Agency/Agentur/Agence – Studio:

517)–522) DELPIRE PUBLICITÉ, PARIS

517) 518) Specimen illustration and open folder drawing attention to fifty features that enhance the safety of *Citroën* ID and DS models. (FRA)
519) 520) Page and double spread from a booklet on the *Citroën* model *Dyane*. (FRA)
521) 522) Specimen illustration and open folder listing the 'great hours of the *Citroën* 2 CV'. (FRA)

517) 518) Ausschnitt und geöffneter Faltprospekt, der auf die fünfzig Vorkehrungen hinweist, die die Sicherheit der *Citroën*-ID- und -DS-Modelle erhöhen. (FRA)
519) 520) Seite und Doppelseite aus einer Broschüre für das *Citroën*-Modell *Dyane*. (FRA)
521) 522) Aus einem Prospekt für den *Citroën* 2 CV, der die «grossen Stunden» dieses Modells aufzählt. (FRA)

517) 518) Illustration et vue ouverture d'un dépliant énumérant les cinquante dispositifs de sécurités des modèles *Citroën* ID et DS. (FRA)
519) 520) Page et double page d'un prospectus en faveur de la *Citroën Dyane*. (FRA)
521) 522) Illustration et vue ouverte d'un dépliant en faveur de la *Citroën* 2 CV. (FRA)

523

523) Cover of a folder about the cargo services of *Swissair*. (SWI)
524) Cover of a folder for *Lipton* foods. (USA)
525) Menu for *Didi's* night club. Three colours. (GB)
526)–529) Spreads and covers of booklets on Germany and Munich, site of the 1972 Olympic Games. (GER)
530) Cover of a booklet on mountaineering issued by the Swiss National Tourist Office. (SWI)
531) Spread from a booklet on four provinces. (CAN)
532) From a booklet on a charity performance. (GB)
533) Cover of a tourist booklet on Greece. (GRE)

523) Umschlag eines Faltprospektes über den Transportdienst der *Swissair*. (SWI)
524) Faltprospekt für eine Nahrungsmittelfabrik. (USA)
525) Menukarte für ein Nachtlokal. Dreifarbig. (GB)
526)–529) Doppelseiten und Umschläge einer Broschüre über Deutschland und München, Schauplatz der Olympischen Spiele 1972. (GER)
530) Broschüre des Schweiz. Verkehrsvereins. (SWI)
531) Doppelseite aus einer Informationsbroschüre über vier kanadische Provinzen. (CAN)
532) Broschüre einer Wohltätigkeitsveranstaltung. (GB)
533) Umschlag eines Touristenprospektes. (GRE)

523) Couverture d'un dépliant pour les services de fret de *Swissair*. (SWI)
524) Couverture d'un dépliant pour les produits alimentaires *Lipton*. (USA)
525) Carte d'une boîte de nuit. Trois couleurs. (GB)
526)–529) Doubles pages et couvertures de prospectus touristiques pour l'Allemagne et Munich, où se dérouleront les jeux Olympiques de 1972. (GER)
530) Couverture d'une brochure sur l'alpinisme. (SWI)
531) Double page d'une brochure touristique. (CAN)
532) D'un prospectus pour une fête de bienfaisance. (GB)
533) Couverture d'un prospectus sur la Grèce. (GRE)

Come to the Pennsylvania Dutch Country and...
GET TO KNOW WHAT GOOD IS

524

525

Artist/Künstler/Artiste:
523) ROLAND GFELLER-CORTHÉSY
524) JOHN TROTTA/ROBERT FROST
525) THOMAS BUND
526)–529) BÜRO AICHER
530) BRUNO GENTINETTA
531) RICHARD BROWN
532) BRIAN TATTERSFIELD
533) AGNI KATZOURAKIS

Art Director/Directeur artistique:
523) ROLAND GFELLER-CORTHÉSY
524) ROBERT FROST
525) RICHARD NEGUS
531) RICHARD BROWN
532) MARCELLO MINALE/BRIAN TATTERSFIELD
533) MICHAEL KATZOURAKIS

526

527

530

528

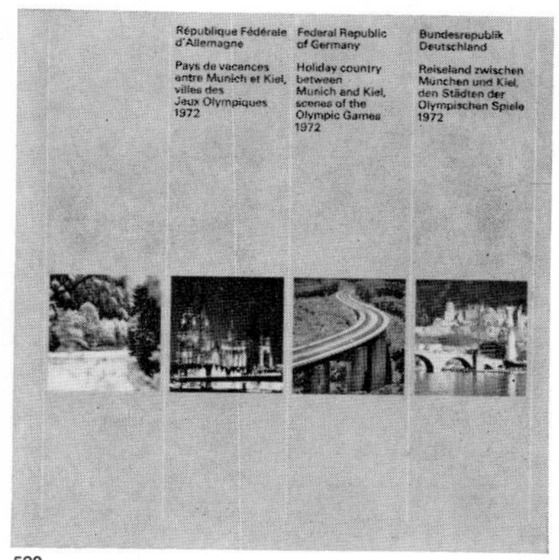

529

AMENITIES

531

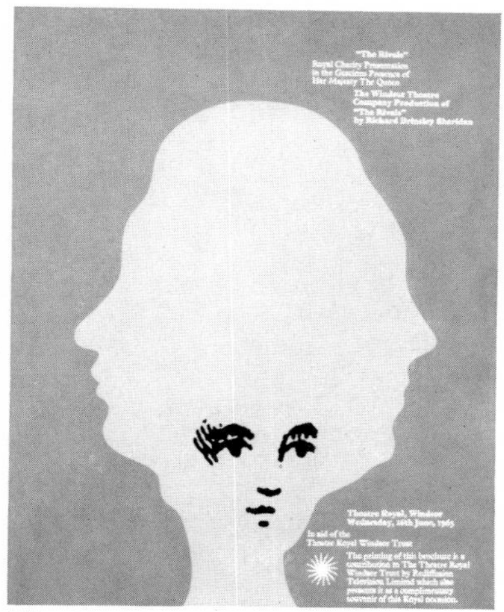

532

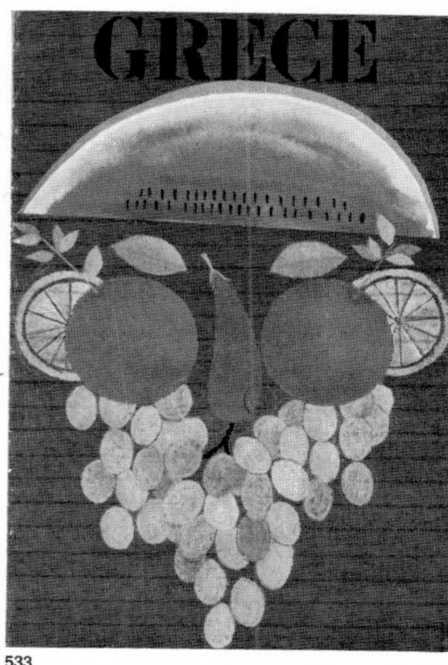

533

Agency/Agentur/Agence – Studio:
523) BLACKBOX AG, ZÜRICH
524) MONOGRAM, INC., NEW YORK
525) NEGUS & NEGUS, LONDON
531) RICHARD BROWN, LONDON
532) MINALE, TATTERSFIELD, PROVINCIALI LTD., LONDON
533) K & K, ATHENS PUBLICITY CENTRE, ATHENS

4

Magazine Covers
House Organs
Book Jackets
Paperbacks
Gramophone Record Covers

Zeitschriften-Umschläge
Hauszeitschriften
Schutzumschläge
Taschenbücher
Schallplatten-Umschläge

Couvertures de périodiques
Journaux d'entreprises
Chemises de livres
Livres brochés
Pochettes de disques

Magazine Covers
Zeitschriften-Umschläge
Couvertures de périodiques

Artist/Künstler/Artiste:

534) SAUL BASS/PAUL BRUHWILER
535) TSUNEHISA KIMURA
536) 537) SHIGEO OKAMOTO
538) SHIGEO FUKUDA
539) HARTMUT JÄGER
540) ARMANDO TESTA

Art Director/Directeur artistique:

534) SAUL BASS
535) TSUNEHISA KIMURA
536) 537) SHIGEO OKAMOTO
538) SHIGEO FUKUDA
539) ANDREW KNER
540) ARMANDO TESTA

Agency/Agentur/Agence – Studio:

534) SAUL BASS & ASSOCIATES, INC., LOS ANGELES
536) 537) SHIGEO OKAMOTO, DESIGN ROOM, TOKYO
540) STUDIO TESTA, TURIN

Publisher/Verleger/Editeur:

534) IDEA MAGAZINE, TOKYO
535) DESIGN MAGAZINE, TOKYO
536) 537) BUNKAZITSUGYO-SHA, TOKYO
538) SANKEI NEWSPAPER CO., TOKYO
539) PRINT MAGAZINE, NEW YORK
540) EDITRICE L'UFFICIO MODERNO, MILAN

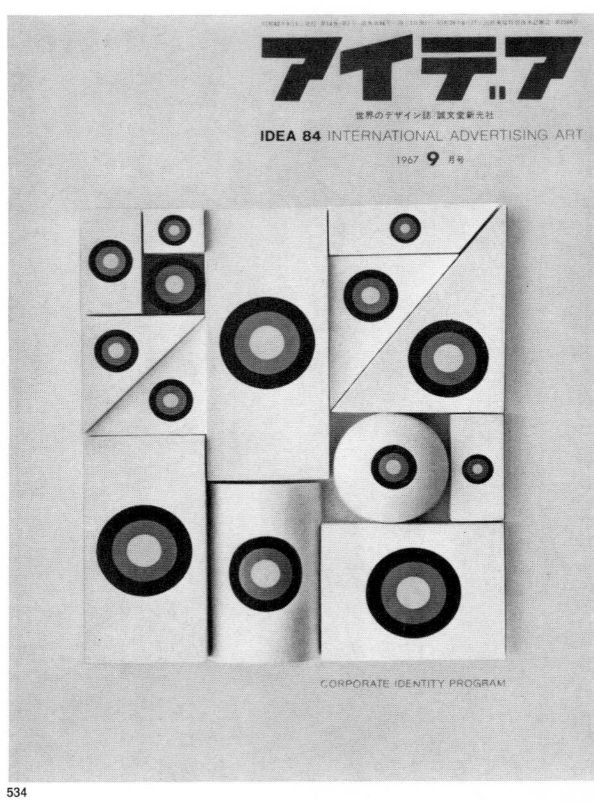

534

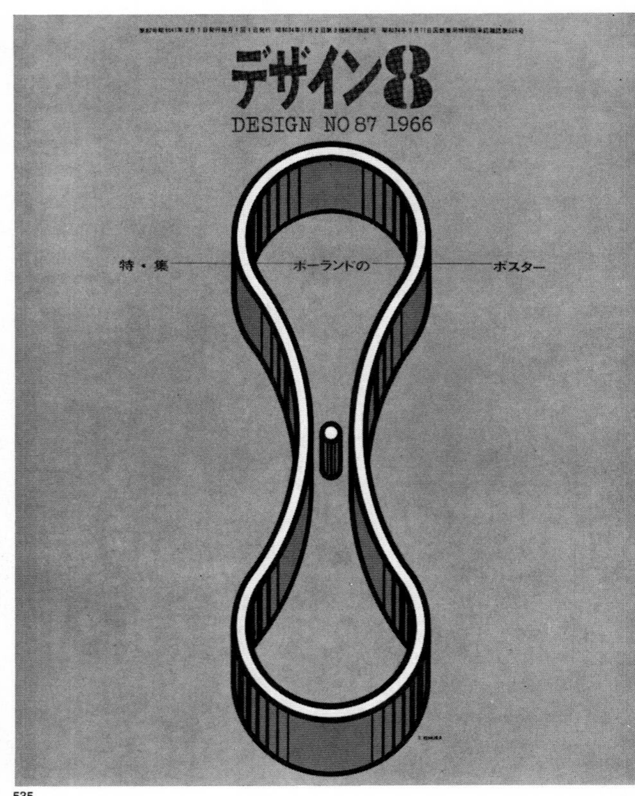

535

538

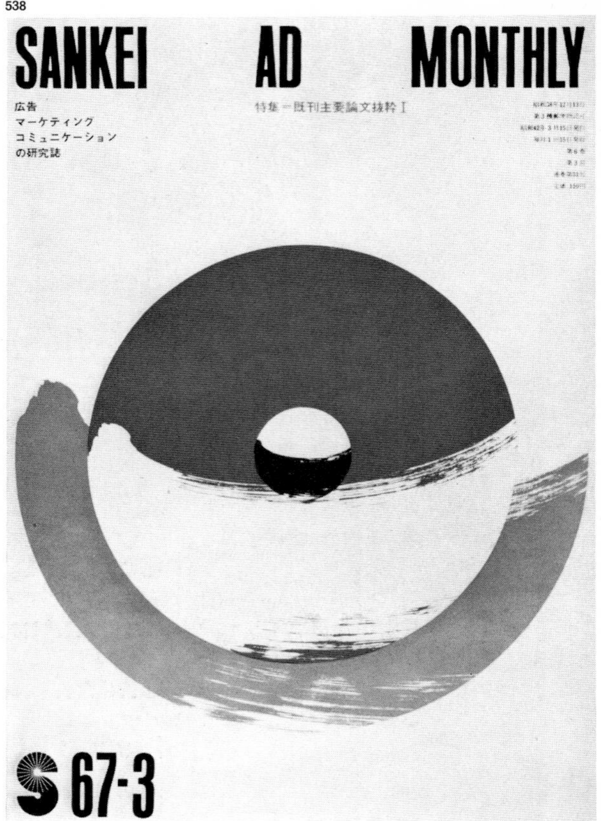

539

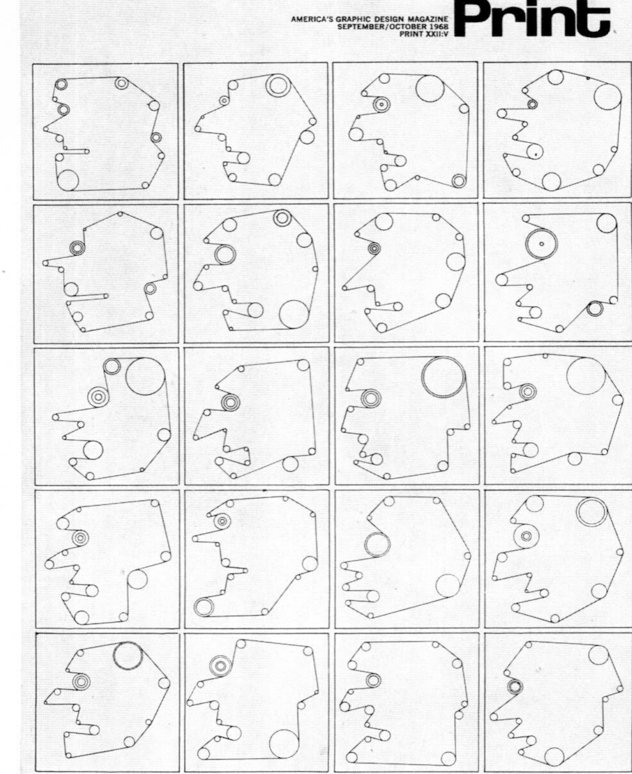

536

537

540

534) Cover of IDEA magazine, symbolizing corporate identity programmes. Emblem in two blues and yellow, beige ground. (JAP)
535) Cover of the monthly magazine DESIGN. Black and orange on green. (JAP)
536) 537) Covers of the monthly magazine SHINFUJIN. Fig. 536 in shades of yellow and green, fig. 537 with yellow rose and purple lettering. (JAP)
538) Cover of SANKEI AD MONTHLY, a magazine of advertising. Three colours. (JAP)
539) Cover of the graphic design magazine PRINT. Red and black. (USA)
540) Cover of LINEA GRAFICA, a bi-monthly graphic design magazine. Black, head and feet of hen in colour. (ITA)

534) Umschlag der Zeitschrift IDEA, der das Gestaltungsprogramm eines Unternehmens darstellt. Das Signet ist in zwei Blautönen und Gelb auf beigem Grund gehalten. (JAP)
535) Umschlag der Monatszeitschrift DESIGN. Schwarz und orange auf Grün. (JAP)
536) 537) Umschläge der Monatszeitschrift SHINFUJIN. Umschlag 536 in gelbgrünen Farbtönen, Schrift orange/schwarz, Umschlag 537 mit gelber Rose und lila Schrift. (JAP)
538) Umschlag von SANKEI AD MONTHLY, einer Zeitschrift für Werbung. Dreifarbig. (JAP)
539) Umschlag von PRINT, Zeitschrift für graphische Gestaltung. Rot und schwarz. (USA)
540) Umschlag von LINEA GRAFICA, einer zweimonatlich erscheinenden Zeitschrift für graphische Gestaltung. Schwarz, Kopf und Füsse des Huhnes farbig. (ITA)

534) Couverture de la revue IDEA. Emblème en deux tons de bleu et jaune sur fond beige. (JAP)
535) Couverture de la revue mensuelle DESIGN. Noir et orange sur vert. (JAP)
536) 537) Couvertures de la revue mensuelle SHINFUJIN. 536) Jaune et vert; 537) rose en jaune, texte en mauve. (JAP)
538) Couverture d'une revue mensuelle de publicité. Trois couleurs. (JAP)
539) Couverture de la revue d'art graphique PRINT. Rouge et noir. (USA)
540) Couverture de LINEA GRAFICA, revue bimensuelle d'art graphique. Noir, tête et pattes de la poule en couleur. (ITA)

Artist/Künstler/Artiste:

541) DOUGLAS MURRAY
542) ROSS
543) GEOFFREY DICKINSON
544) WILLIAM HEWISON
545) 547) 548) ANDRÉ FRANÇOIS
546) SAM ANTUPIT

Art Director/Directeur artistique:

541)-544) 547) 548) WILLIAM HEWISON
545) JAMES GERAGHTY
546) SAM ANTUPIT/DICK HESS

541

542

543

544

Publisher/Verleger/Editeur:

541)–544) 547) 548) PUNCH MAGAZINE, LONDON
545) THE NEW YORKER MAGAZINE, NEW YORK
546) ESQUIRE MAGAZINE, NEW YORK

545

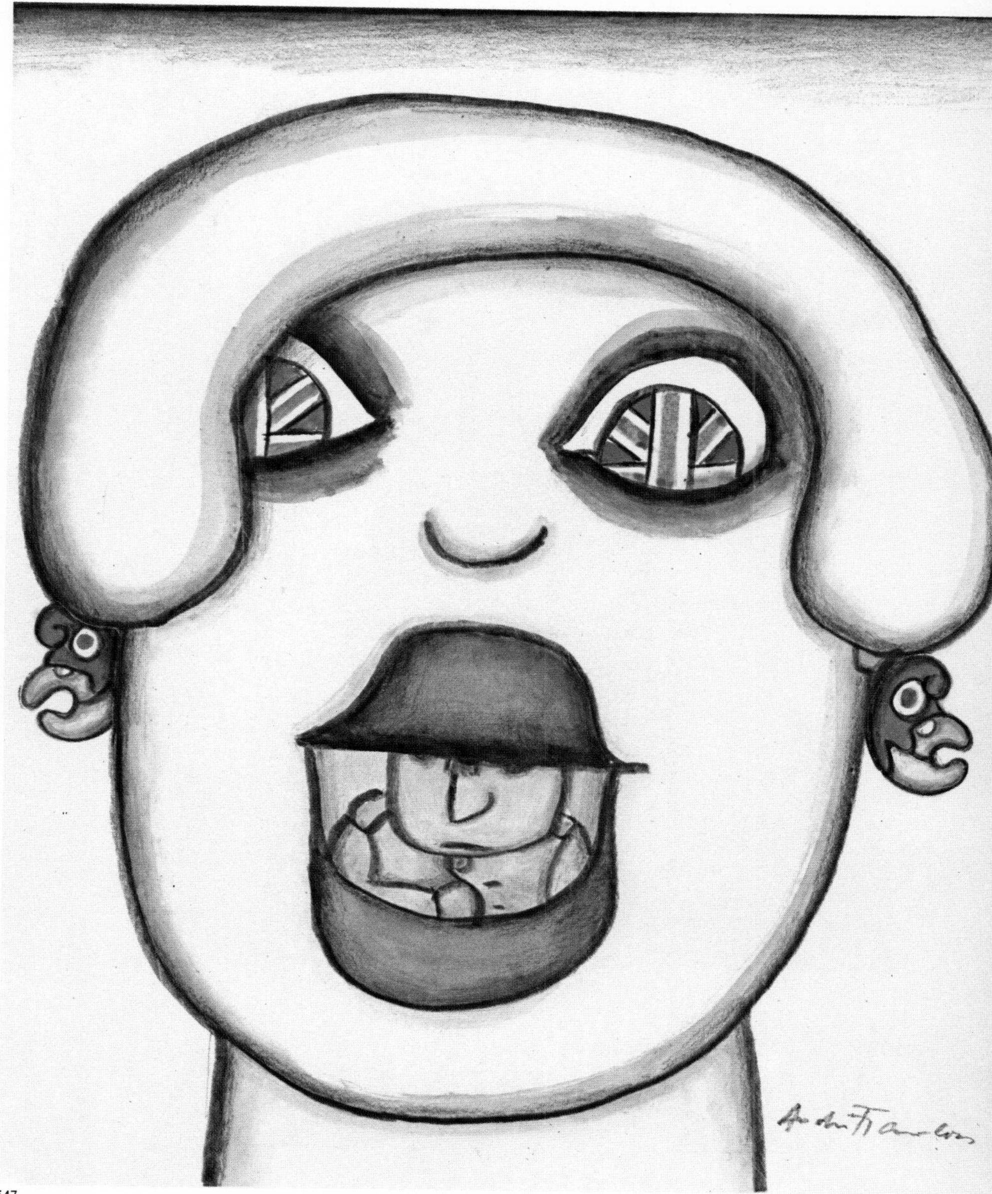

547

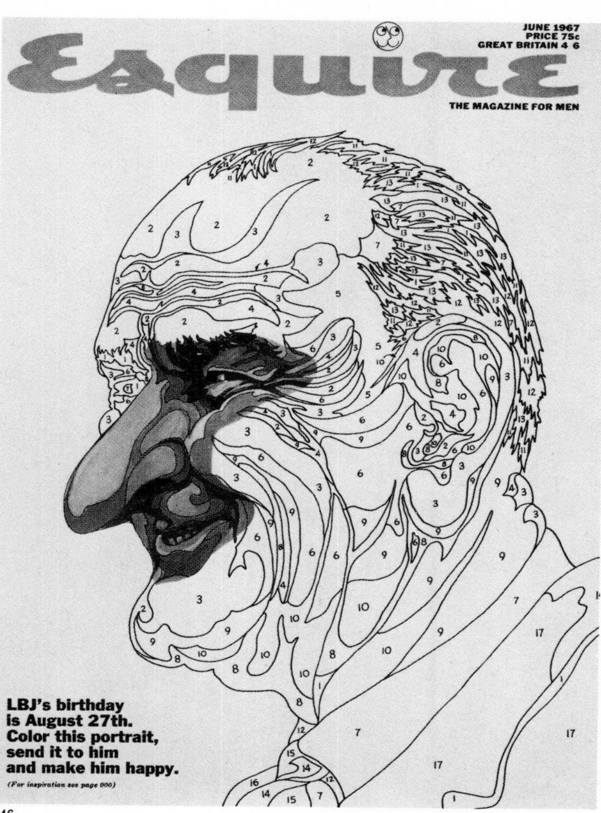

546

548

541)–544) Covers of the humorous magazine PUNCH. Polychrome. (GB)
545) Cover of THE NEW YORKER. Shades of blue and grey, blue lettering. (USA)
546) Cover of the monthly men's magazine ESQUIRE with a 'portrait' of Lyndon Johnson to colour. (USA)
547) 548) Illustration and complete cover of PUNCH magazine. (GB)

541)–544) Umschläge der satirischen Zeitschrift PUNCH. Mehrfarbig. (GB)
545) Umschlag der Zeitschrift THE NEW YORKER. Blaugraue Farbtöne. (USA)
546) Umschlag des Herrenmagazins ESQUIRE mit einer farbig auszumalenden Karikatur von Lyndon Johnson. (USA)
547) 548) Illustration und vollständiger Umschlag der Zeitschrift PUNCH. (GB)

541)–544) Couvertures en couleur de l'hebdomadaire humoristique PUNCH. (GB)
545) Couverture de l'hebdomadaire THE NEW YORKER. Bleu et gris. (USA)
546) Couverture de la revue masculine ESQUIRE, reproduisant un «portrait» de Lyndon Johnson pour colorier. (USA)
547) 548) Illustration et couverture de l'hebdomadaire PUNCH. (GB)

549

550

552

553

551

554

Magazine Covers
Zeitschriften-Umschläge
Couvertures de périodiques

549) Cover of DOMUS, a monthly of architecture and art. (ITA)
550) Cover of IMPACT, magazine of the Student National Education Association. Pale green and black with rose madder lettering. (USA)
551) Full-colour cover of THE REPORTER, a political news magazine. (USA)
552) 553) Covers of AMERYKA, Polish edition of an official magazine about America. Fig. 552 uses a metal sculpture; fig. 553 refers to a feature on American authors. (USA)
554) Cover of the fashion magazine BEAUTY FASHION. Red drawing, grey lettering. (USA)

549) Umschlag für DOMUS, Monatszeitschrift für Architektur, Kunst und Innenausstattung. (ITA)
550) Umschlag für IMPACT, Zeitschrift einer nationalen Bildungsvereinigung Studierender. (USA)
551) Mehrfarbiger Umschlag für THE REPORTER, ein politisches Nachrichtenmagazin. (USA)
552) 553) Umschläge für AMERYKA, polnische Ausgabe eines offiziellen Magazins über Amerika. Abb. 552 zeigt eine Metall-Skulptur; Abb. 553 bezieht sich auf einen Artikel über zeitgenössische amerikanische Autoren. (USA)
554) Umschlag der Modezeitschrift BEAUTY FASHION. (USA)

549) Couverture de DOMUS, revue d'art et d'architecture. (ITA)
550) Couverture d'une revue estudiantine. Vert pâle et noir, texte en rose. (USA)
551) Couverture polychrome d'une revue d'information politique, intitulée THE REPORTER. (USA)
552) 553) Couvertures de AMERYKA, édition polonaise d'une revue officielle consacrée à l'Amérique. L'ill. 552 reproduit une sculpture de métal, 553 s'inspire d'un article sur les auteurs américains. (USA)
554) Couverture de la revue BEAUTY FASHION. Dessin en rouge, texte en gris. (USA)

Artist/Künstler/Artiste:

549) GIULIO CONFALONIERI
550) TED ZEIGLER
551) FERNANDO KRAHN
552) GEORGE GIUSTI
553) ROBERT BANKS
554) EUGENE KARLIN/RAYMOND A. SCHULZE

Art Director/Directeur artistique:

549) GIULIO CONFALONIERI
550) EDDIE BYRD
551) REGINALD MASSIE
552) 553) DAVID MOORE
554) JEFF BABITZ

Agency/Agentur/Agence – Studio:

550) BEVERIDGE & ASSOC., INC., WASHINGTON, D.C.

Publisher/Verleger/Editeur:

549) DOMUS, MILAN
550) STUDENT NATIONAL EDUCATION ASSOC., WASHINGTON, D.C.
551) THE REPORTER, NEW YORK
552) 553) THE UNITED STATES INFORMATION AGENCY, WASHINGTON, D.C.
554) CONCEPT PUBLISHING CORP., NEW YORK

POLSKA

555

556

557

558

559

560

555) Cover of the Polish edition of the cultural magazine POLAND. Full colour. (POL)
556) Cover of the publication G.Q. SCENE. (USA)
557) Full-colour cover of THE NEW MIDDLE EAST, an international monthly magazine. (GB)
558) Cover of the professional magazine BROADCAST MANAGEMENT/ENGINEERING. (USA)
559) Cover of KONTAKT, a magazine for young people. Red and black. (SWI)
560) Cover of the design magazine GRAPHIS. (SWI)
561) 562) Covers of the travel magazine HOLIDAY. Fig. 561 in black and white, fig. 562 in black, green, red and purple. (USA)
563) Cover of an issue of OPERA NEWS devoted to opening nights. Red and black. (USA)

555) Umschlag der polnischen Ausgabe der kulturellen Zeitschrift POLAND. Mehrfarbig. (POL)
556) Umschlag einer Herrenzeitschrift. (USA)
557) Mehrfarbiger Umschlag für THE NEW MIDDLE EAST, eine internationale Monatszeitschrift. (GB)
558) Umschlag für die amerikanische Fachzeitschrift BROADCAST MANAGEMENT/ENGINEERING. (USA)
559) Umschlag für KONTAKT, eine Zeitschrift für junge Leser. (SWI)
560) Umschlag für GRAPHIS, Zeitschrift für graphische Gestaltung. (SWI)
561) 562) Umschläge für das Reisemagazin HOLIDAY. Abb. 561 schwarzweiss, Abb. 562 mehrfarbig. (USA)
563) Umschlag einer Ausgabe von OPERA NEWS, die Eröffnungsabenden gewidmet ist. Rot/schwarz. (USA)

555) Couverture de la revue culturelle POLOGNE, édition polonaise. Polychrome. (POL)
556) Couverture de la revue G.Q. SCENE. (USA)
557) Couverture en couleur de THE NEW MIDDLE EAST, revue mensuelle internationale. (GB)
558) Couverture de la revue professionnelle BROADCAST MANAGEMENT/ENGINEERING. (USA)
559) Couverture de KONTAKT, une revue s'adressant aux jeunes. Rouge et noir. (SWI)
560) Couverture de la revue GRAPHIS. (SWI)
561) 562) Couvertures polychromes de la revue touristique HOLIDAY. L'ill. 561 noir et blanc; 562 noir, vert, rouge et mauve. (USA)
563) Couverture d'un numéro de la revue OPERA NEWS consacré aux soirées de premières. Rouge et noir. (USA)

Magazine Covers
Zeitschriften-Umschläge
Couvertures de périodiques

561

Artist/Künstler/Artiste:

555) GABRIEL RECHOWICZ
556) ROBERT P. SMITH
557) GEORGE HIM
558) ART SUDDUTH
559) FRED BAUER-BENOIS
560) TOMI UNGERER
561) MILTON GLASER
562) GEORGE GIUSTI
563) SEYMOUR CHWAST

Art Director/Directeur artistique:

555) LECH ZAHORSKI
556) ROBERT P. SMITH
558) GUS SAUTER
559) FRED BAUER-BENOIS
560) WALTER HERDEG
561) FRANK ZACHARY/TONY LANE
562) FRANK ZACHARY
563) DOUGLAS BEN EZRA/HOWARD SPERBER

Publisher/Verleger/Editeur:

555) POLONIA VERLAG, WARSCHAU
556) G.Q. SCENE, NEW YORK
557) THE NEW MIDDLE EAST MAGAZINE, LONDON
558) BROADCAST MANAGEMENT/ENGINEERING MAGAZINE, NEW YORK
559) KONTAKT, ZEITSCHRIFT DER JUNGEN, ZÜRICH
560) THE GRAPHIS PRESS, ZÜRICH
561) 562) HOLIDAY MAGAZINE, NEW YORK
563) OPERA NEWS, NEW YORK

562

563

Artist/Künstler/Artiste:

564) 567) CELESTINO PIATTI
565) FREDY SIGG
566) WOLF BARTH
568) WALTER ALLNER
569) DAVID WILCOX/ DUGALD STERMER
570) HERB LUBALIN
571) GEORGE TOOKER/ HERB LUBALIN

Art Director/Directeur artistique:

568) WALTER ALLNER
569) DUGALD STERMER
570) 571) HERB LUBALIN

Agency/Agentur/Agence – Studio:

568) WALTER ALLNER, NEW YORK

Publisher/Verleger/Editeur:

564)-567) NEBELSPALTER-VERLAG, RORSCHACH
568) FORTUNE MAGAZINE, NEW YORK
569) RAMPARTS MAGAZINE, SAN FRANCISCO
570) 571) AVANT GARDE MAGAZINE, NEW YORK

564

565

566

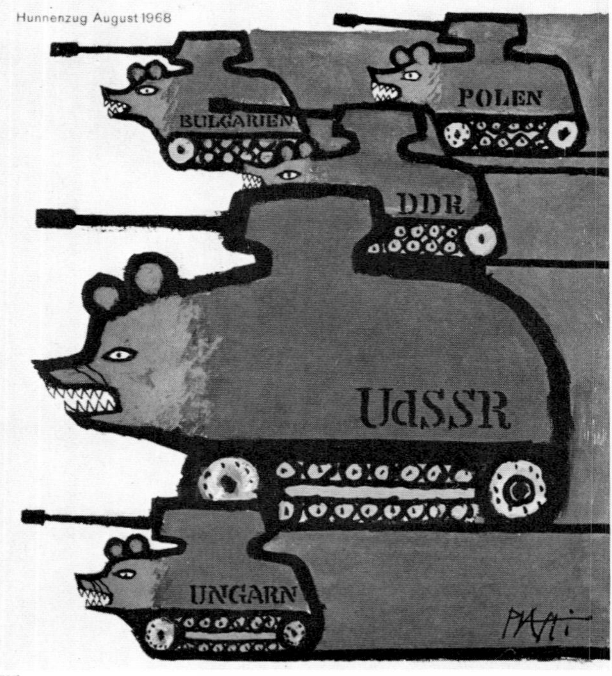

567

564)-567) Covers of the humorous magazine NEBELSPALTER. Fig. 564 refers to British and Russian help for Nigeria, fig. 565 to decorations on ladies' hats, fig. 566 to a 'Landscape Museum' and fig. 567 to the 'march of the Huns' into Czechoslovakia, August 1968. Full colour. (SWI)

568) Cover of the business magazine FORTUNE. Grey, ochre and white on black ground. (USA)

569) Cover of RAMPARTS, an avant-garde political magazine. Black, grey and red, coloured halo. (USA)

570) 571) Covers of the bi-monthly AVANT GARDE. Fig. 570 is a painting by Tom Wesselman. (USA)

564)-567) Umschläge der satirischen Zeitschrift NEBELSPALTER. Abb. 564 bezieht sich auf britische und russische Hilfe für Nigeria, Abb. 567 auf den Einmarsch der Warschauer-Pakt-Mächte in die Tschechoslowakei im August 1968. Alle Umschläge sind mehrfarbig. (SWI)

568) Umschlag für FORTUNE, Zeitschrift für Handel und Wirtschaft. Grau, ocker und weiss auf schwarzem Grund. (USA)

569) Umschlag für RAMPARTS, eine avantgardistische politische Zeitschrift. Schwarz, grau und rot, farbiger Heiligenschein. (USA)

570) 571) Umschläge der Zweimonats-Zeitschrift AVANT GARDE. Abb. 570 zeigt ein Gemälde von Tom Wesselman. (USA)

568

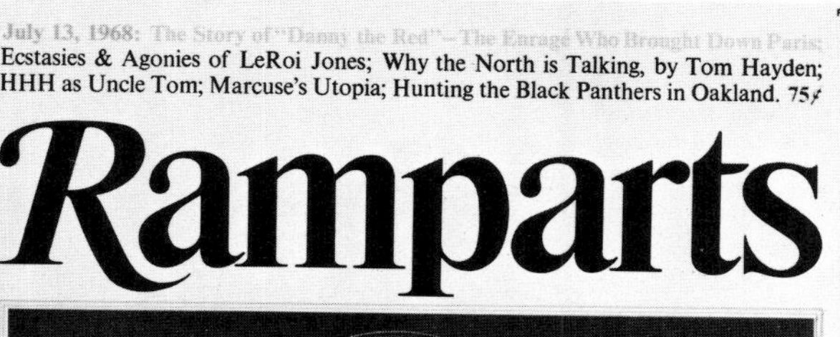

569

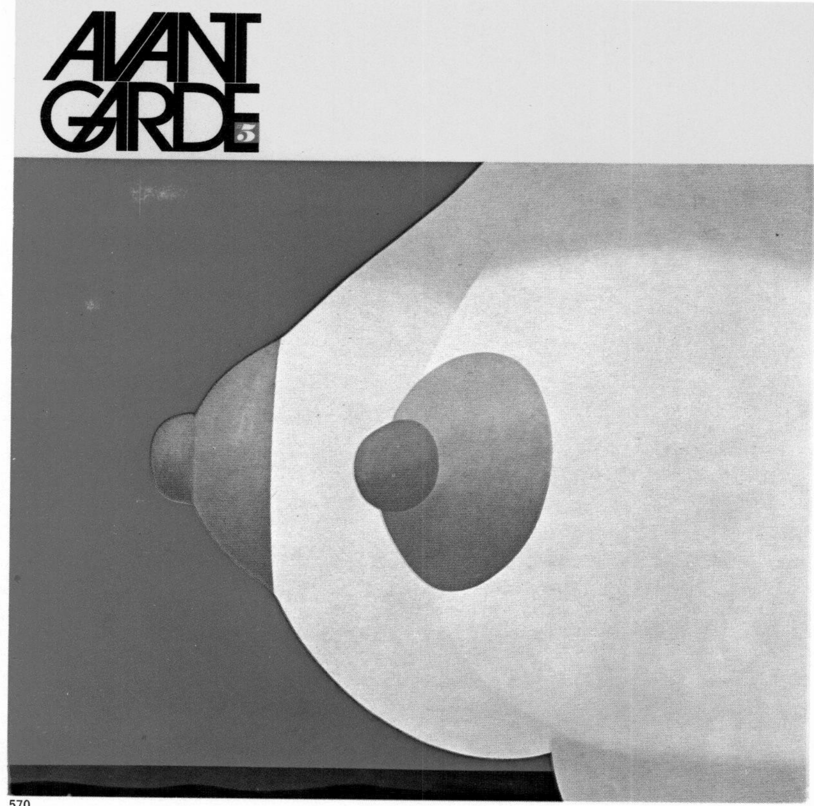

570

571

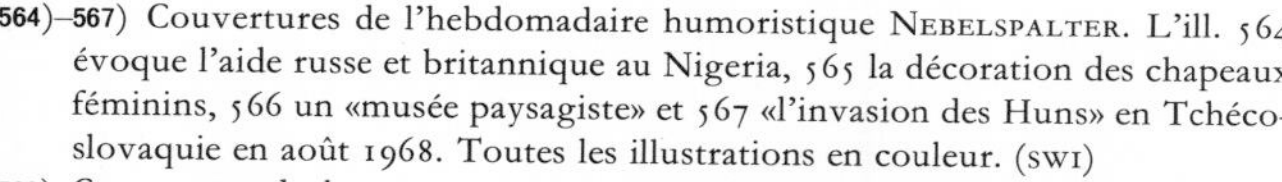

564)–567) Couvertures de l'hebdomadaire humoristique NEBELSPALTER. L'ill. 564 évoque l'aide russe et britannique au Nigeria, 565 la décoration des chapeaux féminins, 566 un «musée paysagiste» et 567 «l'invasion des Huns» en Tchécoslovaquie en août 1968. Toutes les illustrations en couleur. (SWI)

568) Couverture de la revue commerciale et financière FORTUNE. Gris, ocre et blanc sur fond noir. (USA)

569) Couverture de RAMPARTS, revue politique d'avant-garde. Noir, gris et rouge, auréole polychrome. (USA)

570) 571) Couvertures de la revue bimensuelle AVANT GARDE. L'ill. 570 reproduit une toile du peintre Tom Wesselman. (USA)

Magazine Covers
Zeitschriften-Umschläge
Couvertures de périodiques

572

573

572)–574) Illustration, page and cover of the Standard Oil house organ The Lamp, with an account of a Frenchman's visit to the Far West. Our thanks are due to the Case-Hoyt Corp. for loan of the offset films. (USA)
575) Cover of the house organ of Haskins & Sells, management consultants. Full colour. (USA)
576) 577) Colour covers of a magazine for physicians issued by the *Boehringer* pharmaceutical company. (GER)
578) 579) Pages from the *Alfa Romeo* house magazine. Full colour. (ITA)

Artist/Künstler/Artiste:

572)–574) ETIENNE DELESSERT
575) RICHARD DANNE
576) 577) ERWIN POELL
578) 579) RICCARDO MANZI

Art Director:

572)–574) H. O. DIAMOND
575) GIPS & DANNE
576) 577) ERWIN POELL
578) 579) GIUSEPPE GOZZINI

Agency/Agentur:

575) GIPS & DANNE, NEW YORK

Publisher/Verleger/Editeur:

572)–574) STANDARD OIL COMPANY, NEW YORK
575) HASKINS & SELLS, NEW YORK
576) 577) BOEHRINGER, MANNHEIM
578) 579) ALFA ROMEO S.P.A., MILAN

576

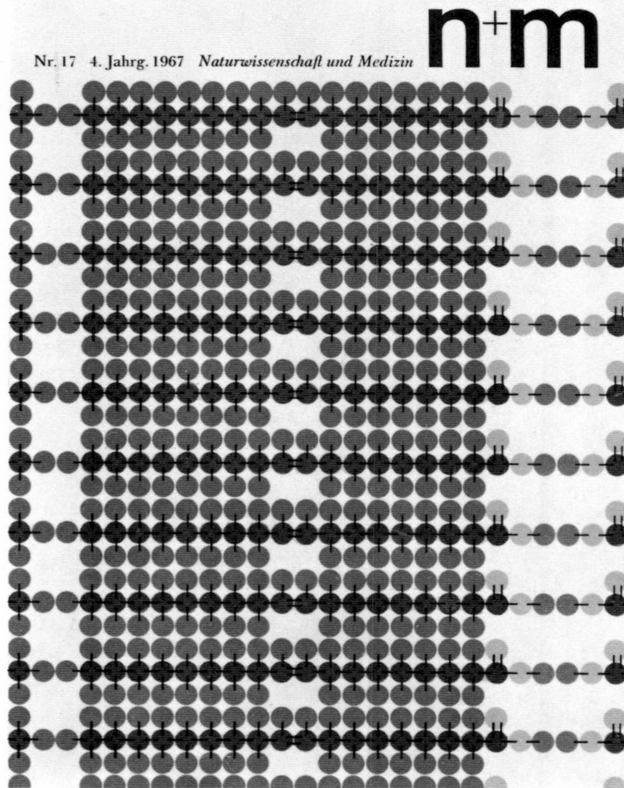

577

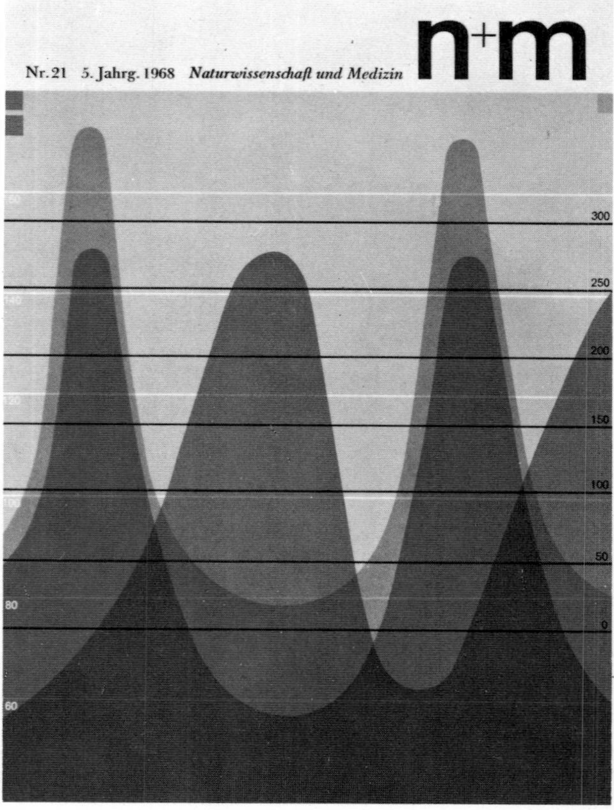

House Organs
Hauszeitschriften
Journaux d'entreprises

574

575

572)-574) Illustration, vollständige Wiedergabe der Seite und Umschlag von THE LAMP, Hauszeitschrift von der Standard Oil Company, mit der Beschreibung der Reise eines Franzosen in den Wilden Westen. (USA)

575) Umschlag der Hauszeitschrift von Haskins & Sells, einer Firma für Betriebsberatung. Mehrfarbig. (USA)

576) 577) Umschläge von einer Zeitschrift für Ärzte, herausgegeben von der Firma Boehringer, Mannheim. Mehrfarbig. (GER)

578) 579) Seiten aus der Hauszeitschrift von *Alfa Romeo*. Mehrfarbig. (ITA)

572)-574) Illustration, page et couverture d'un numéro de THE LAMP, revue de la société *Standard Oil*, contenant un compte rendu de la visite d'un Français au Far West. (USA)

575) Couverture de la revue de l'entreprise Haskins & Sells, conseils en gestion d'entreprises. Polychrome. (USA)

576) 577) Couvertures en couleur d'une revue médicale publiée par les laboratoires pharmaceutiques *Boehringer*. (GER)

578) 579) Pages de la revue des usines *Alfa Romeo*. Polychrome. (ITA)

578

579

House Organs / Hauszeitschriften
Journaux d'entreprises

580

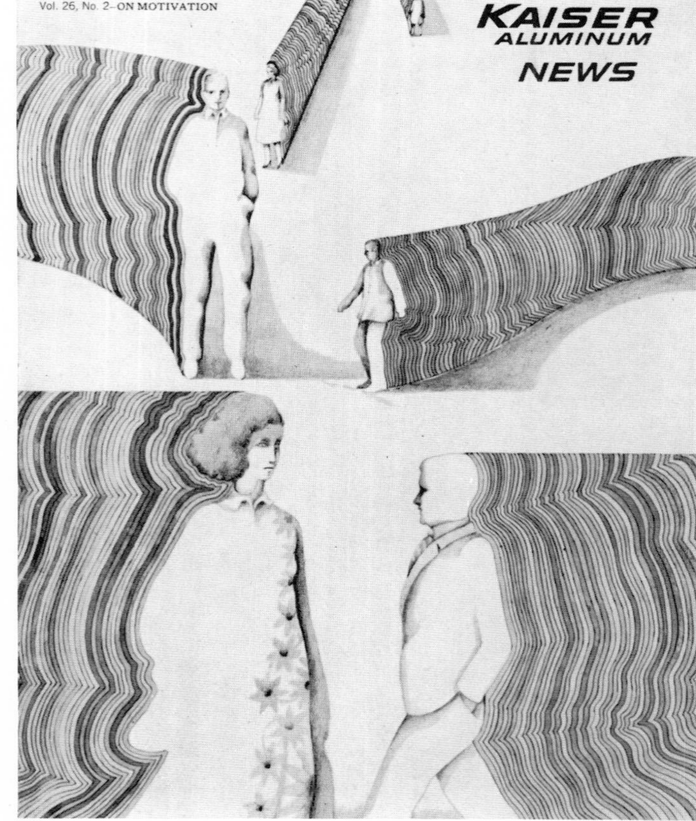

581

Reward and Punishment

584

586

Drivepower

Highlights and sidelights of Texaco's research contributions to automotive performance illustrated by drawings of period cars

585

580) 581) 584) Double spreads and cover of an issue of Kaiser Aluminium News devoted to the subject of motivation. Illustrations in full colour. (USA)
582) 583) Cover and page from an issue of the *Pirelli* review containing an article on the use of colours on motorways. (ITA)
585) Double spread from Texaco Topics. Illustration in black and green to an article on *Texaco's* research contributions to automotive performance. (USA)
586) 587) Double spread and illustration from an article on 'judging the load' in The Texaco Star. (USA)

580) 581) 584) Doppelseiten und Umschlag von Kaiser Aluminium News; diese Ausgabe hat das menschliche Verhalten zum Thema. Illustrationen mehrfarbig. (USA)
582) 583) Umschlag und Seite aus der Hauszeitschrift von *Pirelli.* Thema dieser Ausgabe ist die Verwendung von Farbe für Strassenmarkierungen. (ITA)
585) Doppelseite aus Texaco Topics. Illustration in Schwarz und Grün für einen Artikel über *Texaco's* Beiträge zur Automobilforschung. (USA)
586) 587) Doppelseite und Illustration aus einem Artikel in der Hauszeitschrift The Texaco Star über die Besteuerung in der Ölindustrie. (USA)

580) 581) 584) Doubles pages et couverture d'un numéro de Kaiser Aluminium News consacré à la motivation. Illustrations en couleur. (USA)
582) 583) Couverture et page d'un numéro de la revue *Pirelli* contenant un article sur le marquage en couleur des autoroutes. (ITA)
585) Double page de la revue de la société *Texaco.* Illustration en noir et vert. (USA)
586) 587) Double page et illustration tirées d'un article paru dans la revue d'une société pétrolière. (USA)

582

583

Artist/Künstler/Artiste:

580) 581) 584) PAT MALONEY/ROGER WATERMAN
582) 583) ROBERTO ALDROVANDI
585) SEYMOUR CHWAST/LESLIE A. SEGAL
586) 587) BILL CHARMATZ

Art Director/Directeur artistique:

580) 581) 584) ROGER WATERMAN
582) 583) TERESITA CAMAGNI HANGELDIAN
585)–587) LESLIE A. SEGAL

Agency/Agentur/Agence – Studio:

582) 583) CENTRO S.R.L., MILAN
585) CORPORATE ANNUAL REPORTS, INC., NEW YORK

Publisher/Verleger/Editeur:

580) 581) 584) KAISER ALUMINIUM & CHEMICAL CORP., OAKLAND, CALIF.
582) 583) PIRELLI S.P.A., MILAN
585)–587) TEXACO, INC., NEW YORK

587

588

589

588)–591) Illustrations to a series of articles on accommodation for travellers published in PÉTROLE PROGRÈS, and cover of one issue of this *Esso* house organ. (FRA)
592) Cover of WESTERN ADVERTISING. Full colour. (USA)
593) 594) Full-colour covers of THE MACHI, house organ of the Nippon Shopping Circle. (JAP)
595)–597) Three covers of NOTIZIE IRI, organ of the Istituto per la Ricostruzione Industriale. The subjects are road building, data processing and planning in Rome. Black and white. (ITA)

588)–591) Illustration aus einer Artikelserie in PÉTROLE PROGRÈS über Übernachtungsmöglichkeiten für Reisende, und Umschlag dieser *Esso*-Hauszeitschrift. (FRA)
592) Umschlag von WESTERN ADVERTISING. Mehrfarbig. (USA)
593) 594) Umschläge von THE MACHI, Hauszeitschrift von Nippon Shopping Circle. Mehrfarbig. (JAP)
595)–597) Drei Umschläge von NOTIZIE IRI, Hauszeitschrift des Istituto per la Ricostruzione Industriale. Die Themen sind: Strassenbau, Datenverarbeitung und Stadtplanung in Rom. Schwarzweiss. (ITA)

588)–591) Illustrations tirées d'une série d'articles touristiques, parus dans PÉTROLE PROGRÈS, et couverture d'un numéro de cette même revue *Esso*. (FRA)
592) Couverture en couleur de WESTERN ADVERTISING. (USA)
593) 594) Couvertures en couleur de la revue d'une association commerciale. (JAP)
595)–597) Couvertures de NOTIZIE IRI, revue de l'Istituto per la Ricostruzione Industriale, toutes trois en noir et blanc. (ITA)

590

591

592

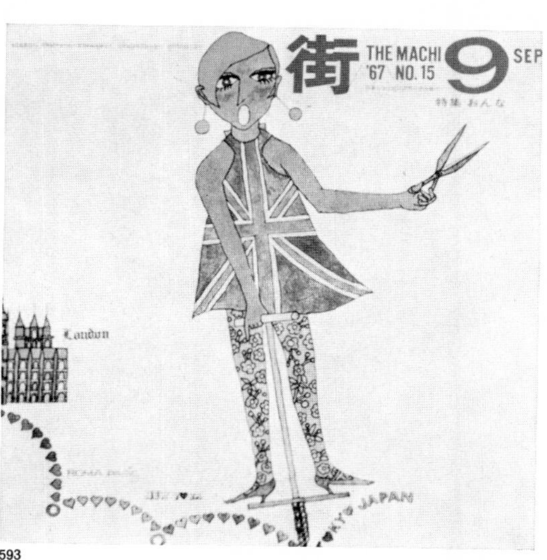

593

594

Artist/Künstler/Artiste:

588)–590) PIERRE PAUL DARIGO/CLAUDE VERNE
591) ALEX RIST/CLAUDE VERNE
592) CAL FREEDMAN
593) 594) KOJI ITO/KYU MIYASHITA
595)–597) ALFRED HOHENEGGER

Art Director/Directeur artistique:

588)–591) MADELEINE ARTHAUD/JACQUES TRIBONDEAU
592) CAL FREEDMAN
593) 594) KOJI ITO

Agency/Agentur/Agence – Studio:

588)–591) MCCANN-ERICKSON, PARIS
592) CAL ART & ASSOC., LOS ANGELES
593) 594) NIPPON SHOPPING CIRCLE, TOKYO

Publisher/Verleger/Editeur:

588)–591) ESSO STANDARD S.A., COURBEVOIE/FRA
592) WESTERN ADVERTISING, LOS ANGELES
593) 594) NIPPON SHOPPING CIRCLE, TOKYO
595)–597) IRI, ROM

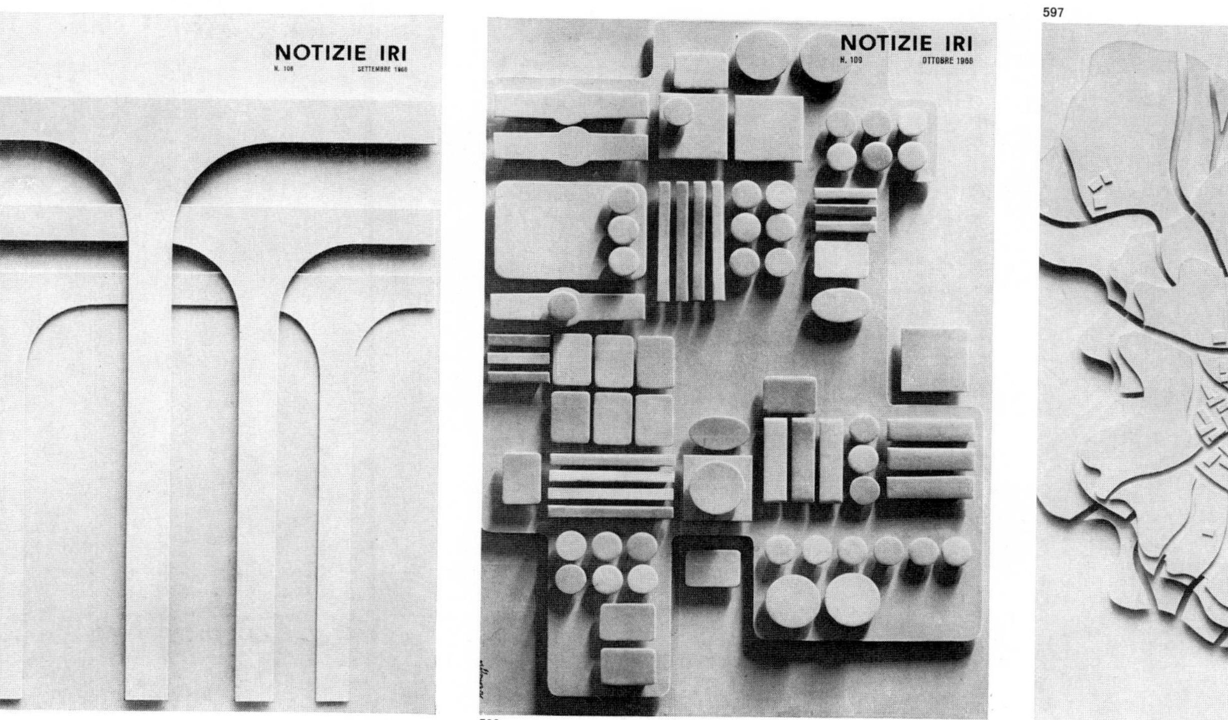

595

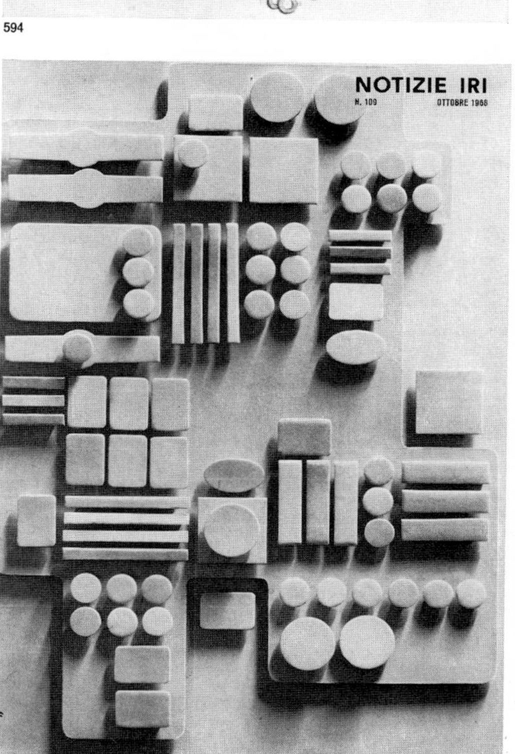

596

597

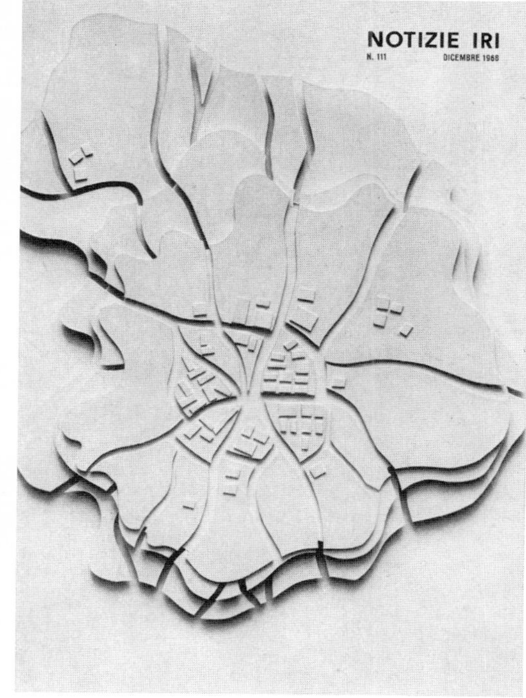

598

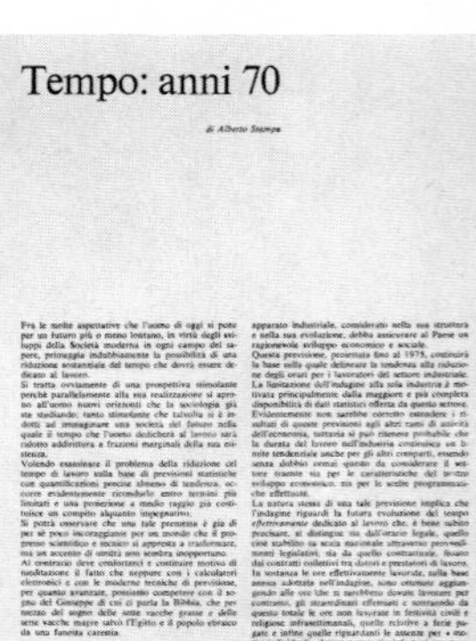
Tempo: anni 70

599

600

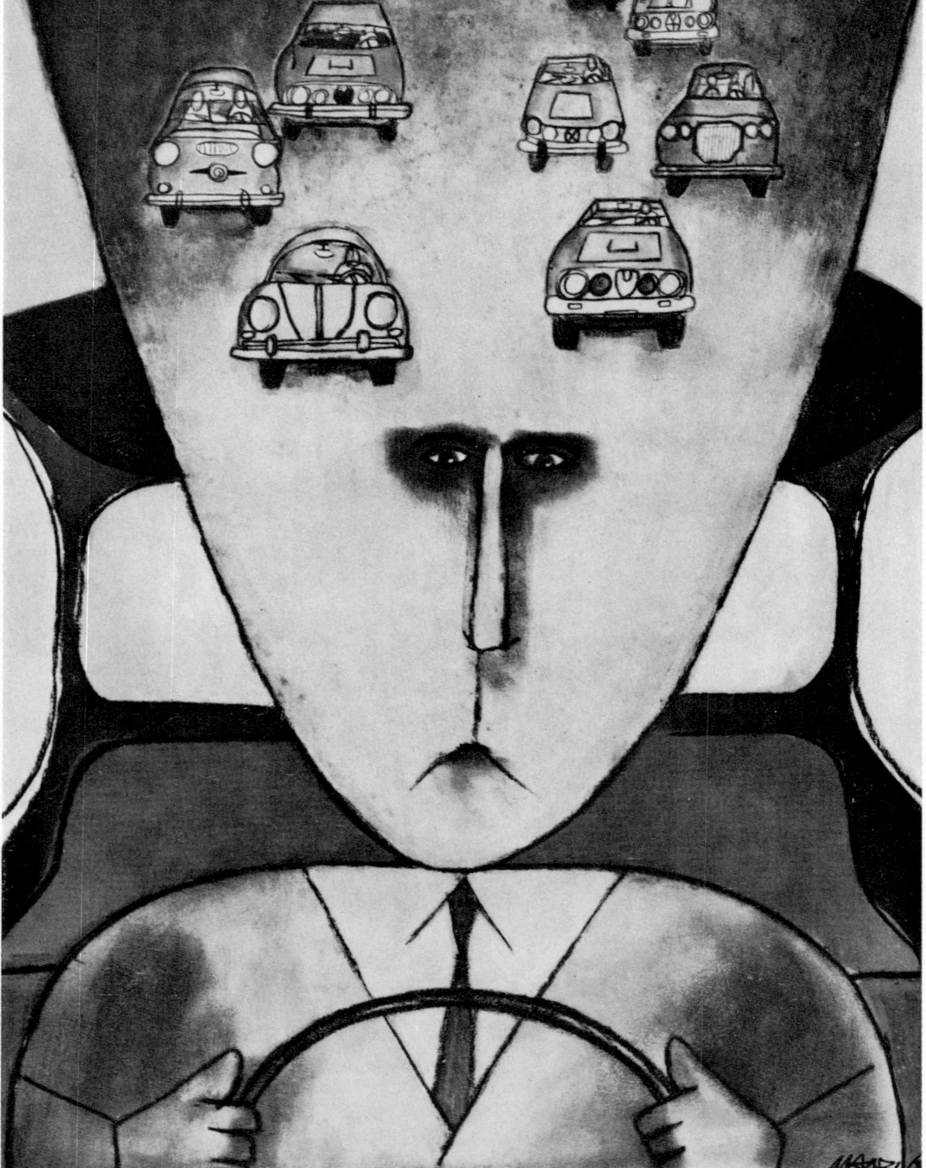

603

604

598)-606) Cover in two shades of black and white, double spread and full-page illustrations in full colour from an issue of PIRELLI RIVISTA containing an article on various aspects of the problem of work and leisure time. The subjects are: 600) the 8.15 lift; 601) short week, lonely Saturday; 602) what to do in a break; 603) weekend; 604) estrangement in the family; 605) a yard of beach; 606) breakfast, Italian style. (ITA)

601

602

605

606

Artist/Künstler/Artiste:
598) PINO TOVAGLIA
599)-606) RICCARDO MANZI

Art Director/Directeur artistique:
598) PINO TOVAGLIA/TERESITA CAMAGNI-HANGELDIAN
599)-606) PINO TOVAGLIA

Agency/Agentur/Agence – Studio:
598) CENTRO, S.R.L., MILAN

Publisher/Verleger/Editeur:
598)-606) PIRELLI S.P.A., MILAN

598)-606) Umschlag in Schwarz und Weiss, Doppelseite und ganzseitige, mehrfarbige Illustrationen aus einer Ausgabe der Hauszeitschrift PIRELLI RIVISTA. Dieses Heft bezieht sich auf die verschiedenen Probleme der Arbeits- und Freizeit. Die Themen sind: 600) der Lift um 8.15; 601) kurze Woche, einsamer Samstag; 602) Beschäftigung in der Pause; 603) das Wochenende; 604) Entfremdung in der Familie; 605) Platzknappheit am Strand; 606) das italienische Frühstück. (ITA)

598)-606) Couverture en noir et blanc, double page et illustrations polychromes sur pages entières, tirées d'un numéro de PIRELLI RIVISTA examinant les différents aspects du problème du travail et des loisirs. Les sujets sont: 600) l'ascenseur de 8 h 15; 601) courte semaine, triste samedi; 602) que faire pendant la pause; 603) week-end; 604) aliénation au sein d'une famille; 605) un mètre de plage; 606) petit déjeuner à l'italienne. (ITA)

Jack & Jill Story

This is a story about security. *My* Jack and Jill Story, that is. The other one is a miserable tale of gross carelessness . . . unless Jack and Jill were so shocked at what they saw over the brow of the hill that in their haste to get down they lost their footing. My story has nothing to do with that sort of nonsense.

Two things began it: a questionnaire in a magazine; and a question from a man at a party. The questionnaire contained 25 questions which a girl was supposed to ask herself before taking the plunge. It seemed to me that it represented a tendency to plan marriage by formula and, while I believe a leap should be preceded by at least a glance, I think there's nothing that can keep you so thoroughly earthbound as too much caution.

The man at the party wanted to know how much security I had. He wasn't impertinent: just puzzled. I was the only actor among fifty people at the party. The man asked me a number of questions about my work, as those outside our profession do, and then said: "You seem to have done pretty well, but just the same—" and he scrutinized me intently "—just the same, aren't you uneasy about having reached your present age without having any security?" While I gathered myself for a reply, he vanished in search of a martini and never came back. I suppose he thought he had security, in the form of a salaried job – but there's nothing you can be fired from so easily as a job.

I would have liked to tell him *my* Jack and Jill story, but as I didn't have the chance then, I'll tell it here. It begins in the traditional way:

Once upon a time there was a girl named Jill, who had two suitors: John and Jack. Since they both wanted to marry her, Jill had been reading everything she could about marriage, and had come upon a questionnaire which contained, among others, one question to which she *must* absolutely answer Yes. "Have you sat down together," it ran, "to list *in detail* the costs that will confront you — not just food and shelter, but transportation of all kinds, and entertainment, and right down to such details as toothpaste and new heels and cigarettes?"

Since Jill hadn't agreed to marry either John or Jack, she thought it more modest to sit down in her imagination with them to answer that question, and she started with John. It was easy. John had it all worked out down to the last cent, and being good with figures, he even had a budget worked out. Next year, he said, barring emergencies, they could get married — and he went on to forecast what they could do each year for the next ten years. There was no doubt about it, John was a man of considerable probabilities.

But in Jill's imaginary conference with poor old Jack, he gave up half way. He had a very unpromising job, and as far as he could see they'd never be able to get married. And while John was a man of probabilities, Jack was only a man of possibilities. But Jill had a weakness for possibilities: to her they didn't seem limited the way probabilities are, and when her friends said to her "You will never have any security with Jack," she smiled and said "It all depends on the kind of security you mean." And when her friends shook their heads and went away, she nodded her head at Jack and they were married.

No doubt about it, their financial life was a hit-and-miss affair. Jill would have everything figured out and suddenly Jack would come home with a bottle of wine and a steak at a dollar a pound (which in those days was the equivalent of three dollars today). She would say they couldn't afford it, but Jack would reply that it was an occasion and what did price matter? and she would kiss him and put candles on the table, because she was a girl with a great sense of occasion.

Now it turned out that Jack had always wanted to be an actor, but nobody had encouraged him…up till now. "Actors!" said Jill's friends. "Why, they're so unpredictable that sometimes they have to pay higher insurance premiums or fifty-dollar deposits before they can get telephones. How do you know where you'll be three years from now?" But Jill smiled quietly as she always did and said that not knowing was half the fun and getting there was the other half (thus anticipating the Cunard slogan). Then her friends would start talking about security, but when she tried to tell them about *her* kind of security they shook their heads again and went away.

Jill knew that Jack had talent, and pretty soon she had him believing it too. And when one day he said: "I'm going to give up my wretched job and take a chance as an actor," instead of replying: "Can we afford it?", she said, "Let's go out and buy a bottle of champagne — this is an occasion."

Long ago they had thrown their budget out of the window, so when one day the rent money was barely in sight, Jill, instead of looking over their finances, looked over Jack's possibilities and saw quite clearly that he was also a writer. It was more than Jack could see at the time, but when he cashed the cheque for his first script she thought he'd forgiven her for saying: "I told you so." And after the rent was paid, you can be sure the rest of the money didn't go into the bank, because as I told you before, Jill was a girl with a sense of occasion.

Now, as the years went by, Jack and Jill became more adventurous. Sometimes Jill's friends would say: "How can you afford it? Where's the money coming from?" and Jill would say: "Your trouble is that you deal in probabilities — you know when the money isn't there; but with possibilities you get the loveliest surprises." And to everyone's astonishment but Jill's, even the bank manager was able to see beyond the solid walls of sound collateral, and conceded that Jack's possibilities were a pretty good investment.

Well, that's the sketchy story of Jack and Jill's early days. If you asked Jack today what the probabilities are for the future, he'd shake his head and say: "I haven't the faintest idea. Who knows what'll happen tomorrow?" And if you said to Jill: "Do you know what will happen tomorrow?" she would say: "I don't want to know," and her eyes would light up as she considered the possibilities.

And when her die-hard friends say: "Yes, we agree, you and Jack are doing very nicely, but surely *now* you must want security," she smiles and says nothing, knowing they will never understand. Because security, to her, is something in the mind: a word built up not by counting the cost but by believing in the possibilities: a world where the probabilities are the flat plains, but the possibilities are the mountain-peaks. You can find your way across the plains by yourself, but it takes two to climb a mountain.

by ALAN KING

9

607

608

OP Electronics

Direct control of the electromagnetic properties of light promises to open new vistas in electronic displays.

by Bruce Shore

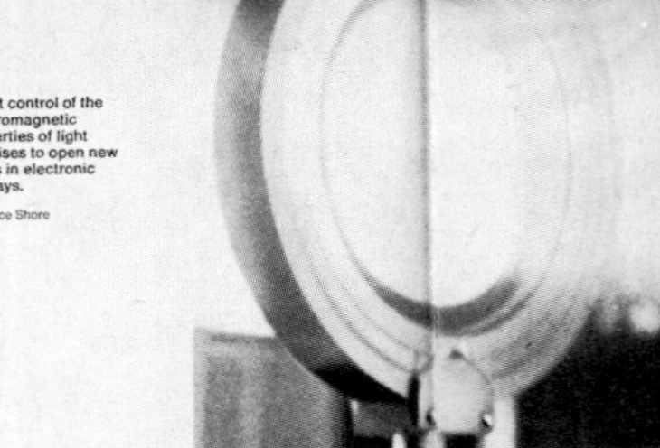

Scientists are making an audacious bid to harness the electromagnetic properties of light directly without first having to convert them to electrical phenomena as is done in the cases of solar cells and television cameras.

Using a variety of new electronic materials and novel effects, they are presently training light to drill holes in diamond dies, carry radio and TV signals, align tunnel-boring equipment, track earth satellites, provide inertial guidance for missiles, and produce optical memory and logic circuits for computers. In the process, they are also fashioning a new optoelectronics technology that has been popularly dubbed "op" electronics.

But nowhere are the potential benefits of this developing technology more evident than in the field of visible displays. A series of recent breakthroughs promises to revolutionize everything from wrist watches and automotive dashboards to computer read-outs, television screens, and phonograph records.

In its strictest sense, "op" electronics is not new. It was derived, originally, from the work of Julius Plucker, a German physicist. In 1859, Plucker discovered the phenomenon of cathodoluminescence: that light is given off when certain phosphors are struck by beams of electrons, which were called cathode rays in his day, hence the name.

Thirty-eight years later, Karl Ferdinand Braun, also a German, employed this and other discoveries to build the first cathode ray oscilloscope: a vacuum tube with a phosphor screen that produced a beam of electrons that could be deflected up, down, or sideways by external magnets. The beam could be followed visually by the bright spot it created on the screen.

Among the direct descendants of this ingenious tube are the laboratory oscilloscope for observing high-speed electrical phenomena, the radarscope for monitoring the flight of airplanes and missiles, and the kinescope for displaying images received by the ubiquitous TV set.

Thus, the Braun tube was the first practical optoelectronic device. And it still serves, 71 years later, as the technological touchstone and inspiration for many of the modern efforts being made to surpass it. This is especially true in those cases where the only change contemplated is in substituting a new material for the phosphor screen found at the viewing end of most display tubes.

Three such changes that have already been demonstrated experimentally might prove revolutionary if they become practical.

The first involves use of a screen composed of lasers of a remarkable cathodoluminescent type – tiny, crystalline flakes of such materials as cadmium sulfide or zinc oxide. These flakes can be activated (pumped) by an electron beam of sufficient energy, causing them to emit intense, coherent light in a flat, 360° halo whose edge remains extremely narrow over relatively long distances.

By substituting these for the phosphors in a conventional TV screen, Dr. Frederick Nicoll of the RCA Laboratories in Princeton, N.J., hopes to produce a bright visual display that can be viewed directly or be intensified still further for projection onto a distant wall or movie screen. He has already built and successfully operated an experimental tube that contains several such lasers in a row and plans to add still more in the future. Eventually, a tube with a full row of such lasers might even be used as a kind of coherent light "flying spot scanner" – a device like that employed by the Lunar Orbiter satellites to convert film of the moon's surface to television signals for relay to earth.

Another approach of equal scientific interest and far-reaching applications potential is that involving the use of a photochromic instead of a phosphor screen.

Since the invention of paint and the development of clothing dyes, it has been known that certain materials change color when exposed to sunlight. Though virtually everyone has experienced these subtle, often exacerbating, effects at one time or another (housewives even take advantage of them by hanging white laundry out to be both dried and bleached by the

Artist's rendition of liquid crystal screen, in which molecules normally are transparent and line up parallel (left of drawing). When subjected to an electric field, however, they become disordered and cause light to scatter (right). This effect can be used to produce any desired graphic image, which, like a printed page, is viewed by reflected light.

Bruce Shore is a staff writer for RCA Public Affairs.

609

4

6

5

610

Artist/Künstler/Artiste:

607) BOB BINKS
608) BRYAN MILLS/DON GRANT
609) SHELDON SEIDLER
610) SHIGEO FUKUDA
611) TADANORI YOKOO
612) LOUIS GUHL
613) HANS KÜCHLER
614) RENÉ CREUX
615) PAUL RAND

Art Director/Directeur artistique:

607) BRYAN MILLS
608) BRYAN MILLS/DON GRANT
609) SHELDON SEIDLER
610) 611) IKKO TANAKA
612) EMIL HÄSLER
613) 614) SCHWEIZ. VERKEHRSZENTRALE
615) WILLIAM MCCAFFERY

Agency/Agentur/Agence – Studio:

609) SHELDON SEIDLER DESIGN, NEW YORK
610) 611) COMART HOUSE, TOKYO
613) 614) SCHWEIZ. VERKEHRSZENTRALE, ZÜRICH

Publisher/Verleger/Editeur:

607) 608) A.C.T.R.A., TORONTO
609) R.C.A., NEW YORK
610) 611) JAPAN PRINTING INK MAKERS' ASSOC., TOKYO
612) CIBA AG, BASEL
613) 614) SCHWEIZ. VERKEHRSZENTRALE, ZÜRICH
615) THE AMERICAN INSTITUTE OF GRAPHIC ARTS, NEW YORK

612

House Organs
Hauszeitschriften
Journaux d'entreprises

Illustrator: Tadanori Yokoo

涯しなき未来の印刷

611

607) 608) Double spread (illustration in lilac, purple and black) and cover (black on brown) of ACTRA, organ of the Association of Canadian Television and Radio Artists. (CAN)
609) Spread from the RCA magazine ELECTRONIC AGE. (USA)
610) 611) Double spreads from PRINTING INK, organ of an association of printing ink manufacturers. (JAP)
612) Cover of CIBA JOURNAL. Insets in full colour. (SWI)
613) 614) Review covers for the National Tourist Office. (SWI)
615) Cover of the JOURNAL OF THE AMERICAN INSTITUTE OF GRAPHIC ARTS. (USA)

607) 608) Doppelseite (Illustration in Lilatönen) und Umschlag (schwarz auf braun) von ACTRA, Hauszeitschrift einer Vereinigung von Fernseh- und Radiomitarbeitern. (CAN)
609) Doppelseite aus der Hauszeitschrift ELECTRONIC AGE. (USA)
610) 611) Doppelseiten aus der Hauszeitschrift einer Vereinigung von Druckfarben-Herstellern. (JAP)
612) Umschlag der Hauszeitschrift CIBA JOURNAL. (SWI)
613) 614) Umschläge der Reisezeitschrift der Schweizerischen Verkehrszentrale. (SWI)
615) Umschlag der Zeitschrift eines Kunstinstitutes. (USA)

607) 608) Double page (illustration en lilas, pourpre et noir) et couverture (noir sur brun) d'ACTRA, revue d'une association d'artistes de radio et de télévision. (CAN)
609) Double page de la revue RCA ELECTRONIC AGE. (USA)
610) 611) Double pages de la revue d'une association de fabricants d'encres d'imprimerie. (JAP)
612) Couverture de la revue CIBA JOURNAL. (SWI)
613) 614) Couvertures de revues de l'Office du tourisme. (SWI)
615) Couverture du JOURNAL OF THE AMERICAN INSTITUTE OF GRAPHIC ARTS. (USA)

613

614

615

FLUCHT IN DIE KISTE

616

Artist/Künstler/Artiste:

616) 617) HANS-JÜRGEN RAU/LOTHAR STAEDLER
618) ANDRÉ AMSTUTZ
619) KOJI ITO
620) ETIENNE DELESSERT
621) REINHART BRAUN

Art Director/Directeur artistique:

616) 617) HANS-JÜRGEN RAU
618) GUY CHALLIS
619) KOJI ITO
620) SHELDON COHEN

Agency/Agentur/Agence – Studio:

616) 617) INTERDESIGN STUDIO GMBH, FRANKFURT/M.

Publisher/Verleger/Editeur:

616) 617) FARBWERKE HOECHST AG, FRANKFURT/M.
618) A. GUINNESS + SON LTD., LONDON
619) NIKKEI ADVERTISING, TOKYO
620) U.S. GOVERNMENT FEDERAL DRUG ADMINISTRATION, WASHINGTON, D.C.
621) EVANG. ST. PETRI-GEMEINDE, HAMBURG

House Organs/Hauszeitschriften
Journaux d'entreprises

617

616) 617) Double spread and illustration from a *Hoechst* house organ about a drug against introversion. (GER)
618) Cover of the *Guinness* house organ. (GB)
619) Cover of the house organ NIKKEI ADVERTISING NOTE. (JAP)
620) Full-colour illustration from the house organ of the Federal Drug Administration. (USA)
621) Cover of the religious house organ STP of St. Peter's Church in Hamburg. Black and green. (GER)

616) 617) Doppelseite und Illustration aus DIE BRÜCKE, Hauszeitschrift der Farbwerke Hoechst AG, Frankfurt/M. (GER)
618) Umschlag für die Hauszeitschrift einer Brauerei. (GB)
619) Umschlag der Hauszeitschrift einer Werbeagentur. (JAP)
620) Mehrfarbige Illustration aus der Hauszeitschrift der Staatlichen Medikamentenkontrolle. (USA)
621) Umschlag einer religiösen Schrift, herausgegeben von der St.-Petri-Kirche, Hamburg. Schwarz und grün. (GER)

616) 617) Double page et illustration d'un article sur un médicament contre l'introversion, paru dans la revue *Hoechst*. (GER)
618) Couverture de la revue de la brasserie *Guinness*. (GB)
619) Couverture d'une revue d'une agence publicitaire (JAP)
620) Illustration en couleur de la revue d'une commission fédérale pour le contrôle des médicaments. (USA)
621) Couverture du journal d'une église de Hambourg. (GER)

618

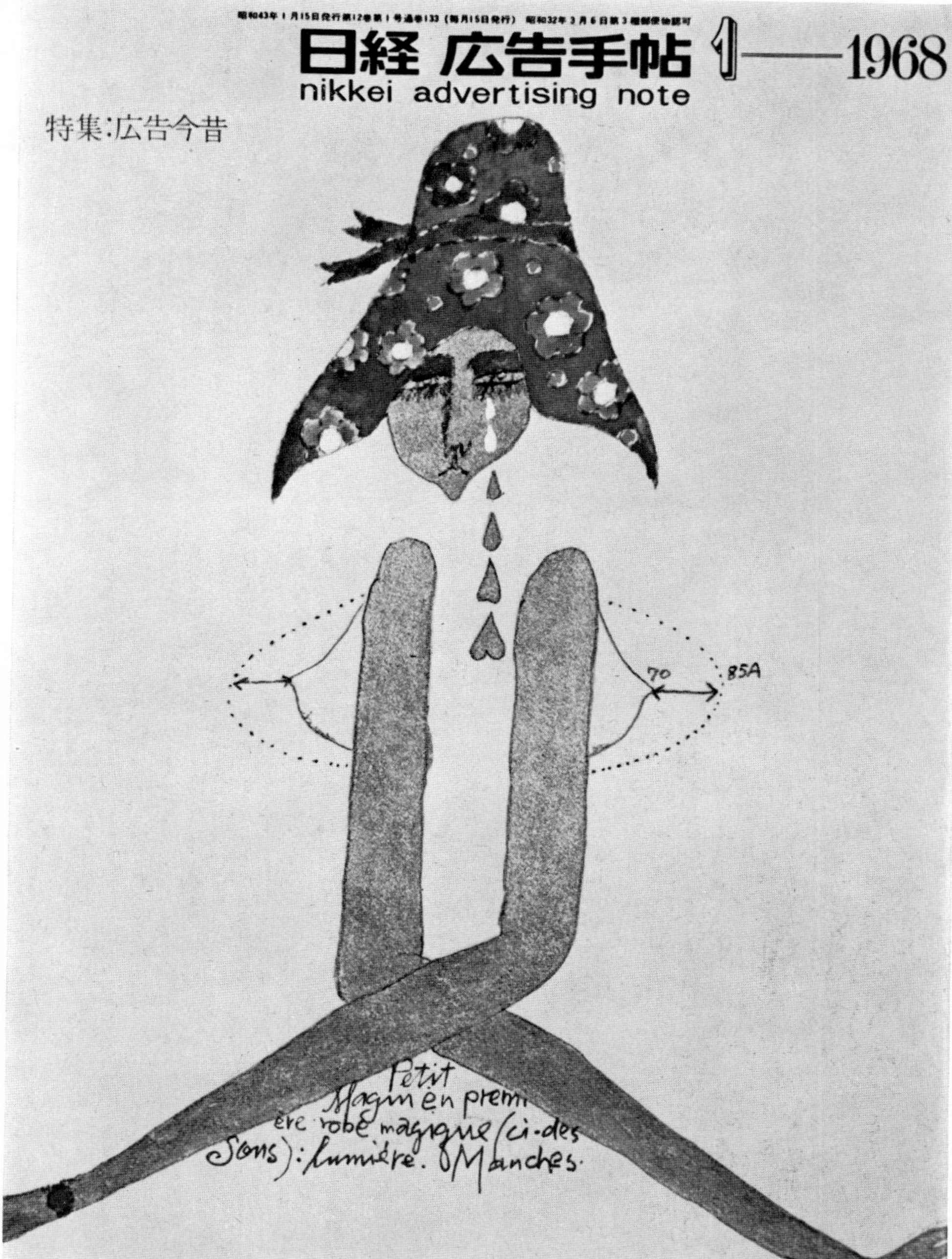

619

620

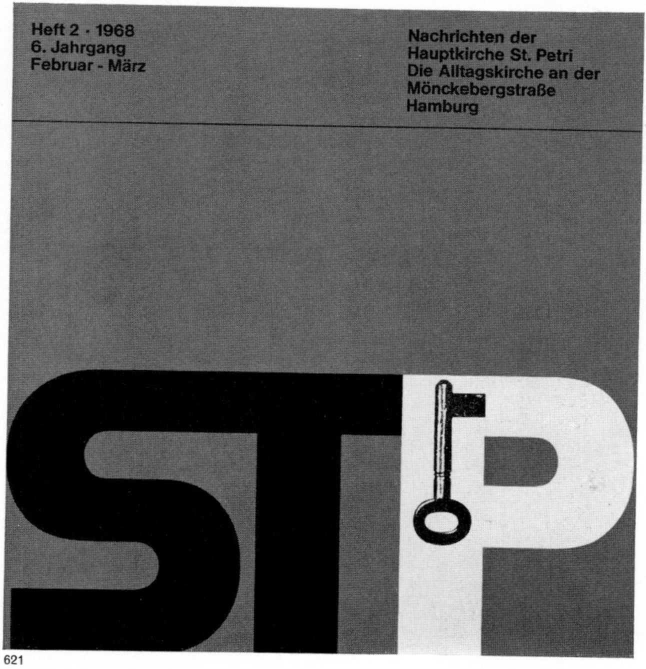

621

622

623

625

626

Artist/Künstler/Artiste:

622) 623) RONALD SEARLE
624) TOM ADAMS
625) BOHDAN BUTENKO
626) ANTONI BORATYNSKI
627) MARIA USZACKA

Art Director/Directeur artistique:

624) ANTHONY COLWELL

Publisher/Verleger/Editeur:

622) DOBSON BOOKS LTD., LONDON
623) WEIDENFELD & NICOLSON LTD., LONDON
624) JONATHAN CAPE LTD., LONDON
625) BIURO WYDAWNICZE «RUCH», WARSCHAU
626) 627) NASZA KSIEGARNIA, WARSCHAU

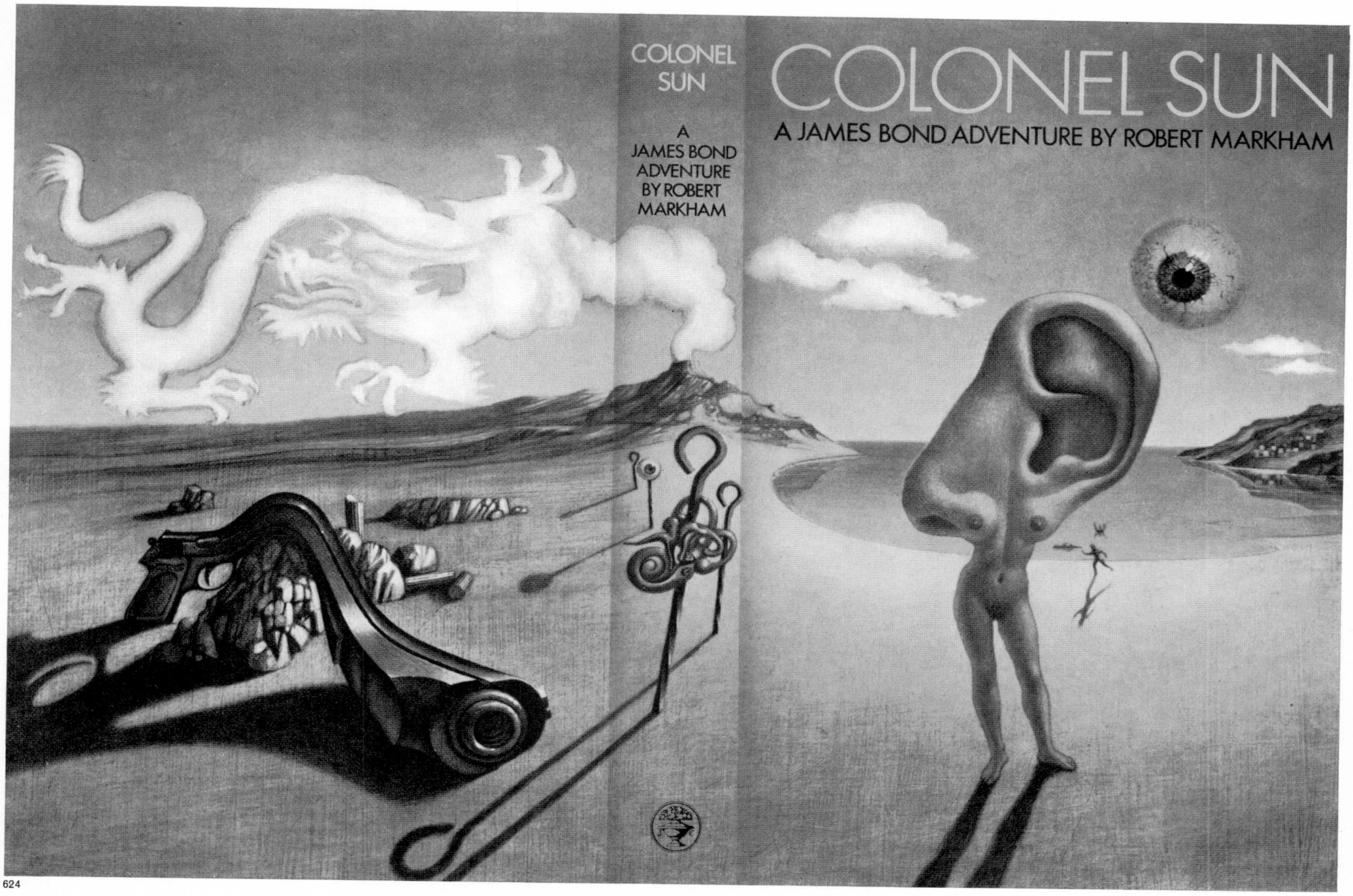

624

627

622) Jacket for a book of ancient medical remedies. Polychrome. (GB)
623) Dust jacket for an album of satirical drawings. Black and white, red and blue hands, red face. (GB)
624) Complete cover of a James Bond novel. Shades of brown and yellow, blue sky, white clouds. (GB)
625) Cover of a children's book about drops of water. (POL)
626) Cover in brown shades for a children's book. (POL)
627) Cover of a children's book. Mainly green shades. (POL)

622) Buchumschlag für eine Sammlung alter medizinischer Rezepte. Mehrfarbig. (GB)
623) Schutzumschlag für ein Album mit satirischen Zeichnungen. Schwarzweiss, rote und blaue Hände, rotes Gesicht. (GB)
624) Vollständiger Umschlag eines James-Bond-Romans. Braun- und Gelbtöne, blauer Himmel, weisse Wolken. (GB)
625) Umschlag für ein Kinderbuch über Wassertropfen. (POL)
626) Umschlag in verschiedenen Brauntönen für ein Kinderbuch. (POL)
627) Umschlag für ein Kinderbuch. Verschiedene Grüntöne. (POL)

622) Chemise d'un recueil de vieux remèdes. Polychrome. (GB)
623) Chemise d'un album de dessins humoristiques. Noir et blanc, mains en bleu et rouge, visage rouge. (GB)
624) Couverture d'un roman «James Bond». Plusieurs tons de brun et jaune, ciel bleu, nuages blancs. (GB)
625) Couverture d'un livre d'enfants sur les gouttes d'eau. (POL)
626) Couverture (plusieurs tons de brun) d'un livre d'enfants. (POL)
627) Couverture (vert dominant) d'un livre d'enfants. (POL)

Artist/Künstler/Artiste:

628) 635) WALTER GRIEDER
629) HANSPETER WYSS
630) EMANUELE LUZZATI
631) ALIKI BRANDENBERG
632) ETIENNE DELESSERT
633) CHRISTINE CHAGNOUX
634) MONIKA LUTZ/PETER SCHUPPISSER

Art Director/Directeur artistique:

628) 635) WALTER GRIEDER
629) OSWALD DUBACHER
631) WALTER OTT
632) ETIENNE DELESSERT/ ELEONORE SCHMID
633) M. CHARLIER
634) ARTHUR HUBSCHMID

Agency/Agentur/Agence – Studio:

628) WALTER GRIEDER, BASEL
634) SEREG, PARIS

Publisher/Verleger/Editeur:

628) JOY-BOOKS AG, BASEL
629) EX LIBRIS VERLAG AG, ZÜRICH
630) EMME EDIZIONI, MILAN/ ZANICHELLI EDITORE, BOLOGNA
631) PRENTICE-HALL, INC., ENGLEWOOD CLIFFS, N.J.
632) NORTON PUBLISHERS, NEW YORK
633) DARGAUD S.A., PARIS
634) EDITIONS DE L'ECOLE, PARIS
635) VERLAG SAUERLÄNDER AG, AARAU

628

629

632

633

628) Cover of a children's book (Brother Ibou). Polychrome. (SWI)
629) Cover of a book of goodnight stories. Polychrome. (SWI)
630) Polychrome cover of *Ali Baba and the Forty Thieves*. (ITA)
631) Complete jacket of an illustrated folk lullaby. (USA)
632) Jacket of a modern fairy tale. Polychrome. (USA)
633) Cover in full colour for a children's book from a series (Little Hippo at the Circus). (FRA)
634) Cover of a French course for children. Cockerel in green shades, red comb and wattles. (FRA)
635) Cover of a children's book (The Enchanted Drum). (SWI)

628) Umschlag für das Kinderbuch *Frère Ibou*. Mehrfarbig. (SWI)
629) Umschlag für ein Buch mit Gute-Nacht-Geschichten. (SWI)
630) Mehrfarbiger Umschlag für *Ali Baba und die vierzig Räuber*. (ITA)
631) Vollständiger Schutzumschlag für ein illustriertes Wiegenlied. (USA)
632) Umschlag für ein modernes Märchen. Mehrfarbig. (USA)
633) Mehrfarbiger Schutzumschlag für ein Kinderbuch (Klein Potam im Zirkus). (FRA)
634) Umschlag für ein Französisch-Buch für Kinder. Hahn in Grüntönen, Kamm und Kehllappen rot. (FRA)
635) Umschlag für das Kinderbuch *Die verzauberte Trommel*. (SWI)

630

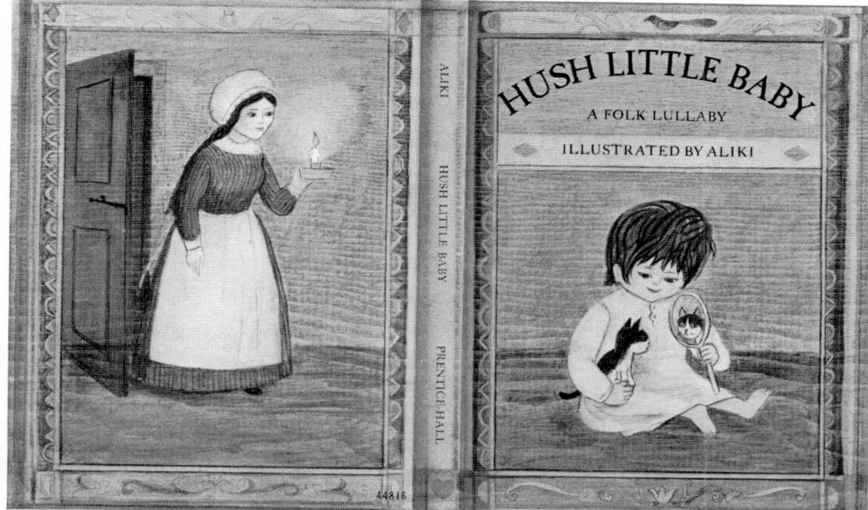

631

634

635

628) Couverture d'un livre d'enfants. Polychrome. (SWI)
629) Couverture d'un recueil d'histoires enfantines. Polychrome. (SWI)
630) Couverture en couleur d'une édition illustrée d'*Ali-Baba et les quarante voleurs*. (ITA)
631) Chemise d'une berceuse populaire, illustrée. (USA)
632) Chemise d'un conte de fées moderne. Polychrome. (USA)
633) Couverture en couleur d'un livre d'enfants. (FRA)
634) Couverture d'un livre d'enfants. Coq en plusieurs tons de vert, crête et barbillons rouges. (FRA)
635) Couverture d'un livre d'enfants (Le tambour enchanté). (SWI)

636

637

638

639

Book Jackets / Schutzumschläge
Chemises de livres

Artist/Künstler/Artiste:

636) 637) 642) JOHN ALCORN
638) 639) 641) 643) SEYMOUR CHWAST
640) PAUL KÖNIG
644) MICHAEL DEMPSEY
645) EUGENE MIHAESCO

Art Director/Directeur artistique:

637) FRANK METZ
638) 639) BOB CHENEY
640) PAUL KÖNIG
641) HARRIS LEWINE
642) MARTHA LEHTOLA
643) BOB REED
644) MICHAEL DEMPSEY
645) ALBERT LORENZETTI

Agency/Agentur/Agence – Studio:

645) EDITIONS RENCONTRE, LAUSANNE

Publisher/Verleger/Editeur:

636) E. P. DUTTON & CO., INC., NEW YORK
637) SIMON & SCHUSTER, INC., NEW YORK
638) 639) HARPER & ROW, INC., NEW YORK
640) VERLAG GEORG OLMS, HILDESHEIM/GER
641) 643) HOLT, RINEHART & WINSTON, NEW YORK
642) LITTLE, BROWN & CO., BOSTON
644) MICHAEL JOSEPH LTD., LONDON
645) EDITIONS RENCONTRE, LAUSANNE

636) Cover of a novel. (USA)
637) Cover of a murder mystery. (USA)
638) Cover of the story of the great Jewish families of New York. Polychrome, pale turquoise background. (USA)
639) Cover of a book about an Italian immigrant in America. (USA)
640) Cover of the journal of G.W. Leibniz's travels in the 17th century. Sepia shades, red lettering. (GER)
641) Cover of a book about the conflict between Catholicism and capitalism in 18th-century France. Black and cream. (USA)
642) Cover of a novel. Ochre, blue-grey and black. (USA)
643) Cover of a novel. Polychrome on white ground. (USA)
644) Jacket (front and spine) of a book about the unsettled life of a simultaneous interpreter. Bright colours, dark blue ground. (GB)
645) Complete cover of a travel book about Chile. Polychrome. (SWI)

636) Umschlag für einen Roman. (USA)
637) Umschlag für einen Kriminalroman. (USA)
638) Umschlag für einen Roman über die berühmten jüdischen Familien von New York. Mehrfarbig. Grund türkis. (USA)
639) Umschlag für ein Buch über einen italienischen Einwanderer in Amerika. (USA)
640) Umschlag für das Reisetagebuch von G.W. Leibniz. (GER)
641) Umschlag für ein Buch über den Konflikt zwischen Katholizismus und Kapitalismus im 18. Jahrhundert. Schwarz und beige. (USA)
642) Umschlag für einen Roman. Ocker, blaugrau und schwarz. (USA)
643) Umschlag für einen Roman. Mehrfarbig auf weissem Grund. (USA)
644) Umschlag (Vorderseite und Rücken) eines Buches über das unstete Leben einer Simultan-Übersetzerin. Mehrfarbig. (GB)
645) Vollständiger Umschlag einer Reisebeschreibung über Chile. (SWI)

636) Couverture de roman. (USA)
637) Couverture d'un roman policier. (USA)
638) Couverture d'un roman retraçant l'histoire des grandes familles juives de New York. Polychrome sur fond turquoise. (USA)
639) Couverture d'un livre sur un émigrant italien en Amérique. (USA)
640) Couverture du journal de voyage de G.W. Leibniz. Sépia, texte en rouge. (GER)
641) Couverture d'un ouvrage sur le conflit ayant opposé en France, au 18e siècle, catholicisme et capitalisme. Noir et beige. (USA)
642) Couverture d'un roman. Ocre, gris-bleu et noir. (USA)
643) Couverture d'un roman. Polychrome sur fond blanc. (USA)
644) Chemise (plat et dos) d'un livre sur la vie vagabonde d'une interprète. Polychrome sur fond bleu. (GB)
645) Couverture d'un ouvrage sur le Chili. Polychrome. (SWI)

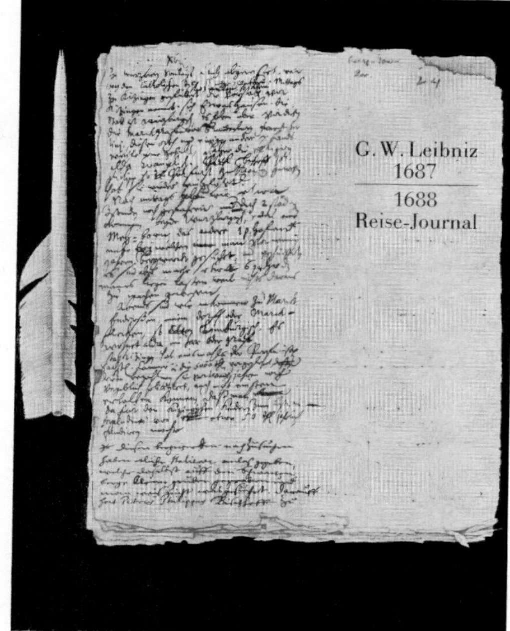

640

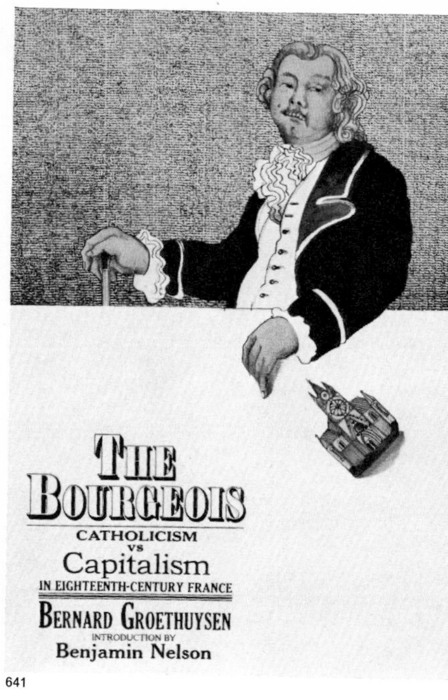

641

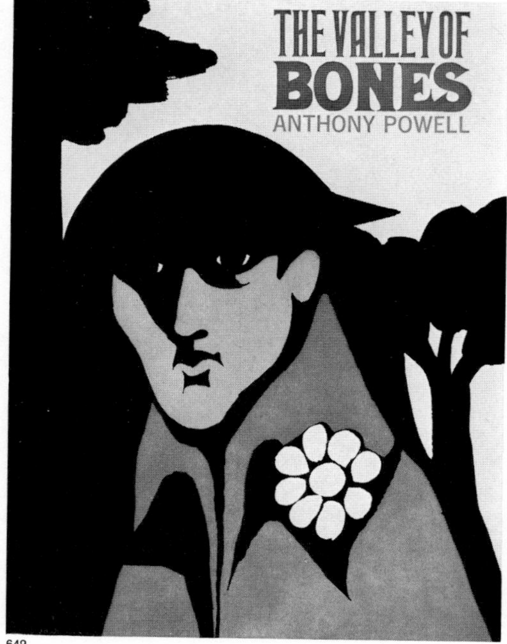

642

643

644

645

Book Jackets
Schutzumschläge
Chemises de livres

Artist/Künstler/Artiste:

646) MARTTI A. MYKKÄNEN
647) HERMANN BONGARD
648) JOHN TROTTA/HARALD PETER
649) HESELER & HESELER
650) KURT WIRTH
651) PETER WEZEL
652) 653) MOGENS ZIELER
654) MICHAEL DEMPSEY/GINGER TILLEY
655) WERNER REBHUHN
656) LEA KOCH
657) ROLF LEHMANN
658) HANS BÄCHER

Art Director:

646) MARTTI A. MYKKÄNEN
647) HERMANN BONGARD
648) HARALD PETER
649) HESELER & HESELER
651) DIOGENES VERLAG
654) DICK O'BRIEN
655) WERNER REBHUHN

Agency/Agentur:

646) MARTTI A. MYKKÄNEN, HELSINKI
648) FOOTE, CONE & BELDING, INC., CHICAGO

Publisher/Verleger/Editeur:

646) OTAVA, HELSINKI
647) J. W. CAPPELEN, OSLO
648) HALLMARK CARDS, INC., KANSAS CITY
649) PETER HAMMER VERLAG, WUPPERTAL/GER
650) VIKTORIA VERLAG, OSTERMUNDIGEN/SWI
651) DIOGENES VERLAG AG, ZÜRICH
652) DECEMBRISTERNE, KOPENHAGEN
653) MUSIKHØJSKOLENS FÖRLAG, EGTVED/DEN
654) BEECHAMS, LONDON
655) ROWOHLT-VERLAG GMBH, HAMBURG
656) DEUTSCHER BÜCHERBUND, STUTTGART
657) 658) VERLAG DER ARCHE, ZÜRICH

646

647

648

649

650

651

652

653

654

655

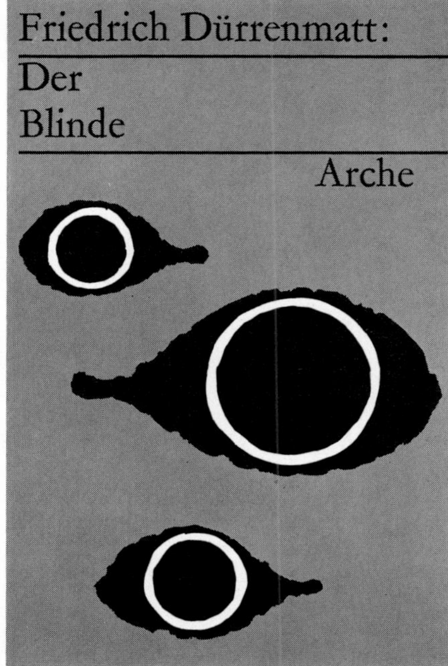

658

656

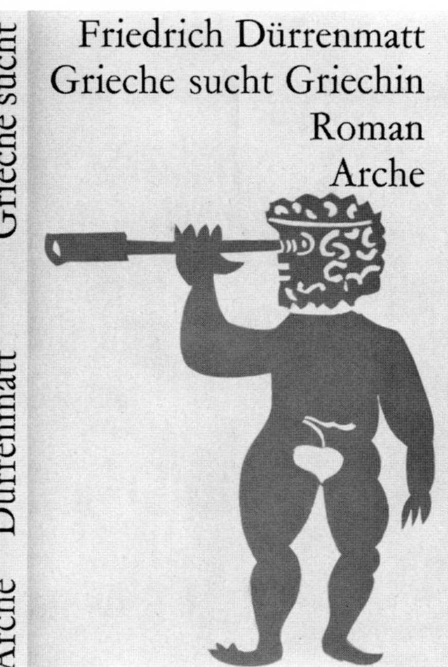

657

646) Cover of a novel. Red and orange on white, red and white lettering. (FIN)
647) Polychrome book jacket. (NOR)
648) Book jacket. Full colour. (USA)
649) Jacket of a book of contemporary German poetry about peace. Green leaf. (GER)
650) Jacket of a book of short stories. (SWI)
651) Jacket of a volume by Sean O'Casey from an autobiographical series. (SWI)
652) Cover of a book containing the work of a group of artists. (DEN)
653) Cover for a music book dedicated to the Aarhus University Choir. (DEN)
654) Cover of a book of cocktail recipes. (GB)
655) Complete cover of a book of short stories. Polychrome. (GER)
656) Polychrome book cover (Blue Haze). (GER)
657) Jacket for a novel. Red figures. (SWI)
658) Jacket for a novel (The Blind Man). (SWI)

646) Umschlag für einen Roman. Rot und orange auf weissem Grund. (FIN)
647) Mehrfarbiger Buchumschlag. (NOR)
648) Buchumschlag. Mehrfarbig. (USA)
649) Umschlag eines Bandes zeitgenössischer deutscher Gedichte. (GER)
650) Umschlag eines Buches mit Erzählungen. (SWI)
651) Umschlag eines Buches von Sean O'Casey aus einer autobiographischen Reihe. (SWI)
652) Umschlag eines Buches mit den Werken einer Gruppe von Künstlern. (DEN)
653) Umschlag für ein Musikbuch, das dem Universitätschor Aarhus gewidmet ist. (DEN)
654) Umschlag für eine Sammlung von Cocktail-Rezepten. (GB)
655) Umschlag für einen Erzählerband. (GER)
656) Mehrfarbiger Schutzumschlag. (GER)
657) Umschlag zu einem Roman. Figuren rot. (SWI)
658) Umschlag zu einem Roman. (SWI)

646) Couverture de roman. Rouge et orange sur fond blanc. (FIN)
647) Chemise de livre en couleur. (NOR)
648) Chemise de livre. Polychrome. (USA)
649) Chemise d'un recueil de poésie allemande contemporaine. Feuille verte. (GER)
650) Chemise d'un recueil de nouvelles. (SWI)
651) Chemise d'une autobiographie de Sean O'Casey, tirée d'une série. (SWI)
652) Couverture d'un recueil des œuvres d'un groupe d'artistes. (DEN)
653) Couverture d'un cahier de musique dédié à une chorale universitaire. (DEN)
654) Couverture d'un recueil de recettes. (GB)
655) Couverture d'un recueil de nouvelles. Polychrome. (GER)
656) Couverture de livre en couleur. (GER)
657) Chemise de roman. Illustrations rouges. (SWI)
658) Chemise de roman (L'Aveugle). (SWI)

GUINNESS BOOK of RECORDS

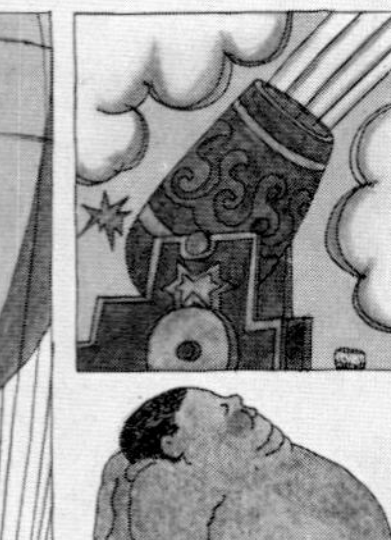

GUINNESS BOOK of RECORDS

LARGEST/SMALLEST/FASTEST/HEAVIEST/LONGEST/HIGHEST/SLOWEST/HOTTEST/OLDEST/RICHEST/DEEPEST/TALLEST/LOUDEST/MOSTEST/IN, ON AND BEYOND THE EARTH

GUINNESS BOOK of RECORDS

LARGEST/SMALLEST/FASTEST/HEAVIEST/LONGEST/HIGHEST/SLOWEST/HOTTEST/OLDEST/RICHEST/DEEPEST/TALLEST/LOUDEST/MOSTEST/IN, ON AND BEYOND THE EARTH

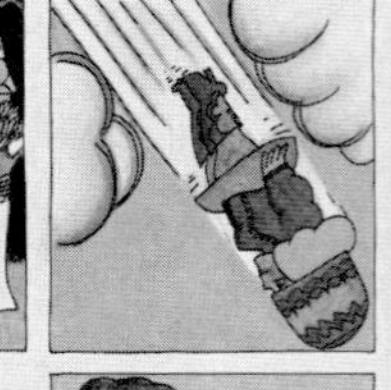

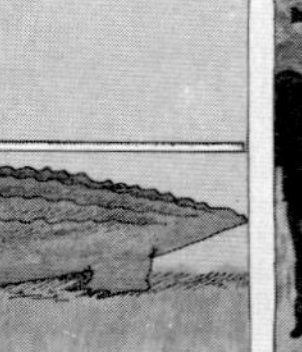

659

Artist/Künstler/Artiste:

659) DAVID MCKEE
660) 661) GIANCARLO BUONFINO
662) IKKO TANAKA
663) EIICHI HASEGAWA
664) SEYMOUR CHWAST/HARALD PETER
665) ART GOODMAN/SAUL BASS
666) HANS ARNOLD
667) KARI GROSSMANN
668) HANS LEHNACKER
669) DORIS BERNATZIK
670) D. SHOZO YORIOKA/I. AKIRA

Art Director/Directeur artistique:

660) 661) GIANCARLO BUONFINO
663) YASUO SHIGEHARA
664) HARALD PETER
665) ART GOODMAN
667) HERMANN BONGARD

Agency/Agentur/Agence – Studio:

660) 661) BUONFINO, MILAN
663) MADISON ADVERTISING, TOKYO

Publisher/Verleger/Editeur:

659) GUINNESS SUPERLATIVES, LONDON
660) 661) FORUM EDITORIALE, MILAN
662) KYUNYUDO, TOKYO
663) YOMIURI SHIMBUN-SHA, TOKYO
664) HALLMARK, INC., NEW YORK
665) WILLIAM MORROW & CO., INC., N.Y.
667) J. W. CAPPELEN, OSLO
668) TYPOGRAPH. GES., MÜNCHEN
669) PAUL ZSOLNAY VERLAG, WIEN
670) TENSEI PUBLICITY, TOKYO

660

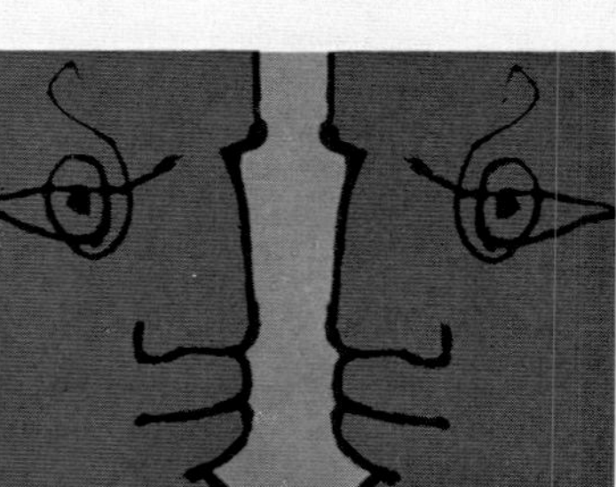

661

659) Complete jacket for a book of world records. Polychrome. (GB)
660) Polychrome cover of a 'classic of surrealism' (The Immaculate Conception). (ITA)
661) Cover of a book by an unknown author (The White Book). Blue, pink and black. (ITA)
662) Book cover. Black, white and orange. (JAP)
663) Jacket of a book entitled 'Travel Beside the River'. Polychrome. (JAP)
664) Jacket of a book of humorous verse. (USA)
665) Jacket of a war-time story. (USA)
666) Jacket of Capote's *In Cold Blood*. Black ground, white lettering, red streak. (GER)
667) Jacket of a novel about London. (NOR)
668) Cover of *Vita Activa*, a book of Georg Trump's typography. One red T among the black. (GER)
669) Cover of a crime story. Black, white, red. (GER)
670) Book jacket. Pastel shades and black, with blue title. (JAP)

紙のフォルム
尾川宏

662

663

664

665

666

667

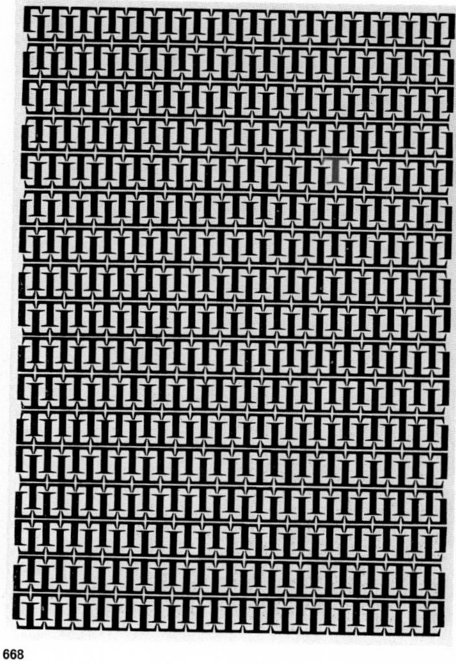

668

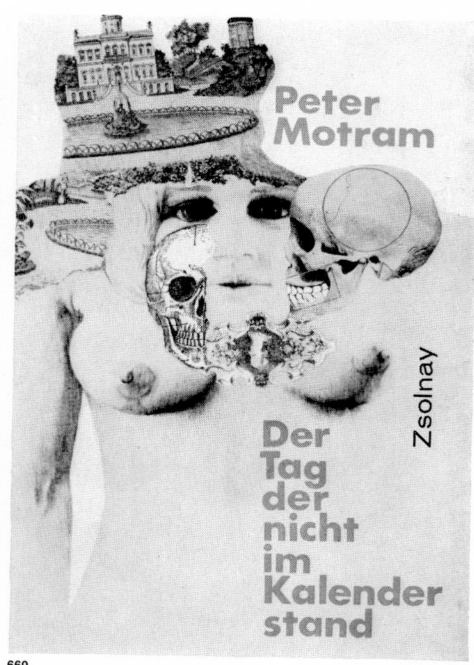

669

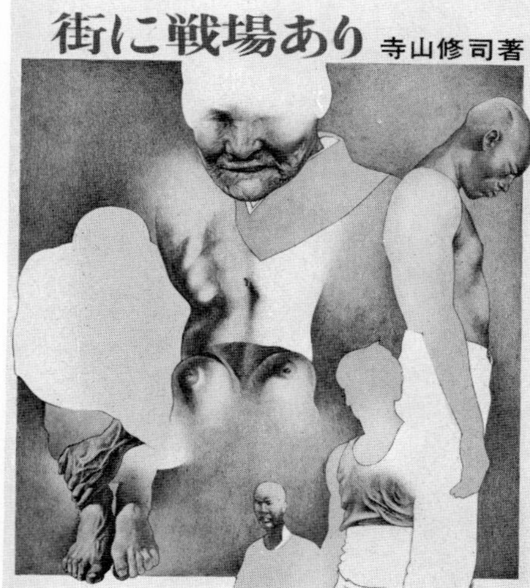

670

659) Vollständiger Umschlag für ein Buch über Weltrekorde. Mehrfarbig. (GB)
660) Mehrfarbiger Schutzumschlag für ein surrealistisches Werk (Die unbefleckte Empfängnis). (ITA)
661) Umschlag für ein Buch (Das weisse Buch) von einem unbekannten Autor. (ITA)
662) Buchumschlag. Schwarz, weiss und orange. (JAP)
663) Umschlag für das Buch *Die Reise entlang des Flusses*. Mehrfarbig. (JAP)
664) Umschlag für ein Buch mit lustigen Versen. (USA)
665) Umschlag für eine Kriegserzählung. (USA)
666) Schutzumschlag für das Buch *Kaltblütig* von Truman Capote. Schwarz, weiss und rot. (GER)
667) Umschlag für einen Roman über London. (NOR)
668) Schutzumschlag für das Buch *Vita Activa*, mit Bildern und Schriften von Georg Trump. (GER)
669) Umschlag für einen Kriminalroman. (GER)
670) Buchumschlag. Pastelltöne und schwarz, blauer Titel. (JAP)

659) Vue de la chemise d'un répertoire de records du monde. Polychrome. (GB)
660) Couverture en couleur d'un «classique du surréalisme» (L'Immaculée conception). (ITA)
661) Couverture d'un livre d'un auteur inconnu (Le Livre blanc). Bleu, rose et noir. (ITA)
662) Couverture de livre. Noir, blanc et orange. (JAP)
663) Chemise d'un livre intitulé «Voyage le long de la rivière». Polychrome. (JAP)
664) Chemise d'un recueil de vers humoristiques. (USA)
665) Chemise d'un conte de guerre. (USA)
666) Chemise du livre de Truman Capote *De sang-froid*. Texte en blanc sur fond noir, trait rouge. (GER)
667) Chemise d'un roman sur Londres. Polychrome. (NOR)
668) Couverture de *Vita Activa*, un ouvrage consacré à la typographie de Georg Trump. (GER)
669) Couverture d'un roman policier. (GER)
670) Chemise de livre. Teintes pastels et noir, titre en bleu. (JAP)

671) 674) Illustration and cover of a book of stories (The Time in W and Elsewhere). (GER)
672) Cover of a modern novel. Black, yellow and ochre. (NLD)
673) Cover of a book of short stories. (GER)
675) Cover of a book from a series (Spies as Politicians). Black, white and pale pink. (SWE)
676) Cover of a novel. Design in greens, blue and orange. (GER)
677) Polychrome cover of a book on health. (GER)
678) Cover of a political book (Why Vietnam?). (ARG)
679) Cover of a book on legal problems. Black, two reds. (USA)
680) Cover of a paperback about a dictator. Polychrome. (GER)
681) Cover of a book of political stories. Coloured glasses. (GER)
682) Cover of a novel. Black, white, green and violet. (GER)
683) Cover of a novel (The Seasick Whale). Polychrome. (GER)

671) 674) Illustration et couverture d'un recueil de nouvelles (Le temps à W et ailleurs). (GER)
672) Couverture d'un roman moderne. Noir, jaune et ocre. (NLD)
673) Couverture d'un recueil d'«Histoires lapidaires». Noir sur fond olive. (GER)
675) Couverture de livre en noir, blanc et rose pâle. (SWE)
676) Couverture de roman. Illustration en couleur. (GER)
677) Couverture en couleur d'un ouvrage sur la santé. (GER)
678) Couverture d'un ouvrage politique. (ARG)
679) Couverture d'un ouvrage sur les problèmes de droit. (USA)
680) Couverture brochée illustrée en couleur. (GER)
681) Couverture d'un recueil d'histoires politiques. (GER)
682) Couverture d'un roman. Noir, blanc, vert et violet. (GER)
683) Couverture d'un roman. Polychrome. (GER)

671) 674) Illustration und Umschlag einer Sammlung von Kurzgeschichten. (GER)
672) Umschlag eines modernen Romans. Schwarz, gelb, ocker. (NLD)
673) Umschlag für den Band *Lapidare Geschichten* von Heinrich Wiesner. Schwarz auf olivgrauem Grund. (GER)
675) Buchumschlag. Schwarz, weiss und blassrosa. (SWE)
676) Umschlag für einen Roman. Illustration mehrfarbig. (GER)
677) Umschlag für ein Taschenbuch über gesundes Leben. (GER)
678) Umschlag für ein politisches Buch (Warum Vietnam?). (ARG)
679) Umschlag für ein Buch über Rechtsprobleme. (USA)
680) Umschlag für ein Taschenbuch. Mehrfarbig. (GER)
681) Umschlag für politische Geschichten moderner Autoren. (GER)
682) Umschlag für eine Erzählung. Schwarz, grün und violett. (GER)
683) Umschlag für eine Erzählung. Mehrfarbig. (GER)

672

671

673

674

675

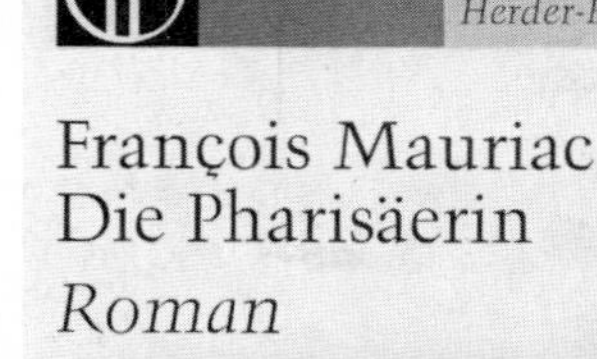

676

677

678

679

680

Strömungen
unter dem Eis
Politische Geschichten
zeitgenössischer deutscher Autoren
Herausgegeben von Arnim Juhre
Peter Hammer Verlag

681

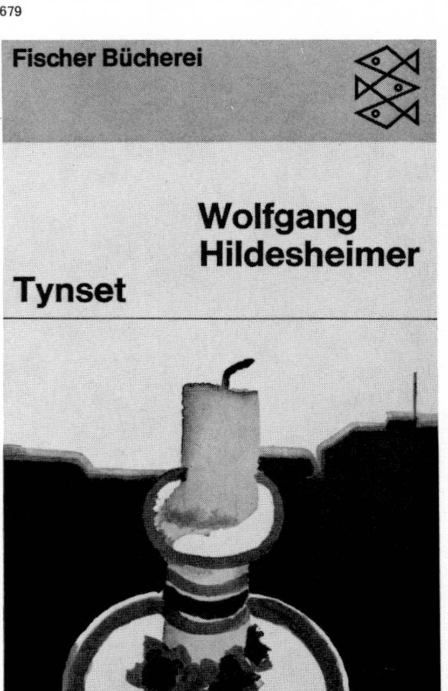

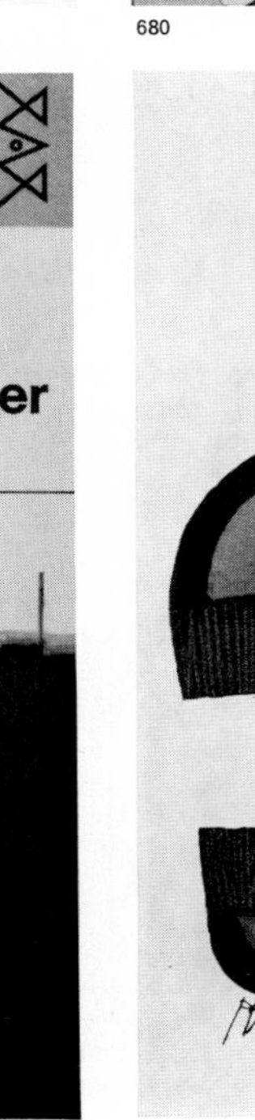
682

683

Artist/Künstler/Artiste:

671) 674) 681) HESELER & HESELER
672) SJOERD DE VRIES/ FRITS STOEPMAN
673) 683) CELESTINO PIATTI
675) KJELL IVAN ANDERSON
676) 677) WALTER GRIEDER
678) ROBERTO PÁEZ
679) GEORGE GIUSTI
680) JAN BUCHHOLZ/ RENI HINSCH
682) HANS HILLMANN

Art Director/Directeur artistique:

671) 674) 681) HESELER & HESELER
676) 677) REINHARD KLEIN
678) ROBERTO PÁEZ
679) DIANA KLEMIN
682) HANS HILLMANN

Publisher/Verleger/Editeur:

671) 674) 681) PETER HAMMER VERLAG, WUPPERTAL
672) MOUSSAULT'S UITGEVERIJ N.V., AMSTERDAM
673) R. PIPER & CO. VERLAG, MÜNCHEN
675) ZINDERMANS FÖRLAG, GÖTEBORG
676) 677) HERDER VERLAG KG, FREIBURG I. BR.
678) EDITORIAL AMERICANA, BUENOS AIRES
679) DOUBLEDAY & CO., INC., NEW YORK
680) ROWOHLT-VERLAG GMBH, HAMBURG
682) S. FISCHER-VERLAG, FRANKFURT/M.
683) DEUTSCHER TASCHENBUCH-VERLAG GMBH & CO., KG, MÜNCHEN

Paperbacks
Taschenbücher
Livres brochés

Gramophone Record Covers
Schallplattenhüllen
Pochettes de disques

684) Cover for a recording of a Berlioz symphony. (USA)
685) Cover for a record by a group of negro singers. (USA)
686) 687) Covers for a series of puppet show recordings for children. (SWI)
688) 689) Covers for a series of recordings of fairy tales. Polychrome. (GER)
690) Cover for a publicity record for a brand of condensed milk. Bright colours. (SPA)
691) Record cover for songs by a folk singer. (USA)
692) 693) Covers for a series of recordings of popular Japanese melodies. (JAP)
694) 695) Illustration and cover for a recording of music by one of the Beatles. (GB)
696) Record cover for two suites conducted by Stravinsky. Black lettering, coloured figures. (USA)
697) Record cover for a one-act English opera. (USA)
698) Cover for a recording of a Dvorák symphony. (USA)

684) Plattenhülle für eine Symphonie von Berlioz. (USA)
685) Schallplattenhülle für Vokalmusik. (USA)
686) 687) Plattenhülle für eine Serie von Aufnahmen aus dem Kasperlitheater. (SWI)
688) 689) Plattenhüllen für Aufnahmen von Märchen der Brüder Grimm. Mehrfarbig. (GER)
690) Umschlag für eine Schallplatte, die für eine neue Kondensmilch wirbt. Mehrfarbig. (SPA)
691) Hülle für die Platte eines Volksliedersängers. (USA)
692) 693) Hüllen für eine Plattenserie mit bekannten japanischen Melodien. (JAP)
694) 695) Illustration und Umschlag für eine Aufnahme der Musik von George Harrison, einem der *Beatles*. (GB)
696) Schallplattenhülle für zwei Suiten, dirigiert von Strawinsky. Schwarze Schrift, farbige Figuren. (USA)
697) Schallplattenhülle für eine englische Oper. (USA)
698) Hülle für eine Dvorák-Symphonie. (USA)

684) Pochette pour un enregistrement d'une symphonie de Berlioz. (USA)
685) Pochette d'un disque de chanteurs nègres. (USA)
686) 687) Pochettes d'une série d'enregistrements de théâtre de marionnettes pour les enfants. (SWI)
688) 689) Pochettes d'une série d'enregistrements de contes de fées. Polychromes. (GER)
690) Pochette pour un disque publicitaire en faveur d'une nouvelle marque de lait condensé. Polychrome. (SPA)
691) Pochette d'un disque de chansons folkloriques. (USA)
692) 693) Pochettes d'une série d'enregistrements de mélodies populaires japonaises. (JAP)
694) 695) Illustration et pochette d'un enregistrement de musique exécutée par un des Beatles. (GB)
696) Pochettes pour deux suites musicales, exécutées sous la direction de Stravinsky. (USA)
697) Pochette pour un opéra anglais en un acte. (USA)
698) Pochette pour un enregistrement d'une symphonie de Dvorák. (USA)

684

685

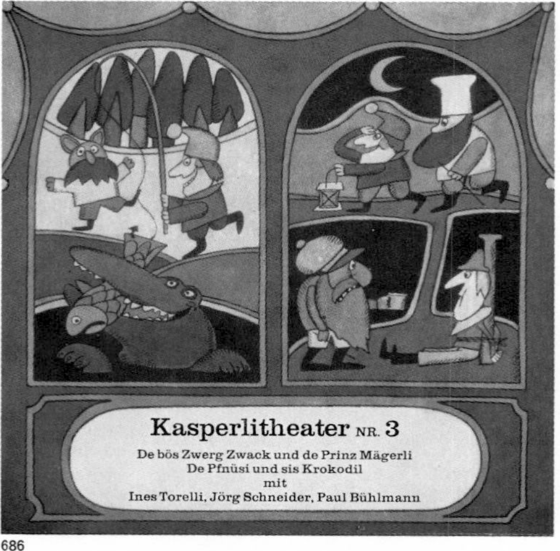

686

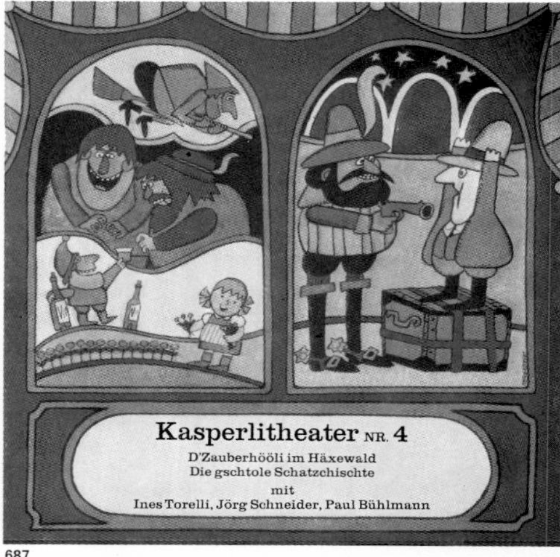

687

688

689

690

691

Artist/Künstler/Artiste:

684) MILTON GLASER/JOHN BERG
685) DON WELLER
686) 687) HEINZ STIEGER
688) 689) HELLA STOLZ
690) ENRIC SATUÈ
691) MILTON GLASER
692) 693) TSUNAO HARADA
694) 695) BOB GILL
696) RICHARD MANTEL
697) MARV SCHWARTZ
698) BYRON GOTO/HENRY EPSTEIN

Art Director/Directeur artistique:

684) 696) JOHN BERG
685) TOM LAZARUS/JOHN C. LE PREVOST
686) 687) OSWALD DUBACHER
688) 689) HELLA STOLZ
690) NÖEL FONTANÈS
691) KEVIN EGGERS
694) 695) BOB GILL
697) MARV SCHWARTZ

Agency/Agentur/Agence – Studio:

690) CLIMAX S.A., BARCELONA

Publisher/Verleger/Editeur:

684) 696) COLUMBIA BROADCASTING SYSTEM, NEW YORK
685) UNIVERSAL CITY RECORDS, A DIVISION OF MCA, INC., LOS ANGELES
686) 687) EX LIBRIS VERLAG AG, ZÜRICH
688) 689) CBS SCHALLPLATTEN GMBH, FRANKFURT/M.
690) NESTLÉ, S.A., BARCELONA
691) POPPY RECORDS, NEW YORK
694) 695) APPLE RECORDS, LONDON
697) CAPITOL RECORDS DISTRIBUTING CORP., HOLLYWOOD
698) ABC RECORDS, INC., NEW YORK

694

692

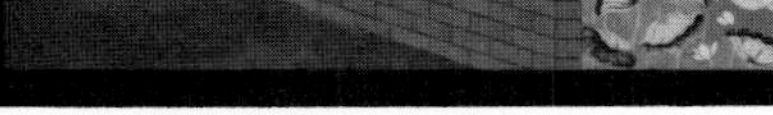

695

696

698

693

697

Record Covers / Schallplattenhüllen
Pochettes de disques

Artist/Künstler/Artiste:

699) 700) KOJI ITO
701) STANISLAW ZAGORSKI
702) 703) KIMIHISA NAKAMURA
704) ROBERT WYSS
705) KURT WIRTH
706) 709) HANS KELLER
707) ARMIN GREDER
708) 711) GEORGE GIUSTI
710) VIRGINIA TEAM
712) 713) HOLGER MATTHIES

Art Director/Directeur artistique:

699) 700) KOJI ITO
701) NESUHI ERTEGUN
704) OSWALD DUBACHER
705) KURT WIRTH
706) 709) GISELA TOBLER
707) ARMIN GREDER
710) JOHN BERG
711) DANIEL PEZZA
712) 713) JOCHEN HINZE

Agency/Agentur/Agence – Studio:

706) 709) GISELA TOBLER, MILAN

Publisher/Verleger/Editeur:

699) 700) COLUMBIA RECORD CO., TOKYO
701) ATLANTIC RECORDING CORP., NEW YORK
704) EX LIBRIS VERLAG AG, ZÜRICH
705) ZYTGLOGGE, SCHALLPLATTEN-VERLAG, BERN
706) 709) RI-FI, MILAN
707) BOUTIQUE NEW SHOP, BIEL
708) 711) COMMAND RECORDS, NEW YORK
710) COLUMBIA BROADCASTING SYSTEM, NEW YORK
712) 713) DEUTSCHE GRAMMOPHON GESELLSCHAFT GMBH, HAMBURG

701

699

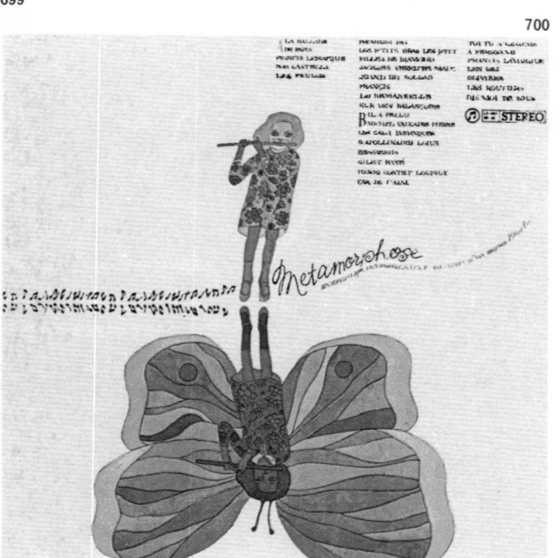

700

704

707

705

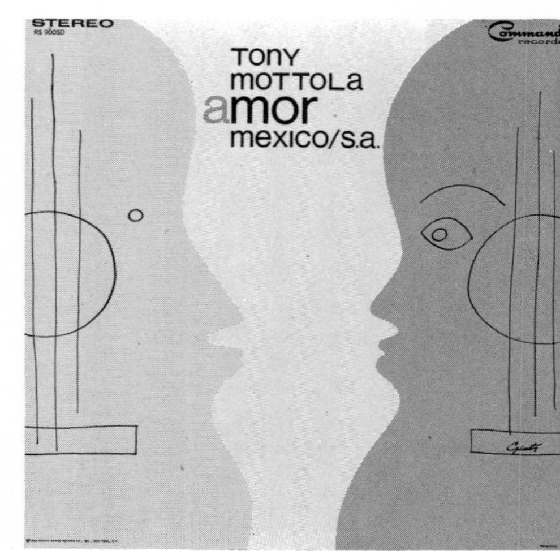

708

702

710

711

703

712

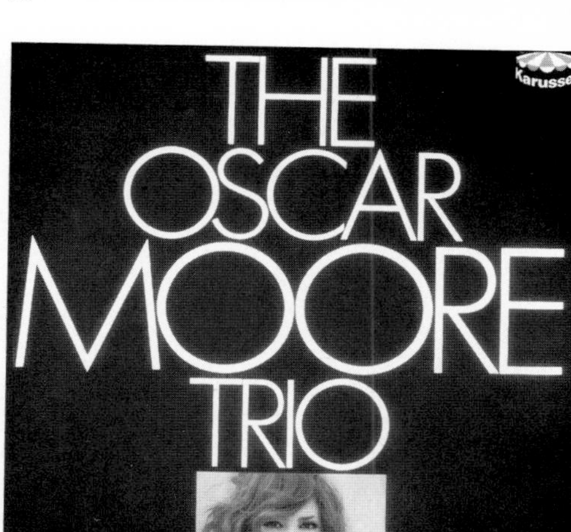

713

706

699) 700) Record cover projects for French chansons. (JAP)
701) Record cover for songs by a popular American soul singer. (USA)
702) 703) Record cover projects for organ music. (JAP)
704) Record cover for a recital of poems for children. Black on yellow. (SWI)
705) Record cover for songs in the Bernese dialect. Black on grey. (SWI)
706) 709) Covers for records retelling Greek legends. Full-colour illustrations. (ITA)
707) Cover for records presented to customers as a gift by a shop in Bienne. Black and white. (SWI)
708) Cover for a recording of songs to the guitar. Green, mauve and black. (USA)
710) Cover for a recording of a symphony and serenade by a British composer. (USA)
711) Record cover for music by a brass choir. (USA)
712) Record cover for music by a soul band. Polychrome circles on green. (GER)
713) Cover for popular hits played by a trio. Dark blue ground, colour inset. (GER)

699) 700) Plattenumschläge für Chansons (Entwürfe). (JAP)
701) Schallplattenhülle für die Lieder eines bekannten amerikanischen Soul-Sängers. (USA)
702) 703) Plattenumschläge für Orgelmusik (Entwürfe). (JAP)
704) Umschlag für eine Sprechplatte mit Gedichten für Kinder. Schwarz auf Gelb. (SWI)
705) Schallplattenumschlag für Chansons, gesungen im Berner Dialekt. Schwarz auf Grau. (SWI)
706) 709) Hüllen für Sprechplatten mit griechischen Sagen. Illustrationen mehrfarbig. (ITA)
707) Hülle für Schallplatten, die die Boutique New Shop in Biel ihren Kunden als Geschenk überreicht. (SWI)
708) Hülle für eine Aufnahme von Liedern mit Gitarrenbegleitung. Grün, lila und schwarz. (USA)
710) Hülle für eine Symphonie und eine Serenade von einem englischen Komponisten. (USA)
711) Schallplattenhülle für Blechmusik. (USA)
712) Schallplattenhülle für Musik von einer Soul-Gruppe. Mehrfarbige Ringe auf Grün. (GER)
713) Schallplattenhülle für Schlager, von einem Trio gespielt. Dunkelblauer Grund. (GER)

709

699) 700) Maquettes de pochettes de disques pour des chansons françaises. (JAP)
701) Pochette d'un disque de Solomon Burke, un chansonnier populaire américain. (USA)
702) 703) Maquettes de pochettes de disques pour de la musique à l'orgue. (JAP)
704) Pochette d'un enregistrement de poèmes pour les enfants. Noir sur jaune. (SWI)
705) Pochette d'un disque de chansons en dialecte bernois. Noir sur gris. (SWI)
706) 709) Pochettes d'enregistrements de légendes grecques. Illustrations polychromes. (ITA)
707) Pochette de disque offert à ses clients par un magasin de Bienne. Noir et blanc. (SWI)
708) Pochette d'un disque de chansons accompagnées à la guitare. Vert, mauve et noir. (USA)
710) Pochette pour un enregistrement d'une symphonie et d'une sérénade d'un compositeur anglais. (USA)
711) Pour un disque par un orchestre de cuivres. (USA)
712) Pochette d'un disque de musique «soul». (GER)
713) Pochette pour des airs à la mode exécutés par un trio. Fond marine. (GER)

5

Trade Marks and Symbols
Letterheads
Packaging

Schutzmarken
Briefköpfe
Packungen

Marques et emblèmes
En-têtes
Emballages

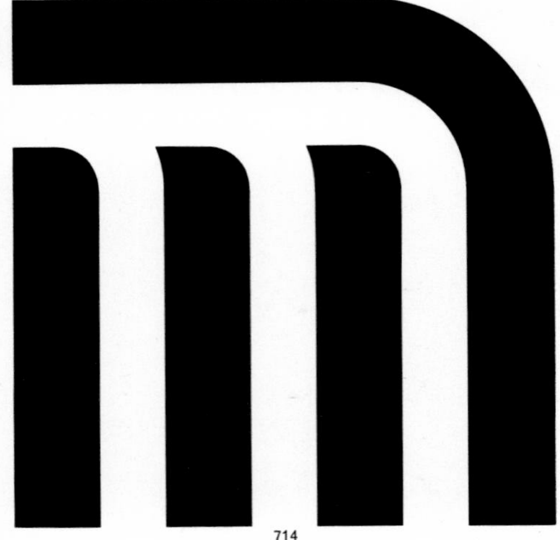
714

Artist/Künstler/Artiste:

714) LANCE WYMAN
715) 721) JACK M. STRICKER
716) FRITZ GOTTSCHALK
717) A. NORMAN LAW, JR.
718) IVAN CHERMAYEFF / HEINER HEGEMANN
719) FELIX BELTRAN
720) TADASHI OHASHI
722) MARKUS J. LÖW
723) STEPHAN KANTSCHEFF
724) BOUDEWIJN DELAERE
725) PETER ULMER
726) CLARENCE LEE
727) HERBERT LEUPIN
728) ROBERT R. OVERBY
729) 730) SUSUMU KIMURA

Art Director/Directeur artistique:

714) LANCE WYMAN
715) 721) JACK M. STRICKER
716) FRITZ GOTTSCHALK
717) A. NORMAN LAW, JR.
718) IVAN CHERMAYEFF
720) TADASHI OHASHI
722) MARKUS J. LÖW
723) STEPHAN KANTSCHEFF
725) PETER ULMER
726) PETER SAPASAP
727) HERBERT LEUPIN
729) 730) SUSUMU KIMURA

714) Symbol for the Metro of Mexico City. (MEX)
715) Trade mark for Gateway Studio, Inc. (USA)
716) Symbol for the Broome County Bus Company. (CAN)
717) Trade mark for East Cleveland Urban Renewal Products, Inc. (USA)
718) Symbol for a Jewish foundation in Washington. (USA)
719) Trade mark for *Aerocarga* air freight. (SPA)
720) Trade mark for Kyowa Bank Ltd. (JAP)
721) Trade mark for Mueller Enterprise, Inc. (USA)
722) Internal symbol (Quality and Safety) for the Geigy Pharmaceuticals Division. (USA)
723) Mark for the steelworks Стомана Силистра. (BUL)
724) Symbol for the VVG, an association of designers. (BEL)
725) Trade mark for Charterways, a transport company. (CAN)
726) Symbol for a Chinese restaurant. (USA)
727) Emblem for a gymnastics meeting in Basle. (SWI)
728) Trade mark for Mel Whitson, Stationers, Inc. (USA)
729) Trade mark for Mochiya, makers of cakes. (JAP)
730) Trade mark for the Japan Lina Carton Co. Ltd. (JAP)

714) Signet für die Untergrundbahn von Mexico City. (MEX)
715) Schutzmarke für Gateway Studio, Inc. (USA)
716) Signet für den Broome County Autobusdienst. (CAN)
717) Schutzmarke für East Cleveland, Inc., eine Produktionsgesellschaft. (USA)
718) Signet für eine jüdische Stiftung in Washington. (USA)
719) Schutzmarke für *Aerocargo* Luftfracht, Madrid. (SPA)
720) Schutzmarke für eine Bank. (JAP)
721) Schutzmarke für Mueller Enterprise, Inc. (USA)
722) Signet (Qualität und Sicherheit) für den internen Gebrauch in einer Abteilung von Geigy. (USA)
723) Marke für die Stahlwerke Стомана Силистра. (BUL)
724) Signet für die VVG, eine Graphikervereinigung. (BEL)
725) Schutzmarke für eine Transportfirma. (CAN)
726) Signet für ein chinesisches Restaurant. (USA)
727) Signet für die 5. Gymnaestrada in Basel. (SWI)
728) Schutzmarke für Mel Whitson, eine Papeterie. (USA)
729) Schutzmarke für die Kuchenbäckerei Mochiya. (JAP)
730) Schutzmarke für die Japan Lina Carton Co. Ltd. (JAP)

714) Emblème pour le métro de Mexico City. (MEX)
715) Marque du Gateway Studio, Inc. (USA)
716) Emblème d'une compagnie d'autobus. (CAN)
717) Marque d'un fabricant de produits de construction. (USA)
718) Emblème d'une association juive de Washington. (USA)
719) Marque des services de fret aérien *Aerocargo.* (SPA)
720) Emblème d'une banque. (JAP)
721) Marque de la société Mueller Enterprise, Inc. (USA)
722) Sigle (qualité et sécurité) utilisé à l'intérieur de la société par la Division pharmaceutique Geigy. (USA)
723) Marque des usines métallurgiques Стомана Силистра. (BUL)
724) Emblème de l'Association de graphistes VVG. (BEL)
725) Marque d'une entreprise de transport. (CAN)
726) Emblème d'un restaurant chinois. (USA)
727) Emblème pour une fête de gymnastique à Bâle. (SWI)
728) Marque de la papeterie Mel Whitson. (USA)
729) Marque d'un fabricant de gâteaux. (JAP)
730) Marque d'une fabrique de carton. (JAP)

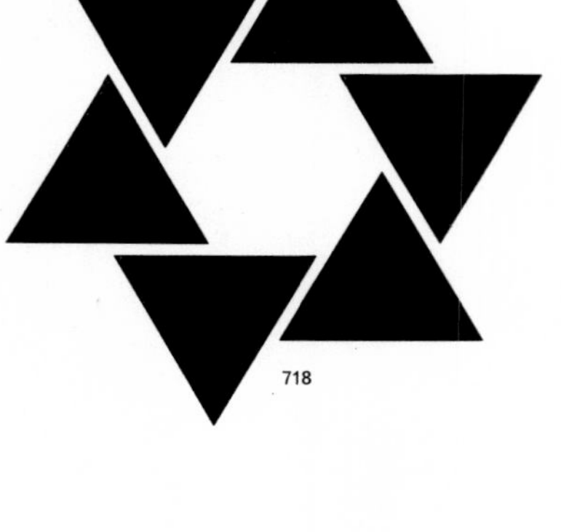
718

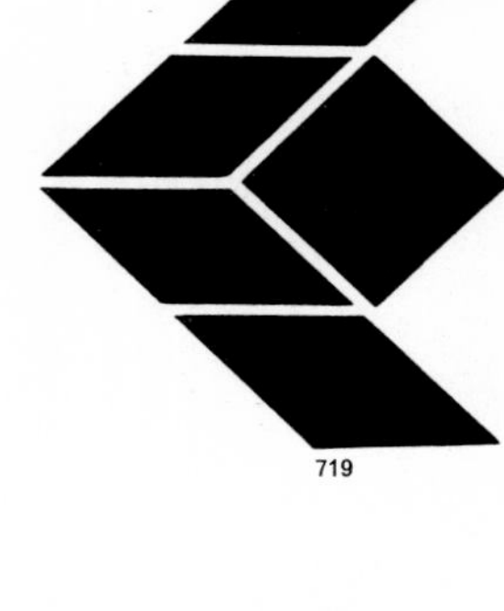
719

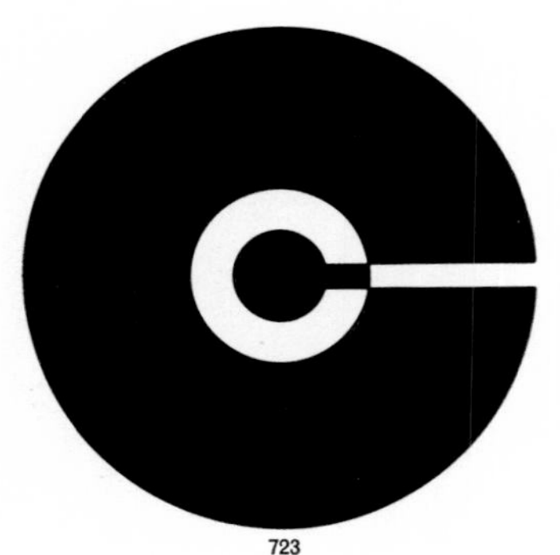
723

724

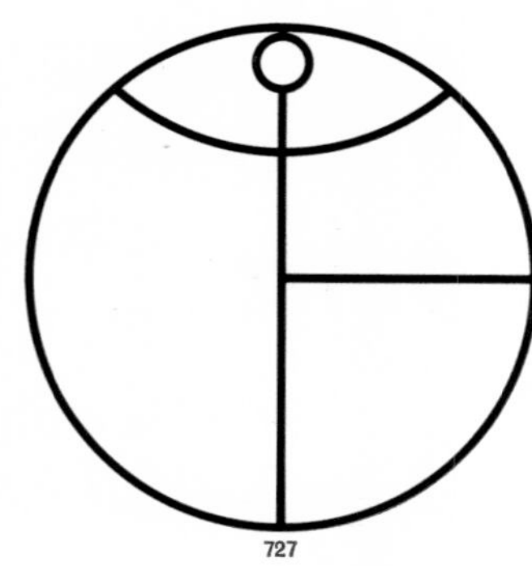
727

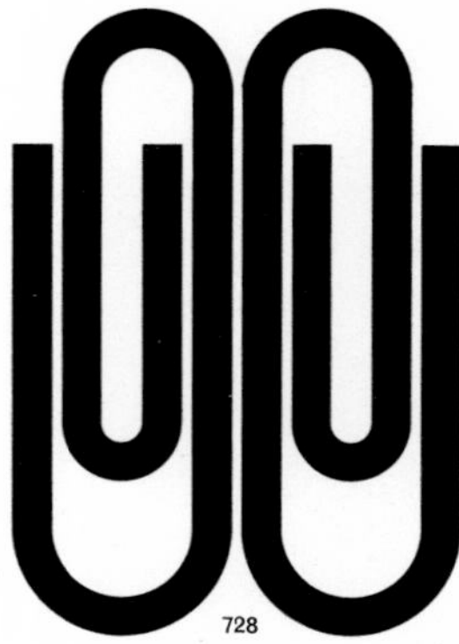
728

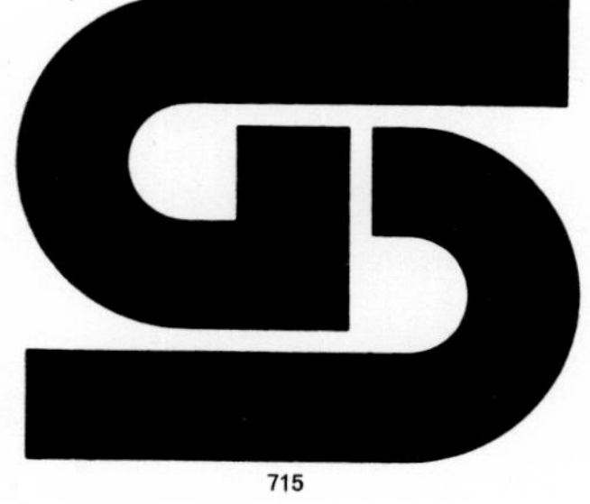
715

716

717

720

721

722

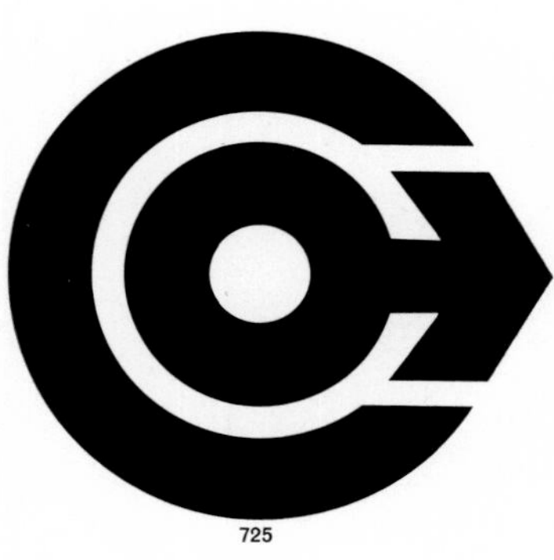
725

726

729

730

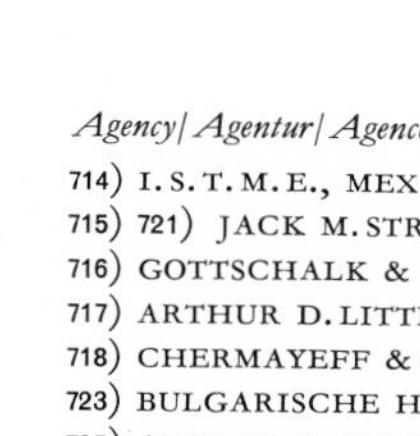

Agency/ Agentur/ Agence – Studio:

714) I. S. T. M. E., MEXICO
715) 721) JACK M. STRICKER ASSOC., PITTSBURGH
716) GOTTSCHALK & ASH LTD., MONTREAL
717) ARTHUR D. LITTLE, INC., CAMBRIDGE/MA.
718) CHERMAYEFF & GEISMAR ASSOC., NEW YORK
723) BULGARISCHE HANDELSKAMMER, SOFIA
725) ARTHUR & SPENCER LTD., TORONTO
726) MILICI ADVERTISING, HONOLULU
727) HERBERT LEUPIN, BASEL
729) 730) PACKAGING DIRECTION CO. LTD., TOKYO

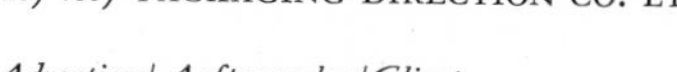

Advertiser/ Auftraggeber/ Client:

714) METRO, MEXICO CITY
715) GATEWAY STUDIO, INC., PITTSBURGH
716) BROOME COUNTY TRANSPORT COMMISSION, MONTREAL
717) ARTHUR D. LITTLE, INC., CAMBRIDGE/MA.
718) THE GREATER WASHINGTON JEWISH COMMUNITY FOUNDATION, WASHINGTON, D. C.
719) AEROCARGA, MADRID
720) KYOWA BANK LTD., TOKYO
721) MUELLER ENTERPRISE, INC., PITTSBURG
722) GEIGY PHARMACEUTICALS, ARDSLEY, N. Y.
723) STAATLICHES INDUSTRIEUNTERNEHMEN «STOMANA», SILISTRA/BUL
724) VVG ORGANISATION DE GRAPHISTES, DEURLE, GENT/BEL
725) CHARTERWAYS, AIR TERMINAL SERVICES AND SCHOOLBUSES, TORONTO + MONTREAL
726) THE DYNASTY RESTAURANT, HONOLULU
727) ORGANISATIONSKOMITEE DER 5. GYMNAESTRADA, BASEL
728) MEL WHITSON, INC., LOS ANGELES
729) MOCHIYA, TOKYO
730) JAPAN LINA CARTON CO., LTD., TOKYO

Letterheads / Briefköpfe / En-têtes

731

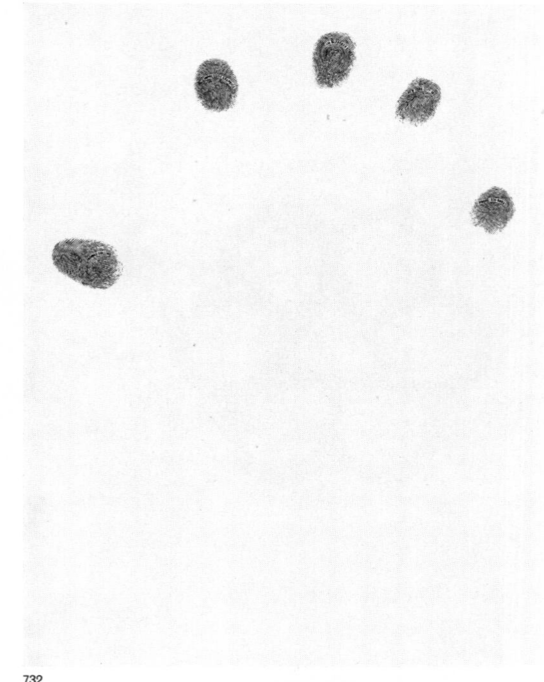

732

733

Jung & Zecca Via Guanella 27 20128 Milano

Studio fotografico

735

736

737

Artist/Künstler/Artiste:

731) 732) ROY SCHLEMME
733) DIETMAR R. WINKLER
734) CROSBY/FLETCHER/FORBES
735) HANS-ULRICH OSTERWALDER
736) ARTHUR BODEN
737) DICK GODFREY/JOHN NASH
738) GARTH BELL
739) HORST LIPPKI
740) OLA LAIHO
741) JOHN NASH
742) OVE SPÄTH
743) BRUCE BLACKBURN/IVAN CHERMAYEFF
744) WHAITE & EMERY
745) TAKESHI OTAKA

739

740

Turun Ylioppilaskyläsäätiö
Rehtorinpellontie 4
Turku 2
Puhelin vaihde 335668
Shekkitilit:
HOP Turku 3390/1/260/7
KOP Turku-Yliopistonrinne 12091/80
PYP Turku 2057/155
TSOk Hämeenkatu 01
TSSp Hämeenkatu 04
TSp 1168
TTSp 619
Postisiirto TU 156261

Lasku

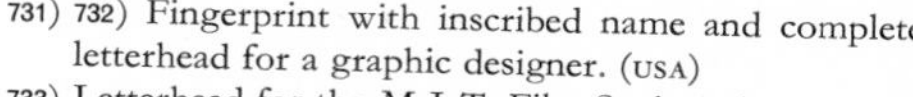

734

738

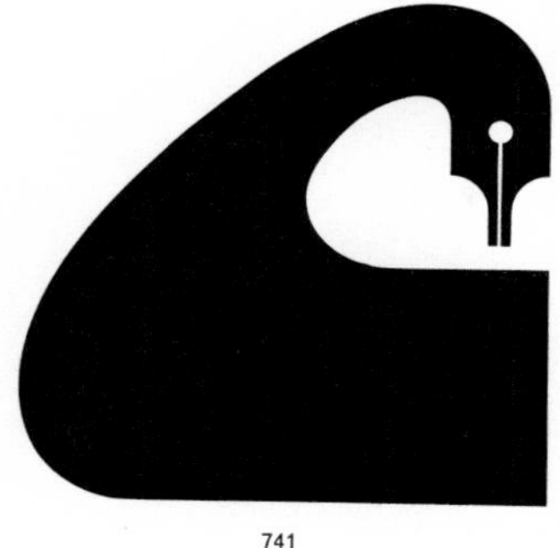
741

742

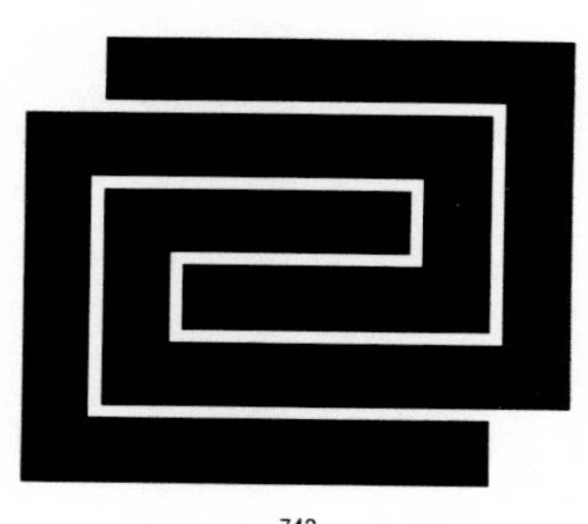
743

744

745

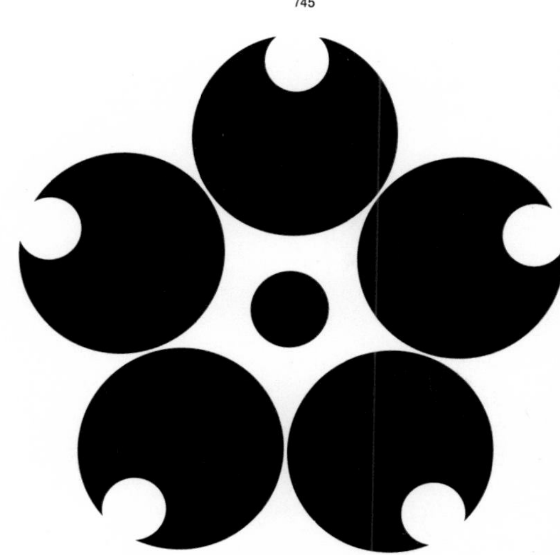

731) 732) Fingerprint with inscribed name and complete letterhead for a graphic designer. (USA)
733) Letterhead for the M.I.T. Film Society. (USA)
734) Letterhead for a night club. Red lettering. (GB)
735) Letterhead for a Milanese photographic studio. (ITA)
736) Letterhead for Herst Litho Inc., New York. (USA)
737) Merchandising bulletin for Guests Biscuits. Design in four colours. (AUL)
738) Letterhead for Cybernetics Research Consultants Ltd., London. Lettering in orange and green. (GB)
739) Letterhead for a children's store in Oldenburg. Red shades and black. (GER)
740) Invoice for a student housing scheme. (FIN)
741) Symbol for Cygnet Publishing Pty. Ltd., Perth. (AUL)
742) Symbol for the European Federation of Brick and Tile Manufacturers, usually printed brick-red. (DEN)
743) Symbol for the Encyclopedia Americana. (USA)
744) Symbol for the Baker Institute, a medical research centre. (AUL)
745) Emblem for EXPO '70 in Osaka. (JAP)

731) 732) Fingerabdruck mit eingezeichnetem Namen und vollständiger Briefkopf für einen Graphiker. (USA)
733) Briefkopf für den Filmklub einer Universität (USA)
734) Briefkopf für einen Nachtklub. Rote Schrift. (GB)
735) Briefkopf für ein photographisches Atelier. (ITA)
736) Briefkopf für Herst Litho Inc., New York. (USA)
737) Briefkopf für die Einkaufsabteilung einer Biskuitfabrik. Illustration mehrfarbig. (AUL)
738) Briefkopf einer Gesellschaft für kybernetische Forschung. Orange und grüne Schrift. (GB)
739) Briefkopf für *Spieltinchen*, ein Laden für Kinder in Oldenburg. Rottöne mit Schwarz. (GER)
740) Rechnungsformular für ein Studentenheim. (FIN)
741) Symbol des Cygnet-Verlags (cygnet = Schwan). (AUL)
742) Schutzmarke (ziegelrot) für die Europäische Vereinigung der Ziegel- und Fliesen-Hersteller. (DEN)
743) Symbol für ein Lexikon. (USA)
744) Symbol für das Baker Institut, ein medizinisches Forschungszentrum. (AUL)
745) Symbol für die EXPO '70 in Osaka. (JAP)

731) 732) Empreinte digitale portant le nom d'un graphiste, et en-tête. (USA)
733) En-tête du club cinéphile d'une université. (USA)
734) En-tête d'une boite de nuit. Texte en rouge. (GB)
735) En-tête des studios de photographie Jung & Zecca, Milan. (ITA)
736) En-tête d'un atelier de lithographie. (USA)
737) En-tête des services d'achat d'une biscuiterie. Illustration en quatre couleurs. (AUL)
738) En-tête d'une société de recherches en cybernétique. Texte en vert et orange. (GB)
739) En-tête d'un magasin pour enfants. Plusieurs tons de rouge et noir. (GER)
740) Facture d'une maison d'étudiants. (FIN)
741) Emblème de la maison d'édition «Cygnet». (AUL)
742) Emblème (rouge brique) de la Fédération européenne des briquetiers et tuilers. (DEN)
743) Emblème de l'Encyclopedia Americana. (USA)
744) Emblème d'un centre de recherches médicales. (AUL)
745) Emblème de l'EXPO '70 à Osaka. (JAP)

Art Director/ Directeur artistique:

731) 732) ROY SCHLEMME
733) DIETMAR R. WINKLER
735) HANS-ULRICH OSTERWALDER
736) ARTHUR BODEN
737) 741) JOHN NASH
738) GARTH BELL
739) HORST LIPPKI
740) OLA LAIHO
742) OVE SPÄTH
743) IVAN CHERMAYEFF
744) WHAITE & EMERY

Agency/ Agentur/ Agence – Studio:

733) M.I.T. OFFICE OF PUBLICATIONS, CAMBRIDGE/MASS.
737) JOHN CLEMENGER PTY. LTD., MELBOURNE
738) UNIT FIVE DESIGN LTD., LONDON
739) WERBESTUDIO HORST LIPPKI, OLDENBURG
741) WEATHERHEAD & STITT PTY. LTD., MELBOURNE
742) OVE SPÄTH, KOPENHAGEN
743) CHERMAYEFF & GEISMAR ASSOC., NEW YORK

746

746) Bottle and boxes for oil of camellia made by Izutsubaki Co. (JAP)
747) Cellophane bags for sticks and pretzels. (SWI)
748) Cigarette pack for the Japan Monopoly Corporation. (JAP)
749) Cigarette pack and match book for IBM. (FRA)
750) Stackable bottles and pack for whisky, gin, brandy and vodka. (JAP)
751) 752) Bottle and label for red Alsatian beer and for London gin sold by the chain of *Prisunic* stores. (FRA)
753) 754) Range of liqueurs in specially shaped space-saving bottles, marketed by the *Prisunic* stores. (FRA)

747

748

Artist/Künstler/Artiste:

746) YORIKAZU HIRATA
747) ARMIN MÜLLER
748) SHIGERU AKIZUKI
749) JEAN PIERRE CREACH
750) SHIGERU AKIZUKI/
MASAKICHI AWASHIMA
751) JACQUES DUDILIEUX
752) CHRISTINE COLLARD
753) 754) GALIZZI/MICHEL BILLIC

Art Director/Directeur artistique:

746) YORIKAZU HIRATA
752)-754) DENISE FAYOLLE

Agency/Agentur/Agence – Studio:

747) JEAN P. WÄLCHLI, ZÜRICH

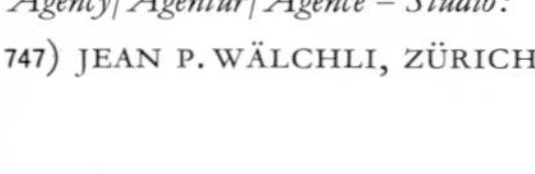

751

752

Packaging / Packungen
Emballages

746) Flasche und Schachteln für Kamelienöl, hergestellt von Izutsubaki Co. (JAP)
747) Cellophansäcke für Bretzel und Sticks von Ch. Singer's Erben AG, Basel. (SWI)
748) Zigarettenverpackung für die Japan Monopoly Corporation. (JAP)
749) Verpackung von Zigaretten und Zündhölzchen für IBM France. (FRA)
750) Stapelbare Flaschen und Verpackungen für Whisky, Gin, Kognac und Wodka. (JAP)
751) 752) Flasche und Etikette für ein Elsässer Bier und für London Gin, verkauft von den Warenhäusern *Prisunic*. (FRA)
753) 754) Reihe von Likören in besonderen platzsparenden Flaschen, die von den Warenhäusern *Prisunic* verkauft werden. (FRA)

746) Flacon et boîtes pour de l'huile de camélia. (JAP)
747) Sachets de cellophane pour des biscuits salés. (SWI)
748) Paquet pour les cigarettes *Luna*. Caractère L en bleu sur fond noir. (JAP)
749) Paquet de cigarettes et étui d'allumettes pour IBM France. (FRA)
750) Bouteilles s'emboîtant les unes sur les autres et emballages pour du whisky, du gin, du cognac et de la vodka. (JAP)
751) 752) Bouteille et étiquette pour une bière alsacienne et du gin en vente dans les magasins *Prisunic*. (FRA)
753) 754) Bouteilles pour les liqueurs en vente dans les magasins *Prisunic*. (FRA)

749

750

753

754

755) Pack for sugar cubes made by the British Sugar Corp. (GB)
756) Folding box for chocolates, with a fable from Aesop. (FRA)
757) Package and instilling container for a veterinary product against mastitis in cattle. (CAN)
758) Folding box for a wine merchant. (FRA)
759) Cylindrical cartons for miscellaneous contents. (JAP)
760) Folding chair of corrugated board printed in two colours. Made by Dymo Products Co. (USA)
761) Gift pack of ginger spice in linen bag, with recipe leaflet, for M. Harland & Son Ltd., Hull. (GB)
762) Container for a mini-toothbrush. Red on white. (SWI)

755) Verpackung für Zuckerwürfel. (GB)
756) Faltschachtel für Pralinen, mit Fabel von Aesop. (FRA)
757) Verpackung und Spritzdose für ein veterinärmedizinisches Produkt gegen Euterentzündung beim Vieh. (CAN)
758) Faltschachtel für einen Weinhändler. (FRA)
759) Zylindrische Kartons für verschiedene Produkte. (JAP)
760) Faltstuhl aus Wellpappe, in zwei Farben gedruckt. (USA)
761) Geschenkverpackung für Ingwer mit Rezepten. (GB)
762) Packung für eine Mini-Zahnbürste der Bürstenfabrik Ebnat-Kappel AG. (SWI)

755) Emballage pour du sucre en morceaux. (GB)
756) Boîte pliante pour des chocolats *Prisunic,* portant une fable d'Esope. (FRA)
757) Emballage et vaporisateur pour une préparation vétérinaire contre la mastite. (CAN)
758) Boîte pliante pour un marchand de vin. (FRA)
759) Cartons cylindriques pour des produits divers. (JAP)
760) Chaise pliante en carton de deux couleurs. (USA)
761) Emballage cadeau avec recette, pour du gingembre. (GB)
762) Emballage pour une brosse à dents miniature. (SWI)

755

759

756

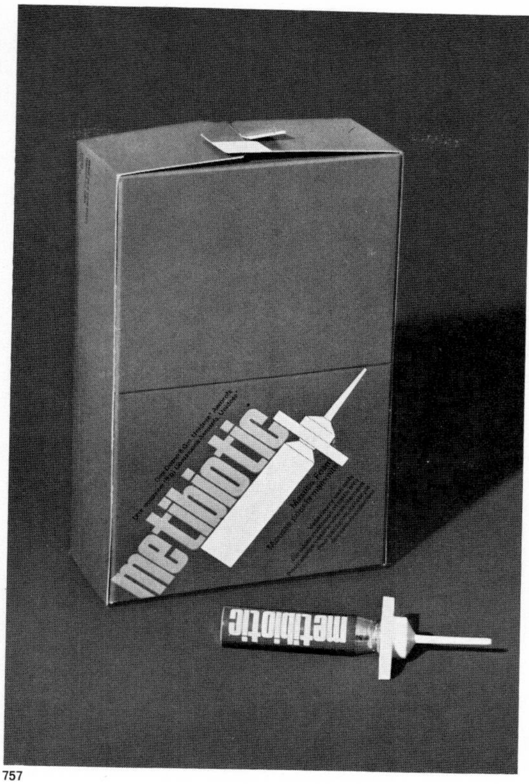

757

758

760

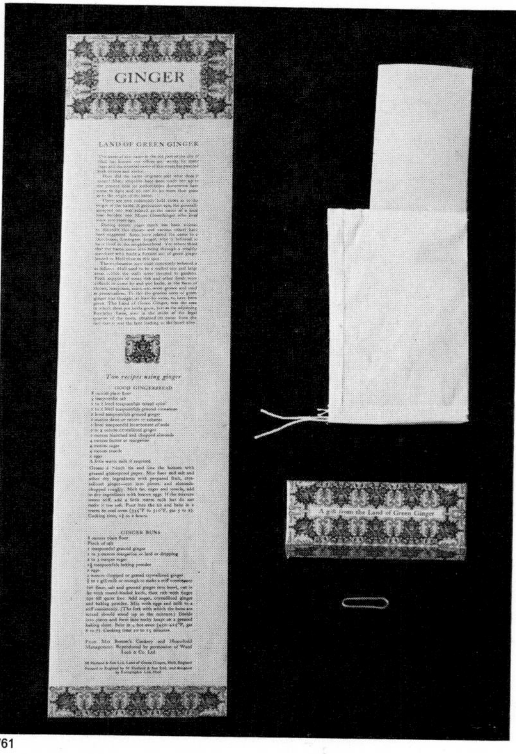

761

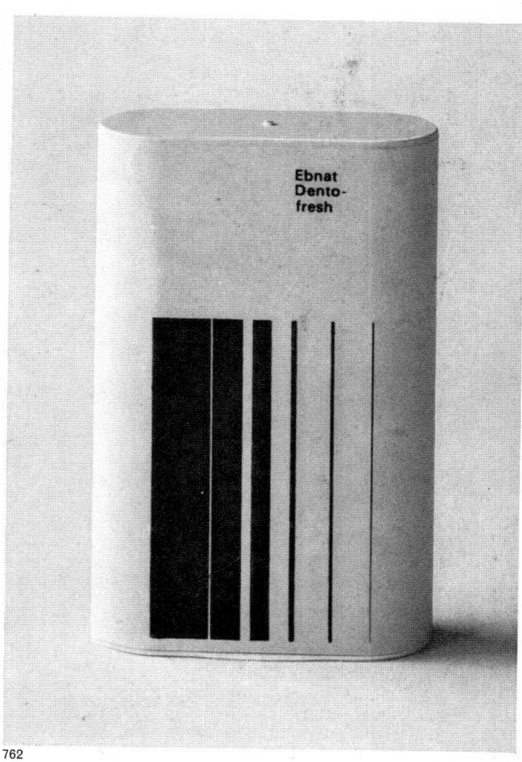

762

Artist/Künstler/Artiste:

755) HANS SCHLEGER & ASSOC.
756) GEORGES LEMOINE
757) STUART ASH
758) STUDIO DRAEGER
759) FUJIKO SUZUKI/MARI MAENO
760) MARGET LARSEN/MICHAEL THONET
761) EUROGRAPHIC LTD.
762) CHRISTIAN LANG

Art Director/Directeur artistique:

755) HANS SCHLEGER
758) RENÉ TONTANI
759) KATSU KIMURA
760) ROBERT FREEMAN

Agency/Agentur/Agence – Studio:

756) PRISUNIC, BUREAU D'ETUDES, PARIS
759) PACKAGING DIRECTION CO. LTD., TOKYO
760) INTRINSICS, INC., SAN FRANCISCO
762) J. P. WÄLCHLI, ZÜRICH

763

764

767

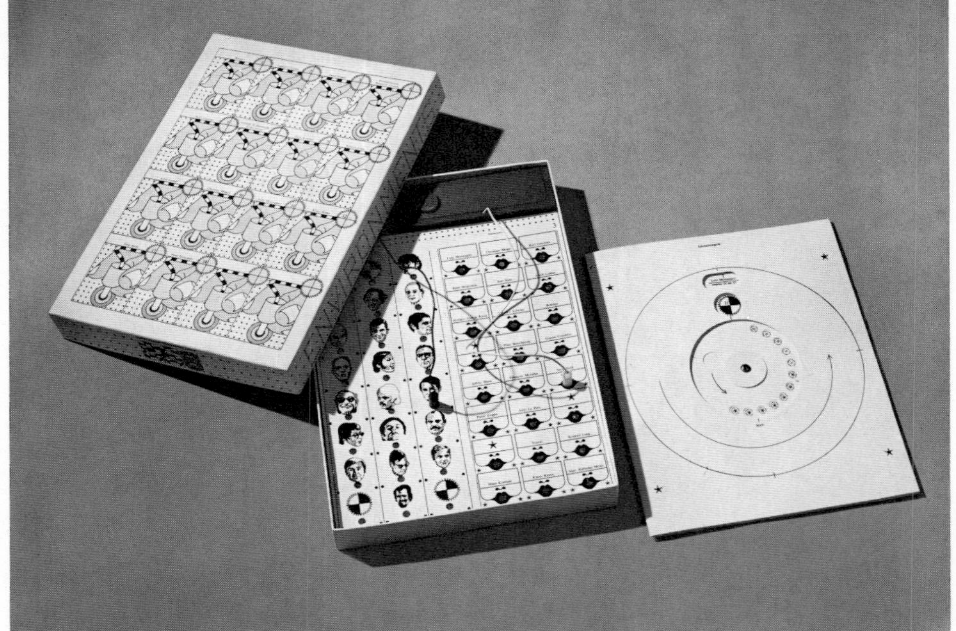

768

Artist/Künstler/Artiste:

763) HELFRIED HAGENBERG
764) 765) STEPHEN DUNNE
766) DONALD & ANNE CREWS
768) SWIP STOLK
769) PETER MEGERT
770) CLAUS KNÉZY
771) ELI GROSS/NIEK HIEMSTRA
772) FELIX MUCKENHIRN

Art Director/Directeur artistique:

763) HELFRIED HAGENBERG
764) 765) STEPHEN DUNNE
766) DONALD & ANNE CREWS
767) HANS-PETER KAMM
768) SWIP STOLK
769) PETER MEGERT
770) CLAUS KNÉZY
771) NIEK HIEMSTRA
772) FELIX MUCKENHIRN

Agency/Agentur/Agence – Studio:

764) 765) UNIMARK INTERNATIONAL, CHICAGO
766) DONALD & ANNE CREWS, NEW YORK
767) PETER V. HEFTI, BERN
770) GLOBUS, WERBEABTEILUNG, ZÜRICH
771) ONTWERPSTUDIO HBM, AMSTERDAM

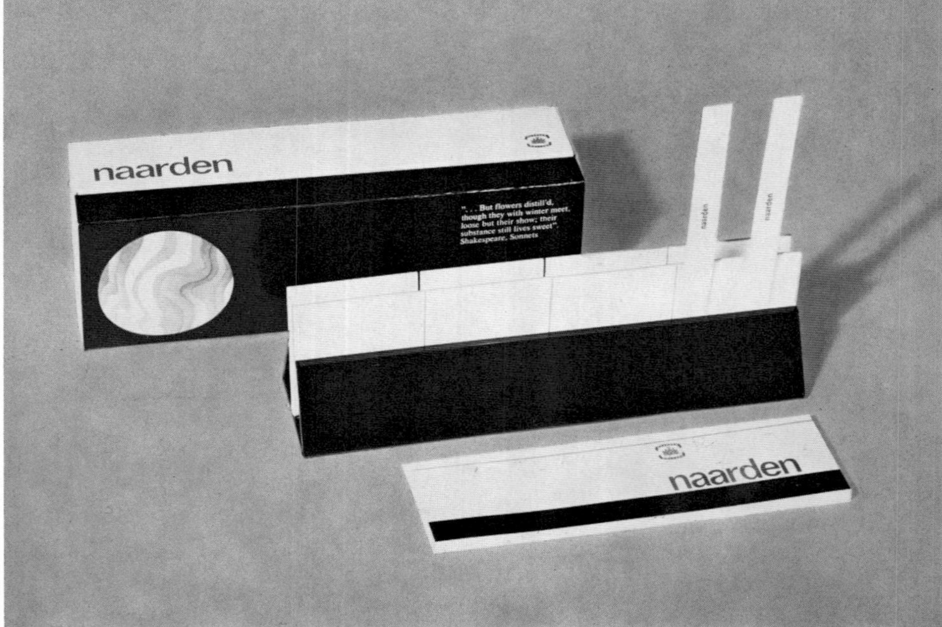

771

765

766

Packaging / Packungen / Emballages

763) Folding box for a clock. Red and black type. (GER)
764) 765) Christmas and general-purpose shopping bags for *Halle's* department stores, Cleveland. (USA)
766) Carrier bag for the 17th Citizens' Committee, handed to voters in a political campaign. (USA)
767) Sealed bag and folding box for flavoured puffed wheat and chocolate-coated corn flakes. (SWI)
768) Set-up box, illuminated game and catalogue of a 'cultural demonstration' of environmental art issued by the State University of Utrecht. (NLD)
769) Carrier bag for an interior decorator. (SWI)
770) Plastic carrier bag for shoes from the *Globus* department store. (SWI)
771) Pack and holder for paper strips used to present perfumes, for the *Naarden* chemical factory. (NLD)
772) Pack for a *Geigy* antidepressant used, for instance, in states of bereavement and loss. (USA)

763) Faltschachtel für eine Uhr. Schrift rot/schwarz. (GER)
764) 765) Einkaufstasche für die Warenhäuser *Halle* in Cleveland. (USA)
766) Tragtasche, die den Wählern in einer politischen Kampagne ausgehändigt wird. (USA)
767) Verpackungen für gepuffte Weizenkörner und Cornflakes-Pralinen von Kentaur AG, Lützelflüh. (SWI)
768) Deckelschachtel mit Spiel und Katalog einer Kultur-Demonstration für Umgebungs-Kunst, herausgegeben von der Staatsuniversität Utrecht. (NLD)
769) Tragtasche für Walter Kilchenmann, Innenarchitekt, Bern. (SWI)
770) Tragtasche aus Plastik für Schuhe von *Globus*. (SWI)
771) Verpackung und Halter für Papierstreifen, die zur Präsentation von Parfums verwendet werden. (NLD)
772) Verpackungen für ein *Geigy*-Medikament gegen Depressionen. (USA)

763) Boite pliante pour une horloge. Texte rouge/noir. (GER)
764) 765) Cabas, dont un de Noël, des grands magasins *Halle* à Cleveland. (USA)
766) Cabas distribué par un comité politique au cours d'une campagne électorale. (USA)
767) Emballages pour des grains de blé soufflés et des corn-flakes enrobés de chocolat. (SWI)
768) Emballage contenant un jeu et un catalogue, pour une «démonstration culturelle» organisée par l'Université d'Utrecht. (NLD)
769) Cabas publicitaire pour un ensemblier. (SWI)
770) Cabas en plastique pour les chaussures des grands magasins *Globus*. (SWI)
771) Emballage et supports pour des banderoles de papier servant à présenter des parfums. (NLD)
772) Emballages pour un tranquillisant *Geigy* utilisé dans le traitement des états dépressifs. (USA)

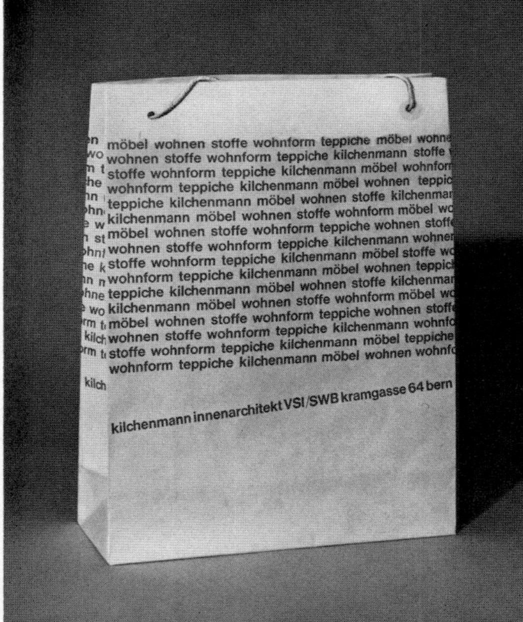

769

770

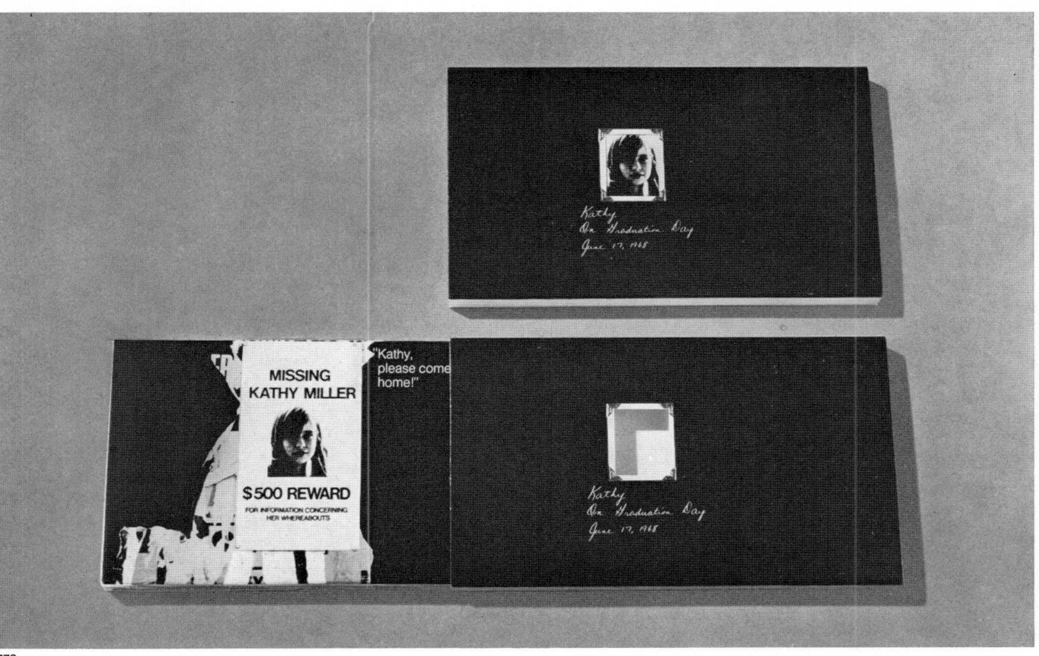

772

773

774

773) Transparent packs for hair brushes. Colours: gold, silver and lilac. (SWI)
774) Pack for a *Minidust* face mask for Industrial Safety Services Pty. Ltd. (AUL)
775) Can for an *Agway* fruit spray liquid from a range of garden products. (USA)
776) Wrapping paper for *Sumiredo* confectionery. (JAP)
777) 780) Boxes with baseball and binoculars for *Mainstay*, a pipe compound. (USA)
778) Cans for an adhesive and a solvent. (GER)
779) Set-up box for a sample of a *Geigy* pharmaceutical against back pain. (USA)
781) Paper bags for a boutique in Tokyo. (JAP)
782) Set-up box for men's shoes. Black on leather-coloured board. (SWI)

773) Sichtpackungen für Kopfbürsten der Bürstenfabrik Ebnat-Kappel AG. (SWI)
774) Verpackung für eine Gesichtsmaske. (AUL)
775) Dose für ein Spritzmittel für Früchte. (USA)
776) Einwickelpapier für *Sumiredo* Konfekt. (JAP)
777) 780) Geschenkschachteln mit Spielball und Feldstecher für Rohrleitungsmaterial. (USA)
778) Dosen für *Atlas Ago* Klebstoff und Lösungsmittel. (GER)
779) Deckelschachtel für ein *Geigy*-Medikament gegen Rückenschmerzen. (USA)
781) Papiertaschen für eine Boutique in Tokyo. (JAP)
782) Schachtel für *Fretz*-Herrenschuhe. Schwarz auf lederfarbenem Grund. (SWI)

773) Emballages transparents pour des brosses à cheveux. (SWI)
774) Emballage pour un masque facial. (AUL)
775) Boite métallique pour un produit à vaporiser sur les arbres fruitiers. (USA)
776) Papier d'emballage d'une confiserie. (JAP)
777) 780) Emballages-cadeaux en faveur d'un matériau pour des conduites. (USA)
778) Boîtes métalliques pour une colle et un dissolvant. (GER)
779) Emballage pour un médicament *Geigy* contre les douleurs dans le dos. (USA)
781) Sacs en papier d'une boutique de Tokyo. (JAP)
782) Boîte pour des chaussures d'hommes. Noir sur fond de couleur cuir. (SWI)

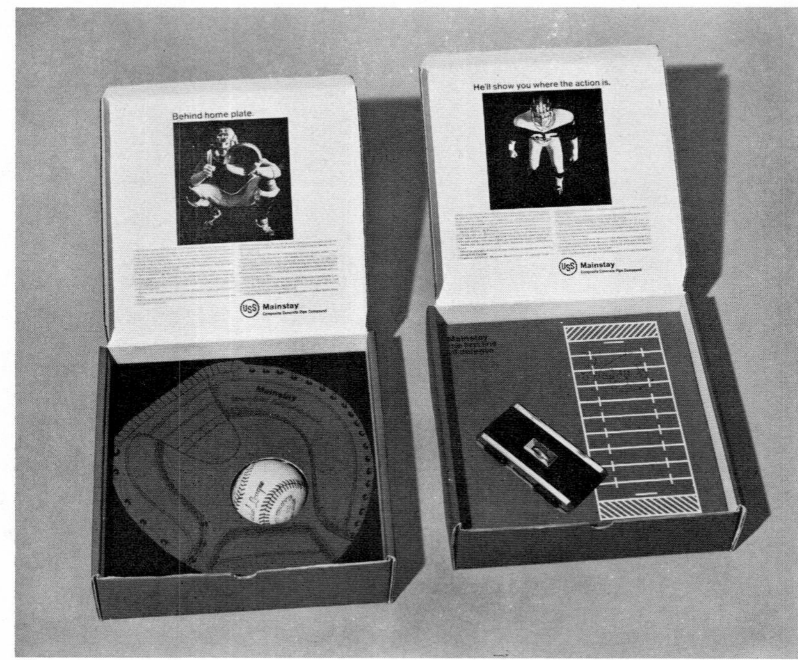

777

Artist / Künstler / Artiste:

773) PAUL GMÜR
774) WHAITE & EMERY
775) JUDITH FALLON
776) KUNI KIZAWA
777) 780) SEBA MICHAELS / GEORGE GAADT / LEN MOSER / MARINI, CLIMES + GUIP, INC.
778) GRAPHICTEAM
779) JOHN DE CESARE
781) KOICHI INAKOSHI
782) KURT BÜCHEL

Art Director / Directeur artistique:

773) PAUL GMÜR
774) WHAITE & EMERY
775) WAYNE BOOTH
778) COORDT VON MANNSTEIN
779) JOHN DE CESARE
781) KAN SANO
782) KURT BÜCHEL

Agency / Agentur / Agence – Studio:

773) J.P. WÄLCHLI, ZÜRICH
775) FALLON, WATSON & GIURLANDO, INC., ROCHESTER, N.Y.
782) SINGER + BÜCHEL, TEUFEN

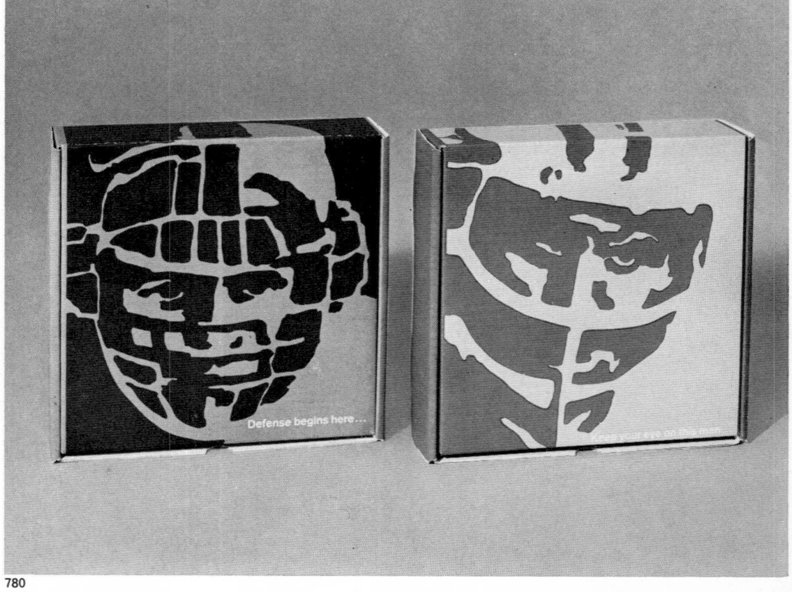

780

775

776

778

779

781

782

783

785

784

788

Artist / Künstler / Artiste:

783) 784) WHAITE & EMERY
785) NOBORU YOSHIMOTO
786) TAKASHI KANOME
787) ALBERT SIRINGO / HARRY LAPOW
788) STUDIO DRAEGER
789) NED HARRIS
790) O. JAEGGI / VOLG PROPAGANDA-ABT. / VOGEL AG

Art Director / Directeur artistique:

783) 784) WHAITE & EMERY
785) NOBORU YOSHIMOTO
786) TAKASHI KANOME
787) ALBERT SIRINGO
788) RENÉ TONTANI
789) NED HARRIS

Agency / Agentur / Agence – Studio:

787) LEHN & FINK PRODUCTS CO., MONTVALE, N.J.
789) WALLACK & HARRIS, INC., NEW YORK

783) 784) Boxes for a welding shield and goggles made by Australian Liquid Air Ltd. (AUL)
785) Dispensers for refreshing pills made by Morishita Jintan Co. Ltd. (JAP)
786) Pack for sheets made by Marushinkeori Co. Ltd. The characters mean 'comfort'. (JAP)
787) Cartons for soap in attractive shapes for little boys. (USA)
788) Box for a *Philips* cassette recorder as a promotional gift. (FRA)
789) Bottle for a *Coty* perfume. (USA)
790) Plastic bottles for a range of shampoos and bath oils. (SWI)

783) 784) Schachteln für Blendschirm und Brillen für Schweisser. (AUL)
785) Verteilerschachteln für Erfrischungstabletten der Morishita Jintan Co. Ltd. (JAP)
786) Verpackung für Leintücher. Die Schriftzeichen bedeuten «Behaglichkeit». (JAP)
787) Kartons für Seifen in attraktiven Formen für Jungen. (USA)
788) Schachtel für ein *Philips* Aufnahmegerät als Werbegeschenk. (FRA)
789) Flasche für ein *Coty* Parfum. (USA)
790) Plastikflaschen für Haarwaschmittel und Badeöle von Volg, Winterthur. (SWI)

783) 784) Boites pour des écrans protecteurs et des lunettes de soudeurs. (AUL)
785) Distributeurs de pastilles rafraîchissantes. (JAP)
786) Emballage pour des draps de lit. Les signes écrits signifient «confort». (JAP)
787) Cartons pour des savonettes de formes amusantes, destinées aux garçonnets. (USA)
788) Emballage pour un enregistreur *Philips* offert à titre publicitaire. (FRA)
789) Flacon pour un parfum *Coty*. (USA)
790) Flacons de plastique pour les shampooings et les huiles de bain d'une société coopérative. (SWI)

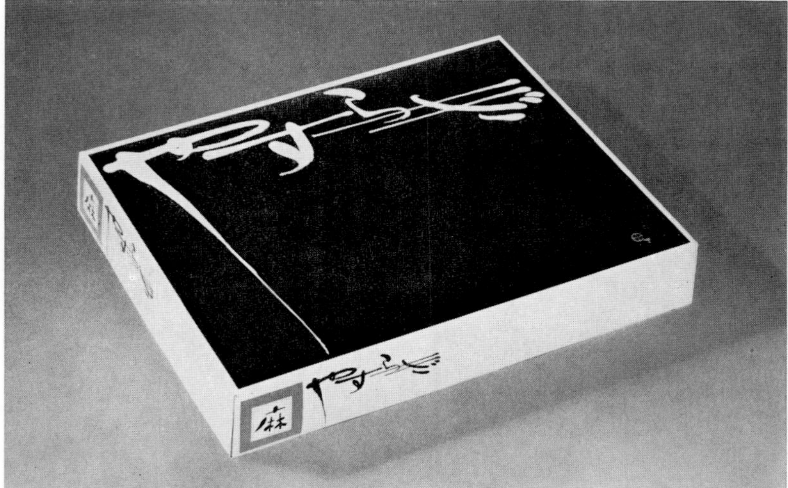

786

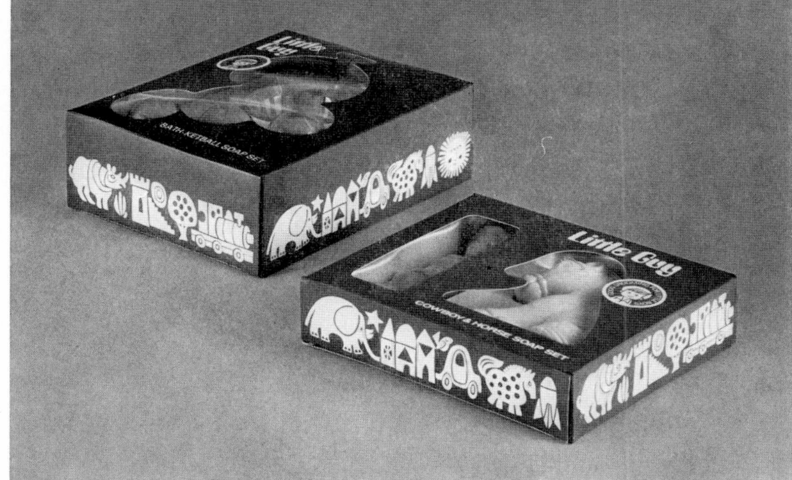

787

789

790

Calendars

Christmas Cards

TV and Film Advertising

Kalender

Glückwunschkarten

Fernseh- und Filmwerbung

Calendriers

Cartes de vœux

TV et films publicitaires

791

792

791) 792) Illustration and sheet from a calendar for a transport firm. (SPA)
793) Do-it-yourself calendar ('the Prang') for Crafton Graphic Co. (USA)
794) Wall calendar for the Morgan Press with polychrome pictures. (USA)
795) Sheet of a calendar for a film company about local festivals. (SPA)
796) Wall calendar for a Bernese printer. (SWI)

791) 792) Illustration und Blatt eines Kalenders für eine Transportfirma. (SPA)
793) Kalender zum Zusammenstecken von einer Offset-Druckerei. (USA)
794) Wandkalender mit mehrfarbigen Illustrationen von einer Druckerei. (USA)
795) Blatt eines Kalenders über Volksfeste für eine Filmgesellschaft. (SPA)
796) Wandkalender für Benteli AG, Druckerei und Verlag, Bern. (SWI)

791) 792) Du calendrier de l'imprimerie Julio Soto, Madrid. (SPA)
793) Calendrier à assembler d'une imprimerie offset. (USA)
794) Calendrier mural d'une imprimerie. Illustrations en couleur. (USA)
795) Feuille du calendrier de la société Rasa Film, Barcelone. (SPA)
796) Calendrier mural d'un imprimeur de Berne. (SWI)

793

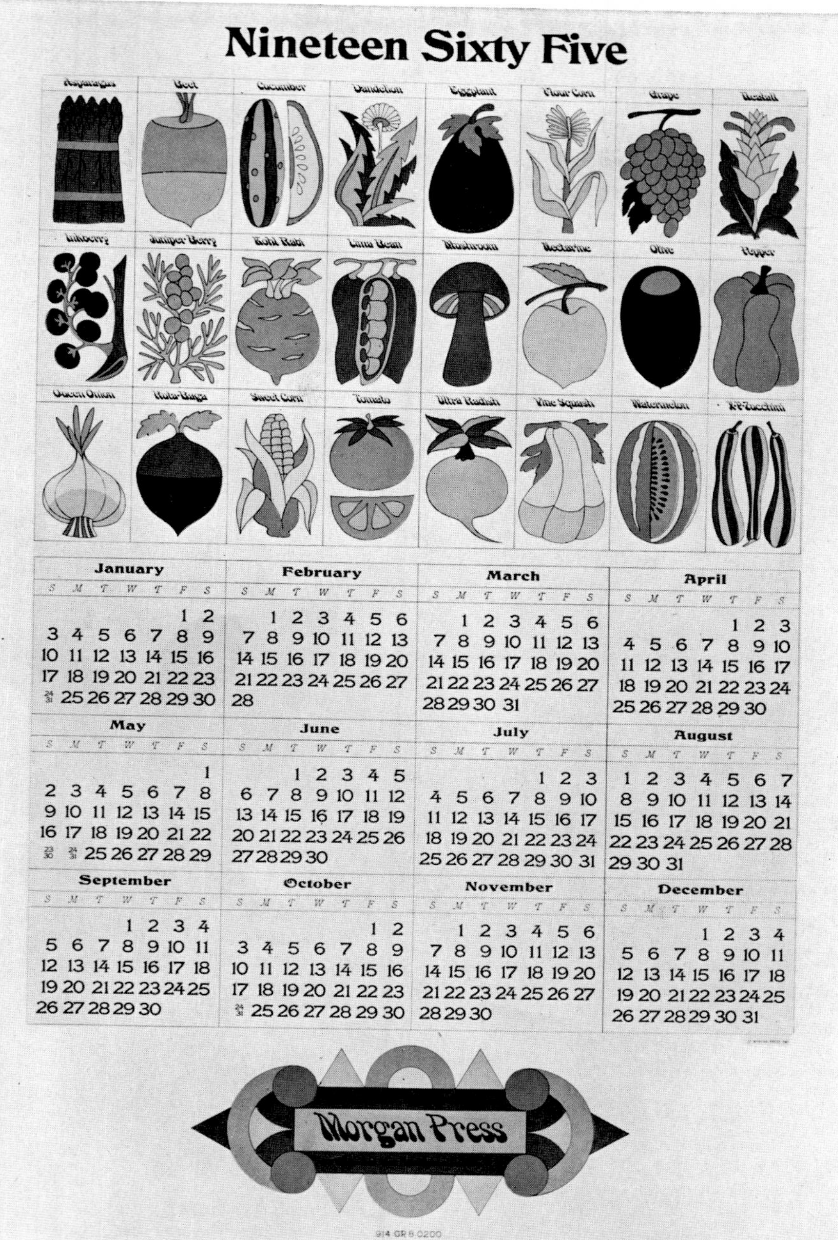

794

795

796

Artist / Künstler / Artiste:

791) 792) JUAN POZA
793) BRUCE BLACKBURN
794) JOHN ALCORN
795) PLA NARBONA
796) TED SCAPA

Art Director / Directeur artistique:

791) 792) JUAN POZA
793) BRUCE BLACKBURN
795) PLA NARBONA

Agency / Agentur / Agence – Studio:

793) CHERMAYEFF & GEISMAR ASSOC., NEW YORK

RAFFREDDAMENTO DEL CUGINO

Raffreddare il cugino richiede innanzitutto una attenta preparazione, specialmente in salita. A La Spezia tutti ricordano il lusso sfarzoso di costumi, fondali e fondaletti messi in opera dal Bergonzi per l'esperimento della Divisione Ligure. È sempre più richiesto. Lo si prenota talvolta a distanza di mesi. E non si dimentichi, prima di tappezzarlo, di prepararlo come per un lungo viaggio. Ma non si creda che tutto riesca facile! Per questo esperimento è necessario avere costanza negli affetti, non bere con sconosciuti e applicare sempre sulla parte alta i segnali d'uso. I parenti devono essere tenuti all'oscuro.

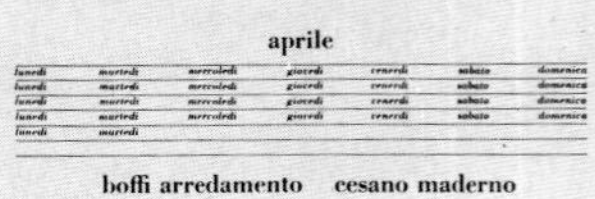

801

797-800

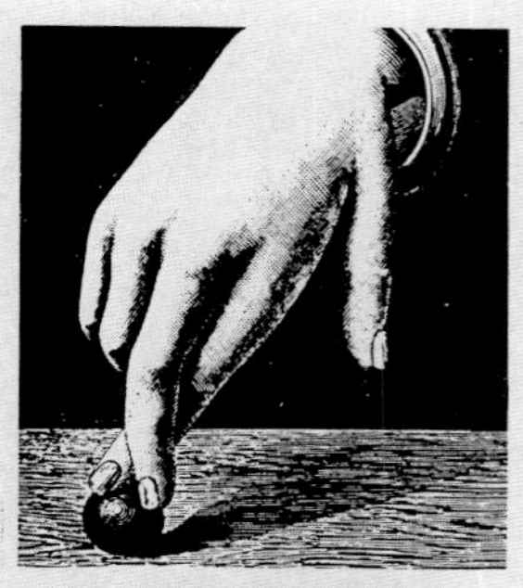

IL MOVIMENTO INCONSULTO

Credo che in Italia non vi sia un'altra città che, come Pinerolo, abbia sentito tanta passione per questo esperimento. Dice il proverbio: «Tu zuu Bertu che nu me n'accorzu». Vi è in ciò qualcosa di eroico. Il movimento va fatto lentamente, ornato in modo da dare l'idea di capitelli, colonne, statue, portichetti, pozzi antichi. La calma e il buonumore abbelliscono il movimento inconsulto, schiariscono l'epidermide, mentre l'astio e la collera fanno più male che bene. A un segnale convenuto, con la mano libera, si imprima la rotazione voluta fino ad abbandonarlo al suo destino. Il grande Marazzi ritornava spesso sul posto dell'esperimento con la Signorina Ginevra Travaglia.

agosto

boffi arredamento cesano maderno

802

Artist / Künstler / Artiste:

797)–800) MARCEL PIJPERS
801) 802) GIULIO CONFALONIERI
803) 804) PAUL FLORA
805) 807) BRUCE BUTTE / ANNE BUTTE / CHUCK WERTMAN
806) OLDRICH HLAVSA / STANISLAV MARSO
808) GEORGES MATHIEU

797)–800) Sheets from a calendar for a paint manufacturer. Each design is in two shades of the same colour and is based on the trade mark. (NLD)
801) 802) Sheet from a calendar for a furnishing company, with conjuring tricks. (ITA)
803) 804) Sheets from a calendar about advertising for a magazine. (GER)
805) 807) Sheet and one of the polychrome illustrations from a calendar of nursery rhymes for Shell Chemical Co. (USA)
806) Sheet from a calendar for a type foundry. Blue and red. (CSR)
808) Wall calendar for a printer. Full colour. (BEL)

797)–800) Blätter aus einem Kalender für einen Farbenhersteller. Jede Illustration ist in zwei Tönen der gleichen Farbe und ist von der Schutzmarke abgeleitet. (NLD)
801) 802) Blätter aus einem Kalender für eine Möbelfabrik, mit Zauberkünsten. (ITA)
803) 804) Blatt aus einem Kalender über Werbung für den Verlag DAS BESTE. (GER)
805) 807) Blatt und eine der mehrfarbigen Illustrationen aus einem Kalender mit Kinderreimen für Shell Chemical Co. (USA)
806) Blatt aus einem Kalender für eine Schriftgiesserei. Blau und rot. (CSR)
808) Wandkalender für eine Druckerei. Mehrfarbig. (BEL)

797)–800) Feuilles du calendrier d'un fabricant de couleurs. Chaque illustration, imprimée en deux tons de la même teinte, est inspirée par l'emblème de la firme. (NLD)
801) 802) Feuilles du calendrier de la fabrique de meubles Boffi Arredamendo, Cesano Maderno, Milan. (ITA)
803) 804) Feuilles d'un calendrier au sujet de la publicité pour une revue. (GER)
805) 807) Feuille et une des illustrations polychromes, tirées d'un calendrier *Shell* contenant des rimes enfantines. (USA)
806) Page du calendrier d'une fonderie de caractères. Bleu et rouge. (CSR)
808) Calendrier mural de l'imprimerie Georges Thone, Liége. Polychrome, (BEL)

805

806

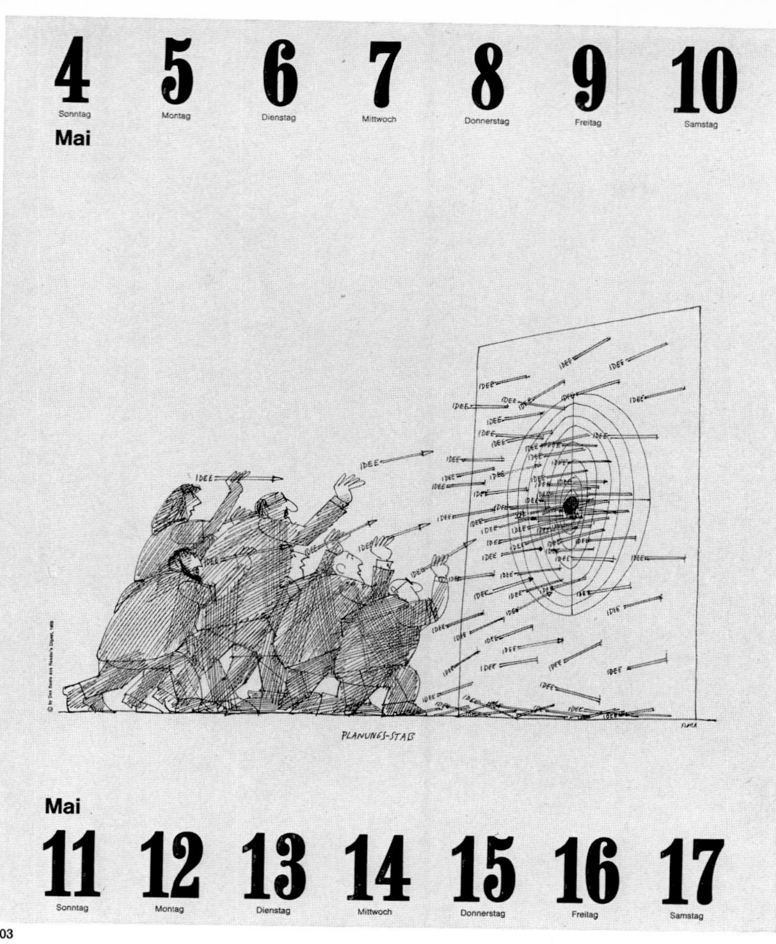

803

804

Art Director / Directeur artistique:

801) 802) GIULIO CONFALONIERI
805) 807) DAVID DAVIES

807

808

Calendars / Kalender
Calendriers

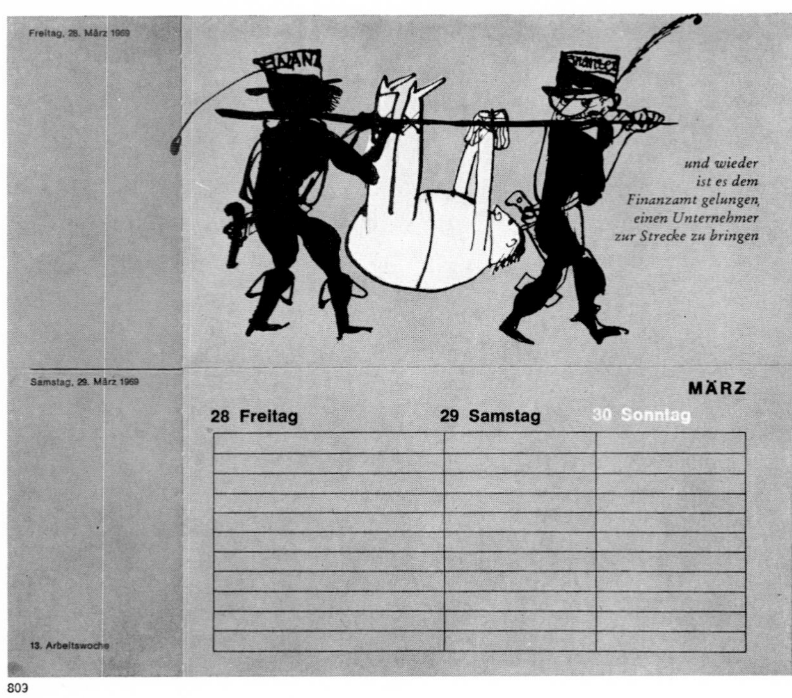

809

Mittwoch, 2. April 1969

Gehen Sie in der Nacht vom 30. April zum 1. Mai nicht auf die Straße. Wir haben Walpurgisnacht!

(Manche Hexen sind jünger und damit noch gefährlicher!)

Donnerstag, 3. April 1969

APRIL

2 Mittwoch — 3 Donnerstag

14. Arbeitswoche

810

Artist | Künstler | Artiste:

809) 810) MICHAEL SCHRIFT
811) ENRIC SATUÉ
812) ENZO MARI
813)–816) JEAN MICHEL FOLON / ENZO MARI

Art Director | Directeur artistique:

812)–816) GIORGIO SOAVI

811

812

9 DOMENICA — 10 LUNEDI — 11 MARTEDI — 12 MERCOLEDI — 13 GIOVEDI — 14 VENERDI — 15 SABATO

809) 810) From a manager's desk calendar with tear-off leaves and a joke on each page. Black and one colour. (GER)
811) Sheet from a calendar entitled 'Ode to Barcelona' for a process engraver. (SPA)
812)–816) Double spread with agenda and four full-page illustrations from a large *Olivetti* desk diary. The drawings are a cartoonist's vision of the technocratic age. (ITA)

809) 810) Aus einer Agenda mit abtrennbaren Witzkärtchen. Schwarz und eine Farbe. (GER)
811) Blatt aus einem Kalender mit dem Titel «Ode an Barcelona» für eine lithographische Anstalt. (SPA)
812)–816) Doppelseite und vier ganzseitige Illustrationen zu dem Zeitalter der Technokraten, aus einer Schreibtischagenda von *Olivetti*. (ITA)

809) 810) D'un agenda de bureau composé de cartes volantes portant chacune une histoire humoristique. Noir et une couleur. (GER)
811) Page d'un calendrier intitulé «Ode à Barcelone», pour l'atelier de photogravure Photochromes Roldan, Barcelone. (SPA)
812)–816) Double page et quatre illustrations d'un agenda de bureau *Olivetti*. (ITA)

813

814

815

816

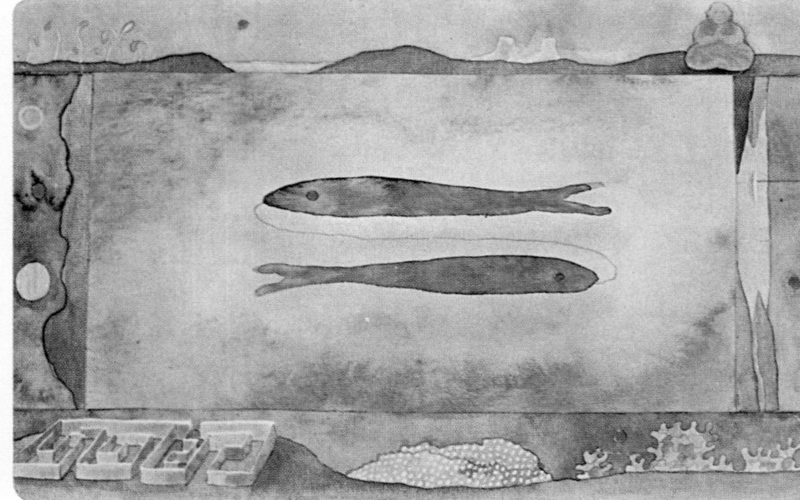

817–820

823

Peter + Sylvia Sollberger-Suri Schlösslistrasse 23 Bern

Ein rosiges neues Jahr wünschen

Artist / Künstler / Artiste:

817) JEAN MICHEL FOLON
818) SOPHIE GRANDVAL
819) MAURICE GARNIER
820) COLETTE PORTAL
821) BAER CORNET
822) JUST REINHOLD
823) PETER + SYLVIA SOLLBERGER
824) FRANCO GRIGNANI
825) VLADIMIR SUCHÁNEK
826) HORST A. RISCHKA / HARTMUT MEISER

Art Director / Directeur artistique:

817)–820) ANTOINE KIEFFER
822) GERHARD MARX
824) FRANCO GRIGNANI
826) HORST A. RISCHKA

Agency / Agentur / Agence – Studio:

817)–820) ÉDITIONS MAFIA, PARIS
824) STUDIO GRIGNANI, MILAN
826) CTR / CREATIVE TEAM RISCHKA, STUTTGART

Christmas Cards / Glückwunschkarten
Cartes de vœux

821

822

817)–820) From a set of cards issued as a gift by a publisher and showing interpretations of the Signs of the Zodiac by twelve different artists: here Aries, Scorpio, Capricorn and Pisces. (FRA)

821) Greetings card from a carpet factory, Koninklijke Tapijtfabrieken Bexgoss N.V. Two reds. (NLD)

822) New Year's greeting from a galvanizing firm. The bell is copper-plated. (GER)

823) Greetings card from an artist wishing recipients a 'rosy New Year'. (SWI)

824) Greetings card from a printer. Black and white, coloured stripes on transparent overlay. (ITA)

825) New Year's card from an artist. Orange, mauve and grey. (CSR)

826) New Year's card with symbols to suit the words of the greeting. Black and white on silver. (GER)

817)–820) Aus einer Serie von Geschenkkarten eines Verlegers, mit Darstellungen der Sternzeichen (hier Widder, Skorpion, Steinbock und Fisch) ausgeführt von verschiedenen Künstlern. (FRA)

821) Glückwunschkarte einer Teppichfabrik. Zwei Rottöne. (NLD)

822) Neujahrsgruss der Firma Schering Galvanotechnik. Das Glöcklein ist glanzverkupfert. (GER)

823) Glückwunschkarte eines Graphikers. (SWI)

824) Glückwunschkarte einer Druckerei. Schwarzweiss, durchsichtiges Deckblatt mit farbigen Streifen. (ITA)

825) Neujahrskarte eines Künstlers. (CSR)

826) Neujahrskarte der Alex Lindner GmbH, Nürtingen. Schwarzweiss auf silbernem Grund. (GER)

817)–820) D'une collection de cartes distribuées par les Editions Mafia, Paris, et portant des interprétations des signes du Zodiaque par douze artistes différents: ici, Bélier, Scorpion, Capricorne et Poisson. (FRA)

821) Carte de vœux d'un fabricant de tapis. (NLD)

822) Carte de Nouvel an d'un atelier de galvanoplastie. (GER)

823) Carte de vœux d'un artiste souhaitant à ses correspondants une «année tout en rose». (SWI)

824) Carte de vœux de l'imprimerie Alfieri & Lacroix, Milan. Noir et blanc, rayures polychromes sur couverture transparente. (ITA)

825) Carte de Nouvel an d'un artiste. (CSR)

826) Carte de Nouvel an. Noir et blanc sur fond argent. (GER)

824

825

826

827

828

830

831

827) Greetings card from the Amsterdam branch of the J. Walter Thompson agency. (NLD)
828) Card from a graphic design studio. Dark blue ground. (USA)
829) Christmas card from a woodcut artist. Gold and green. (GER)
830) Artist's card wishing the recipient skill and luck in 1969. (SWI)
831) Double spread from a Christmas gift book (about printing errors) issued by a typographer. Red illustrations, green type. (USA)
832) New Year's card from a graphic design studio. (ITA)
833) Views of a three-part greetings card for a design studio. (JAP)
834) New Year's card for a film export authority. Green and beige shades. (CSR)

827) Glückwunschkarte der Agentur J. Walter Thompson, Filiale Amsterdam. (NLD)
828) Karte eines graphischen Ateliers. Dunkelblauer Grund. (USA)
829) Glückwunschkarte eines Holzschnittkünstlers. Gold und grün. (GER)
830) Glückwunschkarte eines Künstlers. (SWI)
831) Doppelseite aus dem Geschenkbüchlein einer Druckerei. Rote Illustrationen, grüne Schrift. (USA)
832) Neujahrskarte eines graphischen Ateliers. (ITA)
833) Dreiteilige Glückwunschkarte eines graphischen Ateliers. (JAP)
834) Neujahrskarte für die staatliche Filmexport-Gesellschaft. Grün und beige. (CSR)

827) Carte de vœux de la filiale néerlandaise de l'agence J. Walter Thompson. (NLD)
828) Carte de vœux d'un atelier graphique. Fond bleu marine. (USA)
829) Carte de Noël d'un xylograveur. Vert et or. (GER)
830) Carte de vœux de l'artiste. (SWI)
831) Double page d'un album distribué à Noël par un typographe. Illustrations en rouge, texte en vert. (USA)
832) Carte de Nouvel an d'un atelier graphique. (ITA)
833) Vues de la carte de vœux en trois parties d'un atelier graphique. (JAP)
834) Carte de Nouvel an d'une commission officielle pour l'exportation des films. Tons de vert et beige. (CSR)

829

833

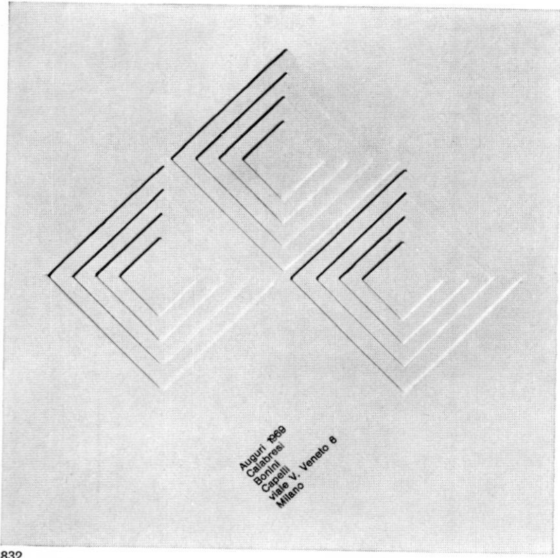

832

834

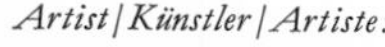

Artist / Künstler / Artiste:

827) DAVID HOUTHUYSE
828) CARL SELTZER
829) HAP GRIESHABER
830) JULIEN VAN DER WAL
831) MILTON GLASER
832) A. CALABRESI / E. BONINI
833) KEISUKE KONISHI
834) VLADIMIR KOUTSKY

Art Director / Directeur artistique:

827) DAVID HOUTHUYSE
828) ADVERTISING DESIGNERS, INC.
831) MILTON GLASER
832) UMBERTO CAPELLI
833) KEISUKE KONISHI

Agency / Agentur / Agence – Studio:

828) ADVERTISING DESIGNERS, INC., LOS ANGELES
834) CESKY FOND VYTVARNÉHO UMÉNI, PRAG

835

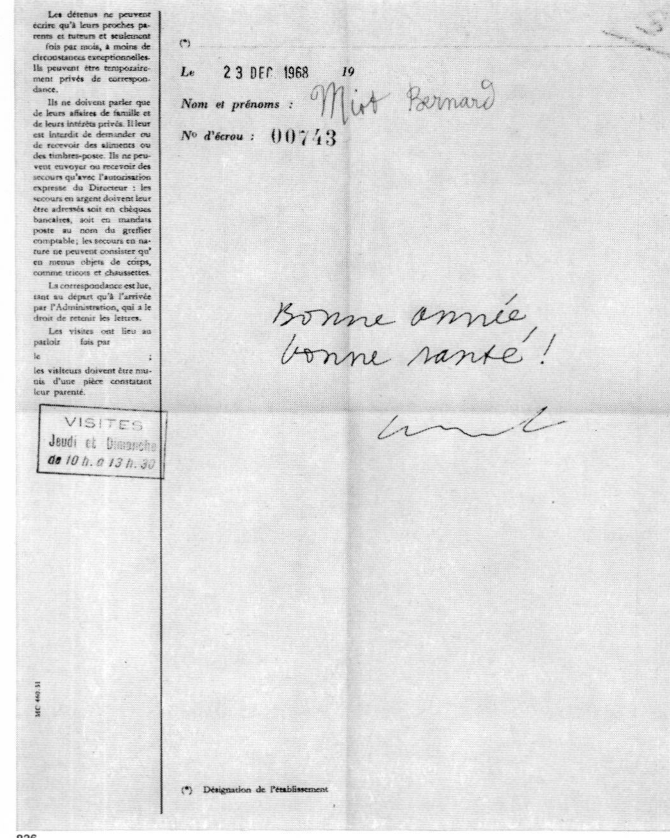
Les détenus ne peuvent écrire qu'à leurs proches parents et tuteurs et seulement fois par mois, à moins de circonstances exceptionnelles. Ils peuvent être temporairement privés de correspondance.

Ils ne doivent parler que de leurs affaires de famille et de leurs intérêts privés. Il leur est interdit de demander ou de recevoir des aliments ou des timbres-poste. Ils ne peuvent envoyer ou recevoir des secours qu'avec l'autorisation expresse du Directeur : les secours en argent doivent leur être adressés soit en chèques bancaires, soit en mandats poste au nom du greffier comptable; les secours en nature ne peuvent consister qu'en menus objets de corps, comme tricots et chaussettes.

La correspondance est lue, tant au départ qu'à l'arrivée par l'Administration, qui a le droit de retenir les lettres.

Les visites ont lieu au parloir fois par le ; les visiteurs doivent être munis d'une pièce constatant leur parenté.

VISITES
Jeudi et Dimanche
de 10 h. à 13 h. 30

(*)

Le 23 DEC 1968 19

Nom et prénoms : Mist Bernard

N° d'écrou : 00743

Bonne année
bonne santé !

(*) Désignation de l'établissement

836

838

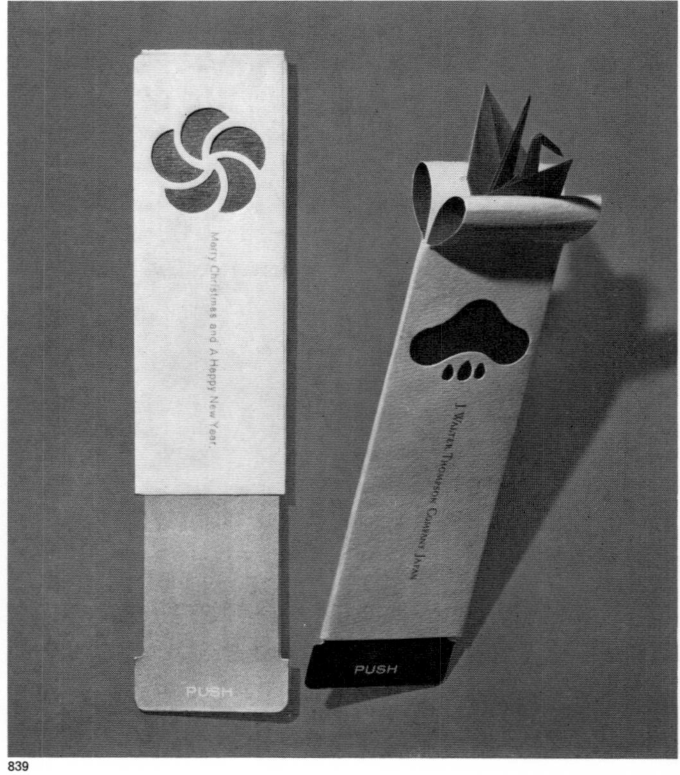

839

841

Vor der Schule standen schon viele Eltern mit ihren Buben und Mädchen. Nie zuvor hatte Karli so viele Leute gesehen, und mit anderen Kindern hatte er selten gespielt. Ganz schüchtern wurde Karli und versteckte sich hinter seinem Vater.

As the trio arrived, many other parents with their boys and girls were already gathered at the school. Never before had Karli seen so many people, and he had seldom played with other children. He became quite shy, and hid behind his father.

Devant l'école se trouvaient déjà de nombreux parents avec leurs enfants, garçons et filles. Jamais auparavant Karli n'avait vu autant de monde, et il avait rarement joué avec d'autres enfants. Karli devint alors tout timide et se cacha derrière le père.

837

840

835) Greetings in the form of a small poster. Blue ground, lettering changing from green to red. (FRA)
836) Artist's card on imitation prison stationery. (FRA)
837) Greetings from a process engraver in the form of a box containing a concertina-type calendar. (GER)
838) Folding card from a silk-screen printer. (MEX)
839) Christmas card from the J. Walter Thompson Co. The 'crane' which appears when the card is pushed upwards symbolizes good fortune. (JAP)
840) Christmas card from a cartoonist. (SWI)
841) Spread from a type foundry's gift booklet, with a story based on the numbers 6 and 9. Blue and red. (GER)

835) Glückwunschkarte in Form eines Plakates. Blauer Grund; die Schrift wechselt von Grün zu Rot. (FRA)
836) Karte eines Künstlers, auf Gefängnis-Briefpapier. (FRA)
837) Glückwunschkarte der Haussmann Reprotechnik Darmstadt, in der Form eines Würfels, der einen Leporello-Kalender enthält. (GER)
838) Osterkarte einer Handdruckerei. (MEX)
839) Weihnachtskarte für J. Walter Thompson Co. Der Kranich symbolisiert das Glück. (JAP)
840) Weihnachtskarte eines Karikaturisten. (SWI)
841) Geschenkbroschüre von D. Stempel AG, Frankfurt/M., mit einer Geschichte über die Nummer 6 und 9. (GER)

835) Carte de vœux sous forme d'affichette. Fond bleu, texte changeant du vert au rouge. (FRA)
836) Carte de l'artiste sur en-tête de prison. (FRA)
837) Carte de vœux d'un atelier de reproduction, sous forme d'un cube contenant un calendrier dépliant. (GER)
838) Carte pliante d'un imprimeur en sérigraphie. (MEX)
839) Carte de Noël de l'agence J. Walter Thompson. La cigogne symbolise le bonheur. (JAP)
840) Carte de Noël d'un dessinateur humoristique. (SWI)
841) Double page d'un album distribué par une fonderie de caractères. Bleu et rouge. (GER)

Artist / Künstler / Artiste:

835) ANDRÉ CHANTE / HOLLENSTEIN-CRÉATION
836) BERNARD MIOT
837) HELMUT LORTZ
838) DAVID KIMPTON
839) YASUYUKI UNO
840) TED SCAPA
841) FOLKHART NEIDIGK

Art Director / Directeur artistique:

838) RICARDO HESKETH

842

843

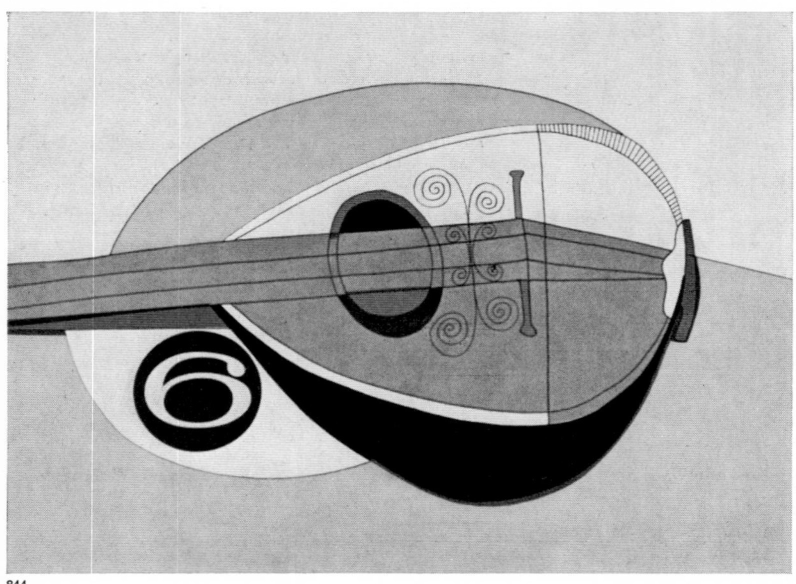

844

845

Artist / Künstler / Artiste:

842) PETER CLARK
843) BRIAN SHIELDS
844) 845) DAVE STRANG
846)–853) ROSEMARY HELD
854)–859) JOHN STAMP
860)–865) ALASTAIR MC MURDO

Art Director / Directeur artistique:

842) DONALD STEVENS
843) PETER GILL
844) 845) DAVE STRANG
846)–853) ROSEMARY HELD
854)–859) JOHN STAMP
860)–865) ALASTEIR MCMURDO

Film / Television / Fernsehen

846–853 →

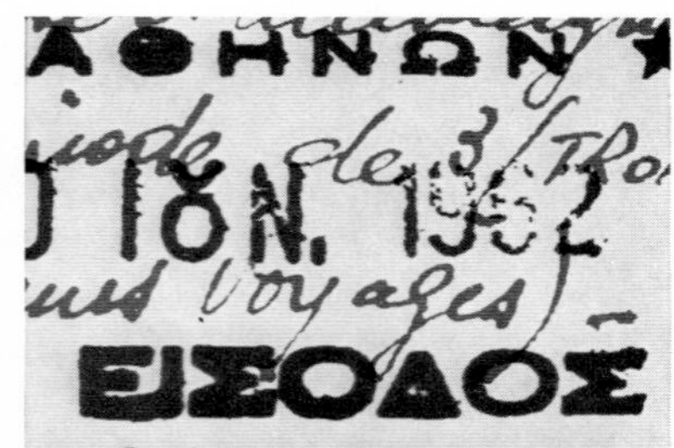

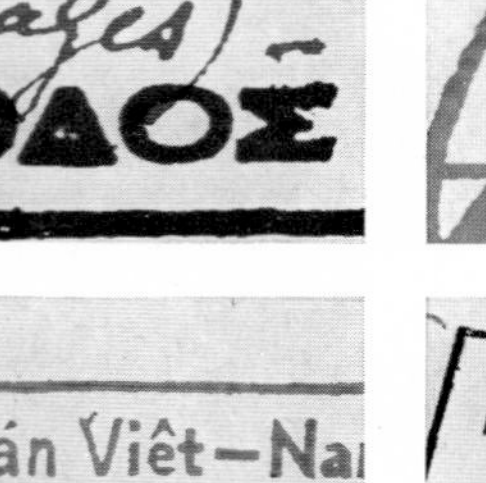

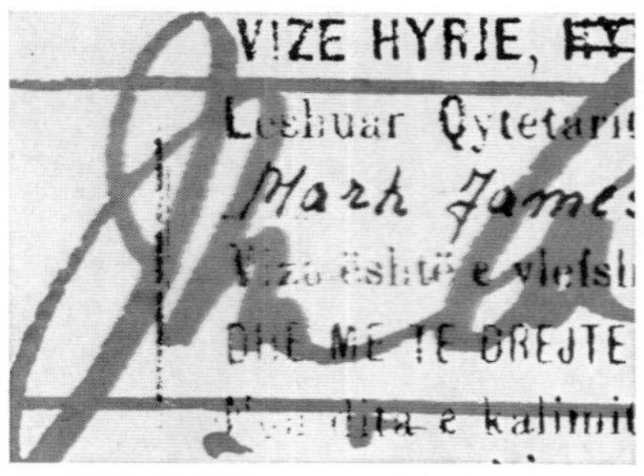

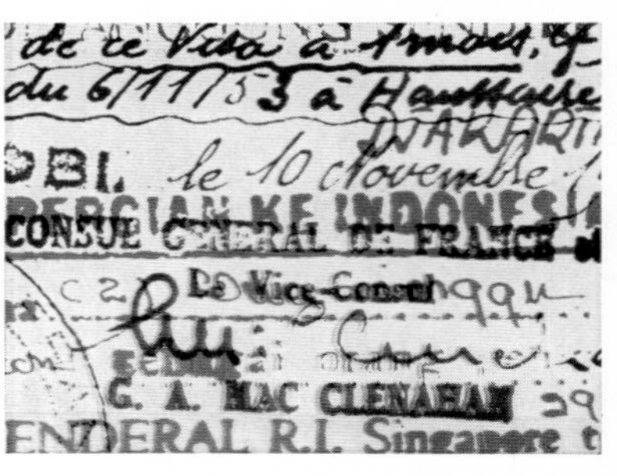

854-859 →

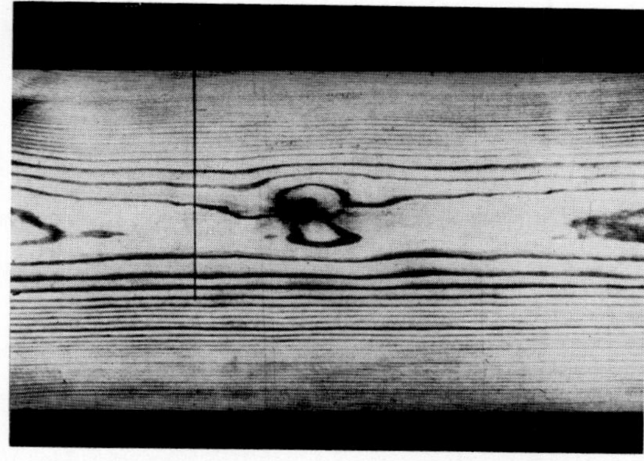

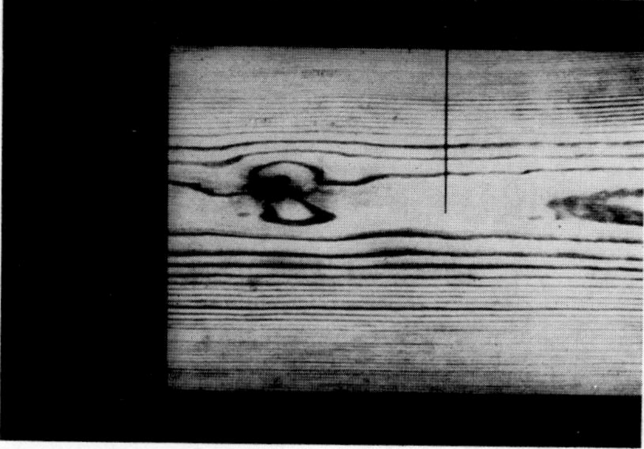

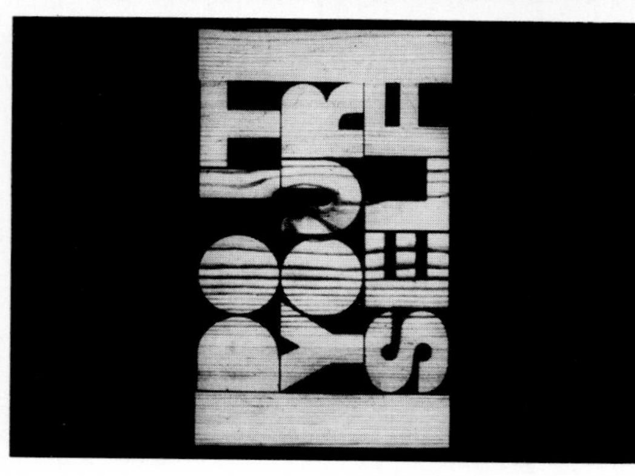

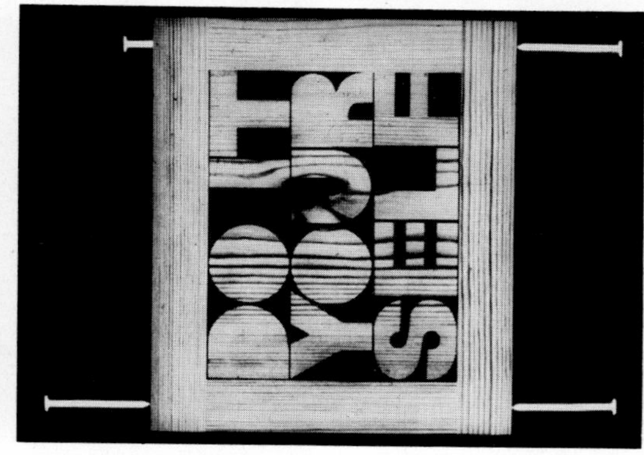

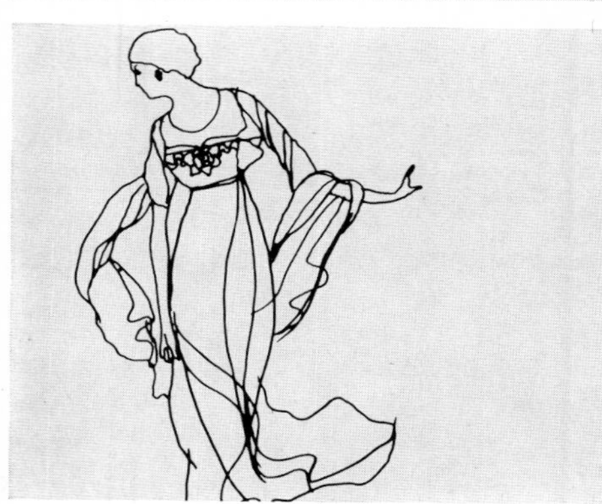

Agency/Agentur/Agence – Studio:

843) BBC GRAPHICS, CARDIFF
844) 845) CBC, WINNIPEG
846)–853) BBC TELEVISION, LONDON
854)–859) ABC TELEVISION, LONDON
860)–865) ATV GRAPHIC DEPT,. LONDON

Producer/Produktion/Production:

842) GRANADA TELEVISION NETWORK LTD., MANCHESTER
843) BRITISH BROADCASTING CORP., CARDIFF
844) 845) CBC TELEVISION GRAPHIC DESIGN, WINNIPEG
846)–853) BRITISH BROADCASTING CORP., LONDON
854)–859) MORENO CARTOONS, LONDON
860)–865) ATV NETWORK LTD., LONDON

842) Promotion slide for Granada Television. (GB)
843) Caption for a BBC Wales television programme. (GB)
844) 845) Slides for musical programmes in colour for the Canadian Broadcasting Company. (CAN)
846)–853) Title sequence for *Cameron Country*, a programme shown on BBC Television. (GB)
854)–859) Title sequence for ABC Television. (GB)
860)–865) Illustrations used for the credits of a period drama set in 1909, for ATV Television. (GB)

842) Voranzeige für ein Fernsehprogramm. (GB)
843) Titel für ein Fernsehprogramm. (GB)
844) 845) Ankündigungen für musikalische Programme in Farbe, ausgestrahlt vom kanadischen Fernsehen. (CAN)
846)–853) Titelfolge für einen vom BBC-Fernsehen ausgestrahlten Reisefilm. (GB)
854)–859) Titelsequenz für ein Fernsehprogramm. (GB)
860)–865) Illustrationen aus der Voranzeige für ein Drama der Jahrhundertwende. (GB)

842) Still publicitaire pour un programme de télévision. (GB)
843) Titre d'un programme de télévision. (GB)
844) 845) Stills pour des programmes de variété en couleur à la TV canadienne. (CAN)
846)–853) Générique de *Cameron Country*, un programme de la TV britannique. (GB)
854)–859) Générique d'un programme de télévision. (GB)
860)–865) Illustrations du générique d'un programme de TV, dont l'action se situe au début du siècle. (GB)

866-875 →

Artist / Künstler / Artiste:
866)–876) RICHARD WILLIAMS / ROY JACKSON

Art Director / Directeur artistique:
866)–876) RICHARD WILLIAMS

Producer / Produktion / Production:
866)–876) RICHARD WILLIAMS ANIMATION PRODUCTIONS, LTD., LONDON

866)–876) Final title sequence for the United Artists colour film *A Funny Thing Happened on the Way to the Forum*, directed by Richard Lester. The only stipulation for the design of these titles was that they should be Roman in style. The idea of having flies walk all over them occurred to the designers because "flies were walking all over the people in the film". Most of the artwork was done in acrylic paints; the backgrounds were painted in oils and "aged" with acrylics. The chief animator spent six weeks on the exclusive task of animating flies. (GB)

866)–876) Schlusstitel des Farbfilms *A Funny Thing Happened on the Way to the Forum.* Regie Richard Lester. Die einzige Bedingung für den Entwurf dieser Titel war, dass sie «römisch» wirken sollten. Die Idee der über die Titel kriechenden Fliegen wurde dem Film selbst entnommen, wo in einigen Sequenzen Fliegen auf der Haut der Akteure umherspazieren. Der Hintergrund der Titel wurde zuerst in Öl gemalt und dann patiniert mit Akrilenfarben. Der Chef-Animator verbrachte sechs Wochen mit dem Zeichnen der sich bewegenden Fliegen. (GB)

866)–876) Générique final du film en couleur *A funny Thing Happened on the Way to the Forum.* La seule directive énoncée quant à la conception de ce générique concernait le style qui devait être «romain». L'auteur a tiré l'idée des mouches se promenant sur les titres du film lui-même, tout au long duquel «les mouches se promènent sur les gens». La plupart des sujets ont été paints à la peinture acrylique; les décors, eux, sont à l'huile et «vieillis» à la peinture acrylique. Il a fallu six semaines pour «animer» les mouches. (GB)

ZERO MOSTEL

PETER BUTTERWORTH
JOHN BENNETT · ANDREW FAULDS
JENNIFER AND SUSAN BAKER · RONNY BRODY
FRANK ELLIOTT · LUCIENNE BRIDOU

MUSICAL DIRECTION AND
INCIDENTAL MUSIC BY
KEN THORNE

2ND UNIT DIRECTOR
BOB SIMMONS
2ND UNIT CAMERAMAN
PAUL WILSON

872–875

PLAYERS

876

877)–882) Frames from the animated film *Egbert Nosh* shown on BBC Television. (GB)
883)–891) Frames from a series of TV commercials based on fairy tales for Jack in the Box drive-in restaurants. (USA)
892)–894) From a series of promotion slides for the programmes of NBC Television. (USA)
895) Promotion slide for a series of colour documentary films on Granada Television. (GB)

877)–882) Bildfolge aus dem Trickfilm *Egbert Nosh*, ausgestrahlt vom BBC-Fernsehen. (GB)
883)–891) Bilder aus einer Serie von Fernsehwerbefilmen mit Neufassungen von Märchen, für Drive-in-Restaurants. (USA)
892)–894) Aus einer Serie von farbigen Ankündigungen für Fernsehprogramme. (USA)
895) Voranzeige für eine Serie von Dokumentarfilmen, die von einer Fernsehgesellschaft in Farbe ausgestrahlt wurden. (GB)

877)–882) Séquence d'un dessin animé présenté à la télévision britannique. (GB)
883)–891) Stills tirés d'une série de films publicitaires pour la TV, inspirés par des contes de fées. (USA)
892)–894) D'une série de stills publicitaires pour des programmes de la chaîne américaine NBC. (USA)
895) Still publicitaire pour un documentaire en couleur à la télévision. (GB)

877–882 →

Artist / Künstler / Artiste:

877)–882) HILARY HAYTON / GRAHAM MCCALLUM
883)–891) ANDRÉ FRANÇOIS
892) 893) FRANK BOZZO / OREST WORONEWYCH
894) JOHN SORJANI / OREST WORONEWYCH
895) RAYMOND M. FREEMAN

892

893

883-891 →

Producer / Produktion / Production:

877)–882) BRITISH BROADCASTING CORP., LONDON
883)–891) JENKYNS, SHEAN & ELLIOTT, INC., LOS ANGELES
892)–894) NATIONAL BROADCASTING CO., NEW YORK
895) GRANADA TELEVISION NETWORK LTD., MANCHESTER

Art Director / Directeur artistique:

892)–894) JOHN GRAHAM
895) RAYMOND M. FREEMAN

894

895

Artist / Künstler / Artiste:

896)–901) MARVIN GLASS / MILTON HERDER / DON FLOCK
902)–907) TONY OLDFIELD / DAVID GILL
908)–923) HANS-OLOF DAHLGREN
924) 925) TIM LEWIS / BILL FEIGENBAUM
926) 927) PIERRE-YVES PELLETIER
928) YVON LAROCHE

Art Director / Directeur artistique:

896)–901) GAYLORD ADAMS / DON FLOCK
902)–907) TONY OLDFIELD / DAVID GILL
908) 923) HANS-OLAF DAHLGREN
924) 925) JOHN GRAHAM
926) 927) PIERRE-YVES PELLETIER

Agency / Agentur / Agence – Studio:

896)–901) ADAMS & STURMAN, INC., NEW YORK
924) 925) PUSH PIN STUDIO, NEW YORK

Producer / Produktion / Production:

896)–901) CYBERNETIC APPLICATIONS, INC., NEW YORK
902)–907) REDIFFUSION & TELEVISION, LONDON
908)–923) SWEDISH BROADCASTING CORP., STOCKHOLM
924) 925) NATIONAL BROADCASTING CO., INC., NEW YORK
926)–928) SOCIÉTÉ RADIO-CANADA, MONTREAL

896-901 →

902–907 →

908-922 →

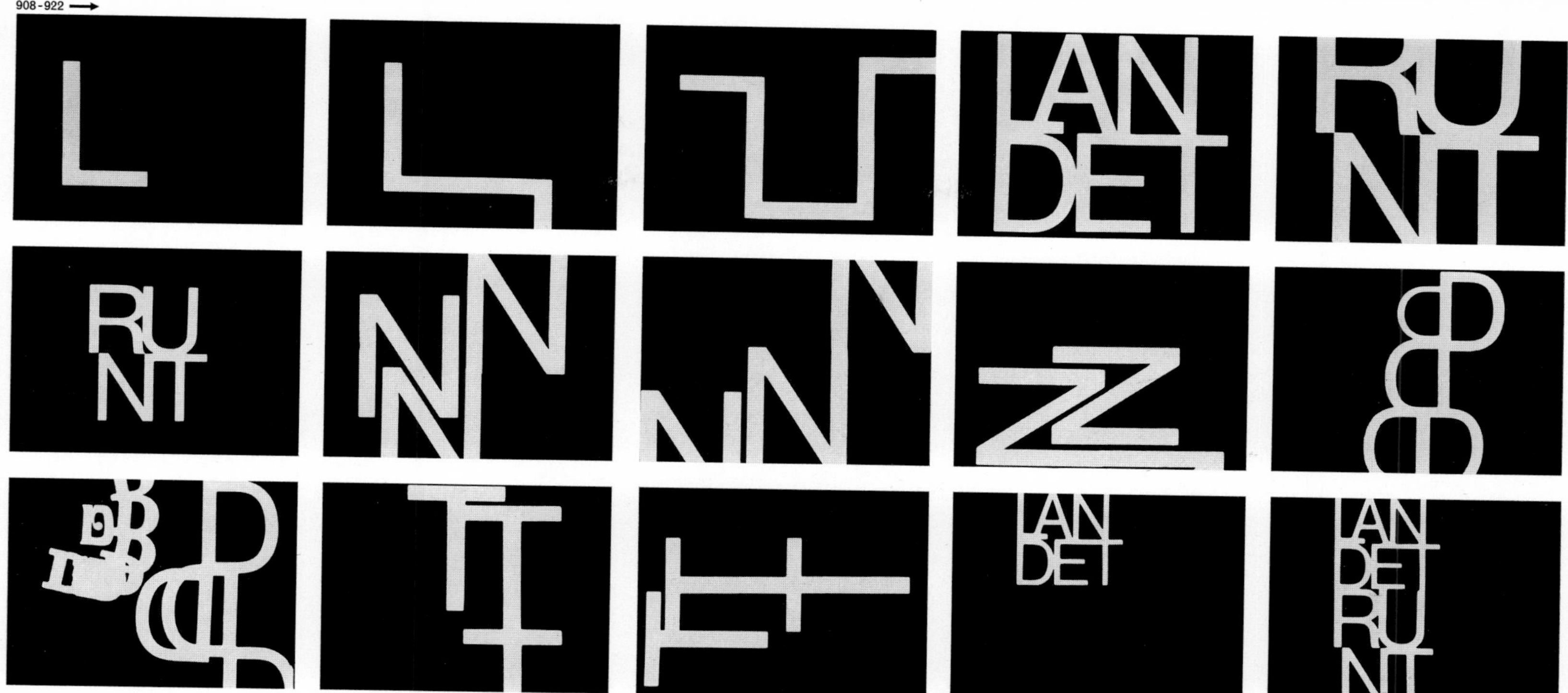

896)–901) Sequence from a commercial film for Cybernetics Applications Inc., showing how their *Prism* system simplifies the use of computers. (USA)

902)–907) Title sequence for a programme shown on Rediffusion Television. (GB)

908)–922) Title sequence for a topical programme on Swedish television. (SWE)

923) Breakdown announcement for Swedish television. (SWE)

924) 925) Frames from a five-minute film on special NBC television features. (USA)

926)–928) Promotion slides and title for programmes shown on Canadian television. (CAN)

896)–901) Sequenz aus einem Werbefilm für eine kybernetische Firma, die zeigt, wie das von ihr entwickelte System die Verwendung von Rechenmaschinen vereinfacht. (USA)

902)–907) Titelfolge für ein Programm, das von der Rediffusion-Fernsehgesellschaft gezeigt wurde. (GB)

908)–922) Titelfolge für ein aktuelles Programm, ausgestrahlt vom schwedischen Fernsehen. (SWE)

923) Einblendbild für Störungen. (SWE)

924) 925) Bildfolge aus einem fünf Minuten dauernden Film über besondere Fernsehsendungen. (USA)

926)–928) Voranzeigen und Titel für Programme, die vom kanadischen Fernsehen gezeigt wurden. (CAN)

896)–901) Séquence d'un film publicitaire présentant un procédé de cybernétique permettant de simplifier l'utilisation des ordinateurs. (USA)

902)–907) Générique d'un programme de télévision. (GB)

908)–922) Générique d'un programme d'actualité à la télévision suédoise. (SWE)

923) Still annonçant une interruption à la suite d'ennuis techniques à la TV suédoise. (SWE)

924) 925) Stills d'un film de cinq minutes sur les programmes spéciaux de la chaine NBC. (USA)

926)–928) Stills publicitaires et titre de programmes présentés à la télévision canadienne. (CAN)

923

924

925

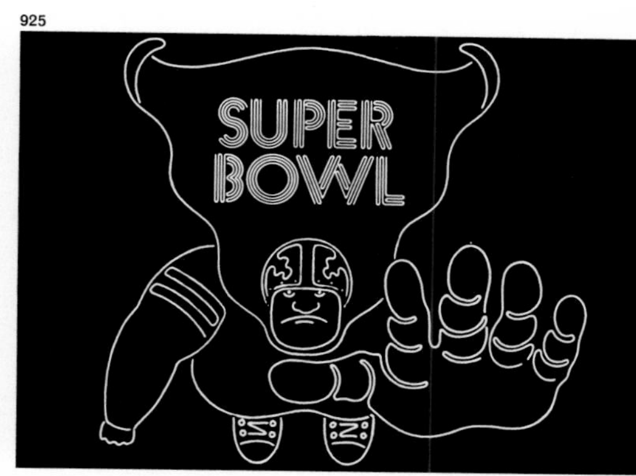

926

927

928

Advertisers
Inserenten
Annonceurs

DESIGNERS'
GOUACHE
WN
321
Flame Red
Rouge de Feu

j. **stemmle** + *co. grossbuchbinderei hardturmstrasse 253/255 zürich*

Steiner + Co.
Clichés
Photolithos
BASEL + ST. GALLEN
Schützenmattstrasse 31
4000 Basel 3
Tel. 061/24 99 10
Rosenbergstrasse 28
9000 St. Gallen
Tel. 071/23 36 73
Ulrich Kemmner

Plakat (Tempera)
Farben
von Talens:
in Tuben
und Tübchen,
in Flacons
und Flaschen,
in Näpfchen
und Tabletten.
In Tönen und
Tönen und Tönen.
In Kästen
und Kästchen.
In einer
einzigen Qualität:
Plakat (Tempera)
Farben von Talens!

Publikation der Königlichen Fabriken Talens & Zoon N.V. Apeldoorn Holland.

The Development of Writing
Die Schriftentwicklung
Le développement de l'écriture

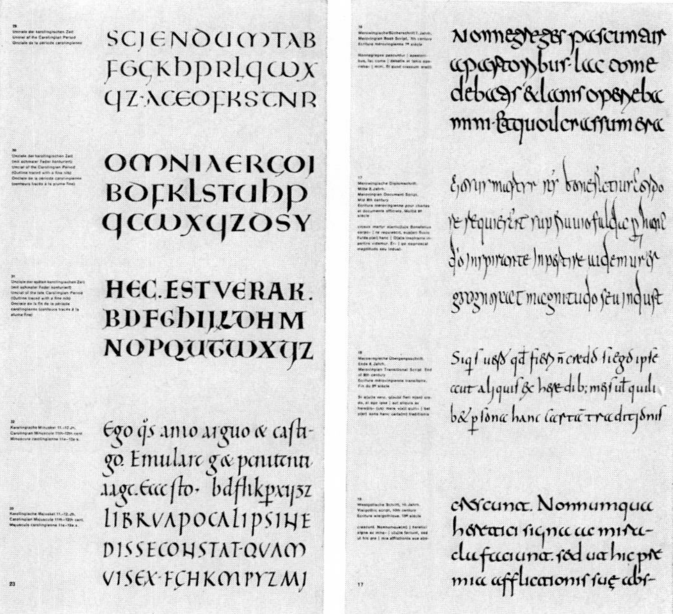

The Development of Writing by Hans Ed. Meyer, Instructor in Lettering at the Zurich School of Arts and Crafts. This small but concise work, now in its fourth edition, will make it possible for any interested person to grasp the essentials of the subject quickly and without involved research, whether as an introduction to profounder studies or as a summary to accompany them. The 71 examples (see specimen pages beside), backed by brief notes, make clear all the main stages in the development of letter forms in the Western world, from Greek and Roman stone-engraved letters by way of the many written scripts to some printers' types of our own time. 11¾ × 6 inches. 48 pages, strongly bound in paper. Price: $ 2.80 / £ 1.2.0.

Die Schriftentwicklung heisst ein bereits in der vierten Auflage erschienenes erfolgreiches Graphis-Buch, mit dem sein Verfasser, Hans Ed. Meyer, Lehrer für Schrift an der Kunstgewerbeschule Zürich, die Kenntnis und Entwicklung der historischen Schriftformen, als Voraussetzung zu schöpferischem Schriftgestalten, vermittelt. Es beginnt mit den römischen Lapidarschriften des 2. und 1. Jh. v. Chr. und enthält alle wichtigen, im Laufe der Zeit entstandenen Schriftarten. Den Schluss bilden die Schriften unserer Zeit: Egyptienne und Grotesk. 71 Beispiele, 48 Seiten (siehe nebenstehende Seitenwiedergabe). Format 15 × 30 cm, broschiert. Preis Fr. 11.— / DM 10.50.

(GA '69/70)

ORDER FORM

I wish to order ______ copy(ies) of THE DEVELOPMENT OF WRITING

Name and address: ______________________

____

____

Signature: ______________________

Date: ______________________

Please send this order form to:
The Graphis Press, 45, Nüschelerstrasse, 8001 Zurich

The Graphis Press Nüschelerstrasse 45, 8001 Zürich

LEONARDI OFFSET

Quality as a constant
Qualität als Konstante

All the reproductions shown here (Nos. 98, 154, 157, 186, 187, 218, 303, 390, 474, 512, 519, 588, 611, 749, 753 in this book) were printed from colour separations by Leonardi Offset-Reproduktionen.

Alle hier gezeigten Farbwiedergaben (Nr. 98, 154, 157, 186, 187, 218, 303, 390, 474, 512, 519, 588, 611, 749, 753 in diesem Werk) wurden nach Farbauszügen von Leonardi Offset-Reproduktionen gedruckt.

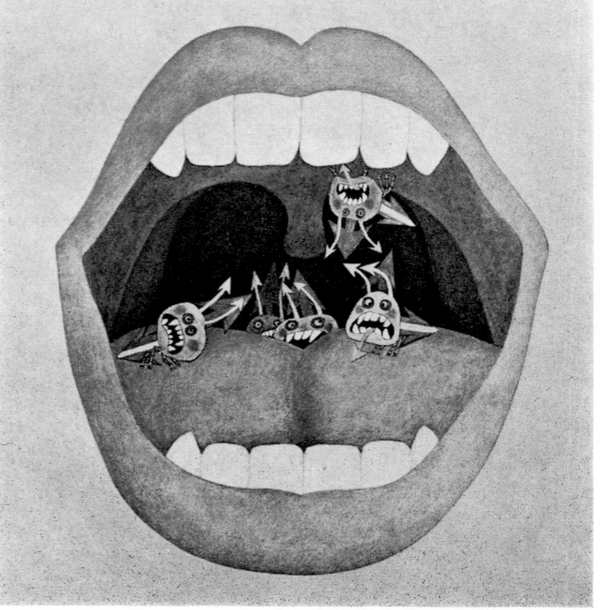

Leonardi Offset Reproduktionen
Zürich, Bändlistrasse 41

REPRODUKTIONEN

The illustrations shown above were taken in different corners of the world — Europe, America, Japan. They are united here in one book and in the high quality of their reproduction. In Leonardi photolithography this high quality is a constant, whatever the source or nature of the illustration. Why not introduce this constant into your own calculations?

Diese Illustrationen stammen aus verschiedenen Teilen der Welt — aus Europa, Amerika und Japan. Sie sind hier vereint — in einem Buch, aber auch in der hohen Qualität der Wiedergabe. Diese photolithographische Qualität ist bei Leonardi eine Konstante, woher die Aufnahmen auch kommen. Beziehen Sie diese Konstante auch in Ihre Berechnungen ein!

U. KEMMNER

GUTE GESTALTUNG UND SORGFÄLTIGER DRUCK
BUCHDRUCKEREI MERKUR AG · LANGENTHAL